CORPORATE BRAND DESIGN

Corporate Brand Design offers a unique and comprehensive exploration of the relationship between companies, their brand design, and their stakeholders.

The book begins its approach with a literature review, to provide an overview of current thinking on the subject and establish a theoretical framework. The following sections cover key stages during the corporate brand development process: Brand signature design, its components and impact on brand reputation; website design and how it builds customer perception of the brand; corporate architecture design and the branding of space and place; brand experience design from a sensuality perspective. International case studies from a range of industries feature in each chapter to demonstrate how the theory translates to practice, alongside case questions to cement learning and definitions of the key constructs.

By combining academic theory with practical case studies and examples, readers will gain a thorough understanding of the corporate brand design process and how it influences customer identification and loyalty to the brand. The book is a useful resource for advanced undergraduate and postgraduate students of strategic brand management, corporate brand design and visual identity, and marketing communications.

Mohammad Mahdi Foroudi is Founder and Managing Director of Foroudi Consultancy. He is also Visiting Lecturer at Middlesex University, UK; Tehran University, Iran; and Azad University, Iran.

Pantea Foroudi is Senior Lecturer in Marketing and Branding at Middlesex University London, UK, and Business Manager and Solution Architect at Foroudi Consultancy.

'This book will be read with interest by corporate brand scholars and practitioners who have an interest in the design dimensions of corporate brand management. As well as covering more traditional areas of the territory such as corporate visual identity and corporate architecture, care has been taken to include new expressions of the field such as website design. This is most welcome addition to the oeuvre.'

Professor John M. T. Balmer, *Professor of Corporate Marketing, Brunel University London, UK; quondam Professor of Corporate Brand/Identity Management, Bradford School of Management, UK*

'With globalisation pervading the farthest reaches of the planet and the onslaught of digital marketing, creating and maintaining a consistent visual identity of the organisation is more critical than ever. This book is a timely endeavour in that regard. It captures all the relevant aspects of corporate brand design creation, evolution and management.'

Paurav Shukla, *Professor of Marketing and Head of Digital of Data Driven Management Department, University of Southampton, UK*

'This book focuses on how visual design communication is intertwined with corporate identity in reflecting the true ethos, personality and spirit of the organisation. Fifteen relevant, practical and contemporary case studies have competently illustrated the phases readers need to understand in designing their own corporate brand. Enjoy reading the multifaceted aspects of corporate design as lucidly presented in this long-awaited book.'

T. C. Melewar, *Professor of Marketing and Strategy and Head of Department of Marketing, Branding and Tourism (MBT), Middlesex University London, UK*

'*Corporate Brand Design: Developing and Managing Brand Identity* lives up to its name as a thoroughly up-to-date and comprehensive guide to the very latest and finest thinking on corporate branding. The compendium focuses comprehensively on all aspects of corporate brand design management, an area critical for brand success. It will be of interest to almost anyone with an interest in developing and successfully managing a brand. The book offers a timely update of the theory and practice of corporate visual identity, through the lenses of established as well as novel perspectives in the domain. It provides academic rigour through systematic analyses and syntheses of research evidence on a wide range of exciting areas, such as corporate brand signature management, corporate brand website design, sensory marketing cues, and visual identity management. Notably, it offers valuable real-world relevance through in-depth business cases that will benefit marketing practitioners and branding students alike. The book is enlightening, thought-provoking, and enormously useful. It belongs on the bookshelf of anyone serious about the art and science of corporate branding theory and practice.'

Jaywant Singh, *Professor of Marketing, University of Southampton, UK*

CORPORATE BRAND DESIGN

Developing and Managing Brand Identity

Mohammad Mahdi Foroudi and
Pantea Foroudi

LONDON AND NEW YORK

First published 2022
by Routledge
2 Park Square, Milton Park, Abingdon, Oxon OX14 4RN

and by Routledge
605 Third Avenue, New York, NY 10158

Routledge is an imprint of the Taylor & Francis Group, an informa business

© 2022 Mohammad Mahdi Foroudi and Pantea Foroudi

The right of Mohammad Mahdi Foroudi and Pantea Foroudi to be identified as authors of this work has been asserted by them in accordance with sections 77 and 78 of the Copyright, Designs and Patents Act 1988.

All rights reserved. No part of this book may be reprinted or reproduced or utilised in any form or by any electronic, mechanical, or other means, now known or hereafter invented, including photocopying and recording, or in any information storage or retrieval system, without permission in writing from the publishers.

Trademark notice: Product or corporate names may be trademarks or registered trademarks, and are used only for identification and explanation without intent to infringe.

British Library Cataloguing-in-Publication Data
A catalogue record for this book is available from the British Library

Library of Congress Cataloging-in-Publication Data
A catalog record has been requested for this book

ISBN: 978-0-367-51499-0 (hbk)
ISBN: 978-0-367-51502-7 (pbk)
ISBN: 978-1-003-05415-3 (ebk)

DOI: 10.4324/9781003054153

Typeset in Bembo
by Newgen Publishing UK

To our lovely father, Dr Mohammad Foroud Foroudi and our lovely mum, Flora Mahdavi

CONTENTS

Contributors   *x*

   Introduction   1
   Pantea Foroudi

PART I
Introduction to corporate brand design management   5

1 The emergence, development, and changing uses of corporate brand design, 1760 to date   7
   Pantea Foroudi

2 Corporate brand design management from different perspectives   15
   Mohammad Mahdi Foroudi, Flora Mahdavi, and Pantea Foroudi

PART II
Corporate brand signature management   41

3 Corporate brand signature management: Logo, design, typeface, and colour   43
   Pantea Foroudi and T. C. Melewar

4 Corporate brand signature: Image and reputation   66
   Pantea Foroudi and Flora Mahdavi

PART III
Corporate architecture design   77

5 Corporate architecture design management   79
Mohammad Mahdi Foroudi, Mohammad Foroud Foroudi, and Pantea Foroudi

6 Corporate architecture design and human factors, needs, and performance   100
Mohammad Mahdi Foroudi, Mohammad Foroud Foroudi, and Pantea Foroudi

7 Corporate architecture design, corporate identity, and identification   124
Mohammad Mahdi Foroudi, John M. T. Balmer, and Pantea Foroudi

PART IV
Corporate brand website design   143

8 Corporate brand website design management   145
Pantea Foroudi, Mohammad Mahdi Foroudi, and Elena Ageeva

9 Corporate brand website design, image, identification, and loyalty   168
Pantea Foroudi, Mohammad Mahdi Foroudi, and Elena Ageeva

PART V
Corporate brand sensuality   181

10 Evolution of branding: Towards an historical understanding of the concept branding, experience, and senses   183
Tugra Nazli Akarsu

11 Evolution of senses: From no-nonsense era to the rise of sensory marketing   203
Tugra Nazli Akarsu

12 Sensory marketing: Environmental psychology theory approach   218
Tugra Nazli Akarsu

13 Sensory marketing: Visual cues and audial cues   231
Tugra Nazli Akarsu

14 Sensory marketing: Olfactory cues and haptic cues 242
   Tugra Nazli Akarsu

15 Gustative signatures as corporate brand identifiers: Exploring the
   sensuality of taste as a marketing strategy 251
   Dongmei Zha

Index *264*

CONTRIBUTORS

Elena Ageeva received her PhD in Business and Marketing from London, United Kingdom. Currently she is working in Kazan, Russia, as Associate Professor in the Department of Marketing at Kazan Federal University, and she is also a Deputy Chairman of Strategic Development in Tatarstan Chamber of Commerce. She has published in top 'marketing' journals such as *Journal of Business Research*, *Journal of Marketing Communications*, and *Qualitative Market Research: An International Journal*.

Tugra Nazli Akarsu is a Lecturer in Marketing at the Southampton Business School, University of Southampton, UK. Tugra's research interests are in the fields of sensory marketing, branding, and consumer psychology. Her research on sensory marketing focuses on the effect of sensory stimuli on consumer perceptions. Within branding and consumer psychology, her research examines the influence of digital platforms and their digital orientations on end-users in different market models for researchers and practitioners. In her research, she applies an interdisciplinary perspective drawing primarily from the field of psychology. Her research has been published in journals including *Journal of Business Research*, *Industrial Marketing Management*, *European Journal of Marketing*, and *International Journal of Hospitality Management*. She has contributed chapters to edited books on various topics and presented her research at various conferences belonging to reputable bodies.

John M. T. Balmer holds a personal chair as Professor of Corporate Marketing. He is quondam Professor of Corporate Brand/Identity Management at Bradford School of Management where he is also a Visiting Professor. He is the 'Father' of the *Corporate Brand Concept* (1995), he also pioneered the corporate marketing, corporate heritage brand/identity, total corporate communications, monarchical marketing, ethical corporate identity, corporate marketing notions, and penned the first academic articles in these aforementioned areas. He also co-conceived the corporate heritage brand/corporate brand with heritage notions and was the originator of the corporate heritage identity and corporate brand orienation notions.

Maria Antonella Ferri is Full Professor of Management at Universitas Mercatorum, Italy, where she teaches Strategy, Marketing and Management. She got a Ph.D. in Business Management at The University Ca' Foscari of Venice; she became researcher at the University of Rome "La Sapienza" and then Associate Professor at the Parthenope University of Naples. She is interested in Strategic Sustainability, Social Responsibility, Business Model and Marketing Plan. She published several books and articles on these items.

Mohammad Foroud Foroudi is an Orthopedic Surgeon and Practitioner Architect.

Mohammad Mahdi Foroudi (PhD, BSc (Honour)) is Founder and Managing Director of Foroudi Consultancy. He is responsible for managing the firm's worldwide interests and enhancing its strategic and creative global offering to his clients in the UK, including the growth and development of the brand, company's corporate identity and architecture since 2013. He earned his PhD from Brunel University London. He has published widely in international academic journals such as *Journal of Business Research*, *European Journal of Marketing*, and so on (Email: mmf_23291@yahoo.com).

Pantea Foroudi (PhD, FHEA, MSc (Honor), MA, BA (Honor) is Business Manager and Solution Architect at Foroudi Consultancy as well as is a member of marketing, branding, and tourism, Middlesex University, London. She earned her PhD from Brunel University, London. Pantea is working in the field of design, branding, and marketing since 1996 and she has experience as a creative innovator and practical problem-solver in visual identity, graphic design, and branding in different sectors. Her primary research interest has focused on consumer behaviour from multidisciplinary approach with a particular focus on the concept of customer perception and its effect on design, image, reputation, identification, and loyalty in the context of retailing and hospitality. Pantea has published widely in international academic journals such as *Journal of Business Research*, *European Journal of Marketing*, *International Journal of Hospitality Management*, and so on. She is the associate/senior/editor of *International Journal of Hospitality Management* (IJHM); *International Journal of Consumer Studies* (IJCS); *Journal of Business to Business* (JBBM); *European Journal of International Management* (EJIM); *Cogent Business and Management, Marketing Session* (CBM); *Iranian Journal of Management Studies* (IJMS), and editorial review board of *Journal of Business Research* (JBR); *International Journal of Information Management* (IJIM). (Email: Pantea.Foroudi@gmail.com)

Flora Mahdavi is a professional fashion designer.

T. C. Melewar is Professor of Marketing and Strategy and the Head of Department (Marketing, Branding and Tourism) at the Business School, Middlesex University London, UK.

Maria Palazzo (PhD, AFHEA, FHEA, MSc (Honours), MA, BA (Honours)) is a research fellow at the Department of Political and Communication Studies, University of Salerno, Italy, and a member of the Sustainability Communication Centre (SCC) (http://dsc.unisa.it/scc/). She is also an academic tutor and a lecturer at the Universitas Mercatorum, Rome. She was a former lecturer at University of Bedfordshire, School of Business. London, a visiting scholar at the University of Granada, Spain, and a visiting lecturer at the Universidad del Norte, Escuela de Negocios, Colombia. She is editor of Cogent Business and Management and International Journal of Sustainable Entrepreneurship and Corporate Social Responsibility. Her articles have been published in *The TQM Journal, European Journal of International Management, Corporate Social Responsibility and Environmental Management, Current Issues in Tourism, International Journal of Bank Marketing, Qualitative Market Research: An International Journal, Land Use Policy, Journal of Business-to-Business Marketing, Journal of Brand Management*, and in other academic outlets.

Alfonso Siano is Professor and Chair of Marketing and of Corporate Communication and Brand Management at the University of Salerno (Italy) where he is Founder of the Doctoral Programme in Marketing Communications. He carries out research in corporate communication and reputation, marketing communications, brand management, CSR communication, sustainable marketing. He has published in a wide range of international academic journals, including the *Journal of Business Research, International Journal of Advertising, Corporate Social Responsibility and Environmental Management, Electronic Commerce Research, International Journal of Tourism Research, Journal of Marketing Communications, Land Use Policy, Current Issues in Tourism, Corporate Communications: An International Journal, Journal of Brand Management, Qualitative Market Research: An International Journal*.

Pierluigi Vitale is a research assistant at the Departement of Political and Communication Sciences (University of Salerno). His current research project is named: 'Integrated Models of Natural Language Processing and Visual Design Tools'. He is Ph.D student since March 2020 with a thesis named 'Itineraries and Communication Design. A semantic issue'. He is author of several papers and chapters in international journals. The research topics are the analysis and visualisation of structured and unstructured data, in particular UGC on the online media, in the fields of cultural heritage, tourism research, digital humanities, and visual communication. He is a member of the Italian Society of Design and of the Laboratories 'Digital Humanities + Information Design' and 'Sustainability Communication Centre' of the University of Salerno, Italy.

Dongmei Zha is presently a Ph.D. candidate at the Business School, Middlesex University, London, having completed her MBA in International Marketing at the University of Coventry London in 2017. She has extensive experience in marketing practise having worked as a sales and marketing manager in technology companies in China. She has recently published in *International journal of Management Review*, and presented research papers at the Academy of Marketing conference in London and MMRA Marketing Congress in Turkey. Her research interests include all aspects of consumption experience, with a special focus on sensory brand experience.

INTRODUCTION

Pantea Foroudi

Corporate Brand Design: Developing and Managing Brand Identity can be employed as a strategic guide to marketing and communication managers who could benefit from promoting an unambiguous corporate design, and audiences will have a clear understanding of what the firm or product represents through a company's visual identity. In addition, entrepreneurs and incubators could use this book to launch their start-ups. The text will serve as an important resource for the design, marketing, identity, and brand practitioners requiring more than anecdotal evidence on the structure and operation of visual/design identity in different geographical areas. Brand designing is the first and essential step for any company to start and expand their businesses, and this book will attract attention in both developed and emerging markets. Readers will find it stimulating to compare and contrast different markets covering important aspects related to companies' design, brands, identity, and reputation. The text will include a mix of theory and practice that will engender confidence in the students, academics, and practitioners of international design, branding, identity, and marketing alike.

Nonetheless, marketers provide consumers with a great deal of vague information. The relevance of the corporate visual identity to companies is its website platforms as a key communication of the desired message to create a profitable and unique position in the marketplace as well as add value to the reputation of an organisation. Corporate visual identity as a key element of corporate identity is used as a company's signature to raise awareness, and help with identification, as well as to be the signs of a promise to the customer that helps differentiate the organisation from its competitors.

By recognising the plurality and complexity of the concept of corporate brand design management as the heart of the branding discipline, this book fills gaps in the global market by proposing a number of innovative research objectives on the fundamental nature of brand design, and suggests manifold answers to objectives in an integrated perspective. This book aims to address the following objectives:

- Explore the multiple stakeholder audiences that corporate brands of all types must address. Branding encompasses many facets, which will be covered throughout the book. Such aspects of corporate brand design management include image, reputation, identification,

DOI: 10.4324/9781003054153-1

and loyalty management. This book will provide examples from a wide range of industries and firms to illustrate the many dimensions of corporate brand design management and theories.
- Readers will be able to understand research studies from different corporate branding points of view. In addition, they gain a good understanding of corporate brand identity design through both theoretical and practical engagement. In this sense, they will be able to compare, contrast, and comprehend whether the 'corporate branding design identity' from different lenses are delivered similarly or otherwise in different parts of the world. This enables readers to understand differences and subsequent application towards managing these corporate brands.
- In this context, readers will be able to acquire 'knowledge and understanding' of: i) the key issues in corporate branding design identity theories; ii) the need for a strategic approach to planning and corporate brand design management; and iii) new developments in corporate branding theories. Also, they will be able to analyse the complex web of stakeholder audiences that corporate brand design management must address.

Corporate Brand Design: Developing and Managing Brand Identity is a mixture of theory and practice with practical case studies, which aims at reaching primarily doctoral, postgraduate, graduate, and final year undergraduate students in business and marketing, but it will be suitable for managers, designers, entrepreneurs, and decision-makers around the world too.

This book will be able to start from the issues related to the development and changing uses of visual identity; corporate brand design: developing and managing brand identity from different perspectives; corporate brand signature management; corporate brand website design management; corporate architecture design management; and corporate brand sensuality. Moreover, this book, proposes a mixture of theory and practice with practical case studies

Corporate Brand Design Management is a textbook aimed at core postgraduate and undergraduate courses which serve as a supplementary text for advanced undergraduates and postgraduates and a key resource for practitioners.

There are five key parts of the book:

Part I: Introduction to corporate brand design management – This explores the history of corporate brand design management and explains the concept from different perspectives. It explains the traditional literature review process as a comprehensive, critical and objective analysis of the current knowledge on a topic which helps to establish a theoretical framework and focus on the research.

Part II: Corporate brand signature management – This part revolves around research studies to understand the corporate brand signature better, the different elements of a corporate brand signature, such as colour, design, typeface, and corporate brand which translated into a physical effect, which helps to develop the corporate brand image and reputation.

Part III: Corporate architecture design – This part revolves around research studies the interrelationships between corporate architecture design management and how a favourable architecture design could influence on customer/company identification.

Part IV: Corporate brand website design – This part explains the importance of corporate brand website design and how it could improve customers' perception and develop customer/company identification and loyalty

Part V: Corporate brand sensuality – This part introduces the concept of corporate brand sensuality as the main five human senses (auditory, visionary, smell, touch, taste); the conceptualisation of the concept and explain each sense which could influence customers' perceptions and emotions to deliver more memorable and meaningful experiences.

The overview of all chapters and their contributors are described in the following text. The Introduction briefly explains the main topics and features of the book.

Chapter 1: The emergence, development, and changing uses of corporate brand design, 1760 to date, by Pantea Foroudi, explores the emergence, development and changing uses of visual identity, 1760 to date.

Chapter 2: Corporate brand design management from different perspectives, by Pantea Foroudi, reviews the literature on the understanding of the corporate brand design and visual identity as a root of corporate identity. Five core disciplines that have contributed to the evolution and study of corporate visual identity are graphic design, integrated-communication, organisational studies, marketing, and multi-disciplinary approaches which discuss in detail and present (a holistic) view of the dimensions of the corporate brand design and visual identity construct.

Chapter 3: Corporate brand signature management: Logo, design, typeface, and colour, by Pantea Foroudi, introduces how to formulate and design a favourable corporate brand signature. Research into the corporate brand signature and corporate image expressed that a favourable corporate brand signature has desirable organisational outcomes such as increased visibility and recognisable products and services for its company's internal and external stakeholders. Corporate brand signature are used to raise awareness, and help with identification, as well as being the signs of a promise to the customer that helps differentiate the organisation from its competitors. Furthermore, a corporate brand signature communicates a company's identity and projects the corporate personality.

Chapter 4: Corporate brand signature: Image and reputation, by Pantea Foroudi, highlights the understanding the relationships between corporate brand signature, image, and reputation and how a company could improve internal and external stakeholders' perception through the corporate brand signature.

Chapter 5: Corporate architecture design management, by Mohammad Mahdi Foroudi and Pantea Foroudi, add insights into the nature and characteristics of corporate architecture design management by recognising the key three main components of the architecture: i) symbolic artifacts/decor and artifacts; ii) physical structure/spatial layout and functionality; and iii) ambient conditions/physical stimuli. These are the main sufficient factors of the physical environment for customer behaviour research in a service context.

Chapter 6: Corporate architecture design and human factors, needs, and performance, by Mohammad Mahdi Foroudi and Pantea Foroudi, reviews architecture and its relationship with human factors by investigating architecture and its expression of social, economic, and technological realities and also the importance of architecture in today's market. Also, it sheds light on architecture and human performance and the association between architecture and human needs. This chapter explains aesthetics as the creation and appreciation of beauty and its influence on architecture. In addition, it overviews the architectural perception, its assessment, and its relation to nature and the human being.

Chapter 7: Corporate architecture design, corporate identity, and identification, by Mohammad Mahdi Foroudi and Pantea Foroudi, explains the key elements of corporate identity which are influencial on corporate architecture design as: i) visual identity; ii) philosophy, mission, and value; and iii) communication, and how these factors could be implemented in the design of favourable architecture. In addition, this chapter describes how a favourable architecture design could improve customer/company identification.

Chapter 8: Corporate brand website design management, by Elena Ageeva and Pantea Foroudi, explains the philosophical understanding of the corporate brand website design management, the key components, antecedents. From the research into corporate brand website designs and corporate image it can be concluded that a favourable corporate brand website design has desirable organisational outcomes. A favourable corporate brand website design is a powerful way for a company to reveal its corporate identity, an avenue to improve the company's image and reputation, leading to the enhancement of identification with the company, and ultimately, development of consumer loyalty. Thus, corporate brand website design represents a crucial element in the corporate identity management.

Chapter 9: Corporate brand website design, image, identification, and loyalty, by Elena Ageeva and Pantea Foroudi, examines how the design of a favourable corporate brand website design could influence on a company's image, identification, and loyalty. The chapter discusses companies' corporate websites and how to communicate and distinguish themselves to their consumers and audience to create favourable images and reputation. A well–designed company's corporate website impacts on company's corporate image. The following section illustrates the concept of corporate image as an important consequences of corporate website favourability. Additionally, corporate website favourability will also be explained as an outcome factor to the corporate image, corporate reputation, consumer – company identification, and loyalty.

Chapter 10: Evolution of branding: Towards an historical understanding of the concept branding, experience and senses, by Tugra Nazli Akarsu, aims to shed light on the concept of branding, as well as to the scrutiny of the concept of 'experience' within the marketing discipline. As the concept of 'senses' are being interchangeably used with 'experience', this chapter aims to provide how the concept of 'experience' paved the way to the introduction of 'senses' throughout the literature.

Chapter 11: Evolution of senses: From no-nonsense era to the rise of sensory marketing, by Tugra Nazli Akarsu, aims to scrutinise the emergence of 'senses' for the last three decades by categorising it into three main eras: (i) 1929–1970 – no-nonsense era; (ii) 1970–1990 – the rise of advertisements; and (3) 1990 to date – the rise of sensory marketing.

Chapter 12: Sensory marketing: Environmental psychology theory approach, by Tugra Nazli Akarsu, aims to present environmental psychology theory (EPT), the widely use theory adopted into the sensory marketing studies. The chapter also illustrates Mehrabian and Russel's (1974) stimulus-organism-response (S-O-R), which is widely applied by scholars as a framework.

Chapter 13: Sensory marketing: Visual cues and audial cues, by Tugra Nazli Akarsu, illustrates an overview to visual and audial cues from sensory marketing literature, where the different elements of those cues and how those cues engage consumers and influence on consumers cognitive, affective attitudes as well as judgements are also discussed via the chapter.

Chapter 14: Sensory marketing: Olfactory cues and haptic cues, by Tugra Nazli Akarsu, highlights an overview to olfactory and haptic cues from sensory marketing literature, where the different elements of those cues and how those cues engage consumers and influence on consumers cognitive, affective attitudes as well as judgements are also discussed via the chapter.

Chapter 15: Gustative signatures as corporate brand identifiers, by Dongmei Zha, introduces the concept of gustative signature as a corporate brand identifier enabling customers to recognise, identify, and recall a brand. By locating the gustative experience in the context of the mouth/brain relationship, the critical role of gustatory activities and the creation of a customer-based brand identity is discussed.

PART I
Introduction to corporate brand design management

1

THE EMERGENCE, DEVELOPMENT, AND CHANGING USES OF CORPORATE BRAND DESIGN, 1760 TO DATE

Pantea Foroudi

Introduction

Chapter 1 explores the emergence, development, and changing uses of corporate brand design from 1760 to the present day. It investigates how the current environment is more visually oriented and how corporate brand design is a language used to communicate independent verbal information to consumers.

Research background

In the years between 1760 and 1949, visual identification and distinctiveness were combined. The social revolution that occurred between 1760 and 1840 (Foroudi et al., 2017; West, 1978) gripped the West and was a radical process that historians refer to as an economic and social revolution. This era reformed the ways in which the world produced its merchandise (Deane, 1979). The Industrial Revolution started in the UK (Vries, 1994) with significant technological advances, but socioeconomic (West, 1978) and cultural problems also resulted. Various industries, such as the chemical, electricity, petroleum, and steel industries, produced vast amounts of goods with the mechanisation of the manufacture of food and drink, clothing and transport, and, with the introduction of the gramophone, even entertainment (Greenwood and Jovanovic, 1999). The trademark protection was developed out of early counterfeiting, forgery, and fraud laws in 1905 in the UK (around 50 years after its formation in France). Civil prosecution was launched against those who used another's mark without authorisation.

The most crucial inventions for the technology of communication were the printing press and the 'endless web' paper-making machine, typography and its mechanisation, the revolution in printing, the wood-type poster, the rise of advertising design, the battle of the signboard, and the development of lithography (Vries, 1994). For example, in the seventeenth and eighteenth centuries, corporate brand designs (e.g., logos) were used by factories to specify the value and origin of porcelain and furniture.

Consequently, cities grew rapidly, as significant numbers of urban workers engaged in industrial labour, and political power shifted from the aristocracy to the capitalist manufacturing and working classes. High fertility rates (Clark, 2004), poor education, and low rates of productivity growth were the most significant characteristics of the Industrial Revolution (Becker et al., 1990). In Western European countries, landowners were the most powerful force, and they invested in machines to enable mass production to take place.

Subsequently, the most important consequences of the Industrial Revolution are understood to be education and literacy (Clark, 2004). Moreover, the availability of design technology through the invention of typography and its mechanisation, the revolution in printing, the growth of lithography, the wood-type poster, and the battle of the signboard, and the overall increase in advertising design led to companies identifying themselves (Raizman, 2003). With the beginning of mass communication, the concept of graphic communication became more significant. In the same era, the nature of visual information was such that using colour lithography brought about a significant transformation.

Pre-industrial society crossed a threshold of literacy that was adequate for industrialisation (Clark, 2004). There was an extraordinary population expansion in the pre-factory environment, and the population in the UK increased by 60 percent between 1781 and 1800. However, the literacy rate was low during the Industrial Revolution. On the other hand, it is believed that there is no connection between economic growth and literacy (West, 1978). The national male illiteracy rate crossed the 60 percent threshold before 1750, whereas the female rate exceeded this around 1795 (West, 1978).

According to Laqueur (1974), who measured marriage register signatures in Britain between 1814 and 1816, 48 percent of men, representing 17 percent of the population, were only able to sign their names. The low level of education was caused by the large-scale factories with workers employed from a young age. This was the start of real social dislocation (West, 1978). There was little association among changes in the literacy rates and modifications in fertility rates (Clark, 2004). Although literacy rates increased noticeably, the skill premium remained constant in the period between 1600 and 1900.

After 1900, fertility rates fell, and the labour market decreased significantly. At that time, education belonged to a specific class of people. Working-class parents did not invest in education for their children, as the need to pay fees in most schools was an important barrier. For this reason, the majority of people were not able to read and write. The number of educated people was low, and producers identified their goods and indicated the quality and origin of their products to the public using a corporate brand design, such as trademarks and logos (Murphy and Rowe, 1988). Merchants used 'production marks' in order to identify their work as distinct from inferior quality goods (West, 1978). This made goods instantly recognisable and memorable to all those members of society who could not read. It is widely thought that trademarks evolved in response to the emergence of a society in which goods circulated in commerce (West, 1978). The significance of corporate identity design was recognised during the Industrial Revolution as a pre-requisite to an organisation's achievement, as numerous developing firms required trademarks to communicate the company's goals. The earliest trademarks, such as Coca Cola, Singer, Kodak, and Heinz, appeared in this time.

However, despite the growth in productive technology and the socioeconomic and cultural advancements, low levels of literacy among people in Western Europe held sway. According to Bowman and Anderson (1963), levels of literacy fell during the Industrial Revolution, and people slowly became more literate (West, 1978).

The first industrial design was made by Peter Behrens who was the first industrial designer in the first decade of the twentieth century (Anderson, 2000). The comprehensive visual identity designed by Behrens was for the German manufacturer, Allgemeine Elektrizitäts Gesellschaft (AEG). This major event in his career occurred in 1907. AEG had grown into one of the world's largest manufacturing companies (Anderson, 2000). Walther Rathenau, a visionary industrialist, sensed the need for a unified visual character for the firm's products, environments, and communications. Thus, Behrens, who was well known for his pioneering abilities and sensitive handling of materials and colour, began to focus upon the design needs of industry, with design responsibility ranging from stationery to buildings. Other companies also began to redesign their products to meet consumers' desires and achieve product differentiation (Collins and Porras, 1994; Pine, 1993; Utterback, 1994).

In the same year, 1907, the German Association of Craftsmen (the *Deutscher Werkbund* in Munich) advocated a marriage of art with technology design in manufactured goods and architecture. A union of artists and craftsmen in industry would elevate the functional and aesthetic qualities of mass production, particularly in low-cost consumer products, and would identify the individual artistic expression (Napoles, 1988). The AEG's graphic identity programme began to use its corporate brand design in all types of advertising (Meggs, 1992).

The First World War (1914–1918) established the importance of visual design (Fiell and Fiell, 2003) due to the need for signs and symbols for military identification and a unique code of status that could be immediately understood. The regimental badge with its heraldic device and its motto had much in common with the equally economical design and the lean, powerful images and slogans of the new posters. Consequently, the government created a visual identity to use as an identification bedrock.

Another important factor at this time was the influence of the Bauhaus School on corporate communication (packaging, the printed page, etc.). Walter Gropius founded the Bauhaus School in Germany in 1919, where he combined his joint knowledge of materials and craft techniques with modern industrial production methods. More schools soon followed his concept (Bayer et al., 1938).

Then, in 1940, with a new widespread globalised communications, organisations realised the crucial need for a visual identity to control the organsiation image through merchants' trade logos, symbols, or prototypes (Napoles, 1988). Lippincott and Margulies created the first design consultancy in 1943.

The years 1950 and 1979 are recognised as turning points in the profession, and design was employed as a decoration, sales, and marketing tool (Napoles, 1988). At this time, many organisations tried to modified their old corporate brand designs to a new design to illustrate the scale and size of the organisation (Capitman, 1976). Also, the trademark was used as a chief characteristics of packaging to encourage the purchaser that the product had a company with a good reputation behind it (Capitman, 1976). In 1956, the visionary behind the first IBM logo, Paul Rand, was convinced that image design would increase the company's strategy (Capitman, 1976). Indeed, Anderson (2000) claimed that the 1970s can be regarded as the decade of the corporate brand design, as it is the time when organisations began to introduce new logos. This era was characterised by imagery with a combination of visual identification and distinctiveness.

In the 1980s, mass marketing intensely improved the power and value of a corporate brand design, what a firm stood for, and how it communicated its identity, product, and services in order to differentiate itself from others by communicating information about its value, reliability, and origin. Visual identities appeared on everything from envelopes to storefronts and were commonly used to identify ownership. The profession of identity design became

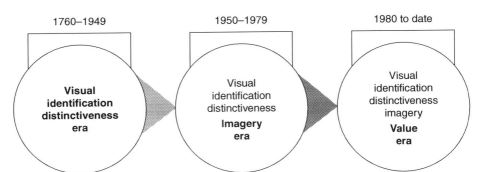

FIGURE 1.1 The emergence, development, and changing uses of corporate brand design, 1760 to date
Source: The researcher

legitimate when business people understood the relationship among favourable design and sales. A corporate brand design should allow consumers to make a decision when faced with choices and should prove an endorsement. Nowadays, organisations use visual expressions to enhance recognisability and differentiate their product and organisation from those of their competitors (Bennett, 1995; Giberson and Hulland, 1994; Gupta et al., 2008; Henderson and Cote, 1998; Zakia and Nadin, 1987). This marks the era characterised by the combination of 'visual identification, distinctiveness, imagery and value'.

The history of corporate brand design, as shown in Figure 1.1, is the main strategic concern for the achievement of a company. Research on the corporate brand design shows that it is the centre of a business's projected image and reputation (Dowling, 1994; Melewar and Saunders, 1998; Olins, 1986). Moreover, a company's corporate brand design communicates with customers and enables them to build up a mental image of the company (Henderson and Cote, 1998). Organisations aim to present a positive image (Napoles, 1988), whether planned or not, and an image can offer success for an organisation and serve to distinguish one company from another (Ferrand and Pages, 1999). Gray and Smeltzer (1985) considered that all this results in the sum of the corporate image, which is communicated through public relations, advertisers, marketers, and designers using images in their activities.

In summary, the evidence from earlier studies shows that the corporate brand design serves as a visual shorthand for communicating a message and promise to its consumers. A company's corporate brand design can act as an indicator to consumers to help them recognise manufacturer's products and services. In addition, corporate brand design can offer other benefits, such as added value to a company, speedy recognition, reaching the consumer through the media clutter, enhancing the company's image and its position, and improving the firm's communication skills. Thus, it is essential to understand the corporate brand design concept and its relationship with people's perception of a company (corporate image and corporate reputation).

Conclusion

Chapter 1 has described the history and the challenges in developing a corporate brand design and identified three eras: i) the visual identification and distinctiveness era (1760–1949); ii) the visual identification, distinctiveness, and imagery era (1950–1979); and iii) the visual identification, distinctiveness and imagery, and value era (1980 to the present day).

CASE STUDY – VIRGIN AND ITS IMAGE: LEVERAGING CORPORATE BRAND DESIGN

Maria Palazzo, University of Salerno, Italy

Discussion around the concept of corporate image developed in the 1950s and was captured by various scholars and practitioners. Definitions of corporate image in early studies are somewhat confusing and blurred; researchers do not agree upon the definition and the operationalisation of the term. However, study of the concept is important because the corporate image is a valuable asset that companies need to manage.

Some authors use the terms 'corporate identity', 'organisational identity', 'organisational image', 'corporate image', and 'corporate reputation' interchangeably. Furthermore, many researchers have discovered a broad range of perspectives to expand and understand these concepts and have defined it differently from the perspective of each paradigm.

On the one hand, the marketing literature stresses that corporate image is the image that external audiences have of an organisation. Marketing scholars focus on corporate brand and claim that a corporate image is about delivering what is promised to multiple audiences.

On the other hand, the graphic design school relied on the work of practitioners and related to the possible forms of a company's physical identification (e.g., corporate logo), transmitting the way in which an organisation is understood by its public. Thus, graphic designers and practitioners have viewed the corporate image as a product.

Starting from these points of view, the next sections, therefore, provide an enhanced understanding of the topic by studying the case of Virgin.

Virgin

According to the available information published on the corporate website:

> The Virgin Group has existed for half a century and now operates more than 40 companies across five business sectors and five continents. For half a century, the Virgin brand has been renowned for providing unique and exceptional customer experiences. From the world class Virgin Atlantic Upper Class lounge and onboarding experience through to pioneering unique group exercise experiences at Virgin Active – the whole business is built around our customers' needs. (…) At Virgin, we're known for challenging the status quo and shaking up markets, while championing people and the planet. Virgin's purpose is to change business for good and it is the very reason we exist. It is the lens through which we make all our decisions. Our values are what keep our people, products and partners on the right path to achieve our purpose while providing incredible experiences.
>
> *www.virgin.com/*

The huge product portfolio of the organisation includes Virgin Orbit, Virgin Oceanic, Virgin O$_2$, Virgin Racing, Virgin Pulse, Virgin Rail Group, Virgin Radio, Virgin Trains USA, Virgin Sports, Virgin Unite, Virgin Vacations, Virgin Startup, Virgin Voyages, and Virgin Voucher. All the brands share the strength of the corporate brand design (Pisano and Corsi, 2012).

Virgin's brand value and image

In order to build brand value, Virgin chooses as a basis for its corporate brand the following items (Batiz-Lazo and Kase, 2010):

1. Fun – Fun is linked with pleasure and entertainment, which is offered to the customer by several products/services typical of the brand.
2. Value for money – This item highlights that Virgin is trying to provide high quality products and services without forgetting that clients are often interested in attaining bargains and discounts.
3. Qualities – Virgin pays high attention to the detail of products and services.
4. Innovations – Virgin's products and services change according with the customers' need.
5. Competitive challenges – the company is able take advantage of external changes and to follow new trends in the selected markets.
6. Intensive customer service – This involves how the quality of the service/product is offered thanks to skilled employees who are able to deal with the clients' complaints and requests.

Under the umbrella of the corporate brand, over the years, Virgin group world has created more than 200 services and products. All of them are strongly associated with Virgin world thanks to the clear corporate brand design: This means that they all share a similar brand value. However, it must be said that not all the products and services are famous or successful; several products typical of Virgin, such as Virgin Radio, Virgin Cola, and Virgin Cosmetics, are no longer available in the current market.

Nevertheless, this does not mean that the Virgin brand is not in line with the new challenges of the market, nor that it is diluted due to saturation caused by the huge number of brand products (Boje and Smith, 2010).

In fact, it must be highlighted that Virgin has always used different marketing and communication techniques to develop and strengthen its brand image among key stakeholders. At Virgin, managers believe that brand building is a daily task. This is the mantra that pushes Richard Branson, Virgin CEO, who is involved every time the company decides to launch another brand or product. In the past, he flew in hot air balloons and promoted a Virgin's service wearing a wedding dress (De Vries, 1998; Shavinina, 2006). All these tactics helped over the years to strengthen the company's value and to position it among the best brands in each market that the organisation decided to reach.

Case questions

1. Please, analyse the emergence, development, and changing uses of corporate brand design taking into account the Virgin case study.
2. Please explore how the visual identity of the Virgin brand evolved over the years.

References

Batiz-Lazo, B. and Kase, K. (2010) Virgin Finance: Sir Richard Branson's Pursuit of a Significant Presence in Retail Financial Services. Available at SSRN 1734011.

Boje, D. and Smith, R. (2010) "Re-storying and visualizing the changing entrepreneurial identities of Bill Gates and Richard Branson", Culture and Organization, Vol. 16, No. 4, pp. 307–331.

De Vries, M. F. K. (1998) "Charisma in action: The transformational abilities of Virgin's Richard Branson and ABB's Percy Barnevik", Organizational Dynamics, Vol. 26, No. 3, pp. 7–21.

Pisano, G. P. and Corsi, E. (2012) "Virgin group: finding new avenues for growth", Harvard Business School Technology & Operations Mgt. Unit Case (612070).

Shavinina, L. V. (2006) "Micro-social factors in the development of entrepreneurial giftedness: the case of Richard Branson", High Ability Studies, Vol. 17, No. 2, pp. 225–235.

References

Anderson, S. (2000) Peter Behrens and a New Architecture for the Twentieth Century, The MIT Press, London.

Bayer, H., Gropius, I., and Gropius, W. (1938) Bauhaus, 1919–1928, Museum of Modern Art, New York.

Becker, G. S., Murphy, K. M., and Tamura, R. F. (1990) "Human capital, fertility, and economic growth", Journal of Political Economy, Vol. 98, No. 5, pp. 12–37.

Bennett, P. D. (1995) Dictionary of Marketing Terms, McGraw-Hill Education, New York.

Bowman, M. J. and Anderson, C. A. (1963) Concerning the Role of Education in Development, in Geertz, C., Old Societies and New States, New York, pp. 247–279.

Capitman, B. B. (1976) American Trademark Designs: A Survey of Seven Hundred and Thirty Two Marks Logos and Corporate Identity Symbols, Peter Smith Pub Inc, New York.

Clark, G. (2004) The Condition of the Working Class in England, 1200–2000, Working Paper, UC-Davis.

Collins, J. C. and Porras, J. I. (1994) Built to Last: Successful Habits of Visionary Companies, Harper Business, New York.

Deane, P. (1979) The First Industrial Revolution, Cambridge University Press, UK.

Dowling, G. R. (1994) Corporate Reputations: Strategies for Developing the Corporate Brand, Kogan Page, London.

Ferrand, A. and Pages, M. (1999) "Image management in sport organisations: the creation of value", European Journal of Marketing, Vol. 33, No. 3/4, pp. 387–402.

Fiell, C. and Fiell, P. (2003) Graphic Design for the 21st Century, Taschen, New York.

Foroudi, P., Melewar, T. C., and Gupta, S. (2017) Corporate logo: History, definition, and components. International Studies of Management & Organization, Vol. 47, No. 2, pp. 176–196.

Giberson, R. and Hulland, J. (1994) Using Logos as Cues to Recognition: A Preliminary Study, Western Business School, Working Paper Series, University of Western Ontario, Ontario.

Gray, E. R. and Smeltzer, L. R. (1985) "Corporate image: an integral part of strategy", Sloan Management Review, Vol. 26, No. 4, pp. 73–77.

Greenwood, J. and Jovanovic, B. (1999) "The Information-Technology Revolution and the Stock Market", American Economic Review, Vol. 89, No. 2, pp. 116–128.

Gupta, S., Grant, S., and Melewar, T. C. (2008) "The expanding role of intangible assets of the brand", Management Decision, Vol. 46, No. 6, pp. 948–960.

Henderson, P. W. and Cote, J. A. (1998) "Guidelines for selecting or modifying logos", Journal of Marketing, Vol. 62, No. 2, pp. 14–30.

Laqueur, T. W. (1974) "Literacy and Social Mobility in the Industrial Revolution in England", Past and Present, Vol. 64 (August), pp. 96–107.

Meggs, P. B. (1992) Type and Image: The Language of Graphic Design, John Wiley and Sons, New Jersey.

Melewar, T. C. and Saunders, J. (1998) "Global corporate visual identity systems: Standardization, control and benefits", International Marketing Review, Vol. 15, No. 4, pp. 291–308.

Murphy, J. M. and Rowe, M. (1988) How to Design Trademarks and Logos, Phaidon, London.

Napoles, V. (1988) Corporate Identity Design, Van Nostrand Reinhold, New York.

Olins, W. (1986) "The strategy of design", Management Today (May), pp. 52–55.

Pine, J. (1993) Mass customisation, Harvard Business School Press, Boston.

Raizman, D. (2003) History of Modern Design, Prentice Hall Art History, New Jersey.

Utterback, J. (1994) Mastering the dynamics of innovation, Harvard Business School Press, Boston.

Vries, J. D. (1994) "The Industrial Revolution and the Industrious Revolution", The Journal of Economic History, Vol. 54, No. 2, pp. 249–270.

West, E. G. (1978) "Literacy and the Industrial Revolution", Economic History Review, Vol 31, No. 3, pp. 369–383.

Zakia, R. D. and Nadin, M. (1987) "Semiotics, Advertising, and Marketing", Journal of Consumer Marketing, Vol. 4, No. 2, pp. 5–12.

2
CORPORATE BRAND DESIGN MANAGEMENT FROM DIFFERENT PERSPECTIVES

Mohammad Mahdi Foroudi, Flora Mahdavi, and Pantea Foroudi

Introduction

Chapter 2 reviews the interpretation in the literature of the corporate brand design and visual identity as a root of corporate identity. Five core disciplines have contributed to the evolution and study of corporate brand design, namely, graphic design, integrated communication, organisational studies, marketing, and multi-disciplinary approaches. In this chapter, we discuss these in detail and present an (holistic) overview of the dimensions of the corporate brand design and visual identity construct.

Background to corporate brand design management

Corporate brand design has attracted the attention of practitioners and academics since 1760 (Foroudi et al., 2017). However, it has become progressively important to differentiate enterprises from their rivals. A corporate brand design helps the business to form an image of the company in people's minds (Foroudi, 2019; 2020; Foroudi et al., 2014), which brings value to an organisation's reputation (Anson, 1988; Green and Loveluck, 1994; Olins, 1989). Corporate brand designs are 'ubiquitous in the marketplace, and the average consumer encounters a multitude of them on any given day' (Hagtvedt, 2011, p. 86). Therefore, organisations invest a significant amount of time, research, and resources to develop a corporate brand design that represents the organisation's identity to form its image in a constructive way (Foroudi et al., 2017).

The corporate brand design is the consumer's first perception of a company, and it encompasses the entire corporate image. According to Foroudi (2019), the corporate brand design is important for decision-makers, who screen developments as well as anticipate potential influences and can advance or modify a favourable design in order to gain a competitive advantage (Melewar and Saunders, 1998). Decision-makers should attempt to enhance customers' favourable attitude towards the organisation through the creation of desirable coordination practices and communication activities.

The concept of corporate brand design is grounded in a number of subject domains. For example, for a long period of time, corporate logo and corporate brand design had been used synonymously with corporate image and corporate identity (e.g., Margulies, 1977). Corporate identity communicates to consumers through different channels (Gray and Balmer, 1998). In other words, when customers adopt a favourable attitude towards a corporate brand design, they acquire a stronger image of the company. Thus, companies often use corporate brands and rituals to create a strong corporate identity (Balmer, 2008).

This statement is based on attribution theory (Foroudi et al., 2014). Social psychologists (Jones et al., 1972; Weiner, 1986) developed the attribution model to study how people make sense of their environment. Attribution theory refers to 'the perception or inference of cause' (Kelley and Michela, 1980, p. 458) and to how individuals manage to excel or fail at dynamic interactions with regard to the implications they draw from specific behaviours (Kelley and Michela, 1980).

Attribution theory (Folkes, 1984) has been widely employed across the marketing and consumer behaviour literature to describe the decision-making process of consumers. The process of attribution defines consumers' likely behaviour, satisfaction, emotion, and cognition (Weiner, 2000). In addition, the customer's desirable perception about an organisation affects their behaviours and attitudes (Sen and Bhattacharya, 2001).

In the literature, there is discussion of how corporate brand design is the key method to produce a consistent image of the company to its audience (Olins, 1986). Attribution theory states that an individual's perception about the failure or success of another person can be attributed to another individual's behaviour (Weiner, 1986). This argument supports the view that a company's brand design can promote a long-term adequate corporate image and corporate reputation as well as the combination of external and internal communicational features of a corporate brand design that can stimulate individuals' perception and interpretation (Van Riel et al., 2001). A satisfying attribute would be seen as favourable and would lead to a more favourable attitude concerning the company's corporate brand design. An original attribute would result in a customer's tendency to react favourably toward the company. Based on this conclusion, the research streams evaluate and present an inclusive overview regarding the paradigms in these fields.

This chapter reviews the publications that consider the understanding of the corporate brand design as a root of corporate identity. Five core disciplines that have contributed to the evolution and study of corporate brand design are the *graphic design, integrated-communication, organisational studies, marketing,* and *interdisciplinary/multi-disciplinary* approaches (Balmer, 1995a; 1998; 2001; Foroudi et al., 2019a; Van Riel and Balmer, 1997) which are discussed in detail, and we present an (holistic) overview of the dimensions of the corporate brand design construct.

Perspective 1: Graphic design – visual and verbal cues

Graphic design is a tangible aspect of an organisation, which is widely accepted, and it is an objectively specified dimension in the early literature (Margulies, 1977). Graphic designers' vision of corporate identity is concerned with the successful use of a corporate logo/trademark (Balmer, 2009). The principal method whereby the company's corporate identities are manifested visually (Bernstein 1984; Olins 1978, 1989; Selame and Selame 1988) is the corporate brand design, which is used to establish a convincing corporate reputation. Corporate identity emerged in the 1930s and 1940s in graphic design. Then, the term 'corporate identity' was used by Margulies in the 1950s to differentiate his work from that of US designers. The company's visual identity is said to be the face of the company (Topalian, 1984). Early scholars in graphic design's domain were practitioners until a primary focus on corporate identity research was undertaken in the 1980s (Balmer, 1995b; Carter, 1982; Simoes et al., 2005). The visual identity paradigm focuses on organisational nomenclature, company name, logos, buildings, company architecture, and on the design and the decor of the corporate retail outlets' architecture, including the exterior design and the interior design, and so on, in fact, anything that could be relevant to graphic design (Bernstein, 1986; Carter, 1982; Hatch and Schultz, 2000; Olins, 1989; 1991; Selame and Selame, 1988). Corporate brand is the core component of the corporate identity that a company can use to portray its image, efficiency, and appearance to stakeholders. Moreover, corporate brand design is a tool that can shape a company with a contemporary touch, and so companies use the visual language to indicate their contemporality (Henderson and Cote, 1998; Martinez, 2006). Kennedy (1977) demonstrated that an organisation's employees play a role in creating an organisational identity and in its communication to external stakeholders and may even help reaffirm trust in the organisation. The research conducted by Kennedy (1977) indicates that the identity of a company influences the values of the organisational participants who create the corporate culture (Balmer, 1995b; Downey, 1986). Therefore, the characteristics of an organisational culture may be reflected through corporate symbolism (Van Riel and Balmer, 1997). Corporate logos that transfer the strategic, visual scopes of corporate identity to a diverse population need management (Balmer, 1997; Hatch and Schultz, 1997; Van Riel and Balmer, 1997).

The role of symbolism 'is assigned a greater role and has grown from its original purpose of increasing organisational visibility to a position where it is seen as having a role in communicating corporate strategy' (Van Riel and Balmer, 1997, p. 340). In this vein, Melewar and Saunders (1998) state that corporate brand design systems are an essential element of an organisation's projected image in a global context. Melewar and Saunders (2000) studied corporate visual identification efficacy and projected the identity of British multinationals and Malaysian subsidiaries. They found that standardising the corporate brand design would have a positive influence on consumers' awareness of recruitment and publicity and on their familiarity with the company and the company's services, sales, products, generosity, and market share, as well as influencing the receptiveness of the local community to its set-up in those specific areas (Foroudi and Marvi, 2020). According to Balmer (1995a) and Van Riel and Balmer (1997), the main focus in this field of study has shifted to evaluating the reason visual representations are structured to mirror the company's core values and beliefs. Identity should be communicated by all corporate features, visible (e.g., buildings, communication material) and invisible (e.g., organisational behaviours towards internal and external audiences). All the features should communicate to internal audiences (Margulies, 1977) and external audiences, which introduce the concept of corporate image (Gioia et al., 2000). Furthermore, corporate identity and corporate image must be coherent (Carter, 1982). Visual identification has commonly been recognised as a means of transmitting a company's identity through visual and tangible aspects, which affect its image in the eyes of different stakeholders. Identity helps in clarifying the organisation's structure. The main intellectual advancement of the visual/graphic school was initiated by Olins (1978; 1991).

Balmer (1995a; 2009) identified seven schools of thought on corporate identity: strategic, behavioural, strategic visual, corporate communications, visual behavioural, strategic communications, and design-as-fashion (Ahmadi Lari et al., 2020). The three non-graphic schools of corporate identity focus on the nature of strategic, cultural (behavioural), or promotional (corporate communications) in relation to social identity, administrative identity, and visual identity/corporate identity (Balmer, 2009). The remaining schools (strategic visual, visual behavioural, strategic communications, and design-as-fashion) relate graphic design to the organisation's strategy, culture, and communications. Graphic design embodies a strategic shift. It can be accomplished by visual means, integrated corporate communication, and multi-disciplinary perspectives (Van Riel and Balmer, 1997). Visual identity is the public face of the company (Topalian, 1984), and it is used consistently across all possible forms of a company's physical identification (e.g., advertisements, letterheads, business cards, buildings, and logos) (Carter, 1982; Margulies, 1977; Olins, 1991, 1978; Pilditch, 1970). It gives an organisation exposure and should be kept up to date (Karaosmanoglu et al., 2011; Van Riel and Balmer, 1997) in order to create a favourable corporate image. The visual school focuses on corporate visual identity. The following quotation from Balmer (2001) summarises the scope of this perspective. Balmer states that with regard to corporate brand design, it

> would be perverse to suggest that visually impaired customers, employees or investors are unable to recognise, differentiate between or form opinions of organisations. Upon reflection it becomes apparent that the non-visual senses can be just as powerful in communicating the identity of a collective group.
>
> *p. 267*

According to Henrion and Parkin (1967), 'The people of these groups build up their idea of the corporation from what they see and experience of it' (p. 7). Experience has been defined as 'displaying a relatively high degree of familiarity with a certain subject area, which is obtained through some type of exposure' (Park and Lessing, 1981). The two main approaches to operationalise and measure the product familiarity are: i) 'in terms of how much a person knows about the product'; and ii) 'to measure familiarity in terms of how much a person thinks she/he knows about the product' (Park and Lessing, 1981, p. 223). A corporate brand design as a product should be carefully constructed in order for it to be effective, to communicate something of the character of corporations, and to increase familiarity towards the brand and the company. When consumers are unfamiliar with an advertised product/brand, they lack any prior knowledge on which to base their perceptions towards the product/brand (Campbell and Keller, 2003). For instance, the corporate logo is the company's official graphic design, and its design's uniqueness demands a considerable degree of creativity that must be in line with the company's strategy: The design should be distinctive and innovative. When a strategy is acknowledged, the nature of the corporate brand design makes the company distinctive and well-known by its corporate logos (Melewar et al., 2017). Furthermore, a strong design may also attract an audience by challenging them to visually relate to the logo. However, in order to develop a new corporate brand design and design improvements, companies must spend considerable amounts of money.

A corporate brand design transmits the visual and strategic aspects of corporate identity to diverse markets (Balmer, 1997; Hatch and Schultz, 1997; Van Riel and Balmer, 1997). For example, McDonalds employs a collection of corporate brand design features comprising the well-designed golden arches and Ronald McDonald, the clown, which results in an image that is coherent and where the different elements convey the same message. According to

DeChernatony (2001), designers need to understand that corporate brand design should inform their decisions about design elements, colours, and typefaces. Furthermore, the fastest growing segment in advertising is corporate giveaways (e.g., T-shirts), which often feature nothing more than the company's corporate brand design. Advertising allows companies to establish a competitive advantage to distinguish themselves from their rivals and to gain goodwill from patrons and stakeholders. Van den Bosch et al. (2006) divided the corporate brand design into three distinct levels: the strategic, the operational, and the design level. All of these stages have a methodological aspect. However, these three levels need to be managed carefully to add any real value to the company:

1. *The strategic level* reflects the organisation's objectives for its visual identity. This level refers to the strategic goals and objectives that organisations have in regard to their visual identity system. It assists companies with the understanding of how to distinguish themselves; the academic literature calls it the corporate branding strategy (Olins, 1989). Different approaches have been established to investigate the corporate identity of organisations (Van Rekom and Van Riel, 2000; Van Riel, 1995; Van Riel and Balmer, 1997).
2. *The operational level*, which is the less visible component of the corporate identity management system, focuses on the expansion and management of corporate brand design systems and how an organisation transforms its strategic objectives into a cohesive, coherent, and efficient visual identity. The focus of this level is integration and alignment with the overall corporate strategy in order to monitor any changes in the internal and external environment to optimise the perceived corporate identity.
3. *The design level* reflects the usefulness and reliability of the basic aspects of a corporate brand design in order to build and preserve an organisation's visual identity. This is the area in which graphic design companies and corporate identity organisations are most active, as they are most familiar with this area.

From a visual identity standpoint, Olins (1978 and 1991) suggested that corporations primarily use three forms of visual identity to convey their corporate culture and corporate strategy; more explicitly, these are: i) monolithic – for example, authors (Foroudi et al., 2019; 2020; Olins, 1989; Van Riel, 1995) refer to the monolithic identification under which the company has its own name and style throughout its organisation; ii) 'endorsed identity' – the organisation has several activities or companies that are endorsed by the group name and identity and the brand is associated with subsidiaries (Holiday Inn Express); and iii) branded identity – the identity under which goods are branded individually and may be unrelated to each other or the company.

Baker and Balmer (1997) identified the introduction to a UK university of a modern graphic identity and explored the role of corporate brand design evaluation and audit in defining an organisation's weakness and dysfunctions. The research findings indicated that visual identity should be integrated into an holistic approach to organisational repositioning. The visual treatment and quality of an organisation's output makes up its visual identity.

This perspective embraces the management of features such as corporate name, corporate logo, architecture, website, and so on. Corporate brand design can be the 'face of the organisation' that transmits the company image to a company's stakeholders. The following section reviews the perspective of integrated communication studies when approaching the corporate brand design concept.

Perspective 2: Integrated communication approach

The integrated communications strategy, as realised by marketers and graphic designers, has led to a number of authors proposing the effectiveness of overall consistency in formal visual and marketing communications (Keller, 1993; Van Riel, 1995; Van Riel and Balmer, 1997). The integrated-communication paradigm has been a concern 'within the marketing, communications and public relations disciplines with the coordination of communications, namely: corporate communications and total corporate communications' (Balmer, 2011, p. 1338). According to Van Riel (1995, 1997), the incorporated communication approach to corporate identity has progressed towards a multi-disciplinary approach as self-presentation.

The integrated marketing communication is defined as 'the strategic co-ordination of all messages and media used by an organisation to influence its perceived brand value' (Duncan and Everett, 1993, p. 33). By integrating their communication strategies, companies can generate synergies between their different forms of communication. Furthermore, companies should place more stress on internal communications. According to Kennedy (1977), looking at the formal communication activities suggested that employees' interactions with external audiences influence the corporate image. Authors (e.g., Abratt, 1989; Bernstein, 1986; Foroudi et al., 2017; Melewar et al., 2018) have studied how a company's corporate identity could be conveyed internally and externally, that is, any communication that expresses an image and attempts to convey the identity of an organisation in cohesive and harmonised expressions through external and internal methods of communication (Simoes et al., 2005). Gilly and Wolfinbarger (1998) studied the effect of advertising on an internal audience and the value of engaging staff in communications emphasising the need for integrated and coherent communication. The efficiency of communication may lead to prior knowledge of the advertised brand or company (Palazzo et al., 2020).

Authors have seen how corporate identity and its elements are internally and externally transmitted (Abratt, 1989; Bernstein, 1986; Gray and Smeltzer, 1987). For example, Abratt (1989) took into consideration the idea of 'interface' for corporate identity and corporate image. Corporate identity is a distinctive attribute that an organisation or brand incorporates to promote its ideals and communicate information about itself.

Organisations align both their internal and external communications to create constructive images for target audiences (Van Riel, 1995). Gray and Smeltzer (1985) referred to the following corporate image communicators: nomenclature, formal statements (e.g., mission), organisational communication, imagery and graphics, permanent media (e.g., stationery, buildings), and promotional media (e.g., advertising, public relations). It is critical that such sources provide the internal and external stakeholders with a consistent image. Indeed, communication is considered to be the bridge that connects the corporate identity with the image of the organisation.

In addition, it is important that organisations harmonise their internal and external communications to facilitate the generation of a favourable image of the company for the stakeholders (Gilly and Wolfinbarger, 1998; Van Riel, 1995). The integrated communications approach advocates that it is critical to develop and manage the impressions that customers and other stakeholders have about the organisation. Moreover, Abratt (1989) states that there is interface consistency among the projected identities and the perceived image. Corporate communication embraces marketing, organisational, and management communication

(Van Riel, 1995). Corporate image can be communicated through nomenclature, formal statements, organisational communication, imagery and graphics, permanent media (e.g., stationery, buildings), and promotional media (e.g., advertising, public relations) (Gray and Smeltzer, 1985). These forms of communication should be consistent and coherent to external audiences in the environment (Gilly and Wolfinbarger, 1998). Total corporate communications include primary, secondary, as well as tertiary communications (Balmer and Gray, 2000). It is important that the corporate identity of an enterprise is identified to ensure that the organisation's stakeholders perceive it as expected (Bick et al., 2003). Bernstein's (1986) study shows that the integrated communication paradigm emphasises the need for efficient communication with all the company's stakeholders. Stakeholders can include employees or even competitors (Hatch and Schultz, 1997). The integrated communication approach is related to corporate identity as total corporate communication and is necessary for managing associations with stakeholders. Communications also play an important role in relation to other factors, such as brand personality and corporate visual identity, which are recognised in the corporate identity context (Van Riel and Balmer, 1997). The marketers and graphic designers have acknowledged the efficacy of consistency in the area of visual and marketing communications, such that formal corporate communications would have to be consistent (Bernstein, 1986; Van Riel and Balmer, 1997). This approach is encapsulated in Balmer and Wilson's (1998) description: 'Corporate identity is the total of visual and non-visual means applied by a company to present itself to all its relevant target groups on the basis of a corporate identity plan' (p. 15). Hence, the corporate identity mix can be defined as 'communications' that need to be 'integrated'.

Abratt (1989) identifies the notion of the corporate identity and corporate image interface. Corporate personality is outlined as 'the sum total of the characteristics of the organisation. These characteristics – behavioural and intellectual – serve to distinguish one organisation from another' (Abratt, 1989, p. 413). Authors (Baker and Balmer, 1997; Balmer, 1995a; 1998; Balmer and Soenen, 1999; Balmer and Wilson, 1998; Bernstein, 1984; Markwick and Fill, 1997; Van Riel and Balmer, 1997) claim that these traits are the behaviours and values held by the employees of the organisation. According to Cornelissen and Harris (2001), corporate identity is a 'tangible representation of the personality, the expression as manifest in the behaviour and communication of the organisation' (p. 56).

The Abratt (1989) paradigm, also known as the corporate image management process (p. 203), was the first attempt to demonstrate that the correlation between corporate personality, corporate identity, and corporate image is the foundation of corporate image. Stuart (1999) states that Marwick and Fill (1997) 'considered that both organisational and marketing communications were the dominant forms of communication between identity and image, and management communication formed the link between corporate personality and corporate identity' (p. 204). Van Rekom (1997) points out how the aim of corporate communications is to create such a desirable corporate image within target audiences (p. 411): 'Gaining a competitive advantage from messages requires the integration of internal and external communications' (Simoes et al., 2005, p. 156). Corporate communication is integrated in organisational messages; hence, consistency in all types of external and internal communication is needed in order to transmit the desired identity (Van Riel, 1995).

The next section reviews the perspective of organisational studies when approaching the organisational identity concept.

Perspective 3: Organisational approach

The organisational literature centres on organisational members' perceptions (member identification), identity (Kennedy, 1977), and organisational behaviour (Dutton and Dukerich, 1991; Elsbach and Kramer, 1996; Foroudi et al., 2019; 2020; Gioia and Thomas, 1996; Gioia et al., 2000; Whetten and Mackey, 2002), which are connected to organisational identity by focusing on the association between employees and organisations (Hatch and Schultz, 1997). Employees of corporations can perceive their own company and understand how they interpret their own external perceptions by perceiving the importance of the identity of the corporation (what it stands for and where it aims to be) and internalising a cognitive structure. The organisational perspective on the organisation's identity is connected to organisational and managerial cognition. Cognitive connection with the organisation and the employees' behaviours suggests the notion of organisational identification as stated by Dutton et al. (1994) as follows: 'When a person's self-concept contains the same attributes as those in the perceived organisational identity, we define this cognitive connection as organisational identification' (p. 239). The emphasis on cognitive theory and research in corporate identity can only be a result of the 'cognitive revolution' in psychological research.

Research on organisational behaviour constituted by corporate identity management primarily draws on organisational culture studies (Hatch and Schultz, 1997). The related terms to this approach are organisational identity (identity of an organisation), image, reputation, and organisational identification. Indeed, there is an overlap between corporate identity and the multi-disciplinary approach to organisational identity (Balmer 2001; Balmer and Wilson, 1998; Van Riel and Balmer, 1997). The identity of the organisation is an organisation's understanding of itself.

Scholars (Albert and Whetten, 1985) have identified organisational identity as what constitutes a core institution (i.e., character), trait, and lasting characteristics of importance in corporate identity management. Ashforth and Mael (1989) focus on the identity in an organisation and identification with an organisation as two perspectives of identity studies. Gioia et al. (2000) comments:

> We might characterise extant approaches to studying identity as involving three ways of thinking about the concept: (1) concern with the identity of organisations, (2) concern with the identity of people within organisations, and (3) concern with people's identification with organisations. The first of these related domains is the area most in need of innovative thinking and also is the area with the most potential for becoming a definitive area for organisational study, rather than another eclectic handmaiden of psychology and sociology.
>
> *p. 146*

Organisational identity is bound to a particular form of the individual's social identity, which highlights the significance of organisational membership to the individual. The perceived organisational identity of employees and the interpreted external image of organisations represent the insider's perception of that organisation by external parties as positive/negative (Dutton et al., 1994). Organisational members use images like a gauge to assess how external people judge organisations. Dutton and Dukerich (1991, p. 518) clarify the matter as follows: 'Our interpretation is that some organisational actions are tied to sets of concerns that we call issues. Issues are developments, events, and trends that an organisation's members collectively recognise as having some benefits to the organisation'. Dutton and Dukerich (1991) outline organisational identity, image, and reputation as follows:

> An organisation's identity describes what its members believe to be its character; an organisation's image describes attributes members believe people outside the organisation use to distinguish it. Organisational image is different from reputation: reputation describes the actual attributes outsiders ascribe to an organisation, but image describes insiders' assessments of what outsiders think. Both organisational image and identity are constructs held in organisation members' minds.
>
> p. 547

Authors (Dutton et al. 1994; Ashforth and Mael 1989) have suggested that attempts by employees to internalise their organisations' core characteristics are a means of social identity. Drawing on the social identity concept, authors (Ashforth and Mael, 1989; Elsbach and Kramer, 1996; Gioia and Thomas, 1996) have claimed that the employees of an organisation are identified in relation to their own workplaces (Ashforth and Mael, 1989; Elsbach and Kramer, 1996; Gioia and Thomas, 1996). Employees attempt to internalise their organisation's core characteristics as a means of social identification (Ashforth and Mael, 1989; Dutton et al., 1994). Dutton et al. (1994) viewed it as 'the degree to which a member defines him- or herself by the same attributes that he or she believes define the organisation' (p. 239). Organisational studies underlie the concept of social identity (Ashforth and Mael, 1989). According to social identity theory, there is a psychological link between organisational and social identities and the way employees try to identify with their workplace. Ashforth and Mael (1989) verified that organisational identification is a form of social identification and that there are multiple identities inside the organisation.

Ashforth and Mael (1989) note that an employee's behaviour and their identification could have an influence on the identity of the company for external stakeholders. They believe that social identification could initiate an employee's beliefs, group values and standards, and homogeneity with regard to their attitudes and behaviour. Ashforth and Mael (1989) address social identification as being

> distinguishable from internalisation. Whereas identification refers to self in terms of social categories (I am), internalisation refers to the incorporation of values, attitudes, and so forth within the self as guiding principles (I believe). Although certain values and attitudes typically are associated with members of a given social category, acceptance of the category as a definition of self does not necessarily mean acceptance of those values and attitudes. An individual may define herself in terms of the organisation she works for, yet she can disagree with the prevailing values, strategy, system of authority, and so on.
>
> pp. 21–22

Corporate identity and organisational identity are complex concepts, and three perspectives can be recognised in organisational and identity studies as follows: i) the identity of the organisation (organisation's identity) is related to an individual's identity and represents the essence of that identity, which can answer the questions about who we are and what we are; ii) the identity (of people) in the organisation (individual's organisational identity) is a metaphor arising from an organisation's identity or social identity (Ashforth and Mael, 1989) whereby an individual defines him/herself by resorting to his/her membership of the focal organisation either spatially or temporally. Individuals have a personal identity (who I am), as well as a social identity (Ashforth and Mael, 1989; Tajfel and Turner, 1985); iii) the identity with the organisation (organisational identification) is used interchangeably with organisational identity. Organisational identity is used to describe a state and organisational identification to describe a process. Organisational identification takes place once an individual's opinions about her/his organisation become self-referential or self-defining.

Top managers play a fundamental role in influencing internal and external stakeholders' identification with the organisation. For organisations to differentiate themselves in the eyes of managers and stakeholders, they aim to promote favourable organisational images to achieve organisational goals, mission, practices, values, and action; this contributes to shaping the organisational identity (Scott and Lane, 2000). A damaged managerial image affects the target audiences' trust in the organisation. Regarding the artefacts of identity, managers are responsible for creating and managing symbols, such as physical settings, to express an organisation's identity. The expression of behaviours and artefacts should be consistent in all internal and external forms in order to convey the desired identity. Ashforth and Mael (1989) assert:

> It is tacitly understood by managers that a positive and distinctive *organisational* identity attracts the recognition, support, and loyalty of not only organisational members but other key *constituents (e.g. stakeholders,* customers, job seekers), and it is this search for a distinctive identity that induces *organisations* to focus so intensely on advertising, names and logos, jargon, leaders and mascots, and so forth.
>
> *p. 28*

Accordingly, corporate identity management should be conceived within multiple disciplines and should be seen to represent three major dimensions: i) visual identity/symbolism (Carter, 1982; Melewar and Saunders, 1998, 1999, 2000; Olins, 1991; Pilditch, 1970); ii) communication (Van Riel, 1995); and iii) philosophy, mission, and values (Abratt, 1989; Balmer, 1994).

Visual identity, as a hard tangible fundamental of corporate identity, shapes the physical symbols and generates physical recognition of the organisation (Carter, 1982; Melewar and Saunders, 1998; Olins, 1991; Pilditch, 1970). The intangibility of services, however, magnifies the complexity of maintaining visual components. For instance, the architecture (physical evidence, environmental design, and decor) and employee presentation help to convey the tangible clues that influence customer behaviour. Thus, the visual identity of an organisation can be viewed as identification (Downey, 1986). Furthermore, the design components indicate the company's culture and values and should be recognised by the organisation's employees (Berry, 2000). In the context of a service encounter, the physical environment will affect how users interpret service failure.

From the marketing perspective, everything in and about a company is concerned with communication. According to some authors (Van Riel, 1995), communication is the keystone for representing an image. Marketing messages should be consistent and coherent in all forms of communication to create a cohesive corporate identity and corporate image. The company's philosophy, mission, and values dimension gives the organisation a degree of consistency and attempts to bring a strategic basis to the corporate identity construct. The corporate concept is a crucial stage of identity creation, and the key element of this philosophy is the corporate mission. Balmer (2001) states:

> The acquisition of a favourable corporate image is dependent upon an understanding of, and, where appropriate, the nurturing by management of a distinct corporate culture which reflects the corporate mission and philosophy and as such becomes one of the dominant cultures within the organisation (i.e., the desired corporate personality) which results in the desired corporate identity (i.e., where the innate character of the organisation mirrors the corporate strategy and philosophy).
>
> *p. 254*

Corporate identity is related to corporate values and sharing them with organisational members. The company's philosophy indicates the company's decisions, policies, and actions. Every organisation has a vision and a mission statement (Dowling, 1994), which transmit the company's purpose and aspirations. Levin (2000) defines the vision and mission statements as follows: The mission is an explanation of what the organisation is and does – the business and beliefs about how it ought to be conducted and its contribution in general and usually last over time. However, the vision is 'a high lucid story of an organisation's preferred future in action. A future that describes what life will be like for employees, customers, and other key stakeholders'.

Perspective 4: Marketing paradigm

Evaluating the marketing studies on corporate brand design over the past few decades is likely to show a variety of significant changes in attention. Researchers have emphasised corporate image management and analysed the significance of corporate identity (in particular, corporate design visual identity) for corporate image creation (Balmer, 2008, p. 882). As corporate brand design is highly important to the reputation and image of the organisation, the layout of the corporate brand design is vital for the marketing efficacy of the company. Marketing effectiveness can build on brand management and integrated communications studies (DeChernatony, 1999; Duncan and Everett, 1993).

The concept of corporate identity has strong supporters, and it exerts a significant influence in marketing. From this perspective, corporate identity is grounded in corporate-level theories, including corporate branding, communications, image, and reputation (Melewar et al., 2020). Connecting the notion of identity and marketing philosophy is linked with the organisation (Balmer, 2008). The early literature of marketing scholarship (e.g., Martineau, 1958; Tucker, 1961) focuses on customers' and stakeholders' perceptions of corporate identity and its advantage to organisations and stakeholders (Balmer, 2011).

Marketing researchers often link the visual identification with the organisation's stakeholder/customer perceptions (Abratt, 1989, Balmer, 2008; Dacin and Brown, 2002; Tourky et al., 2020). Thus, marketing researchers have drawn attention to the role of visuals and, especially, the role of corporate and brand logos (Balmer, 1995a; Foroudi et al., 2016); they believe that strong corporate brand design guidelines and consistent marketing communication should be supported (Van Riel, 2000). The consequences of individual design elements on customer responses have been investigated in the marketing research (e.g., Pittard et al., 2007; Van der Lans et al., 2009). This approach explores the theory of corporate brand design as the basis of corporate identity and addresses how corporate identity is conveyed to the organisation's public (Hatch and Schultz, 1997), which is primarily focused on the branding literature (Simoes et al., 2005).

Marketing scholars have labelled the corporate brand design as a 'vision-driven approach' to management, and this concept is a mix of soul, mind, and voice. This approach highlights how identity management has evolved from a dominant visual expression to the management of strategic change (Balmer and Soenen, 1999; Hatch and Schultz, 2003; Van Riel, 1995). Moreover, integrated communication and the marketing perspective are vital to understand how the marketing field addresses the corporate brand design and its components; marketing managers and scholars understand how design can influence recipients (Van der Lans et al., 2009).

The marketing approach is centred on the corporate image as the external perception of corporate identity (especially corporate visual identity) and is directed at defining the notion of the corporate image (Balmer, 2008). Marketing scholars also focus on deeper notions of corporate identity, which contribute to a related concern about corporate identity management and development (Balmer, 2008; Melewar and Karaosmanoglu, 2006). According to Hankinson et al. (2007), corporate brand design can signal an organisation's rebranding process and reflect the identity of a company; it should be in association with the corporate identity. The design of the corporate brand is used to increase its significance as a product and services differentiator to enable customers to build an image of the company in their minds (Foroudi, 2020); advertising is an opportunity for a corporation to display its corporate image. Attitudes concerning an advertisement can be conceived of as a consumer's general approval for, or displeasure with, an advertisement.

Communication follows on from the brand-building process and occurs wherever there is contact with audiences. Brown and Reingen (1987), for example, believe that information about a product or a company can be a main determinant of consumer behaviour and attitude and can create a favourable corporate image (Dacin and Brown, 2002). Managers should create a belief to interact with the market (Van den Bosch et al., 2005) and with the customers. In addition, management has to consider the design process to engage with designers by using a shared language with a similar perspective. According to Wheeler (2003), 'The main challenge to the designer is to translate vision into a tangible expression and a visual language that resonates with all stakeholders' (p. 16).

Marketing scholars believe that the corporate brand design is a key element of a marketing strategy (Cohen, 1991; Pitta and Franzak, 2008) and of marketing communication (Ewing, 2006; Kohli et al., 2002; Pittard et al., 2007). The corporate brand design could be used as an effective management tool for the arrangement of preferred features. Furthermore, an organisation's corporate brand design is also used to illustrate (Van Riel, 1995; Van Riel et al., 2001) who the organisation is and what its aims are (Balmer, 2006; Stuart, 1997; Van Rekom, 1997). This simplifies the role of formal corporate communication (Baker and Balmer, 1997). Henderson and Cote (1998) observe that corporate brand design is a consistent, recognisable benchmark for an organisation, and it can establish a clear sense of familiarity.

Corporate brand design as a symbol will allow the company to develop a market advantage or brand differentiation from its rivals (Montes and Foroudi, 2017) as well as providing consumers with reassurance. A corporate brand design is used to evoke the set of associations to communicate one clear desirable message to the consumers (Durgee and Stuart, 1987; Keller, 1993; Kropp et al., 1990; Schmitt, 1995; Van Riel, 1995). Accordingly, marketing academics (e.g., Balmer and Gray, 2003; Simoes et al., 2005) regard the corporation as a brand. The branding notion can be clearly implemented at the corporate level (Aaker, 1996).

The organisation, which has grown into a strategic factor in branding and corporate branding, incorporates the company's vision and culture explicitly as part of its unique selling points. Van den Bosch et al. (2006) indicate that employees will have to grasp the logic and the visual identity of an organisation so they can identify it and endorse it, which may provide an incentive for customers to increase their awareness of a company's product brands.

Keller (1999) identifies the ways in which the brand can be communicated and explained. The concept of a brand 'mantra' is a short expression to explain brand positioning and core brand values, a valuable instrument to convey the brand's meaning. According to Keller (2003), a brand is a 'name, term, sign, symbol, or a combination of them, intended to identify the goods and services of one seller or group of sellers and to differentiate them from those of competition' (p. 3). The corporate brand design is the most powerful element of the brand, and it is used to identify the firm or brand and represent the company in marketing efforts to its target audiences and to provide customers with positive associations and enhance their willingness to purchase (Bennet, 1995; Dowling, 1994; Henderson and Cote, 1998). Keller (2003) highlight the significance of selecting brand elements to characterise the brand's identity.

According to Aaker (1996), brand identity provides a brand with strategic direction, purpose, and meaning. Aaker (1996) outlines brand identity as

> a unique set of brand associations that the brand strategist aspires to create or maintain. These associations represent what the brand stands for and imply a promise to customers from the organisation members. Brand identity should help establish a relationship between the brand and the customer by generating a value proposition involving functional, emotional, or self-expressive benefits.
>
> *p. 68*

Aaker's (1996) model contains the brand essence, core identity, and extended identity. The brand essence captures the brand values and vision in an timeless identity statement (Aaker, 2000). The central identity reflects the eternal existence of the brand and includes the associations (the soul, brand values and beliefs, organisational competencies, and organisational mission) that will possibly remain stable overtime. Brand identification for the consumers is a full package that incorporates the business's service reputation, features, product quality, welfare, value, and performance. The core identity elements make the brand sustainable, exclusive, and valued (Aaker, 1996), while the extended brand identity represents completeness and gives texture to the brand (e.g., visible associations with the brand) and transforms the ambivalent core identity into a consistent direction of the brand. Regarding this development, Aaker (2004) states, 'The corporate brand is special because it explicitly and unambiguously represents an organisation as well as a product' (p. 10), while Ind (1997) asserts that 'a corporate brand is more than just the outward manifestation of an organisation its name, logo, visual presentation. Rather it is the core of values that defines it' (p. 13).

Balmer and Greyser (2003) provide many valuable comparisons between the identification and naming of a corporation's corporate identity and corporate branding. Corporate branding is far more externally oriented and aims to achieve a profile vis-à-vis identity. Corporate brands should be financially respected or amortised in a manner that does not preclude corporate identity. As Schmitt and Pan (1994) argue, corporate identity can be viewed as branding at the corporate level. Branding for services is different from branding for goods because it is the organisation that is the primary brand (Berry and Parasuraman, 1991). Thus, in service organisations, such as financial services, hotels, and airlines, customers' multiple interactions with the staff of the brand are presented across various parts of a service delivery (Bitner et al., 1994), and each organisation develops a corporate brand image. Corporate identity promotes corporate branding (Balmer, 1995a), which Balmer and Greyser (2003) is a means of demonstrating corporate identity. For all the above reasons, corporate identity can be seen as an antecedent of corporate branding. Berry (2000) explained:

> Branding plays a special role in service companies because strong brands increase customers' trust of the invisible purchase. Strong brands enable customers to better visualise and understand intangible products. They reduce customers' perceived monetary, social, or safety risk in buying services, which are difficult to evaluate prior to purchase. Strong brands are the surrogates when the company offers no fabric to touch, no trousers to try on, no watermelons or apples to scrutinise, no automobile on test-drive.
>
> *p. 128*

The business branding involves using the assets of a company to establish the ideal identity perception of the internal and external stakeholders of a company (Van Riel and Balmer, 1997). The marketing approach builds on brand management and incorporates communications research (DeChernatony, 1999; Duncan and Everett, 1993). Kennedy (1977) pioneered observational studies on the significance of personnel in image formation; development of a positive corporate image goes beyond formal communications with personnel as the touchstone.

Extending the scope of the corporate brand may shape customers' perceptions of the expected corporate identity by communicators, such as publicity, corporate logo, or buildings. The essence, as representing the major features of the brand, would shape the brand. It can be a corporate brand design, which is always present from the point of production through communication and increases its significance as a commodity and corporate differentiator to raise a favourable corporate image (Foroudi et al., 2020) against competitors (Kotler, 2000).

Marketers have focused on customers as key beneficiaries, and so have studied the antecedents as well as the consequences of consumers' overall impression (corporate image) of companies. The design of corporate brands in marketing is seen as a way of encapsulating a company's identity and values such that the company is represented successfully to stakeholders. Another stream of research in marketing states that the corporate brand design stimulates pleasure, arousal, and domination in patrons. It functions as a cognitive 'switch' to evoke an image in the audience's mind (Balmer, 2005; Ewing, 2006; Kay, 2006; Van den Bosch et al., 2005) and cuts through clutter to gain attention.

The design of the corporate brand can also create a first impression (van Heerden, 1999) that evokes both positive and negative emotional responses (Baker and Balmer, 1997; Bloch, 1995; Henderson and Cote, 1998; Van Riel, 1995; Van Riel et al., 2001). The corporate logo can remind the beholder of his/her attitudes, desires, perceptions, expectations, thoughts, experiences, and even aversion to the company behind the logo (Van Heerden and Puth, 1995). Furthermore, the design of a corporate logo as a symbol will allow the organisation to develop a business advantage or differentiation from its rivals and the environment (Abratt and Mofokeng, 2001; Kotler, 2000) and will provide reassurance for the customer. Thus, leading brands are prompted to react to environmental dynamics.

Keller (1999) mentions the importance of employees to the outward image of the company. Harris and DeChernatony (2001) developed the frameworks that link employees' perception of their organisation's corporate brand and brand performance. The perceptions and experiences of a company depend considerably on personal contact with employees (Kennedy, 1977). Indeed, some marketing scholars consider employees to be a communicator of corporate values to external audiences.

According to Van den Bosch et al. (2006), the visual identity should initially be recognised and endorsed internally by the workforce of the company before being exhibited externally. Their research reveals how the design of a corporate brand is interpreted internally. First, all the employees of the company have to be familiar with the rationale and objectives behind the design so that they can fully respect it. Second, the organisation's employees need to be trained to use the corporate visuals both formally and informally. Corporate brand design should contain the characteristics, future goals, and direction of the organisation (Van den Bosch et al., 2006). In order to differentiate the organisation from competitors, the visual identity should reflect what the organisation actually stands for (Baker and Balmer, 1997). Marketing scholars view the characteristics of the corporate brand design in the development as a symbol that represents the corporate reputation and that can expand upon consumers' perception of the corporate reputation (Hatch and Schultz, 2001; Omar and Williams, 2006; Van den Bosch et al., 2005; Van Riel et al., 2001). Thus, the reputation of a company can spread if a corporate brand design aligned with the other corporate identity mixes elements such as behaviour and communication.

Marketing research focuses on customers as key beneficiaries and suggests that the corporate logo can be used to establish favourable attitudes towards the organisation and specifically influence buying intentions that may affect the financial performance of an organisation (Bloch, 1995; Henderson et al., 2004). In addition, the corporate logo is seen as a primary economic asset for consumers to reduce their search costs (Cohen, 1991) and to effectively overcome global boundaries and language barriers due to its visual character (Kohli et al., 2002). Hence, favourable corporate brand design can influence an audience, carry tremendous amounts of aesthetic value (Mollerup, 1999, p. 75), and make aesthetic responses (Bloch, 1995; Pittard et al., 2007; Schmitt et al., 1995).

Perspective 5: Interdisciplinary/multi-disciplinary approach paradigm

Several marketing approaches advocate a more eclectic view of corporate identity (Hatch and Schultz, 1997; Moingeon and Ramanantsoa, 1997; Van Riel and Balmer, 1997). Corporate identity and management have been discussed for decades, and there seem to be several ways of interpreting the phenomenon (Balmer, 1995b, 1998). Academics have made a valuable effort to conduct research on corporate identity in recent years (Foroudi et al., 2019a; 2019b; 2020; Melewar et al., 2017; 2018; 2020; Tourky et al., 2020). However, organisational and corporate identity boundaries (internal and external) are becoming increasingly blurred, overlapping, or interconnected in areas such as marketing and organisation studies (Hatch and Schultz, 1997). The 'inter-disciplinary' paradigm emphasises 'marshalling' the corporate identity mix (Van Riel and Balmer, 1997). The corporate identity mix within the multi-disciplinary approach entails four fundamentals: behaviour/communications/symbolism, mind/soul/voice, communication/visual identity, and behaviour/corporate culture/market conditions (He and Balmer, 2007, p. 768), and employees' sense making about their organisation's identity in order to bring about a promising corporate reputation (Fombrun, 1996).

The corporate mind is the conscious decisions made by the companies; it consists of managerial vision, strategy and product performance, corporate philosophy, and corporate history (Balmer and Soenen, 1999; He and Balmer, 2007). Soul is a subjective element of corporate identity, comprising the beliefs shared by employees and shaped by the combination of subcultures and the mix of identity forms found within organisations (Balmer, 2001). Balmer (2001) employs the term 'voice', which refers to the total corporate communication, and (2001) maintains:

> Every organisation has an identity. It articulates the corporate ethos, aims and values and presents the sense of individuality that can help to differentiate the organisation within its competitive environment. When well managed, corporate identity can be a powerful means of integrating the many disciplines and activities essential to an organisation's success. It can also provide the visual cohesion necessary to ensure that all corporate communications are coherent with each other and result in an image consistent with the organisation's defining ethos and character.
>
> By effectively managing its corporate identity an organisation can build understanding and commitment among its diverse stakeholders. This can be manifested in an ability to attract and retain customers and employees, achieve strategic alliances, gain the support of financial markets and generate a sense of direction and purpose. Corporate identity is a strategic issue. Corporate identity differs from traditional brand marketing since it is concerned with all of an organisation's stakeholders and the multifaceted way in which an organisation communicates.
>
> *Balmer, 2001, p. 291*

Corporate identity is embodied in the presence of several versions of corporate identity within an organisation. The ACID test is a comprehensive framework that has undergone a range of innovations and refinements in corporate identity management (Balmer, 2009). The variations of the ACID test related to multiple categorisations of corporate identity are ACID, AC2ID, and AC3ID (Balmer and Greyser, 2003; He and Balmer, 2007). Corporate identity management requires alignment between identity types. There are six identity categories: actual identity, communicated identity, ideal identity, desired identity, conceived identity (Balmer, 2001; Balmer and Gray, 2003; He and Balmer, 2007), and covenanted or corporate brand identity (He and Balmer, 2007).

Actual identity (what we really are) as the particular characteristics of the organisation can be formed by a variety of elements consisting of purposes, the leadership style of management, organisational structure, commercial operations, corporate style and ethos, covered markets, and overall business efficiency. Actual identity includes the set of values held by those who 'make' the company (management and employees).

Communicated identity (what we say we are) includes controlled (advertising, sponsorship, and public relations), and non-controlled communications (word-of-mouth, media commentary), and overall corporate communications (primary, secondary, and tertiary communications) (Balmer, 2009; Balmer and Gray, 2000; Balmer and Greyser, 2002).

Ideal identity (what we ought to be) is the optimum strategic (future-oriented) placing of the corporation in the marketplace. The ideal identity includes organisational competencies and prospects assets, corporate rivalry, and changes in the economic, political, ethical, technological, and social environment. It also refers to strategic planning leadership, environmental and corporate analysis, and the corporate structure's actual identity (Balmer, 2001; Balmer and Gray, 2003; Balmer and Greyser, 2002; He and Balmer, 2007).

Desired identity (what we wish to be) is often misunderstood and is frequently viewed as being almost indistinguishable from ideal identity (Balmer and Greyser, 2002). However, desired identity exists in the hearts and minds of the company's CEO; it is the vision, personality, and ego of the corporate leader. In addition, desired identity is cognitive/aspirational in character whereas ideal identity is strategic in nature and usually emerges by following a rational assessment of the organisation's research and analysis in a particular time and (Balmer, 2009; Balmer and Greyser, 2002).

Conceived identity (what we are seen to be) refers to corporate image, the corporate reputation of the organisation (which held by customers and other stakeholder groups), and corporate branding. Management must determine the most significant perceptions of external publics to the organisation (Balmer, 2009; Balmer and Greyser, 2002).

Covenanted or corporate brand identity (what the brand stands for) underpins a corporate brand and is associated with the architecture. It is 'owing to the power and strength of association with a corporate brand by customers, employees, and others (which sometimes has a religious like fervour), the term covenant appears to be appropriate'. The identity of the brand, in essence, acts as a bridge between the internal identity and the identity that consumers experience. According to Van Riel and Balmer (1997) and Foroudi et al. (2017), an interdisciplinary approach focuses on marketing, including studies on human resources, organisational studies, graphic design, public relations, and communication studies. Van Riel and Balmer (1997) formulated the following statement:

> Academics acknowledge that corporate identity refers to an organisation's unique characteristics which are rooted in the behaviour of members of the organisation… management of an organisation's identity is of strategic importance and requires a multi-disciplinary approach.
>
> *p. 341*

A multidisciplinary (Van Riel and Balmer, 1997) approach discusses 'what we are as an organisation' and the elements that distinguish corporate identity (He and Balmer, 2007, p. 772). This approach draws heavily on organisational behaviour. Some scholars (Olins, 1978; Van Riel, 1995; Van Riel and Balmer, 1997) have expressed ideas for progressively expanding the understanding of corporate identity to indicate how an organisation's identity is exposed by communicative and behavioural practices and a strategically planned symbolism for internal and external audiences.

Corporate identities and corporate brands are inseparable and should be aligned. Corporate branding can be related to multiple stakeholders, and the management of corporate identity requires formal communication with them internally and externally. Therefore, some authors (Balmer, 2001; Bick et al., 2003; Dacin and Brown, 2002) emphasise corporate brand design management, which needs to be accompanied by a multi-disciplinary approach.

Authors (e.g., Balmer, 2001, 2009; Dacin and Brown, 2002; Karaosmanoglu et al., 2011; Melewar and Karaosmanoglu, 2006; Powell et al., 2009; Simoes et al., 2005) highlight that corporate identity management (e.g., corporate logo) and corporate image should be driven by a multi-disciplinary approach. The multi-disciplinary school also places importance on stakeholder communication. For example, Balmer's (1995) communications model is analogous to the integrated communications model and can be interpreted as an Interdisciplinary School of Communications (Van Riel and Balmer, 1997). Van Riel and Balmer (1997) categorise the 'integrated communication paradigm' and the 'inter-disciplinary model' as being on the same level. According to Van Riel (1995), a company's communication involves visual and verbal signals, whereas symbolism contains visual cues that designate what the brand wants to stand for.

For several years, scholars have ascribed corporate identity as a visual concept (Pilditch, 1970) and have identified it as the visual and verbal communications of organisational characters that incorporate the communication model (Bernstein, 1986; Van Riel, 1995). To develop the corporate identity, organisations have recruited graphic designers to emphasise the visual identity and make it more modern. Balmer (1995) points to the connections between the visual schools and the graphical paradigm (Van Riel and Balmer, 1997), described in a multidisciplinary paradigm by the symbolism principal. Visual identity metaphors have attracted the attention of academic researchers in advertising and marketing. Simoes et al. (2005) proposes that marketing researchers should base their studies' evaluation on a number of different disciplines.

Several articles (Balmer, 2001; Hatch and Schultz, 1997; Van Riel and Balmer, 1997) highlight the intertwined relations between identity and image positioning. To obtain a favourable image, corporate brand design needs to be handled across a multi-disciplinary field. The areas that can be managed include corporate brand design (e.g., corporate logo) and communication (e.g., marketing communications).

Conclusion

Chapter 2 has shown how a company develops a corporate brand design in order to project a desired identity and vice versa. In addition, the four main classifications by authors (Balmer, 1995a; 1998; 2001, Foroudi et al., 2014; 2016; 2017; Simoes et al., 2005; Van Riel and Balmer, 1997) are the visual/graphic design, organisational studies, integrated communication, marketing, and multi-disciplinary standpoints, and these are clarified in the subsequent sections. The *marketing perspective* concerns the corporate brand design through brand management and integrated communications research. The focus is on the management of how the corporate brand design is transmitted to the organisation's public. *Graphic design studies* centres on a company's visual identity and refers to the concept of all the visual tangible aspects of a company to express the identity of the corporation to various audiences. The *multi-disciplinary approach* places significance on stakeholder communication and identifies the overlap in various areas of knowledge. This perspective advocates that corporate brand design management should be a tenet across various domains. Finally, the *organisational perspective* acknowledges the internal aspects of identity and its members' identification. This perspective underlines the effect of corporate visual identity on organisational identification.

CASE STUDY – SAMSUNG

Maria Palazzo, University of Salerno, Italy

Samsung is one of the leading international electronics brands in the world. It has the following vision statement:

> Samsung is committed to complying with local laws and regulations as well as applying a strict global code of conduct to all employees. It believes that ethical management is not only a tool for responding to the rapid changes in the global business environment, but also a vehicle for building trust with its various stakeholders including customers, shareholders, employees, business partners and local communities. With an aim to become one of the most ethical companies in the world, Samsung continues to train its employees and operate monitoring systems, while practicing fair and transparent corporate management.
>
> *www.samsung.com/uk/aboutsamsung/vision/philosophy*

The company has several competitors in the market such as Apple, Sony, Panasonic, and many others (Seungkwon et al., 2002).

Logo

As the company was aiming to become the leader in its sector, it decided to make several amendments to its logo (Djatmiko and Pradana, 2016). During the 1990s, the organisation changed its logo drastically: it abandoned the logotype and the red stars preferring a more innovative blue background and white lettering. The added oval shape was representative of concepts such as modernisation and interactivity.

From 2005, when the company saw its target market becoming more international, designers decided to simplify the logo by deleting the oval. The organisation decided to show only the word 'Samsung' painted in blue. Moreover, the characters are characterised by right angles and the absence of serifs (the 'A' does not have the horizontal stroke).

In addition, Samsung has chosen to communicate the logo with a very recognisable slogan: 'Turn on Tomorrow'.

Origin of the brand: From Korea to the world

The main objectives of restructuring the Samsung brand were to strengthen the brand image of the company while trying not to link the organisation with its country of origin (Magnusson et al., 2011), namely, South Korea. In fact, the organisation has tried to exert leverage on its international features to reinforce the corporate reputation and identity (Lee and Slater, 2007); consumers do not usually associate expensive and high quality products, in the electronic area, with Korea, as they often consider Japanese goods to be superior in terms of innovation and technology (Chang, 2011).

Future analyses will show if Samsung will be able to preserve its image and reliability as a genuine brand related to the electronics sector and whether it will succeed in connecting with international consumers without showing its connection to its country of origin.

Case questions

1. After changing the logo, what did Samsung do to strengthen its brand image?
2. What kind of strategies were implemented by Samsung in order to structure a successful corporate brand design?

References

Chang, S. J. (2011) Sony vs Samsung: The Inside Story of the Electronics Giants' Battle for Global Supremacy, John Wiley & Sons, Singapore.

Djatmiko, T. and Pradana, R. (2016) "Brand image and product price; its impact for Samsung smartphone purchasing decision", Procedia-Social and Behavioral Sciences, Vol. 219, pp. 221–227.

Lee, J. and Slater, J. (2007) "Dynamic capabilities, entrepreneurial rent-seeking and the investment development path: The case of Samsung", Journal of International Management, Vol. 13, No. 3, pp. 241–257.

Magnusson, P., Westjohn, S. A., and Zdravkovic, S. (2011) "'What? I thought Samsung was Japanese': accurate or not, perceived country of origin matters", International Marketing Review, Vol. 28, No. 5, pp. 454–472.

Seungkwon, J., Kilpyo, H., Gee, W. B., and Ilhwan, K. (2002) "Knowledge management and process innovation: the knowledge transformation path in Samsung SDI", Journal of Knowledge Management, Vol. 6, No. 5, pp. 479–485.

Key terms and definitions

Corporate brand design is an assembly of visual cues to make an expression of the organisation by which an audience can recognise the company and distinguish it from others; it serves to remind customers of the corporate's real purpose (Foroudi, 2019).

Corporate identity is the features, characteristics, traits, or attributes of a company that are presumed to be central, distinctive, and enduring; it serves as a vehicle for expression of the company's philosophy, values, and mission, communications, and corporate brand design to all its audience (Foroudi et al., 2019; 2020).

Paradigm is a cluster of beliefs that, for scientists in a particular discipline, influences what should be researched, how the study should be done, and how the results should be interpreted (Bryman, 2004; Tashakkori and Teddlie, 1998).

Acknowledgement

Many thanks to Helnaz Ahmadi Lari for editing the chapter.

References

Aaker, D. (1996) Building Strong Brands, Free Press, New York.
Aaker, J. L. (2000) "Accessibility or diagnosticity? Disentangling the influence of culture on persuasion processes and attitudes", Journal of Consumer Research, Vol. 26, No. 4, pp. 340–356.
Aaker, J. L. (2004) "Leveraging the corporate brand", California Management Review, Vol. 46, No. 3, pp. 6–18.
Abratt, R. (1989) "A new approach to the corporate image management process", Journal of Marketing Management, Vol. 5, No. 1, pp. 63–76.
Abratt, R. and Mofokeng, T. N. (2001) "Development and management of corporate image in South Africa", European Journal of Marketing, Vol. 35, No. 3, pp. 368–386.
Ahmadi Lari, H., Foroudi, P., and Imani, S. (2020) "Behavioral intentions in the UK fashion industry: The impact of perceived fashion innovativeness on fashion brand image with the moderating role of social media marketing and lovemark", in Melewar, T. C., Dennis, C., and Foroudi, P. (Eds.), Building Corporate Identity, Image and Reputation in Digital Era, Routledge, London.
Albert, S. and Whetten, D. A. (1985) "Organisational identity", Research in Organisational Behaviour, Vol. 7, pp. 263–295.
Anson, W. (1988) "Determining your identity's asset value", Identity Management Conference, Dallas, Texas.
Ashforth, B. E. and Mael, F. (1989) "Social identity theory and the organization", Academy of Management Review, Vol. 14, No. 1, pp. 20–39.
Baker, M. J. and Balmer, J. M. T. (1997) "Visual identity: trappings or substance?", European Journal of Marketing, Vol. 31, No. 5, pp. 366–382.
Balmer, J. M. T. (1994) "The BBC's corporate identity: Myth, paradox and reality", Journal of General Management, Vol. 19, No. 3, pp. 33–49.
Balmer, J. M. T. (1995a) "Corporate branding and connoisseurship", Journal of General Management, Vol. 21, No. 1, pp. 22–46.
Balmer, J. M. T. (1995b) "Corporate identity: the power and the paradox", Design Management Journal, Vol. 6, No. 1, pp. 39–44.
Balmer, J. M. T. (1997) Corporate Identity: Past, Present and Future, Department of Marketing, Working Paper Series, University of Strathclyde, UK.
Balmer, J. M. T. (1998) "Corporate identity and the advent of corporate marketing", Journal of Marketing Management, Vol. 14, No. 8, pp. 963–996.
Balmer, J. M. T. (2001) "Corporate identity, corporate branding and corporate marketing seeing through the fog", European Journal of Marketing, Vol. 35, No. 3/4, pp. 248–291.
Balmer, J. M. T. (2005) "Corporate Brand Cultures and Communities", in Schroeder, J. E. and Salzer-Morling, M. (Eds.), Brand Culture, Routledge, London, pp. 34–49.
Balmer, J. M. T. (2006) "Comprehending corporate marketing and the corporate marketing mix", working paper, Bradford School of Management, Bradford, UK.
Balmer, J. M. T. (2008) "Identity based views of the corporation: Insights from corporate identity, organisational identity, social identity, visual identity, corporate brand identity and corporate image", European Journal of Marketing, Vol. 42, No. 9/10, pp. 879–906.
Balmer, J. M. T. (2009) "Corporate marketing: Apocalypse, advent and epiphany", Management Decision, Vol. 47, No. 4, pp. 544–572.
Balmer, J. M. T. (2011) "Corporate heritage identities, corporate heritage brands and the multiple heritage identities of the British Monarchy", European Journal of Marketing, Vol. 45, No. 9/10, pp. 1380–1398.
Balmer, J. M. T. and Gray, E. R. (2000) "Corporate identity and corporate communications: creating a competitive advantage", Industrial and Commercial Training, Vol. 32, No. 7, pp. 256–262.
Balmer, J. M. T. and Gray, E. R. (2003) "Corporate Brands: What are they? What of them?", European Journal of Marketing, Vol. 37, No. 7/8, pp. 972–997.
Balmer, J. M. T. and Greyser, S. A. (2003) Revealing the Corporation, Routledge, London.

Balmer, J. M. T. and Soenen, G. B. (1999) "The acid test of corporate identity management", Journal of Marketing Management, Vol. 15, No. 1/3, pp. 69–92.

Balmer, J. M. T. and Wilson, A. (1998) "Corporate identity: There is more to it than meets the eye", International Studies of Management and Organisation, Vol. 28, No. 3, pp. 12–31.

Bennett, P. D. (1995) Dictionary of Marketing Terms, McGraw-Hill Education, New York

Bernstein, D. (1984) Company Image and Reality: A Critique of Corporate Communications, Cassell Educational Ltd, London.

Bernstein, D. (1986) Company Image and Reality: A Critique of Corporate Communications, Cassell Educational Ltd, London.

Berry, L. L. (2000) "Cultivating service brand equity", Journal of the Academy of Marketing Science, Vol. 28, No. 1, pp. 128–137.

Berry, L. L. and Parasuraman, A. (1991) Marketing Services: Competing through Quality, Free Press, New York.

Bick, G., Jacobson, M. C., and Abratt, R. (2003) "The corporate identity management process revisited", Journal of Marketing Management, Vol. 19, No. 7/8, pp. 835–855.

Bitner, M. J., Booms, B. H., and Mohr, L. A. (1994) "Critical service encounters: The employee's viewpoint", Journal of Marketing, Vol. 58, No. 4, pp. 95–106.

Bloch, P. H. (1995) "Seeking the ideal form: product design and consumer response", Journal of Marketing, Vol. 59, No. 3, pp. 16–29.

Brown, J. J. and Reingen, P. H. (1987) "Social ties and word-of-mouth referral behaviour", Journal of Consumer Research, Vol. 14, No. 3, pp. 350–362.

Bryman, A. (2004) Social Research Methods, Oxford University Press, Oxford.

Carter, D. E. (1982) Designing Corporate Identity Programs for Small Corporations, Art Direction Book Company, New York.

Cohen, D. (1991) "Trademark strategy revisited", Journal of Marketing, Vol. 55, No. 3, pp. 46–59.

Cornelissen, J. and Harris, P. (2001). "The corporate identity metaphor: Perspectives, problems and prospects", Journal of Marketing Management, Vol. 17, No, 1–2, pp. 49–71.

Dacin, P. and Brown, T. (2002) "Corporate identity and corporate associations: A framework for future research", Corporate Reputation Review, Vol. 5, No. 2/3, pp. 254–253.

DeChernatony, L. (1999) "Brand management through narrowing the gap between brand identity and brand reputation", Journal of Marketing Management, Vol. 15, No. 1/3, pp. 157–179.

DeChernatony, L. (2001) "A model for strategically building brands", Brand Management, Vol. 9, No. 1, pp. 21–44.

Dowling, G. R. (1994) Corporate Reputations: Strategies for Developing the Corporate Brand, Kogan Page, London.

Downey, S. M. (1986) "The relationship between corporate culture and corporate identity", Public Relations Quarterly, Vol. 31, No. 4, pp. 7–12.

Duncan, T. and Everett, S. (1993) "Client perceptions of integrated marketing communications", Journal of Advertising Research, Vol. 33, No. 3, pp. 30–39.

Durgee, J. F. and Stuart, R. W. (1987) "Advertising symbols and brand names that best represent key product meanings", The Journal of Consumer Marketing, Vol. 4, No. 3, pp. 15–24.

Dutton, J. E. and Dukerich, J. M. (1991) "Keeping an eye on the mirror: Image and identity in organisational adaptation", The Academy of Management Journal, Vol. 34, No. 3, pp. 517–554.

Dutton, J. E., Dukcrich, L M., and Harquail, C. V. (1994) "Organisational images and member identification", Administrative Science Quarterly, Vol. 39, No. 2, pp. 239–263.

Elsbach, K. D. and Kramer, R. M. (1996) "Members' responses to organisational identity threats: Encountering and countering the Business Week rankings", Administrative Science Quarterly, Vol. 41, No. 3, pp. 442–476.

Ewing, T. M. (2006) "Brands, artifacts and design theory: A call to action", Journal of Product and Brand Management, Vol. 15, No. 4, pp. 255–256.

Folkes, V. S. (1984) "Consumer reactions to product failure: An attributional approach", Journal of Consumer Research, Vol. 10, No. 4, pp. 398–409.

Fombrun, C. J. (1996) Reputation: Realizing value from the corporate image, Harvard Business School Press, Boston, MA.

Foroudi, M. M., Balmer, J. M., Chen, W., Foroudi, P., and Patsala, P. (2020) "Explicating place identity attitudes, place architecture attitudes, and identification triad theory", Journal of Business Research, Vol. 109 (March), pp. 321–336.

Foroudi, M. M., Balmer, M. T., Chen, W., and Foroudi, P. (2019) "Corporate identity, place architecture, and identification: an exploratory case study", Qualitative Market Research: An International Journal, Vol. 109 (May), pp. 321–336.

Foroudi, P. (2019) "Influence of brand signature, brand awareness, brand attitude, brand reputation on hotel industry's brand performance", International Journal of Hospitality Management, Vol. 76 (Jan), pp. 271–285

Foroudi, P. (2020) "Corporate brand strategy: Drivers and outcomes of corporate brand orientation in international marketing", International Journal of Hospitality Management, Vol. 88 (July), pp. 1–14.

Foroudi, P. and Marvi, R. (2020) "Some like it hot: The role of identity, website, co-creation behavior on identification and love", European Journal of International Management.

Foroudi, P., Cuomo, M. T., Foroudi, M. M., Katsikeas, C. S., and Gupta, S. (2020) "Linking identity and heritage with image and a reputation for competition", Journal of Business Research, Vol. 113 (May), pp. 317–325.

Foroudi, P., Dinnie, K., Kitchen, P. J., Melewar, T. C., and Foroudi, M.M. (2017) "IMC antecedents and the consequences of planned brand identity in higher education", European Journal of Marketing, Vol. 51, No. 3, pp. 528–550.

Foroudi, P., Foroudi, M. M., Nguyen, B., and Gupta, S. (2019a) Conceptualising and managing Corporate Logo: A Qualitative Study from Stakeholders Perspectives, Qualitative Market Research: An International Journal, Vol. 22, No. 3, pp. 381–404

Foroudi, P., Gupta, S., and Melewar, T. C. (2017) "Corporate logo: History, definition, and component", International Studies of Management and Organization, Vol. 47, No. 2, pp. 176–196.

Foroudi, P., Hafeez, K., and Foroudi, M. M. (2016) "Evaluating the impact of corporate logos towards corporate reputation: a case of Persia and Mexico, Qualitative Market Research", An International Journal, Vol. 20, No. 2, pp. 158–180.

Foroudi, P., Melewar, T. C., and Gupta, S. (2014) "Linking corporate logo, corporate image, and reputation: An examination of consumer perceptions in the financial setting", Journal of Business Research, Vol. 67, No. 11, pp. 2269–2281.

Foroudi, P., Yu, Q., Gupta, S., and Foroudi, M. M. (2019b) "Enhancing university brand image and reputation through customer value co-creation behaviour", Technological Forecasting and Social Change, Vol. 138 (Jan), pp. 18–227.

Gilly, M. C. and Wolfinbarger, M. (1998) "Advertising's internal audience", Journal of Marketing, Vol. 62, No. 1, pp. 69–88.

Gioia, D. A. and Thomas, J. B. (1996) "Identity, image and issue interpretation: Sensemaking during strategic change in academia", Administrative Science Quarterly, Vol. 41, pp. 370–403.

Gioia, D. A., Majken, S., and Corley, K. G. (2000) "Organisational identity, image, and adaptive instability", The Academy of Management Review, Vol. 25, No. 1, pp. 63–81.

Gray, E. R. and Smeltzer, L. R. (1985) "Corporate image: An integral part of strategy", Sloan Management Review, Vol. 26, No. 4, pp. 73–77.

Gray, E. R. and Smeltzer, L. R. (1987) "Planning a face-lift: Implementing a corporate image program", The Journal of Business Strategy, Vol. 1, No. 1, pp. 4–10.

Green, D. and Loveluck, V. (1994) "Understanding a corporate symbol", Applied Cognitive Psychology, Vol. 8, No. 1, pp. 37–47.

Hagtvedt, H. (2011) "The impact of incomplete typeface logos on perceptions of the firm", Journal of Marketing, Vol. 75 (July), pp. 86–93.

Hankinson, P., Lomax, W., and Hand, C. (2007) "The time factor in re-branding organisations: Its effects on staff knowledge, attitudes and behaviour in UK charities", Journal of Product and Brand Management, Vol. 16, No. 4, pp. 236–246.

Harris, H. and DeChernatony, L. (2001) "Corporate branding and corporate brand performance", European Journal of Marketing, Vol. 35, No. 3/4, pp. 441–456.

Hatch, M. J. and Schultz, M. (1997) "Relations between organisational culture, identity and image", European Journal of Marketing, Vol. 31, No. 5/6, pp. 356–365.

Hatch, M. J. and Schultz, M. (2000) "Scaling the Tower of Babel: Relational Differences Between Identity, Image and Culture in Organisations", in Schultz, M. Hatch, M. J., and Larsen, M. H. (Eds.), The Expressive Organisation: Linking Identity, Reputation, and the Corporate Brand, Oxford University Press, Oxford, pp. 13–35.

Hatch, M. J. and Schultz, M. (2001) "Are the strategic stars aligned for your corporate brand", Harvard Business Review, Vol. 69 (February), pp. 128–134.

Hatch, M. J. and Schultz, M. (2003) "Bringing the corporation into corporate branding", European Journal of Marketing, Vol. 3, No. 7/8, pp. 1041–1064.

He, H. and Balmer, J. M. T. (2007) "Identity studies: multiple perspectives and implications for corporate-level marketing", European Journal of Marketing, Vol. 41, No. 7/8, pp. 765–785.

Henderson, P. W. and Cote, J. A. (1998) "Guidelines for selecting or modifying logos", Journal of Marketing, Vol. 62, No. 2, pp. 14–30.

Henderson, P. W., Giese, J., and Cote, J. A. (2004) "Impression management using typeface design", Journal of Marketing, Vol. 68, No. 4, pp. 60–83.

Henrion, F. and Parkin. A. (1967) Design Coordination and Corporate Image, Reinhold Publishing Corporation, London.

Ind, N. (1997) The Corporate Brand, New York University Press, New York.

Jones, E. E., Kanouse, D. E., Kelley, H. H., Nisbett, R. E., Valins, S., and Weiner, B. (1972) Attribution: Perceiving the Causes of Behaviour, General Learning Press, Morristown, NJ.

Kay, M. J. (2006) "Strong brands and corporate brands", European Journal of Marketing, Vol. 40, No. 7/8, pp. 742–760.

Keller, K. L. (1993) "Conceptualizing, measuring, and managing customer-based brand equity2", Journal of Marketing, Vol. 57 (January), pp. 1–22.

Keller, K. L. (1999) "Brand mantras: Rationale, criteria and examples", Journal of Marketing Management, Vol. 15, No. 1/3, pp. 43–51.

Keller, K. L. (2003) Strategic Brand Management: Building, Measuring, and Managing Brand Equity, Prentice Hall, Hoboken, NJ.

Kelley, H. H. and Michela, J. L. (1980) "Attribution theory and research", Annual Review of Psychology, Vol. 31, No. 1, pp. 457–501.

Kennedy, S. H. (1977) "Nurturing corporate images", European Journal of Marketing, Vol. 11, No. 3, pp. 120–164.

Kohli, C., Suri, R., and Thakor, M. (2002) "Creating effective logos: Insights from theory and practice", Business Horizons, Vol. 45, No. 3, pp. 58–64.

Kotler, J. P. (2000) How to Create, Win and Dominate Market, The Free Press, New York, pp. 18–151.

Kropp, H. R., Warren A. F., and French, J. E. H. (1990) "Trademark management-not brand management", Business, Vol. 40 (October–December), pp. 17–24.

Levin, M. L. (2000) "Vision revisited", The Journal of Applied Behavioural Science, Vol. 36, No. 1, pp. 91–107.

Margulies, W. P. (1977) "Make the most of your corporate image", Harvard Business Review, Vol. 55, No. 4, pp. 66–74.

Martineau, P. (1958) "Sharper focus for the corporate image", Harvard Business Review, Vol. 36 (November/December), pp. 49–58.

Martinez, J. G. (2006) "Designing symbols: The logos of the Spanish autonomous communities", Journal of Spanish Cultural Studies, Vol. 7, No. 1, pp. 51–74.

Melewar, T. C. and Karaosmanoglu, E. (2006) "Seven dimensions of corporate identity: A categorization from the practitioners' perspectives", European Journal of Marketing, Vol 40, No. 7/8, pp. 846–869.

Melewar, T. C. and Saunders, J. (1998) "Global corporate visual identity systems: Standardization, control and benefits", International Marketing Review, Vol. 15, No. 4, pp. 291–308.

Melewar, T. C. and Saunders, J. (1999) "International corporate visual identity: Standardisation or localisation?", Journal of International Business Studies, Vol. 30, No. 3, pp. 583–598.

Melewar, T. C. and Saunders, J. (2000) "Global corporate visual identity systems: Using an extended marketing mix", European Journal of Marketing, Vol. 34, No. 5, pp. 538–550.

Melewar, T. C., Foroudi, P., Dinnie, K., and Nguyen, B. (2018) "The role of corporate identity management in the higher education sector: an exploratory case study", Journal of Marketing Communications, Vol. 24, No. 4, pp. 337–359.

Melewar, T. C., Foroudi, P., Kitchen, P., Gupta, S., and Foroudi, M. M. (2017) "Integrating identity, strategy and communications for trust, loyalty and commitment", European Journal of Marketing, Vol. 51, No. 3, pp. 572–604.

Melewar, T. C., Foroudi, P., and Jin, Z. (2020) "Corporate branding, identity, image and reputation: Current and future trends", Developments and Challenges (Editorial Notes), Journal of Business Research.

Moingeon, B. and Ramanantsoa, B. (1997) "Understanding corporate identity: The French school of thought", European Journal of Marketing, Vol. 31, No. 5/6, pp. 383–395.

Mollerup, P. (1999) Marks of Excellence, History and Taxonomy of Trademarks, Phaidon Press, London.

Montes, E. and Foroudi, P. (2017) "Corporate e-communication: Its relationship with the corporate logo in the construction of the consumers online interaction", The Bottom Line, Vol. 30, No. 3, pp. 201–215.

Olins, W. (1978) The Corporate Personality: An Inquiry into The Nature of Corporate Identity, Kynoch Press, Birmingham.

Olins, W. (1986) "The strategy of design", Management Today (May), pp. 52–55.

Olins, W. (1989) Corporate Entity: Making Business Strategy Visible through Design, Thames and Hudson, London.

Olins, W. (1991) Corporate Identity, Toledo, Thames and Hudson, Spain.

Omar, M. and Williams, R. L. J. R. (2006) "Managing and maintaining corporate reputation and brand identity, HAIER co-operation group logo", Journal of Brand Management, Vol. 13, No. 4/5, pp. 268–275.

Palazzo, M., Foroudi, P., Kitchen, P. J., and Siano, A. (2020) "Developing corporate communications in Italian firms: An exploratory study", Qualitative Market Research: An International Journal.

Park, C. W. and Lessig, V. P. (1981) "Familiarity and its impact on consumer decision biases and heuristics," Journal of Consumer Research, Vol. 8 (September), pp. 223–230.

Pilditch, J. (1970) Communication by Design: A Study in Corporate Identity, McGraw-Hill, London.

Pitta, D. A. and Franzak, F. J. (2008) "Foundations for building share of heart in global brands", Journal of Product and Brand Management, Vol. 17, No. 2, pp. 64–72.

Pittard, N., Ewing, M., and Jevons, C. (2007) "Aesthetic theory and logo design: Examining consumer response to proportion across cultures", International Marketing Review, Vol. 24, No. 4, pp. 457–473.

Powell, S. M., Elving, W., Dodd, C., and Sloan, J. (2009) "Explicating ethical corporate identity in the financial sector", Corporate Communications: An International Journal, Vol. 14, No. 4, pp. 440–455.

Schmitt, B. (1995) "Experimental marketing", Journal of Marketing and Management, Vol. 15, No. 1/3, pp. 53–67.

Schmitt, B. and Pan, Y. (1994) "Managing corporate and brand identities in the Asia Pacific Region", California Management Review, Vol. 36, No. 4, pp. 32–48.

Schmitt, B. H., Simonson, A., and Marcus, J. (1995) "Managing corporate image and identity", Long Range Planning, Vol. 28, No. 5, pp. 82–92.

Scott, S. G. and Lane, V. R. (2000) "A stakeholder approach to organisational identity", Academy of Management Review, Vol. 25, No. 1, pp. 43–62.

Selame, E. and Selame, J. (1988) The Company Image: Building your Identity and Influence in the Marketplace, John Wiley & Sons, New York.

Sen, S. and Bhattacharya, C. B. (2001) "Does doing good always lead to doing better? Consumer reactions to corporate social responsibility", Journal of Marketing Research, Vol. 38, No. 2, pp. 225–243.

Simoes, C., Dibb, S., and Fisk, R. (2005) "Managing corporate identity: An internal perspective", Journal of the Academy of Marketing Science, Vol. 33, No. 2, pp. 153–168.

Stuart, F. I. (1997) "The influence of organisational culture and internal politics on new service design and introduction", International Journal of Service Industry Management, Vol. 9, No. 5, pp. 469–485.

Stuart, H. (1999) "Towards a definitive model of the corporate identity management process", Corporate Communications: An International Journal, Vol. 4, No. 4, pp. 200–207.

Tajfel, H. and Turner, J. C. (1985) "The Social Identity Theory of Intergroup Behaviour", in Worchel, S. and Austin, W. G. (Eds.), Psychology of Intergroup Relations, Nelson-Hall, Chicago.

Tashakkori, A. and Teddlie, C. (1998) Mixed Methodology: Combining the Qualitative and Quantitative Approaches, Sage Publications, Thousand Oaks, CA.

Topalian, A. (1984) "Corporate identity: beyond the visual overstatements", International Journal of Advertising, Vol. 3, No. 1, pp. 55–62.

Tourky, M., Foroudi, P., Gupta, S., and Shaalan, A. (2020) "Conceptualising corporate identity in a dynamic environment", Qualitative Market Research: An International Journal.

Tucker, W. T. (1961) "How much of the corporate image is stereotype?", Journal of Marketing, Vol. 25, No. 3, pp. 61–65.

Van den Bosch, A. L. M., De Jong, M. D. T., and Elving, W. J. L. (2005) "How corporate visual identity supports reputation", Corporate Communications: An International Journal, Vol. 10, No. 2, pp. 108–116.

Van den Bosch, A. L. M., Elving, W. J. L., and De Jong, M. D. T. (2006) "The impact of organisational characteristics on corporate visual identity", European Journal of Marketing, Vol. 40, No. 7/8, pp. 870–885.

Van der Lans, R., Cote, J. A., Cole, C. A., Leong, S. M., Smidts, A., Henderson, P. M., Bluemelhuber, C., Bottomley, P. A., Doule, J. R., Fedorikhin, A., Janakiraman, M., Ramaseshan, B., and Schmitt, B. H. (2009) "Cross-national logo evaluation analysis: An individual-level approach", Marketing science, Vol. 28, No. 5, pp. 968–985.

Van Heerden, C. H. (1999) "Developing a corporate image model", South African Journal of Economic and Management Sciences, Vol. 2, No. 3, pp. 492–508.

Van Heerden, C. H. and Puth, G. (1995) "Factors that determine the corporate image of South African banking institutions: an explanatory investigation", International Journal of Bank Marketing, Vol. 31, No. 3, pp. 340–355.

Van Rekom, J. (1997) "Deriving an operational measure of corporate identity", European Journal of Marketing, Vol. 31, No. 5/6, pp. 410–421.

Van Rekom, J. and Van Riel, C. B. M. (2000) "Operational measures of organisational identity: A review of existing methods", Corporate Reputation Review, Vol. 3, No. 4, pp. 334–350.

Van Riel, C. B. M. (1995) Principles of Corporate Communication, Prentice Hall, Hoboken, NJ.

Van Riel, C. B. M. (2000) "Corporate Communication Orchestrated by a Sustainable Corporate Story", in Schultz, M., Hatch, M. J., and Larsen, M. H. (Eds.), The Expressive Organisation: Linking Identity, Reputation and the Corporate Brand, Oxford University Press, Oxford, pp. 157–181.

Van Riel, C. B. M. and Balmer, J. M. T. (1997) "Corporate identity, concept, its measurement and management", European Journal of Marketing, Vol. 31, No. 5/6, pp. 340–355.

Van Riel, C. B. M. and Van den Ban, A. (2001) "The added value of corporate logos; an empirical study", European Journal of Marketing, Vol. 35, No. 3/4, pp. 428–440.

Weiner, B. (1986) An Attribution Analysis of Achievement Motivation, Springer-Verlag, New York.

Weiner, B. (2000) "Intrapersonal and interpersonal theories of motivation from an attribution perspective", Educational Psychology Review, Vol. 12, No. 1, pp. 1–14.

Wheeler, A. (2003) Designing Brand Identity: A Complete Guide to Creating, Building and Maintaining Strong Brands, John Wiley & Sons, New York.

Whetten, D. A. and Mackey, A. (2002) "A social actor conception of organisational identity and its implications for the study of organisational reputation", Business and Society, Vol. 41, No. 4, pp. 393–414.

PART II
Corporate brand signature management

3
CORPORATE BRAND SIGNATURE MANAGEMENT

Logo, design, typeface, and colour

Pantea Foroudi and T. C. Melewar

Introduction

Chapter 3 introduces how to formulate and design a favourable corporate brand signature. Research into the corporate brand signature and corporate image expressed that a favourable corporate brand signature has desirable organisational outcomes such as increased visibility and recognisable products and services for its company's internal and external stakeholders. Corporate brand signatures are used to raise awareness, and help with identification, as well as being the signs of a promise to the consumer that helps differentiate the organisation from its competitors. Furthermore, a corporate brand signature communicates a company's identity and projects the corporate personality.

Background to corporate brand signature management

The review of literature in the previous chapter on corporate brand signature and corporate image from different disciplines considered the concepts of corporate brand signature and of corporate image from their own perspective and emphasised certain aspects of corporate brand signature management. Among prevailing studies, those in marketing and design have provided the greatest amount of evidence about the corporate brand signature as an imperative element in creating a visual identity for the organisation (Foroudi, 2019) and its effect on the economic performance of organisations. Corporate brand signatures are the most well-organised management asset for arranging the features that organisations necessitate to articulate to the stakeholders (Foroudi, 2019).

Organisation studies paradigm argues that an organisation is a social actor with distinct, unique, and enduring qualities to distinguish them from other companies in the industry; it relies on social identity theory (Foroudi et al., 2014). Moreover, using social identity theory, marketing researchers (Bhattacharya and Sen, 2003; Bhattacharya et al., 1995; Gwinner and Swanson, 2003; Karaosmanoglu et al., 2011) have explored identity from the perspectives of external audiences. The effective management of corporate identity results in a favourable corporate image. In turn, having a long-lasting, favourable corporate image results in the company developing a favourable reputation and it leads to stakeholders having a positive attitude with regard to the organisation (Carter, 1982).

The marketing approach grounded itself in branding that extends beyond the traditional marketing field. Corporate identity is a basis for positioning the company as a brand. Understanding the relationship between consumers and companies to an association between corporate image and corporate performance outcome such as customer loyalty and purchase intention is the focus of this paradigm. Advertising and marketing researchers focus on visual expressions of corporate brand signature (McQuarrie and Mick, 2003; Mulvey and Medina, 2003). The corporate brand signature can affect consumers' awareness of advertising and can also influence how memorable the advertisements are.

Academics in the field of marketing and corporate branding consider the corporate brand signature to be a concept that is developed based on the corporate brand promise of an organisation, and it can be used to identify the particular characteristics or features of a brand, a product, and services (Aaker, 1991; Johansson and Hirano, 1999; Kay, 2006; Van Heerden, 1999). Research in marketing regards the corporate brand signature as a useful device to produce more effective responses, and it has been shown that word-mark logos generate a higher number of cognitive responses. For consumers, a corporate brand signature stimulates arousal and pleasure dominance, and this serves as a cognitive 'switch' whereby the consumers can recall an image (Balmer, 2005; Ewing, 2006; Kay, 2006) as it avoids distractions while gaining consumers' attention. Also, a corporate brand signature can create a first impression (Van Heerden, 1999) that evokes positive and negative emotional reactions (Bloch, 1995; Van Riel, 1995). A corporate brand signature can recall to the beholder her/his perceptions of the corporation that are linked with the corporate brand signature (Van Heerden and Puth, 1995). Furthermore, using the corporate brand signature as a symbol can be helpful to the firm by assisting it in the creation of a position in the market or by developing brand differentiation from its rivals and making it stand out in the environment (Hatch and Schultz, 2001; Kotler, 2000). This, in turn, provides reassurance for consumers (Douglas, 2001).

Bernstein (1986) states that customers look for a symbol that can reassure them of experienced customer satisfaction. Bernstein (1986) believes that the corporate brand signature is a condition of consistency in the wider context of a company's identity. Identity is often disseminated through official documents, the corporate brand signature, and the logo (Bhattacharya and Sen, 2003). Corporate brand signatures are part of an overall brand/corporate meaning to provide differentiation and influence choice. It can help a corporate/brand in two ways: i) it can be used in combination with the name for fast recognition of a brand/firm; ii) it can be used instead of the name when there are constraints of space or time. A firm can benefit from assigning a corporate brand signature to their corporation (Henderson and Cote, 1998).

A corporate brand signature can give a firm a competitive advantage as it can be used to project quality, to convey strength, and to differentiate the firm from its rivals (Olins and Selame, 2000; Schmitt, 1995). According to Van Heerden and Puth (1995), they can expand the market share, keep customers, and maintain a profitable position, develop business survival and profitability, and attain differentiation in the minds of audiences (Gupta et al., 2008).

Studies show that corporate identity and corporate image focus on two main levels: first, the organisation level is concerned with the way a company creates a unique and long-lasting corporate identity to communicate internally and externally (Brown et al., 2006; Foroudi et al., 2020). The second, which is used in this study, is the investigation at the individual level, which is intended to provide an explanation of the stakeholders' opinions of the company. A corporate brand signature should be chosen carefully as logos symbolise the desired identifying characteristics of the organisation. Therefore, organisations spend substantial amounts of money, time, and research on developing a corporate brand signature that will convey the organisation's identity and that will help to mould its image in a favourable way (Foroudi, 2019). This research considers the second level and explores the factors that may influence how consumers assess companies (corporate image).

The message sources, which are external to organisations and which give individuals indications regarding a company's identity, are in keeping with the inter-disciplinary perspective (Dacin and Brown, 2002). The multi-disciplinary paradigm views corporate identity as managed by organisations. Marketing tended to expense the depth and breadth of literature in sociology and psychology (Palmer and Bejou, 2006). Corporate identity is related to an organisation's behaviour, marketing, and psychology. It focuses on how decision-makers decide to communicate an organisation's identity internally and promote the company's characteristics externally. Simoes et al. (2005) assert that to attain a desirable image, the logo, as a part of the corporate identity, can be drawn and managed from several disciplines.

Dacin and Brown (2002) state that the mental image people maintain of the company is one of the factors that define the company's actual identity. Can a corporate brand signature communicate a corporate image? A corporate brand signature can communicate in a very subtle way. Henderson and Cote (1998) developed 'guidelines to assist managers in selecting or modifying corporate brand signatures to achieve their corporate image goals' (p. 14). Their research was related to aesthetics and the findings were limited as they used corporate brand signatures without company names and examined how the influence of design can transmit the evaluations of the brand or company. In contrast with theoretical assumptions and anecdotal evidence, data showing empirical evidence of the impact of specific antecedents of corporate brand signatures explaining variations in external corporate reputation data are limited (Van Riel et al., 2001, p. 439). Accordingly, this study takes into account this gap in the literature and devises a conceptual model based on the consumers' viewpoint.

Corporate brand signature can also enhance the company's image (Balmer, 2005; Ewing, 2006; Kay, 2006). Firms understand the need to measure their visual identity to manage the company's image, including logos and trade symbols as well as prototypes of contemporary identity design (Ageeva et al., 2019; Napoles, 1988). Researchers of the visual school believe that corporate brand signatures should provide visibility and reflect any change in corporate strategy, culture, and communication. The graphic design paradigm highlights the symbolism of organisations to provide visibility to the company and influence any changes in corporate culture, communication, and strategy. The researchers in this field studied an organisation's value, which reflects a company's visual identity such as the logo, name, slogan, and its changes after a merger or acquisition. The corporate brand is recognised by its design, and the visual identity should be fashionable and up-to-date (Balmer and Gray, 2000; Foroudi, 2020; 2019; Tucker, 1961). Brand and design consultants have studied the effect of design elements, identifying the important responses to the visual characteristics of corporate brand signatures (Henderson and Cote, 1998) that can promote a favourable image in the audience's mind (Mollerup, 1999).

A corporate brand signature's impact comes from repetition, seeing it continually in places such as television commercials, stationery, and flyers: The list is endless in the marketplace. Corporate brand signatures have meaning, and present to the subconscious mind of the consumer a message about the product and corporation. Studies also consider the corporate brand signature to be 'a assets of the organisation' that can be employed to convey a required communication to customers (Balmer and Gray, 1999). Abratt (1989) suggests that integrating the efforts to produce company-driven communication can help organisations gain consistency regarding what they choose to communicate and what communication is attributed to them. When it is difficult to distinguish the services and products of one company from those of another, the use of a symbol (logo) can be a key factor in making one company stand out (Aaker, 1991). The corporate identity mix (symbolism, communication, and behaviour) should be integrated to convey a consistent message so that corporate identity is perceived as it was intended.

Furthermore, a corporate brand signature can elicit different responses from people to serve as a competitive advantage and also provides an organisation with the means of building its reputation (Olins, 1989). A corporate brand signature also affects consumers' familiarity not only with the company but also with its products and services (Henderson and Cote, 1998; Peter, 1989), and presents the company's culture. In the following sections the definitions of the corporate brand signature and its elements (typeface, graphic design, colour, and corporate name) are provided. Furthermore, the corporate image and corporate reputation are depicted.

Corporate brand signature concept

In the literature, the terms 'corporate brand signature', 'corporate brand signature', 'trade figure', 'trademark', 'symbol', 'brand logo', and 'logotype' are frequently used interchangeably as the definitions for the terms seem to suggest an overlap. Nonetheless, in this research, the decision was made to use the phrase 'corporate brand signature'. In particular, the definition and the application of this term are central to this chapter.

Each paradigm provides a specific lens through which the corporate brand signature is defined. For instance, academics in the field of marketing pay more attention to the corporate and human personality and claim that the corporate brand signature is an indication of what the company represents to the customer. Therefore, it can be used as a way to represent the organisation's personality and values. Indeed, each company develops its own unique personality, that is, a distinctive and intellectual behaviour that can be used to distinguish one company from others in the same field. The corporate brand signature is at the heart of corporate identity, as it is a key element in corporate visual identity (Foroudi et al., 2019). Corporate brand signature is used to epitomise the firm's personality and its values so that it can be presented in a concise and effective way to stakeholders. Based on the definition by Balmer (2008) a brand signature is a 'distinctive way in which an organisation's name is rendered, principally in typographic form' (p. 899).

Marketing scholars highlighted the particular attributes of a corporate brand signature when they developed the definition of the corporate brand signature, which could then be used as a symbol not only to convey the corporate reputation but also to expand upon consumers' perception of the company. The graphical characteristics of a corporate brand signature can help increase the familiarity of a firm. Familiarity defined by Herrera and Blanco (2011) as 'the number of product related experiences that have been accumulated by the consumer' (p. 286). The referential properties of a corporate brand signature may describe the effect corporate brand signatures have on reputation (Green and Loveluck, 1994). A company can enhance its reputation when the corporate brand signature aligns with the various components of corporate identity (behaviour and communication).

Diverse studies have given a range of definitions of the concept of corporate brand signature with different authors offering different meanings. A significant number of these meanings have been developed from design and marketing perspectives (Melewar et al., 2000).

Academics in the field of marketing and advertising have conducted research into the visual expressions of the corporate brand signature, which can also be seen as a company's signature. However, there is a range of outlooks in the marketing literature with regard to the corporate brand signature. For example, some researchers view the corporate brand signature as being the public's first impression of a firm (Henderson and Cote, 1998; Henderson et al., 2004; Hutton, 1997; Van Heerden, 1999). In addition, researchers in the marketing field state that the company's brand signature as a sensory cues which is associated with company's identity with the aim of producing positive and negative emotional reactions. Therefore, the aim for a range of stakeholders to have positive associations with regard to the company and brand (Dowling, 1994; Kotler, 2000; Topalian, 1984).

Corporate brand signatures increase the significance of a company as a product or a corporate identifier (Van den Bosch et al., 2005) and influence purchase intentions (Cohen, 1991; Siegel, 1989; Wallace, 2001) to create a positive corporate reputation and image. Kohli et al. (2002) state that 'a logo provides instant recognition for the brand and the product. Logos help transcend international boundaries and language barriers because of their "visual" character' (p. 58). Dowling (2001) argues that a company's identity can be conveyed in a range of ways, such as typefaces, logos, names, and colour schemes. Though, in the marketing research, there is a lack of any systematic research on the impact of design on consumers' assessment of corporate brand signatures (Foroudi, 2019).

Research from the perspective of marketing focuses on customers as main receivers and claims which the company's brand signature can result in favourable company attitudes as well as having a direct impact on purchase intentions, which subsequently, can then have an impact on a company's financial performance. Furthermore, the corporate brand signature can be considered a key economic advantage in that it can be used to reduce customer search costs and can help overcome the problems of language barriers and global boundaries (Kohli et al., 2002). The corporate brand signature is used to make aesthetic responses (Bloch, 1995). Marketing literature is very similar to design literature and will be discussed in the next section.

The design literature refers to the corporate brand signature as a set of elements (typeface, colour, design, and name) that highlight a company's products and services; it allows customers to identify a particular company or brand and distinguish it from others (Bennett, 1995; Leitch and Motion, 1999; Mollerup, 1999). They view the corporate brand signature as a crucial element in provoking an emotional reaction from consumers (Berlyne, 1971; Lewicki, 1986). Graphic designers and consultants consider the idea of the corporate brand signature as the method an organisation can use to communicate with the public.

In a similar way to the marketing research, the organisational literature focuses on the corporate brand signature as a clear tool to convey the characteristics of the organisation. Corporate visual identity (CVI) 'plays a significant role in the way an organisation presents itself to both internal and external stakeholders' (Van den Bosch et al., 2006, p. 871). The researchers in the organisational literature view the corporate brand signature as more than merely a visual presentation of the organisation; instead, they consider it to be fundamental for the organisation to communicate with consumers.

The different elements of a corporate brand signature's operational definition have to explain the dynamics of the way people position a company. The perspective of organisational studies, which to some extent is grounded in social identity theory (Dutton et al., 1994), offers a valuable viewpoint for explaining how a customer views an organisation; others' perceptions of an organisation also affect an individual's overall assessment of that organisation. Concluding this discussion, the concept of the corporate brand signature can communicate a necessary message and signals the company's individuality, which can convey a company's image.

The elements of the corporate brand signature

Early research into corporate identity and corporate image focused on corporate identity as communicating a company's culture, values, and principles through visual identity tools, for example, the company logo, specific colours, typeface and so on (Balmer, 2001).

In this section, to understand the corporate brand signature better, the different elements of a corporate brand signature, for example, colour, design, typeface, and corporate name (Henderson et al., 2003; Melewar, 2003), are discussed. Building a favourable image through corporate brand signature design needs the main tools, such as design, fonts, corporate name, and colour. Other audible aspects may also be relevant (Mollerup, 1999, p. 74). These key components, translated into a physical effect, facilitate the development of the corporate identity.

Corporate brand typeface

Typeface design is a significant visual tool to achieve the objectives of corporate communication (Childers and Jass, 2002; Henderson et al., 2004; Hutton, 1987; McCarthy and Mothersbaugh, 2002; Pan and Schmitt, 1996; Tantillo et al., 1995) and plays a crucial role in the way an organisation presents itself to both external and internal stakeholders. As paradigms involved in the field of corporate brand signature, a typeface can communicate numerous messages to the audience. Wheeler (2003) suggests that a typeface can express feelings that reflect a company's personality and a company's culture. A company's typeface is important in helping people to recognise the organisation and call to mind its image. It may even confirm consumers' trust in the organisation (Dowling, 1993) and can influence people's behaviour and judgements (Doyle and Bottomley, 2002; Gabrielsen et al., 2000; Van Riel et al., 2001).

The corporate typeface is central to how an organisation presents the physical facet that depicts sophistication. According to Rowden (2000), typeface is the voice of character and 'the best typography has grace and a certain invisibility' (p. 185). Based on aesthetics research, a link has been found between the specific features of a typeface's and how the typeface influences consumers' responses. Typeface design can be based on consumers' understanding of a specific cultural heritage, the nuances of which are not accessible in other cultures. Childers and Jass (2002, p. 2) defined corporate typeface as 'the art or skill of designing communication by means of the printed word'.

The preliminary evidence indicates that the design dimensions (harmony, elaborateness, and naturalness) are significant for understanding reactions to typeface. The choice of a typeface can affect the definition of the term and can assist the viewers in understanding what the new organisation represents and where it is heading (Childers and Jass, 2002). The voice employed in the communication as a written word and the typeface is its physical appearance. Hence, typefaces are employed to communicate with the customer in circumstances in which it is not feasible to use the spoken word.

Both practitioners and academics have claimed that the design of the typeface can affect consumers' perceptions of advertised brands due to their readability and memorability (Childers and Jass, 2002; Henderson et al., 2004). Readability can be defined as how easily we can comprehend text by recognising the words as shapes. Researchers assert that typefaces can have an effect on the suitability of a typeface for different products and different companies (Pan and Schmitt, 1996). A certain typeface may be able to refer to a specific trade or may relate to the company or the product in question. If this reference exists only due to habit or agreement, then the selection of the typeface is arbitrary (according to Mollerup, 1999, p. 109). Hagtvedt (2011) investigates how an incomplete typeface can affect consumer perceptions of the firm and shows that, although an incomplete typeface can result in a negative effect on the perceived trustworthiness of the firm, in contrast, it can have a positive effect on the perceived innovativeness of the firm. However, an incomplete typeface can also have a negative impact on consumers' overall attitude toward and perception of the firm.

A typeface can generate significant impressions and an optimistic image with the public. Spaeth (1999) discussed how firms change their company's corporate brand signature, it is necessary to modify the company's typeface, which helps to communicate their company's goals. Some researchers stated that fonts and name can possess an inherent meaning (Bottomley and Doyle, 2006; Klink, 2003). The company's message should communicate consistency and, since a corporate brand signature cannot communicate by itself, it is appropriate to generate a written communication.

It is important for managers to choose typefaces that promote strategically valued impressions. In particular, a carefully selected typeface indicates a company's identity by supporting a range of other elements of corporate visual identity systems (Jenkins, 1991; Kapferer, 1992). Typefaces can also improve the probability of the company becoming more visible (Melewar and Saunders, 2000). According to marketing researchers, a typeface plays a significant and important role in conveying an organisation's visual identity and can become sufficiently individualistic that they function without the need for a symbol, such as Coca Cola.

Corporate typeface is the essential component of organisational and communication purposes. The corporate typeface is conveyed via the design identity or brand signature and is embraced by the managers (Leuthesser and Kohli, 1997). Childers and Jass (2002) believe that the effects of typefaces at the consumer level are not very well understood, when there are so many typeface choices available. Typefaces create significant and strategic impressions, and promote a favourable image. Moreover, researchers discuss the appropriateness of a typeface for different products (Henderson et al., 2004; Walker et al., 1986), and claim that typefaces may affect a company's financial performance (Wallace, 2001).

Corporate brand colour

Today, companies have become aware of the power and the value of a corporate brand signature and its colour to identify their products or services and distinguish them from those of other companies or other products in addition to communicating information about their value, quality, and reliability. Colour 'induces moods and emotions, influences consumers' perceptions and behaviour and helps companies position or differentiate from the competition' (Aslam, 2006, p. 15). Colour is an expressive tool with regard to visual identity and depends for its effect on two quite different considerations: The first is an association with natural phenomena, and the second is an association with received cultural references (Baker and Blamer, 1997). Colours can influence consumers' responses based on their associations and instincts and thus are also able to predict consumer behaviour. Consumer behaviour research states that communication impacts on individuals' behaviours and attitudes (Brown and Reingen, 1987).

Colour is significant and research has shown that it can elicit different responses from people (Bellizzi and Hite, 1992). Colour helps products stands out from the crowd (Tavassoli, 2001). It has a powerful influence and causes reactions based on associations and instincts that maintain corporate identities (Madden et al., 2000) and consumer perceptions (Grossman and Wisenblit, 1999). Colour is fundamental in attracting the consumers' attention towards the corporate brand signature. Colour has been associated with various consumer rituals (Bellizzi and Hite, 1992). Sophisticated colours denote elegance and intimate communication. In addition, well-chosen colours in corporate brand signatures contribute to the exchange of meaning between the sender and the receiver in the process of their perception and processing of an incoming message.

Bellizzi and Hite (1992) explored how the individual uses multiple senses when reacting to and understanding colour stimuli. People frequently 'like stimuli more as familiarity increases'. Gabrielsen et al. (2000) demonstrated that people can differentiate between design elements, and that of these, it is colour that gives the strongest results. Colour also has an impact on other elements of brand design, for instance, typeface. It is centred on the symbolic workings of form and colour.

Colour is a language that is essential for religious or cultural reasons in some countries. It evokes emotions and moods, affects consumers' perceptions and behaviours, and helps a company improve its position or differentiate itself from its competitors (Aslam, 2006). Moreover, colour is an important component of corporate visual identity (Alessandri, 2001; Balmer, 2001; Melewar and Saunders, 2000; Van den Bosch et al., 2005). Hatch and Schultz (1997) believe that corporate brand signature and colours create a monolithic identity for the firm, and are big contributors, which affect perceptions. On the other hand, Tavassoli (2001) inspected the effect of printing brand names in colour and found that colour did not have a strong effect on brand name ratings.

Studies on corporate strategy show that when used as an element of corporate promotion applied across business units over extended periods (Aaby and McGann, 1989), it can convey to stakeholders not only the value of the company but also the values of each country's strategy and mission statement as well as the characteristics of the company (Baker and Balmer, 1997; Seifert, 1992). Companies use colours they have selected as appropriate to communicate signals by assisting the strategy of visual recognition and so capture a competitive advantage. The symbolisms of colours are an essential part of the global marketer's encyclopaedia (Cateora, 1990). Colours are a crucial component of a company and play an important role in marketing communications. A brand's physical appearance can be conveyed to the company's audience through the use of colour in the design of the corporate brand signature. Colour helps the company to establish a position or differentiate the brand from those of its rivals (Schmitt and Pan, 1994). In addition, it can provoke and influence reactions based on the consumers' associations and instincts, which, in turn, can help to maintain distinct corporate identities (Madden et al., 2000) and support customer perceptions (Grossman and Wisenblit, 1999). Colour as an instrument can help to attract consumers' attention to the corporate brand signature.

The appropriate use of colour was tested by Bottomley and Doyle (2006) to demonstrate the 'effects of colours and products on perceptions of brand logo appropriateness' (p. 63). It was found that colours were more significantly congruent with products. The results also showed that blue logos were found to be more suitable than red logos for those brands that need to promote a functional image. In contrast, red logos were found to be more suitable for those brands that wish to promote a sensory social image. Madden et al. (2000) explored inter-cultural dissimilarity in consumer preferences for colours and colour combinations for product logos.

The choice of colour in a corporate brand signature is in accordance with the company's marketing objectives, cultural values, corporate communications, and desired customer relationship levels. Colour preferences, however, call for high-involvement decisions. Furthermore, the product quality is a critical determinant for consumer satisfaction and the visual appearance of the brand is also important. According to Wheeler (2003), 'colour is used to evoke emotion, express personality, and stimulate brand associations' (p. 84). Ughanwa and Baker (1989) state that colour can influence design in three main ways: i) centre of attention; ii) separation/association; and iii) proportion and orientation.

Research into colour has found that reactions to colour can be native or instinctual in origin, or they can be learned or associative in origin (Humphrey, 1976). When measured on evaluative scales, there is clearly a significant type of communication between colour and product that reinforces the needs.

In addition, colour is useful for conveying the position of the company and for focusing on information the company wishes to highlight in order to attract attention. This, in turn, can be effective in provoking individuals to respond in specific ways. The significance of different colours is vital and it is necessary to explore the meaning and effects before launching the product or using the colour on corporate brand signatures. Different colours can have different meanings in different cultures, and therefore, their visual appeal when communicating with the audience will also be different. Simple colours are vibrant and intense, and hence they are selected for use in traffic signs. Investigations into the use of colour have shown that colour can provoke a range of reactions from different individuals, and so it is an expressive tool for use in establishing brand identity and conveying both its connection with natural phenomena and with received cultural references (Jenkins, 1991).

Bottomley and Doyle (2006) investigate colour appropriateness and demonstrate the 'effects of colours and products on perceptions of brand logo appropriateness' (p. 63). The test by Gabrielsen et al. (2000) demonstrated that people are able to discriminate between different elements of design, and colour gives the strongest result. The use of colour requires that the targeted audience has a comprehend of value (dark to light) and hue (red, blue). It is the value that creates legibility and contrast. Shepard and Cooper (1992) agree that visual abilities are divided into light and colour reception, brain functions, acuity, motility, and visual fields. According to Bellizzi et al. (1983), large sections of the research into the use of colour in advertisements and products and on packages has yet to be published due to the level of competition in the world (how does colour influence corporate brand signature perception?). Drawing on this discussion, the colour concept can be defined as follows: Colour is a medium of communication and can form a central component of corporate and marketing communications, which evokes moods and emotions in consumers and thus has an impact on their perceptions and behaviour, while helping organisations to position themselves or to establish their difference from rival companies (Aslam, 2006; Tavassoli, 2001).

Corporate brand design

The design of corporate brand signature is becoming increasingly significant as a method of differentiating between companies and their competitors. Corporate brand signature selection is a challenge for a company (Henderson and Cote, 1998) and a company brand signature facilitates easy as well as rapid recognition and a quick association with the company. A corporate brand signature is crucial in terms of what it can convey about the company in the market and to its customers.

The corporate brand signature can convey formal characteristics (Van Riel et al., 2001), which, as Henderson and Cote (1998) show, depend upon the company's objective. Cohen (1991), Peter (1989), Robertson (1989) and Vartorella (1990) believe that a well-designed corporate brand signature and all desired goals are high on correct recognition, effect, and a familiar, clear meaning. Bloch (1995) stated that corporate brand signature perception can be an aesthetic response and generates a fundamental element of a stimulus that may attract the attention of and evoke an emotional response in customers.

Henderson and Cote (1998) have developed a set of guidelines for selecting and modifying corporate brand signatures to help firms select a corporate brand signature that evokes the desired responses from their target customers, thus helping them to distinguish between the different corporate brand signature objectives. Corporate brand signatures have main three characteristics, which are high recognition, low-investment, and high-image communication objectives. Henderson et al. (2004) studied typeface and developed four measures and guidelines to help managers choose those typefaces that will create strategically valued impressions. They discussed the possible trade-offs among the impressions a typeface creates, such as engaging, prominent, reassuring, pleasing, and they researched the effect of elaborate, harmonious, flourished, weighted, compressed, and natural typefaces. Studies on design have centred on specific audiences (Henderson et al., 2004).

Design characteristics affect reactions towards corporate brand signature. Henderson and Cote (1998) found that the design of corporate brand signatures consists of three major dimensions: elaborateness, naturalness, and harmony. Corporate visual identity managers need a simple guideline to know how to best utilise the visual elements of their marketing stimuli. The following section describes the design characteristics, such as natural, representativeness, organic, elaborate, complexity, active, depth, harmony, symmetric, balance, parallel, proportion, and repetition, which are essential for designing logos, and the influence on consumers' responses towards the corporate brand signatures, and the impact of the level of recognition, subject familiarity, clear meaning, and effect.

In addition, changing geographical emphasis, acquisitions, mergers, restructuring, take-overs, and marketplaces may lead to a new corporate brand signature (Balmer and Dinnie, 1999). Companies alter their corporate brand signature, because of changes in strategy (Brun, 2002), and corporate identity modification (Huppatz, 2005; Melewar and Akel, 2005). Organisations alter the company's design to communicate a favourable image and to modernise the brand design. In addition, several researchers have made assumptions about the effects of changes to the corporate brand signature. However, there are no empirical findings to support their views.

Martinez (2006) clarified the distinction between coats of arms and logos, and the elements clearly belong to the two distinguishable categories; though, their design generally coincides, making this separation indistinct. He added that coats of arms are elements mainly based on heraldic rules, with a design that belongs to a particular group of people, to be used by them in a wide variety of ways. All matters relating to the duties and responsibilities connect the institutions closely to territory (place) and history (time) by using calligraphic designs.

Aesthetic appeal is an element of corporate brand signature design. 'A positive association could be an aesthetically pleasing visual presentation of the firm's logo' (Alessandri, 2001, p. 179). The visual aesthetic is a crucial element of corporate marketing and the identity building process, which creates a positive effect. This object draws attention to its beauty and attractiveness.

The reaction to corporate brand signature design is linked to various aspects of non-conscious processing. These include how an individual develops sensitivity to stimuli (Lewicki, 1986) and the effects of implicit exposure (Berlyne, 1971; Harrison, 1977; Veryzer, 1993, 1999). The theory of aesthetic, by Verzer (1993), describes responses analysed on non-conscious processing of visual stimuli. The role played by non-conscious algorithms in evaluating a range of design aspects has been studied by Lewicki (1986).

Pythagoras was the first of the great teachers of ancient Greece who discovered the divine proportion, and the ancient Greeks followed him in using it but, surprisingly, there was no name for this fundamental proportion of nature until, early in the sixteenth century, when Pacioli (1445–1514), a geometer, rediscovered the golden secret. Pacioli published a book entitled *De Divina Proportione*, which was illustrated by Leonardo da Vinci in 1509, and this was the first to propose the golden ratio. Renaissance artists used this 'divine proportion' to design paintings, sculpture, and architecture (from the Mona Lisa to the Parthenon and the great pyramids, which are the finest example of proportion in the history of architecture). The term 'golden section' was first used by Martin Ohm in 1835 (Livio, 2002, p. 6).

Using divine proportion as a guide to compositions can improve design communication by creating a natural language that understands which artefacts are most pleasing to the human eye. The divine proportions, golden mean, and golden sections are expressions of the same concept (Pittard et al., 2007). Henderson and Cote (1998) emphasise that the divine proportions used in art over the centuries have been employed as a way to measure proportion, and preference is dependent on whether the stimuli are orientated on the vertical or the horizontal axis. Practical information is available as to how to create designs based on simple rules and logical thought, rather than just a feeling.

According to Pittard et al. (2007), culture has no important influence on the respondent's preference for the divine proportion. However, the level of uniqueness in a society is a key value for designing an aesthetic strategy. Ewing (2006) and Pittard et al. (2007) believe that the nature of a corporate brand signature is expressed in the divine proportion in three different cultures that react similarly to corporate brand signature designs when compared with other fields of marketing. The aesthetic primacy of the divine proportion in corporate brand signature design is restricted to designing characteristics and natural phenomena, which provide a bridge across cultures (Pittard et al., 2007). Schechter (1993, p. 34) states:

> image contribution is the degree to which a corporate brand signature design influences perception of a company or brand name as trustworthy and reputable, offering high quality, a product (or service) for today's lifestyles, and a product (or service) I would use.

Kohli et al. (2002) believed that a logo design should be carefully chosen, since 'a strong image may take a long time to build but an even longer time to shed' (p. 62). Giberson and Hulland

(1994) stated that since the product category is cued in a corporate brand signature and the corporate brand signature is retrieved quicker from memory.

In addition, the design and development of a corporate brand signature as a key component of the company's visual identity increases questions regarding issues such as company's identity and strategic choices. A company will establish a corporate brand signature to improve organisational visibility and so convey the corporate strategy to consumers. When the strategy is established, the company's corporate brand signature aims to fix it in the consumers' memory and, in this way, the business develops uniquely in the minds of the audience.

The association amongst the specific basics of an organisation and the design of a company's corporate brand signature has an important communicative value. Therefore, a well-designed corporate brand signature impacts the consistency and overall picture both over time and among the many components. Based on the above argument, in this study, design is defined as a creative process that communicates a message or that creates effective communications for companies.

Corporate brand name

It could be assumed that a corporate brand signature helps consumers to identify the product or company by reading the company's name. Researchers in design and marketing (Henderson et al., 2003; Melewar, 2003) have dedicated much time and attention to use of the company name as an element of the corporate brand signature. Psychologists, sociologists, and economists have investigated the concept of name via investigating symbology to devise theories on the power of corporate brand signatures and names to attract attention and to evoke desired responses. The corporate name is closely connected to the company's expected attributes and promises.

Corporate names are intangible assets, which the company can use as a significant competitive advantage among its competitors. The corporate name is viewed as a key and central part of any marketing programme. The company's name can position the company in the stakeholders' minds (Selame and Selame, 1988). It can summarise the company's reputation and develop into a valuable asset. From a marketing perspective, the corporate name is the components of brand design identity (Chun, 2005; Dowling, 1994; Melewar and Saunders, 1998). Gray and Balmer (1998) state that a company's name is the main element of the organisation's communication system (Koku, 1997).

Poon and Fatt (1997) claim that the company's name as the greatest recognisable component of the company's identity, should be easily identifiable by consumers. Association/recognition is the degree to which consumers associate the visual elements of corporate brand signature with the company or brand, and conversely, the degree to which use of the name evokes the visual elements of the corporate brand signature (Schechter, 1993).

The corporate name should be internationally acceptable and hence care should be taken to ensure that it does not convey any embarrassing meanings when used in major foreign languages (Margulies, 1977). This is because when companies start to develop their operations on an international basis, the image that they developed as national producers often becomes inappropriate. Therefore, companies aiming to operate on an international basis should take care with managing their corporate identity.

Researchers have demonstrated that corporate visual identity gives a strong indication of the corporate name (Dowling, 1994) and therefore, employees should be particularly aware of a company's corporate brand signature and its meanings. The corporate name is a context within which a corporate identity can be interpreted, and it can affect the corporate image through the use of cultural artefacts (Hatch and Schultz, 1997). Managers have an important role to play in the development of the organisation, and physical artefacts are becoming an increasingly important element of the vocabulary of management thinking that exists at a visible level of the organisation.

Moreover, it can be useful in shaping the consumer's expectations and, in turn, it can influence the corporate image. Company's identity is closely linked with the company name and the corporate brand signature. Childers and Houston (1984) and Lutz and Lutz (1977) acknowledged the main features of brand symbols that can affect awareness of a brand name. For example, a name may convey a specific message and communicate the quality of the organisation to customers, and so it can be used to distinguish an organisation from competitors. Corporate names are a method whereby corporations can convey messages to customers and so, are objects of communication. Company name changes would convey to the public the steps taken by the business to progress the company's performance and quality and should indicate how the new version of the company differs from the old version.

A corporate brand signature has many communication objectives, and it influences awareness of the company's name. The company's name is the an easily recognisable component of the company's identity. It is a crucial element in constructing a company's acceptance and international recognition (Jefkins, 1990; Smith, 1990) and in helping to form the customer's prospects once developing a corporate image.

It is easier to remember meaningful names that are represented in a visual manner, as a word and design/graphic express design/visual statements. In this way, a name could convey to consumers a specific communication and give an indication of the organisation's quality while forming the foundation for characteristic among one organisation and competitors. In addition, it is used to illustrate the quality and performance of a company's services/products. The role of the corporate brand signature and corporate name is to help to identify a firm through its design to increase the speed of recognition (Kohli et al., 2002). They state that content and style are two features of corporate brand signature design. Content features concentrate on the graphical and worded elements in a corporate brand signature and style focuses on how these elements are formed.

Changing a corporation's name is increasingly common. For instance, Federal Express (cargo airline) changed to FedEx (Koku, 1997). Horsky and Swyngedouw (1987) studied the effects of name change on banks and believe that a corporate name change can enhance the value of a firm. Firms should make their corporate name synonymous with the firm's image and an assurance of quality that encourages consumers to differentiate their companies against their competition (Brachel, 1999). The name of a company can express confidence to the consumers and provide value (Grace and O'Cass, 2002).

According to Mollerup (1999), the understanding of proper names is arguable, because an appropriate name should be categorised as a symbol. Descriptive names give an indication of the nature of the business (Mollerup, 1999). A metaphoric name can be related to the nature of the industry and use a shared quality to convey its object (Mollerup, 1999). In addition, a found name is a name which is already known and has no previous association with either the company or with the product it represents (Mollerup, 1999, p. 115). Artificial names are completely new words that are coined specifically for the company or for the product they represent (Mollerup, 1999, p. 116). Abbreviation names are used when the name of a company is excessively long, such as ABC or BBC (Mollerup, 1999, p. 117). Furthermore a company's name can be based on the phonetic content of an abbreviated form of the novel name.

Kohli and Thakor (1997) gave the following five name categorisations: descriptive, generic, arbitrary, coined, and suggestive. Descriptive and suggestive names are strong, and they can be used to create an immediate image; due to this, less advertising is required than is necessary with coined and arbitrary names. Though, suggestive and arbitrary names have additional profits since they need not be restricted to a specific organisation or product, and therefore, it is easier to transfer the name to other products. A name can have an aura for original service/product through the globe. Therefore, names should be selected to encourage values in the solidity of the company, to play an essential role in the hierarchy of the brand and signify the organisation's field of action.

The study by MacInnis et al. (1999) shows that brand name and symbols signify effective communication tools to communicate to stakeholders the corporate structure or identity (Olins, 1989): 'Consumers would prefer products that have a brand and a corporate name' (Saunders and Guoqun, 1996, p. 30). The company's name can be used to assist with raising initial awareness of products, and subsequently, the link between the organisation and the brand name upsurges the company's value, assist to raise the audience view toward the company and increase their preference. If corporate branding promotes the corporate name, it could help to create more value.

In many cases the corporation is the brand. IBM or Christian Dior, for instance, use their corporate name across their product range. Firms prefer their logos to be identical with the company's names and, therefore, generating a corporate brand signature can be an efficient way for the company to attract peoples' interest. Furthermore, the company name should be unique, easily recognisable and understandable at an international level and should be associated with a logo. Most companies initially decide to use English names to advance the quality insight and to create and develop a global image. Thus, the company's name is a key factor in promoting a company, particularly, when consumers have little knowledge of or awareness regarding the product or company. In addition, the corporate name should function on an international level if the company decides to do business with foreign consumers.

Language is the chief expression of culture, and if insufficient care is taken when selecting a name for the company, it can cause significant problems in the target audience. Language can influence the choice and use of corporate names, and indeed, a significant number of global businesses are concerned about the language they use when deciding on their company name. Based on this discussion, it can be concluded that the definition of corporate name is the most ubiquitous element in corporate and brand communications as it identifies a company and increases the speed of recognition (Foroudi, 2019; Foroudi et al., 2017; 2020).

Conclusion

Chapter 3 provides a clear explanation and definition of the concept of corporate brand signature and the various components (logo, name, design, and typeface). Academics and practitioners alike are aware of the value and power of corporate brand signatures and how their designs can be useful for identifying company products or services, for differentiating the company from others and for communicating information about their qualities, values, and reliability to the consumers. The corporate brand signature has attracted significant attention from both practitioners and academics in the last 50 years. A large body of literature surrounding these areas exists. In this theoretical examination of the corporate brand signature, the literature described the significance and value of a corporate brand signature as an effective means of communication, making a corporate brand signature's main task to deepen and integrate the company's total image.

CASE STUDY – CADBURY

Maria Palazzo, University of Salerno, Italy

In 1824, John Cadbury opened Cadbury, a chocolate brand that is still loved nowadays, in the UK and around the world. The company has succeeded in creating an iconic brand, that was affected by many changes during its history, but surely Cadbury still have an important place in the chocolate lovers' mind (Jones, 1984; Barthel, 1989).

Cadbury states:

> We've been inventing, inspiring and investing in a nation of chocolate lovers for nearly 200 years. Delve into the company's fascinating history and you'll find a wealth of interesting facts and information on subjects including how the nation's favourite chocolate was born, the Cadbury family, packaging, and so much more!
>
> *www.cadbury.co.uk/our-story*

Cadbury produces a wide variety of products, such as: Dairy Milk, Twirl, Wispa, Crunchie, Twisted, Bournville, Chomp, Boost, Double Decker, Fudge, Flake, Starbar, Picnic, Time Out, Snack, Dream, Curly Wurly, Brunchbar, Freddo Frog, etc. (Child and Smith, 1987).

The most well-known and appreciated product is the Dairy Milk, that acts as the flagship of Cadbury brand and product.

Cadbury communication: Glass and a half full

Cadbury has been always associated with the slogan: 'Glass and a half full'. This statement is due to the fact that the company puts 'a glass and a half full' of milk in every product: It has been seen as a thriving tactic for Cadbury, and its latest communication campaigns are inspired by the 'glass and a half full' productions, too.

Nevertheless, in 2010, Cadbury tried to change the well-known slogan, in favour of the message: 'the equivalent of 426ml of fresh liquid milk in every 227g of milk chocolate'. The new promotional phrase was considered by consumers not to be in line with their expectations, in fact, they were hesitant to allow changes to their loved British company (Hasian, 2008).

It must be said that this transformation was added exclusively to the packaging and wrappers. This was also stated during an interview to *Marketing Week*, by a manager of the company, who said that no changes were made to the brand, and that some new information about ingredients would be added only to the wrappers, in order to fulfil the EU regulation.

Focus on competitors

Several competitors in the confectionary sector have to be taken into consideration by Cadbury (Rowlinson, 1995; 2002; Sahoo and Garg, 2012; Wood & Grosvenor, 1997). The main competitor is Mars corporation and its brand portfolio (Mars, Snickers, M&Ms, Galaxy, etc.).

Another competitor in the UK, is the confectionary organisation, Thorntons. Set in Derbyshire, it specialises in chocolate, and creates high quality/high price products.

The Swiss company, Nestlé, is the third competitor. Its brands in the chocolate sector are: Butterfinger, Aero, Crunch, Cailler, Orion, KitKat, Smarties, Wonka, etc. Half of these brands are very famous among the customers, and are really successful.

Kraft is considered to be another competitor of the company.

Nevertheless, in 2010, Cadbury agreed to an aggressive takeover bid made by an American company. In fact, Kraft offered a price for Cadbury, that was below the stock exchange value: Many experts highlighted that it was an attempt to 'buy Cadbury on the cheap'.

Moreover, journalists and employees at Cadbury were worried about the future of the organisation due to the fact that Kraft had many debts and was renowned for moving the manufacturing processes of purchased corporations in Eastern European countries. This fear, regrettably, was shared by the customers too.

Once more, clients were irritated by Cadbury's decisions. Consumers, in fact, were annoyed by the fact that a British organisation was being sold abroad, and they felt that a British icon was damaged.

Case questions

1. What does the change in the slogan mean for Cadbury's brand personality?
2. How does Kraft takeover affect Cadbury's brand image?
3. Analyse the logo, design, typeface, and colour of Cadbury

References

Barthel, D. (1989) "Modernism and marketing: the chocolate box revisited", Theory, culture and society, Vol. 6, No. 3, pp. 429–438.

Child, J. and Smith, C. (1987) "The context and process of organizational transformation – Cadbury limited in its sector", Journal of Management Studies, Vol. 24, No. 6, pp. 565–593.

Hasian Jr, M. (2008) "Critical memories of crafted virtues: The Cadbury chocolate scandals, mediated reputations, and modern globalized slavery", Journal of Communication Inquiry, Vol. 32, No. 3, pp. 249–270.

Jones, G. (1984) "Multinational chocolate: Cadbury overseas, 1918–39", Business History, Vol. 26, No. 1, pp. 59–76.

Rowlinson, M. (1995) "Strategy, structure and culture: Cadbury, divisionalization and merger in the 1960s", Journal of Management Studies, Vol. 32, No. 2, pp. 121–140.

Rowlinson, M. (2002) "Public history review essay – Cadbury World", Labour History Review, Vol. 67, No. 1, pp. 101–119.

Sahoo, D. and Garg, S. (2012) "Buying motives in the purchase of Cadbury chocolate among young Indians", Romanian Journal of Marketing, Vol. 4.

Wood, L. J. and Grosvenor, S. (1997) "Chocolate in China: The Cadbury experience", The Australian Geographer, Vol. 28, No. 2, pp. 173–184.

Key terms and definitions

Colour is a medium of communication and is an integral element of corporate and marketing communications, which induces emotions and moods, impacts on consumers' perceptions and behaviour, and helps organisations position or differentiate themselves from competitors.

Corporate logo is the signature of a company with an essential communication, distinctiveness, which can reflect a company's image.

Corporate name is the most pervasive element in corporate and brand communications that identifies a company and increases recognition speed.

Design is a creative process that conveys a message or creates effective communications for companies.

Icon is a picture to be communicated to people.

Symbol is a pictorial sign with no letter or combination of letters.

Trademark is a letter or combination of letters, pictorial sign, or non-graphic – even non-visual – sign, or any combination of these.

Typeface is the visual perceptual property of a company, which is the art, or skill of designing communication by means of the printed word.

References

Aaby, N. E. and McGann, A. F. (1989) "Corporate strategy and the role of navigational strategy", European Journal of Marketing, Vol. 23, No. 10, pp. 18–31.

Aaker, D. (1991) Managing Brand Equity, Free Press, New York.

Abratt, R. (1989) "A new approach to the corporate image management process", Journal of Marketing Management, Vol. 5, No. 1, pp. 63–76.

Ageeva, E., Melewar, T. C., Foroudi, P., and Dennis, C. (2019). Evaluating the factors of corporate website favorability: a case of UK and Russia. Qualitative Market Research: An International Journal.

Alessandri, S. W. (2001) "Modelling corporate identity: a concept explication and theoretical explanation", Corporate Communications: An International Journal, Vol. 6, No. 4, pp. 173–182.

Aslam, M. (2006) "Are you selling the right colour? A cross-cultural review of colour as a marketing cue", Journal of Marketing Communications, Vol. 12, No. 1, pp. 15–30.

Baker, M. J., and Balmer, J. M. T. (1997) "Visual identity: Trappings or substance?", European Journal of Marketing, Vol. 31, No. 5, pp. 366–382.

Balmer, J. M. T. (2001) "Corporate identity, corporate branding and corporate marketing seeing through the fog", European Journal of Marketing, Vol. 35, No. 3/4, pp. 248–291.

Balmer, J. M. T. (2005) "Corporate brand cultures and communities", in Schroeder, J. E., Salzer-Morling, M. (Eds.), Brand Culture, Routledge, London, pp. 34–49.

Balmer, J. M. T. (2008) "Identity based views of the corporation: Insights from corporate identity, organisational identity, social identity, visual identity, corporate brand identity and corporate image", European Journal of Marketing, Vol. 42, No. 9/10, pp. 879–906.

Balmer, J. M. T. and Dinnie, K. (1999) "Corporate identity and corporate communications: The antidote to merger madness", Corporate Communications: An International Journal, Vol. 4, No. 4, pp. 171–176.

Balmer, J. M. T. and Gray, E. R. (1999) "Corporate identity and corporate communications: creating a competitive advantage", Corporate Communications: An International Journal, Vol. 4, No. 4, pp. 171–176.

Balmer, J. M. T. and Gray, E. R. (2000) "Corporate identity and corporate communications: creating a competitive advantage", Industrial and Commercial Training, Vol. 32, No. 7, pp. 256–262.

Bellizzi, J. A. and Hite, R. E. (1992) "Environment colour, consumer feelings, and purchase likelihood", Psychology and Marketing, Vol. 9, No. 5, pp. 347–363.

Bellizzi, J. A., Crawley, A. E., and Hasty, R. W. (1983) "The effects of colour in store design", Journal of Retailing, Vol. 59, No. 1, pp. 21–45.

Bennett, P. D. (1995) Dictionary of Marketing Terms, McGraw-Hill Education, New York.

Berlyne, D. E. (1971) Aesthetics and Psychobiology, Appleton Century Crofts, New York.

Bernstein, D. (1986) Company Image and Reality: A Critique of Corporate Communications, Cassell Educational Ltd, London.

Bhattacharya, C. B. and Sen, S. (2003) "Consumer-company identification: A framework for understanding consumers, relationships with companies", Journal of Marketing, Vol. 67, No. 2, pp. 76–88.

Bhattacharya, C. B., Rao, H., and Glynn, M. A. (1995) "Understanding the bond of identification: An investigation of its correlates among art museum members", Journal of Marketing, Vol. 59, No. 4, pp. 46–57.

Bloch, P. H. (1995) "Seeking the ideal form: Product design and consumer response", Journal of Marketing, Vol. 59, No. 3, pp. 16–29.

Bottomley, P. A. and Doyle, J. R. (2006) "The interactive effects of colours and products on perceptions of brand logo appropriateness", Marketing Theory, Vol. 6, No. 1, pp. 63–83.

Brachel, J. V. (1999) "Make your firm a household name", Journal of Accountancy, Vol. 187, No. 5, pp. 43–48.

Brown, J. J. and Reingen, P. H. (1987) "Social Ties and word-of-mouth referral behaviour", Journal of Consumer Research, Vol. 14, No. 3, pp. 350–362.

Brown, T. J., Dacin, P. A., Pratt, M. G., and Whetten, D. A. (2006) "Identity, intended image, construed image, and reputation: an inter-disciplinary framework and suggested terminology", Journal of the Academy of Marketing Science, Vol. 34, No. 2, pp. 99–106.

Brun, M. (2002) Creating a new identity for France Telecom – Beyond a visual exercise? Routledge, London.

Carter, D. E. (1982) Designing Corporate Identity Programs for Small Corporations, Art Direction Book Company, New York.

Cateora, P. R. (1990) International Marketing, Irwin, Boston, MA.

Childers, T. L. and Jass, J. (2002) "All dressed up with something to say: Effects of typeface semantic associations on brand perception and consumer memory", Journal of Consumer Psychology, Vol. 12, No. 2, pp. 93–106.

Chun, R. (2005) "Corporate reputation: Meaning and measurement", International Journal of Management Reviews, Vol. 7, No. 2, pp. 91–109.

Cohen, D. (1991) "Trademark strategy revisited", Journal of Marketing, Vo. 55, No. 3, pp. 46–59.

Dacin, P. and Brown, T. (2002) "Corporate identity and corporate associations: A framework for future research", Corporate Reputation Review, Vol. 5, No. 2/3, pp. 254–253.

Douglas, S. (2001) "Executive insights; integrating branding strategy across markets: Building international brand architecture", Journal of International Marketing, Vol. 9, No. 2, pp. 97–115.

Dowling, G. R. (1993) "Developing your company image into a corporate asset", Long Range Planning, Vol. 26, No. 2, pp. 101–109.

Dowling, G. R. (1994) Corporate Reputations: Strategies for Developing the Corporate Brand, Kogan Page, London.

Dowling, G. R. (2001) Creating Corporate Reputations, Oxford University Press, Oxford.
Doyle, J. R. and Bottomley, P. A. (2002) "Font appropriateness and brand choice", Journal of Business Research, Vol. 57, No. 8, pp. 873–380.
Dutton, J. E., Dukcrich, L M., and Harquail, C.V. (1994) "Organisational images and member identification", Administrative Science Quarterly, Vol. 39, No. 2, pp. 239–263.
Ewing, T. M. (2006) "Brands, artifacts and design theory: A call to action", Journal of Product and Brand Management, Vol. 15, No. 4, pp. 255–256.
Foroudi, M. M., Balmer, J. M., Chen, W., Foroudi, P., and Patsala, P. (2020) "Explicating place identity attitudes, place architecture attitudes, and identification triad theory", Journal of Business Research, Vol. 109, March, pp. 321–336.
Foroudi, M. M., Balmer, M. T., Chen, W., and Foroudi, P. (2019) "Corporate identity, place architecture, and identification: an exploratory case study", Qualitative Market Research: An International Journal.
Foroudi, P. (2019) "Influence of brand signature, brand awareness, brand attitude, brand reputation on hotel industry's brand performance", International Journal of Hospitality Management, Vol. 76, Jan, pp. 271–285.
Foroudi, P. (2020) "Corporate brand strategy: Drivers and outcomes of corporate brand orientation in international marketing", International Journal of Hospitality Management.
Foroudi, P., Cuomo, M. T., Foroudi, M. M., Katsikeas, C. S., and Gupta, S. (2019a) Linking identity and heritage with image and a reputation for competition. Journal of Business Research.
Foroudi, P., Cuomo, M., and Foroudi, M.M. (2019b) Continuance Interaction Intention in Retailing: Relations between Customer Values, Satisfaction, Loyalty, and Identification, Information Technology and People
Foroudi, P., Foroudi, M. M., Nguyen, B., and Gupta, S. (2019c) Conceptualising and managing Corporate Logo: A Qualitative Study from Stakeholders Perspectives, Qualitative Market Research: An International Journal.
Foroudi, P., Gupta, S., and Melewar, T. C. (2017) "Corporate logo: History, definition, and component", International Studies of Management and Organization, Vol. 47, No. 2, pp. 176–196.
Foroudi, P., Melewar, T. C., and Gupta, S. (2014) "Linking corporate logo, corporate image, and reputation: An examination of consumer perceptions in the financial setting", Journal of Business Research, Vol. 67, No. 11, pp. 2269–2281.
Foroudi, P., Nazarian, A., Ziyadin, S., Kitchen, P. J., Hafeez, K., Priporas, C., and Pantano, E. (2020) « Co-creating brand image and reputation through stakeholder's social network", Journal of Business Research.
Foroudi, P., Yu, Q., Gupta, S., and Foroudi, M. M. (2019d). Enhancing university brand image and reputation through customer value co-creation behaviour. Technological Forecasting and Social Change, Vol. 138, No. Jan, pp. 218–227.
Gabrielsen, G., Kristensen, T., and Hansen, F. (2000) "Corporate design: A tool for testing", Corporate Communications: An International Journal, Vol. 5, No. 2, pp. 113–118.
Giberson, R. and Hulland, J. (1994) Using Logos as Cues to Recognition: A Preliminary Study, Western Business School, Working Paper Series, University of Western Ontario, Ontario.
Grace, D. and O'Cass, A. (2002) "Brand Associations: Looking through the eye of the beholder", Qualitative Market Research, Vol. 5, No. 2, pp. 96–111.
Gray, E. R. and Balmer, J. M. T. (1998) "Managing corporate image and corporate reputation", Long Range Planning, Vol. 31, No. 5, pp. 695–702.
Green, D. and Loveluck, V. (1994) "Understanding a corporate symbol", Applied Cognitive Psychology, Vol. 8, No. 1, pp. 37–47.
Grossman, R. P. and Wisenblit, J. Z. (1999) "What we know about consumers' colour choices", Journal of Marketing Practice, Vol. 5, No. 3, pp. 78–88.
Gupta, S., Grant, S., and Melewar, T. C. (2008) "The expanding role of intangible assets of the brand", Management Decision, Vol. 46, No. 6, pp. 948–960.

Gwinner, K. P. and Swanson, S. R. (2003) "A model of fan identification: Antecedents and sponsorship outcomes", The Journal of Services Marketing, Vol. 17, No. 2/3, pp. 275–294.

Hagtvedt, H. (2011) "the impact of incomplete typeface logos on perceptions of the firm", Journal of Marketing, Vol. 75 (July), pp. 86–93.

Harrison, A. A. (1977) "Mere exposure", in Berkowitz (Ed.), Advances in Social Psychology, Academic Press, New York.

Hatch, M. J. and Schultz, M. (1997) "Relations between organisational culture, identity and image", European Journal of Marketing, Vol. 31, No. 5/6, pp. 356–365.

Hatch, M. J. and Schultz, M. (2001) "Are the strategic stars aligned for your corporate brand", Harvard Business Review, Vol. 69 (February), pp. 128–134.

Henderson, P. W. and Cote, J. A. (1998) "Guidelines for selecting or modifying logos", Journal of Marketing, Vol. 62, No. 2, pp. 14–30.

Henderson, P. W., Cote, J. A., Meng, L, S., and Schmitt, B. (2003) "Building strong brands in Asia: Selecting the visual components of image to maximize brand strength", International Journal of Research in Marketing, Vol. 20, No. 4, pp. 297–313.

Henderson, P. W., Giese, J., and Cote, J. A. (2004) "Impression management using typeface design", Journal of Marketing, Vol. 68, No. 4, pp. 60–83.

Herrera, C. F. and Blanco, C. F. (2011) "Consequences of consumer trust in PDO food products: The role of familiarity", Journal of Product and Brand Management, Vol. 20, No. 4, pp. 282–296.

Horsky, D. and Swyngedouw, P. (1987) "Does it pay to change your company's name? A stock market perspective", Marketing Science, Vol. 6 (Fall), pp. 320–335.

Humphrey, N. K. (1976) "The Colour Currency of Nature", in Porter, T. and Mikelides, B. (Eds.), Colour for Architecture, Van Nostrand, New York.

Huppatz, D. J. (2005) "Globalising corporate identity in Hong Kong: Rebranding two banks", Journal of Design History, Vol. 18, No. 4, pp. 357–369.

Hutton, J. (1987) "How to think corporate identity", Public Relations Journal, Vol. 43 (May), pp. 25–28.

Hutton, J. (1997) "The influence of brand and corporate identity on consumer behaviour: A conceptual framework", Journal of Brand Management, Vol. 5 (November) pp. 428–439.

Jefkins, F. (1990) Modern Marketing Communications, Blackie, London.

Jenkins, N. (1991) The Business of Image: Visualising the Corporate Message, Kogan Page, London.

Johansson, J. K. and Hirano, M. (1999) "Brand reality: The Japanese perspective", Journal of Marketing Management, Vol. 13, No. 1/3, pp. 93–106.

Kapferer, J. N. (1992) Strategic Brand Management, Kogan Page, London.

Karaosmanoglu, E., Bas, A. B. E., and Zhang, J. (K) (2011) "The role of other customer effect in corporate marketing Its impact on corporate image and consumer-company identification", European Journal of Marketing, Vol. 45, No. 9/10, pp. 1416–1445.

Kay, M. J. (2006) "Strong brands and corporate brands", European Journal of Marketing, Vol. 40, No. 7/8, pp. 742–760.

Klink, R. R. (2003) "Creating meaningful new brand names: The relationship between brand name and brand mark", Marketing Letters, Vol. 14, No. 3, pp. 143–157.

Kohli, C. and Thakor, M. (1997) "Branding consumer goods: Insights from theory and practice", Journal of Consumer Marketing, Vol. 14, No. 3, pp. 206–219.

Kohli, C., Suri, R., and Thakor, M. (2002) "Creating effective logos: insights from theory and practice", Business Horizons, Vol. 45, No. 3, pp. 58–64.

Koku, P. S. (1997) "Corporate name change signaling in the services industry" Journal of Services Marketing, Vol. 11, No. 6, pp. 392–408.

Kotler, J. P. (2000) How to Create, Win and Dominate Market, The Free Press, New York, pp. 18–151.

Leitch, S. and Motion, J. (1999) "Miplicity in corporate identity strategy", Corporate Communications: An International Journal, Vol. 4, No. 4, pp. 193–200.

Leuthesser, L. and Kohli, C. (1997) "Corporate identity: The role of mission statements", Business Horizons, Vol. 40, No. 3, pp. 59–66.

Lewicki, P. (1986) "Processing information about co variations that cannot be articulated", Journal of Experimental Psychology: Learning, Memory and Cognition, Vol. 12, No. 1, pp. 135–146.

Livio, M. (2002) The Golden Ratio: The Story of Phi, the World's Most Astonishing Number, Broadway Books, New York.

Lutz, K. A. and Lutz, R. J. (1977) "Effects of interactive imagery on learning: Application to advertising", Journal of Applied Psychology, Vol. 72, No. 2, pp. 493–498.

MacInnis, D. J., Shapiro, S., and Mani, G. (1999) "Enhancing brand awareness through brand symbols", Advances in Consumer Research, Vol. 26, No. 1, pp. 601–608.

Madden, T. J., Hewett, K., and Roth, M. S. (2000) "Managing images in different cultures: A cross-national study of colour meanings and preferences", Journal of International Marketing, Vol. 8, No. 4, pp. 90–107.

Margulies, W. P. (1977) "Make the most of your corporate image", Harvard Business Review, Vol. 55, No. 4, pp. 66–74.

Martinez, J. G. (2006) "Designing symbols: The logos of the Spanish autonomous communities", Journal of Spanish Cultural Studies, Vol. 7, No. 1, pp. 51–74.

McCarthy, M. S. and Mothersbaugh, D. L. (2002) "Effects of typographic factors in advertising-based persuasion: A general model and initial empirical tests", Psychology and Marketing, Vol. 19 (July/August), pp. 663–691.

McQuarrie, E. F. and Mick, D. G. (2003) "Visual and verbal rhetorical figures under directed processing versus incidental exposure to advertising", Journal of Consumer Research, Vol. 29, No. 4, pp. 579–587.

Melewar, T. C. (2003) "Determinants of the corporate identity construct: A review of literature", Journal of Marketing Communications, Vol. 9, No. 3, pp. 195–220.

Melewar, T. C. and Akel, S. (2005) "Corporate identity in the higher education sector: A case study", Corporate Communications: An International Journal, Vol. 10, No. 1, pp. 41–27.

Melewar, T. C. and Saunders, J. (1998) "Global corporate visual identity systems: Standardization, control and benefits", International Marketing Review, Vol. 15, No. 4, pp. 291–308.

Melewar, T. C. and Saunders, J. (2000) "Global corporate visual identity systems: Using an extended marketing mix", European Journal of Marketing, Vol. 34, No. 5, pp. 538–550.

Melewar, T. C., Saunders, J., and Balmer, J. M. T. (2000) "The saliency of Olins' visual identity structure in relation to UK companies operating in Malaysia", Corporate Reputation Review, Vol. 3, No. 3, pp. 194–200.

Mollerup, P. (1999) Marks of Excellence, History and Taxonomy of Trademarks, Phaidon Press, London.

Mulvey, M. S. and Medina, C. (2003) Invoking the rhetorical power of character to create identifications, Persuasive imagery, Mahwah, Erlbaum, NJ.

Napoles, V. (1988) Corporate Identity Design, Van Nostrand Reinhold, New York.

Olins, W. (1989) Corporate Entity: Making Business Strategy Visible through Design, Thames and Hudson, London.

Olins, W. and Selame, E. (2000) The Corporate Identity Audit. A Company Selfassessment Tool, *Financial Times*, Prentice Hall, London.

Palmer, A. and Bejou, D. (2006) "The future of relationship marketing", Journal of Relationship Marketing, Vol 4, No. 3/4, pp. 1–10

Pan, Y. and Schmitt, B. H. (1996) "Language and brand attitudes: Impact of script and sound matching in Chinese and English", Journal of Consumer Psychology, Vol. 5, No. 3, pp. 263–277.

Peter, J. P. (1989) "Designing logos", Folio, Vol. 18, No. July, pp. 139–141.

Pittard, N., Ewing, M., and Jevons, C. (2007) "Aesthetic theory and logo design: Examining consumer response to proportion across cultures", International Marketing Review, Vol. 24, No. 4, pp. 457–473.

Poon, J. and Fatt, T. (1997) "Communicating a winning image", Industrial and Commercial Tradining, Vol. 29. No. 5, pp. 158–165.

Robertson, K. R. (1989) "Strategically desirable brand name characteristics", Journal of Consumer Marketing, Vol. 6 (Fall), pp. 61–71.

Rowden, M. (2000) The Art of Identity: Creating and Managing a Successful Corporate Identity, Gower Publishing, Aldershot.

Saunders, J. and Guoqun, F. (1996) 'Dual branding: How corporate names add value", Marketing Intelligence and Planning, Vol. 14, No. 7, pp. 29–34.

Schechter, A. H. (1993) "Measuring the value of corporate and brand logos", Design Management Journal, Vol. 4 (Winter), pp. 3–39.

Schmitt, B. (1995) "Experimental marketing", Journal of Marketing and Management, Vol. 15, No. 1/3, pp. 53–67.

Schmitt, B. and Pan, Y. (1994) "Managing corporate and brand identities in the Asia Pacific Region", California Management Review, Vol. 36, No. 4, pp. 32–48.

Seifert, L. S. (1992) "Pictures as means of conveying information", Journal of Gestalt Psychology, Vol. 119, No. 3, pp. 279–287.

Selame, E. and Selame, J. (1988) The Company Image: Building your Identity and Influence in the Marketplace, John Wiley & Sons, New York.

Shepard, R. N. and Cooper, L. A. (1992) "Representation of colours in the blind, colour blind, and normally sighted", Psychological Science, Vol. 3, No. 2, pp. 97–104.

Siegel, L. B. (1989) "Planning for a long-life logo", Marketing Communications, Vol. 14 (March), pp. 44–49.

Simoes, C., Dibb, S., and Fisk, R. (2005) "Managing corporate identity: An internal perspective", Journal of the Academy of Marketing Science, Vol. 33, No. 2, pp. 153–168.

Smith, P. (1990) "How to present your firm to the world", Journal of Business Strategy, Vol. 11 (January/February), pp. 32–36.

Spaeth, T. (1999) "Powerbrands", Across the Board, Vol. 36, No. 2, pp. 23–28.

Tantillo, J., Janet, D., and Richard E. M. (1995) "Quantifying perceived differences in type styles: An exploratory study", Psychology and Marketing, Vol. 12, No. 5, pp. 447–457.

Tavassoli, N. T. (2001) "Colour memory and evaluations for alphabetic and logographic brand names", Journal of Experimental Psychology: Applied, Vol. 7, No. 2, pp. 104–111.

Topalian, A. (1984) "Corporate identity: Beyond the visual overstatements", International Journal of Advertising, Vol. 3, No. 1, pp. 55–62.

Tucker, W. T. (1961) "How much of the corporate image is stereotype?", Journal of Marketing, Vol. 25, No. 3, pp. 61–65.

Ughanwa, M. O. and Baker, M. J. (1989) The Role of Design in International Competitiveness, Routledge, London.

Van den Bosch, A. L. M., De Jong, M. D. T., and Elving, W. J. L. (2005) "How corporate visual identity supports reputation", Corporate Communications: An International Journal, Vol. 10, No. 2, pp. 108–116.

Van den Bosch, A. L. M., Elving, W. J. L., and De Jong, M. D. T. (2006) "The impact of organisational characteristics on corporate visual identity", European Journal of Marketing, Vol. 40, No. 7/8, pp. 870–885.

Van Heerden, C. H. (1999) "Developing a corporate image model", South African Journal of Economic and Management Sciences, Vol. 2, No. 3, pp. 492–508.

Van Heerden, C. H. and Puth, G. (1995) "Factors that determine the corporate image of South African banking institutions: an explanatory investigation", International Journal of Bank Marketing, Vol. 31, No. 3, pp. 340–355.

Van Riel, C. B. M. (1995) Principles of Corporate Communication, Prentice Hall, London.

Van Riel, C. B. M. and Van den Ban, A. (2001) "The added value of corporate logos: An empirical study", European Journal of Marketing, Vol. 35, No. 3/4, pp. 428–440.

Vartorella, R. W. (1990) "Doing the bright thing with your company logo", Advertising Age, Vol. 61, No. 26, p. 31.

Veryzer, R. W. (1993) "Aesthetic response and the influence of design principles on product preferences", Advances in Consumer Research, Vol. 20, No. 1, pp. 224–228.

Veryzer, R. W. (1999) "A nonconscious processing explanation of consumer response to product design", Journal of Psychology and Marketing, Vol. 6, No. 6, pp. 497–522.

Walker, P., Smith, S., and Livingston, A. (1986) "Predicting the appropriateness of a typeface on the basis of its multi-modal features", Information Design Journal, Vol. 5, No. 1, pp. 29–42.

Wallace, R. (2001) "Proving our value: Measuring package design's return on investment", Design Management Journal, Vol. 12 (Summer), pp. 20–27.

Wheeler, A. (2003) Designing Brand Identity: A Complete Guide to Creating, Building and Maintaining Strong Brands, John Wiley & Sons, New York.

4
CORPORATE BRAND SIGNATURE
Image and reputation

Pantea Foroudi and Flora Mahdavi

Introduction

Chapter 4 highlights the relationships between corporate brand signature, image, and reputation and how a company could improve the perception of internal and external stakeholders' through the corporate brand signature.

Background to corporate brand image and reputation

A corporate brand design serves as a mark of quality, a form of identification, and as a method of enhancing a company's image. The reputation of a company helps to increases the company's distinctiveness, positive visibility, authenticity, transparency, and consistency. For example, the corporate brand design is mainly concerned with the impression or appearance of management as well as the visibility of the company through the use of the corporate brand design and the corporate name.

A company's corporate brand design influences positive and desired attributes, and this, in turn, can improve an organisation's reputation. For this reason, companies are willing to dedicate significant amounts of money, research, and time to design and develop a corporate brand; this, in turn has a positive effect on the perceptions of the firm's customers. It can improve a company's unique offering, increase its visibility, and have a positive impact on the impression the firm makes on the public (Foroudi, 2020). Organisations are keen for shareholders to make an investment in the company, and corporate reputation is an important factor when the corporate audience is making decisions regarding investment and product selection (Dowling, 1986).

Authors (Dowling, 1993; Foroudi, 2020) state that because corporate reputation takes the form of a collection of corporate images that customers use to make an overall evaluation of a company over time, therefore, the emotional association an individual stakeholder has to an organisation affects the image he/she has of it. According to Dowling (2001), a company's reputation is based on a combination of respect, confidence, and admiration, as well as trust in the organisation's future actions. Furthermore, companies can distinguish themselves and make

DOI: 10.4324/9781003054153-5

themselves known among investors through the company corporate brand design in order to build up a favourable business reputation (Balmer, 2001; Fombrun and Van Riel, 2004). Corporate reputation comprises the perceptual representation not only of a company's actions in the past but also its prospects for the future, as the combination forms the company's overall appeal with regard to its main constituents in comparison with other leading competitors. Customers view themselves as being similar to those organisations that demonstrate appealing actions, such as providing compliments. Individuals make a conscious decision to evaluate the reputation of the organisation when assessing a company; nonetheless, they have a tendency to make their ultimate assessment based on the organisation's emotional appeal for them. Therefore, an organisation can also be viewed as the object of emotional evaluations.

Corporate reputation is the result of images, beliefs, experiences, and facts an individual comes into contact with over time. Moreover, consumers' perception of a company as trustworthy can be due to their experience with the company and its services and products and so is based on the corporate reputation. This can influence the probability of a stakeholder identifying with the organisation. Corporate image is deemed to be a product of individuals' own perception of reality on the basis of their beliefs, feelings, and emotions, whereas corporate reputation is viewed as the picture of an organisation instantly conjured up by the many images accumulated by both internal and external stakeholders over time.

The relationship between image and reputation is one of stability and dynamism, or selection and variation, and image can be attained relatively quickly but a good reputation takes time to build. A favourable corporate reputation is a snapshot that combines the range of images of a company that are maintained by all of its component parts. An individual's view of the company's reputation is strongly dependent on the relationship between the organisation and the individual, with customers being the stakeholders most likely to establish a 'relationship' with a company.

Based on the findings from previous studies, if the clients' image of a company is favourable, this will have a positive impact on how they evaluate the company and what they feel about it. In this way, the company's reputation will be enhanced.

Corporate image concept

Discussion regarding the concept of corporate image developed in the 1950s was captured by various scholars and practitioners. Definitions of corporate image in early works are rather confusing and blurred; researchers (Balmer, 2001; Gioiaet al., 2000) do not agree upon the definition and the operationalisation of the term. However, study of the concept is important because the corporate image is a valuable asset, and so companies need to manage it carefully.

Some authors use the terms corporate identity, organisational identity, organisational image, corporate image, and corporate reputation interchangeably. Then, many researchers discovered a broad range of perspectives to expand and understand these concepts and defined it differently from each paradigm. For example, marketing literature focuses on customers and the corporate image represents the impressions, associations, attitudes, and beliefs customers hold. According to O'Shaughnessy and O'Shaughnessy (2000), 'the term image is used loosely in marketing as a synthesis of impressions' (p. 57). A corporate image can vary within different geographical marketplaces or within the same market (Dowling, 1986). The corporate image focuses on perceptions of the organisation's members, customers, stakeholders, and the media (Hatch and Schultz, 2003).

The marketing literature stresses that corporate image is the image of an organisation external audiences hold (Abratt, 1989; Chun, 2005). Marketing scholars focus on corporate brand and claim that a corporate image that has been referred to as being most admired is about delivering what is promised to multiple audiences (Balmer, 2001; Balmer and Soenen, 1999; Henrion and Parkin, 1967; Keller, 1999; 2003). The graphic design school relied on the work of practitioners (Carter, 1982; Olins, 1991; Pilditch, 1970) and related to the possible forms of a company's physical identification (e.g., corporate brand design), transmitting the way in which an organisation is understood by its public (Carter, 1982). According to social identity theory (Tajfel and Turner, 1985) identification can be viewed as a perceptual cognitive construct.

The graphic designers and practitioners have viewed the corporate image as a product and how a company communicates their identity through the company's icon or name. Image does not depend on the company and what it considers itself to be; instead, it is formed from the beliefs and feelings the audience has about the company. Organisational studies indicate its influence within organisations by focusing on an organisation's internal members and how they perceive the identity of their organisation (Hatch and Schultz, 1997; Whetten and Mackey, 2002). Image is an intangible and important part of the creation and success of a company. However, Kennedy (1977) states that corporate image relates to tangible and intangible characteristics.

Marketing authors stress the external foundation of the image and refer to the corporate image concept through two different viewpoints. First, it refers to a corporate image as an individual's total impression of an organisation that is held by several segments of the public (Dowling, 1986; Hatch and Schultz, 1997). Second, a stream of authors uses the terms corporate image to mean: Construction of public impressions created to appeal to an audience. This seems to indicate that it is not just an attempt to infer outsiders' perceptions but, instead, that it is possible for insiders to consciously manipulate the image for their consumption.

Based on the social identity theory, from the perspective of the organisation, corporate image is what an organisation's managers want external stakeholders to perceive about the organisation or what an organisation's employees believe external stakeholders perceive from the organisation.

Brown et al. (2006) stated that it is difficult to define the image concept within its own parameters. The concept of the corporate image is a set of general characteristics, feelings or impressions, experiences, beliefs, knowledge that each stakeholder has about an organisation (Bernstein, 1986; Margulies, 1977). A corporate image is the perception of how the organisation is influenced by corporate identity; the way the company actually exists or is, and a strong corporate image gives the company a long-term sustainable competitive advantage. Corporate image is commonalities: first, image is an impression or perception located in the minds of stakeholders; second, that different groups form different images; and third, that image is an 'overall' or gestalt impression. However, corporate image as the set of meanings generated by the known object by which public describe, remember, and relate to it, which is a result of the interaction of a person's impressions ideas, beliefs, and feelings. Dacin and Brown (2002) defined the term 'corporate associations' as any types of beliefs, moods and emotions, evaluations, etc., about an organisation that are held by individuals and that are mentally associated with the organisation. Corporate associations may (or may not) include individuals' interpretations of the corporate identity as wished for by an organisation's managers. In principle, corporate associations show individuals' thoughts and feelings about the organisation.

Corporate associations serve as a generic label for all the facts and information a person holds about a company.

A corporate image consists of functional quality and psychological attributes (Martineau, 1958) and can be analogised among the human and corporate personality. Moreover, the corporate image is the image connected with the name of the organisation. It is related to public image or organisational image, what an organisation's managers want external stakeholders to perceive about the company (Hatch and Schultz, 2003) or what their staff believe is the external stakeholders' perception of the organisation (Dutton et al., 1994; Hatch and Schultz, 2003). Based on the discussion above, in this study, corporate image is defined as 'corporate image is the instant mental picture an individual gets of the organisation. It can have a practical effect on the sense of association the individual has with an organisation and is likely to influence behavior'.

The corporate reputation concept

Even though for the last 50 years, marketing academics and practitioners have been debating the conceptualisation of corporate reputation, the terms 'corporate identity' and 'corporate image' are used interchangeably with 'corporate reputation'. Nonetheless, in a business context, researchers have frequently employed different, sometimes even contradictory definitions for the concept. The main aim of corporate identity is to devise and develop a favourable reputation among organisational stakeholders. Image has a significant impact on consumers' attitudes toward a company's products; this has an external foundation since it depends on how the public perceive an organisation and/or its selling elements. Herbig and Milewicz (1994) claim that corporate reputation can be seen as an image imbued with a judgement and that it is underpinned by an entity's ability and willingness to consistently undertake an activity.

A favourable corporate reputation has a positive impact on the profitability of a company (Chun, 2005), retains customers, and is associated with greater overall returns (Roberts and Dowling, 1997). Corporate reputation can attract high-quality employees and the corporate audience depends on the corporate reputation when making investment decisions and product choices (Dowling, 1986; Fombrun et al., 2000) as the reputation of an organisation impacts on organisational performance.

According to Fombrun and Rindova (1996), the definition of 'corporate reputation' is derived mostly from the wide range of relevant literature, which investigates the construct from a variety of disciplinary perspectives (Barnett et al., 2006; Gotsi and Wilson, 2001). For example, from the strategists' point of view, reputations are regarded as accumulations of firms' dealings with stakeholders, as it is these interactions that indicate to observers what values companies have and what they stand for. Accounting researchers define reputation as an important intangible asset. In management studies corporate reputation is interchangeable with image. Marwick and Fill (1997) provide a conclusive definition of corporate reputation as 'observers' collective judgements and repeated impression of a corporation which [is] created over time'. Balmer (2001) states that the multiplicity of perspectives requires a would-be researcher in the area: 'to show a good deal of perspicacity not only in accommodating the rich variety of concepts in use, but also in exerting acute vigilance in their assessment of what he or she understands by the concept' (p. 267).

An evaluative element in the definition presents corporate reputation as a collective representation of a firm's previous actions and results that describes the firm's capacity to deliver valued outcomes to a wide range of stakeholders. A corporate reputation, it is suggested, calibrates a company's relative standing internally with company's stakeholders externally and externally.

Van den Bosch et al. (2006) explored the relationship between corporate visual identity and corporate reputation by using the five reputation dimensions (distinctiveness, transparency, visibility, authenticity, and consistency). Corporate visual identity supports visibility in the reputation model by the use of the corporate brand design, corporate name, and logo. Visibility is an indication of how important the customers consider the brand or company to be. Distinctiveness is the unique position of the company in the stakeholders' minds and can be achieved through emotionally attractive features in combination with strategic alignment, and by attracting consumers' attention through the use of favourable messages (Fombrun and Van Riel, 2004). The design's distinctiveness needs significant creativity and has to be in keeping with the corporate strategy. Authenticity tries to create a persuasively constructed corporate identity, followed by external and internal expression. Authenticity is seen as the features of the company that are considered to be real, accurate, genuine, trustworthy, and reliable. Transparency is created by corporate visual identity. Findings from the research indicate that 'the more transparent an organisation is, the more likely it is that stakeholders will rely on its disclosures' (Van den Bosch et al., 2005, p. 112) and increase trust. Based on the above discussion, in this study, corporate reputation is defined as corporate reputation imbued with a judgement and is the overall evaluation of a company over time.

Corporate brand design, corporate image, and corporate reputation

Many organisations are becoming concerned about their corporate brand design because of changes in the competitive environment and the need to differentiate themselves in various ways to create distinctive images among diverse stakeholder groups. The corporate brand design is a key factor to encourage the companies to communicate with consumers and their stakeholders. In essence, an outstanding favourable corporate brand design will certainly lead to a favourable corporate image.

Corporate image studies have concentrated on how corporate brand design and advertising influence a company's image. As a component of corporate identity management, managers should aim to project their companies' corporate brand design so as to establish or maintain a positive image in their customers' minds. People may have varied views of a company's identity based on their emotions, feelings, and beliefs. Van Heerden and Puth (1995) stated that a corporate brand design creates measurable images in consumers' minds and acts as a stimulus or mental switch. Initially, the marketing literature focuses on customers and the corporate image to demonstrate customers' impressions, attitudes, associations, and beliefs (Belt and Paolillo, 1982; Keller, 1993; Van Heerden and Puth, 1995). The way people perceive a company should be in alignment with the organisational identity and should represent the shared beliefs of what is enduring and distinctive about, and central to the organisation.

Marketing studies show that image can influence people. Image is 'what comes to mind when one hears the name or sees the logo' (Gray and Balmer, 1998, p. 696). Image is created by corporate identity (Gray and Balmer, 1998). Balmer (1998, 2001) asserts that organisations should encompass all the organisation's stakeholders (constituencies) and articulate their identities (communication) via their organisation's total efforts at communication ranging from public relations to visual identity. Communication tools can convert corporate identity into an image in the public's mind (Gray and Balmer, 1998). Melewar and Saunders (2000) identify the practical communicative aspects of the corporate visual identity system for managing corporate identity effectively. Visual expressions of an organisation can offer an important means of identifying the distinctive qualities of a firm to distinguish it from its competitors (Bernstein, 1986).

According to Cornelissen and Lock (2001), consistency in communication can be viewed as an essential condition. Accordingly, the key factor is the influence of the corporate image that the stakeholders experience from the organisation (Dowling, 1986). Balmer and Greyser (2003, 2006) claim that a positive corporate image can have a favourable influence on how the company performs. The corporate image is the perceived image and can be defined as 'perceptions, feelings and relationships' (p. 23). The above studies showed that the corporate identity and corporate image go beyond a corporate brand design.

According to the marketing research (Van Riel, 1995), consumer evaluations of the corporate image have been discussed as the basis of messages the corporate brand design conveys about corporate identity. A well-thought-out corporate brand design may trigger an emotional response. Corporate brand design can inspire a positive reaction and lead to organisations receiving a more favourable evaluation. It is suggested in the literature that the corporate brand design prompts awareness and recognition of the company in the minds of consumers. Consumer assessments of the corporate image have been discussed as forming the basis of messages about corporate identity, which are conveyed by the corporate brand design (Van Riel, 1995). The corporate brand design influences a company's verbal and visual communications and has external influences (Fisher, 1986).

Based on this discussion, it can be argued that the attitudes consumers display towards a design of an organisation indicate their evaluation of the firm. Therefore, based on the previous literature, it can be claimed that the corporate brand design has a major influence on corporate image and corporate reputation.

Conclusion

A corporate brand design can add value for stakeholders and must serve as a signature of the company, by clearly connecting the corporate brand design to the organisation it represents. For the corporate brand design to be managed effectively, an understanding is needed of the company identity (in terms of the corporate brand design as a root of corporate visual identity). Various academics and practitioners have voiced their support for more attention on the importance of the corporate brand design. This has resulted in an increased volume of conceptual literature on the corporate brand design since the 1950s. However, very little research has been done on the impact of corporate brand design on the factors required for designing a suitable design. The literature shows the significance of the corporate brand design as a differentiator to develop a positive corporate image and reputation and to differentiate the company from its rivals.

CASE STUDY – PAMPERS: IMAGE AND REPUTATION DURING THE CRISIS

Maria Palazzo, University of Salerno, Italy

The case analyses what happens when Cathy Valentine and other mothers tried to boycott Procter & Gamble (P&G) products as they were affected by a negative experience with Pampers' brand.

Pampers is Procter & Gamble's brand (www.pampers.co.uk/history).

The company states that:

> At Pampers, our responsibility and passion is simple: to serve families and their little ones. That is why we remain committed to ensuring that babies have the brightest beginnings, that parents love the changes that parenthood brings (and have the resources they need to succeed) and that we're doing everything we can to give back and create products that lead to a more sustainable world.
>
> www.pampers.com/en-us/about-us/pampers-purpose

Pampers creates nappies of all sizes for premature babies up to toilet training pants for grown-up children (aged two to four). This highlights that parents who select Pampers as a brand will grow their children together with the brand and will be able to recognise the brand signature for years (Boothby, 2003).

Pampers promoted its corporate brand signature basing in on the characteristic of ease of use and value for money. Actually, the company states that the products and the brands are all created around the user' requests, thus it bridges the needs of 'mom and kid' by producing valuable diapers.

The crises

The biggest issue Pampers had to face was the fact that it was often highlighted by several paediatricians that the use of diapers delays toilet training. Dr. Brazelton become Pampers' consultant and acted as a testimonial in several communication campaign. Dr. Brazelton said that the kids should decide on his own when it is time for starting potty training. Moreover, Brazelton said that Rosemond's viewpoint was creating negative pressure on parents. Nevertheless, Rosemond said that the use of Pampers' products beyond the age of two was fostering gratification for kids. Therefore, extending the disposable diaper use means that the usual evolution could prove to be shocking for kids (Neuhaus, 2013).

Whilst this critical period can be said to be contentious, during the 2010, Pampers and Procter & Gamble were affected by an even worse crisis.

It must be said that at the beginning of 2010, a research in different markets highlighted that Pampers and Nokia were the two most reliable brands internationally.

Nevertheless, only a couple of month after, Pampers created the product: Pampers with Dry Max technology and promoted this diaper as the best innovation in the last 20 years. The matter was started when some mothers stated that Pampers and the new technology have caused diaper rashes on their kids. These mothers created a Facebook page called: 'Pampers bring back the old Cruisers/Swaddlers' which reached many members in a few weeks. Two class-actions were made against Pampers, which were followed by the U.S. Consumer Product Safety Commission investigation on the issue.

The managers of Pampers said that the matter was receiving huge attention inside the company, nevertheless, Pampers stated that there was no connection between the new diaper technology and the regrettable cases.

At that time, Pampers gave coupons for new Dry Max products: This made the mothers even more disappointed. In fact, they said that such conduct is inexcusable, particularly being implemented by a brand like Pampers, which has several associations with positive features such as trust, reliability, innovation, and safety.

Pampers decided to communicate its brand in a different way in late 2010, and focussed its promotion on dads (Payaud, 2014). Several managers of Pampers stated that fathers play a huge role in the family and they have to be praised wherever possible. Moreover, Pampers created the 'Daddy Play Date' in the USA with famous fathers showing their skills with their children.

Any strategies and tactics implemented by Pampers are taken to restore its reputation, that involves setting a positive relation between the brand and customers' need. It means being trusted and being able to deliver what the brand promises. These are the features which made Pampers one of the most acknowledged brands in the past years.

Case questions

1. After you have written down what Pamper does to sustain its reputation, including all of the benefits that the company has achieved thanks to this branding strategy, analyse what a positive reputation has to offer to the company and to its relevant stakeholders.
2. After you have written down what the brand reputation is, analyse what this topic has to offer during the critical period mentioned in the case study.
3. After you have written down what corporate brand signature is, analyse how international companies successfully implement it.

References

Boothby, K. (2003) "Case study: Pampers – Relationship building using multiple channels", Interactive Marketing, Vol. 5, No. 2, pp. 166–170.

Neuhaus, J. (2013) "'A little bit of love you can wrap your baby in:' Mothers, fathers, race, and representations of nurturing in 1960s–1970s pampers advertising", Advertising & Society Review, Vol. 14, No. 3.

Payaud, M. A. (2014) "Marketing strategies at the bottom of the pyramid: Examples from Nestle, Danone, and Procter & Gamble", Global Business and Organizational Excellence, Vol. 33, No. 2, pp. 51–63.

Key terms and definitions

Corporate brand design is an assembly of design cues by which people can recognise the company and distinguish it from others.

Corporate image is the immediate mental picture an individual holds of the organisation. It can materially affect individuals' sense of association with an organisation and is likely to have an impact on behaviour.

Corporate reputation endowed with a judgement and is the overall evaluation of a company over time.

References

Abratt, R. (1989) "A new approach to the corporate image management process", Journal of Marketing Management, Vol. 5, No. 1, pp. 63–76.

Balmer, J. M. T. (1998) "Corporate identity and the advent of corporate marketing", Journal of Marketing Management, Vol. 14, No. 8, pp. 963–996.

Balmer, J. M. T. (2001) "Corporate identity, corporate branding and corporate marketing seeing through the fog", European Journal of Marketing, Vol. 35, No. 3/4, pp. 248–291.

Balmer, J. M. T. and Greyser, S. A. (2003) Revealing the Corporation, Routledge, London.

Balmer, J. M. T. and Greyser, S. A. (2006) "Corporate marketing: Integrating corporate identity, corporate branding, corporate communications, corporate image and corporate reputation", European Journal of Marketing, Vol. 40, No. 7/8, pp. 730–741.

Balmer, J. M. T. and Soenen, G. B. (1999) "The acid test of corporate identity management", Journal of Marketing Management, Vol. 15, No. 1/3, pp. 69–92.

Barnett, M. L. L., Jermier, J. M., and Lafferty, B. A. (2006) "Corporate reputation: The definitional landscape", Corporate Reputation Review, Vol. 9, No. 1, pp. 26–38.

Belt, J. A. and Paolillo, J. G. P. (1982) "The influence of corporate image and specificity of candidate qualifications on response to recruitment advertisements", Journal of Management, Vol. 8, No. 1, pp. 105–112.

Bernstein, D. (1986) Company Image and Reality: A Critique of Corporate Communications, Cassell Educational Ltd, London.

Brown, T. J., Dacin, P. A., Pratt, M. G., and Whetten, D. A. (2006) "Identity, intended image, construed image, and reputation: An inter-disciplinary framework and suggested terminology", Journal of the Academy of Marketing Science, Vol. 34, No. 2, pp. 99–106.

Carter, D. E. (1982) Designing Corporate Identity Programs for Small Corporations, Art Direction Book Company, New York.

Chun, R. (2005) "Corporate reputation: Meaning and measurement", International Journal of Management Reviews, Vol. 7, No. 2, pp. 91–109.

Cornelissen, J. P. and Lock, A. R. (2001) "The appeal of integration: Managing communications in modern organisations", Marketing Intelligence and Planning, Vol. 19, No. 6, pp. 425–431.

Dacin, P. and Brown, T. (2002) "Corporate identity and corporate associations: A framework for future research", Corporate Reputation Review, Vol. 5, No. 2/3, pp. 254–253.

Dowling, G. R. (1986) "Managing your corporate images", Industrial Marketing Management, Vol. 15, No. 2, pp. 109–115.

Dowling, G. R. (1993) "Developing your company image into a corporate asset", Long Range Planning, Vol. 26, No. 2, pp. 101–109.

Dowling, G. R. (2001) Creating Corporate Reputations, Oxford University Press, Oxford.

Dutton, J. E., Dukcrich, L. M., and Harquail, C. V. (1994) "Organisational images and member identification", Administrative Science Quarterly, Vol. 39, No. 2, pp. 239–263.

Fisher, S., (1986) Development and Structure of the Body Image, Hillsdale, New Jersey.

Fombrun, C. J. and Rindova, V. (1996) "Who's tops and who decides?", The Social Construction of Corporate Reputations, Stern School of Business, Working Paper, New York University.

Fombrun, C. J. and Van Riel, C. B. M. (2004) Fame and Fortune: How Successful Companies Build Winning Reputation, *Financial Times*, Prentice Hall, New Jersey.

Fombrun, C. J., Gardberg, N. A., and Sever, J. M. (2000) "The reputation quotient: A multi-stakeholder measure of corporate reputation", The Journal of Brand Management, Vol. 7, No. 4, pp. 241–255.

Foroudi, P. (2020) "Corporate brand strategy: Drivers and outcomes of corporate brand orientation in international marketing", International Journal of Hospitality Management, Vol. 88 (July), pp. 1–14.

Gioia, D. A., Majken, S., and Corley, K. G. (2000) "Organisational identity, image, and adaptive instability", The Academy of Management Review, Vol. 25 No. 1, pp. 63–81.

Gotsi, M. and Wilson, A. M. (2001) "Corporate reputation: Seeking a definition", Corporate Communications: An International Journal, Vol. 6, No. 1, pp. 24–30.

Hatch, M. J. and Schultz, M. (1997) "Relations between organisational culture, identity and image", European Journal of Marketing, Vol. 31, No. 5/6, pp. 356–365.

Hatch, M. J. and Schultz, M. (2003) "Bringing the corporation into corporate branding", European Journal of Marketing, Vol. 3, Vol. 7/8, pp. 1041–1064.

Henrion, F. and Parkin. A. (1967) Design Coordination and Corporate Image, Reinhold Publishing Corporation, London.

Herbig, P. and Milewics, J. (1994) "Marketing signals in service industries", Journal of Services Marketing, Vol. 8, No. 2, pp. 19–35.

Keller, K. L. (1993) "Conceptualizing, measuring, and managing customer-based brand equity2", Journal of Marketing, Vol. 57 (January), pp. 1–22.

Keller, K. L. (1999) "Brand mantras: Rationale, criteria and examples", Journal of Marketing Management, Vol. 15, No. 1/3, pp. 43–51.

Keller, K. L. (2003) Strategic Brand Management: Building, Measuring, and Managing Brand Equity, Prentice, New Jersey.

Kennedy, S. H. (1977) "Nurturing corporate images", European Journal of Marketing, Vol. 11, No. 3, pp. 120–164.

Margulies, W. P. (1977) "Make the most of your corporate image", Harvard Business Review, Vol. 55, No. 4, pp. 66–74.

Martineau, P. (1958) "Sharper focus for the corporate image", Harvard Business Review, Vol. 36 (November/December), pp. 49–58.

Melewar, T. C. and Saunders, J. (2000) "Global corporate visual identity systems: Using an extended marketing mix", European Journal of Marketing, Vol. 34, No. 5, pp. 538–550.

Olins, W. (1991) Corporate Identity, Toledo, Thames and Hudson, Spain.

O'Shaughnessy, J. and O'Shaughnessy, N. J. (2000) "Treating the nation as a brand: Some neglected issues", Journal of Macromarketing, Vol. 20, No. 1, pp. 56–64.

Pilditch, J. (1970) Communication by Design: A Study in Corporate Identity, McGraw-Hill, London.

Roberts, P. and Dowling, G. (1997) "The value of a firm's corporate reputation: How reputation helps attain and sustain superior profitability", Corporate Reputation Review, Vol. 1, No. 1/2, pp. 72–75.

Tajfel, H. and Turner, J. C. (1985) "The Social Identity Theory of Intergroup Behaviour", in Worchel, S. and Austin, W. G. (Eds.), Psychology of Intergroup Relations, Nelson-Hall, Chicago, IL.

Van den Bosch, A. L. M., De Jong, M. D. T., and Elving, W. J. L. (2005) "How corporate visual identity supports reputation", Corporate Communications: An International Journal, Vol. 10, No. 2, pp. 108–116.

Van den Bosch, A. L. M., Elving, W. J. L., and De Jong, M. D. T. (2006) "The impact of organisational characteristics on corporate visual identity", European Journal of Marketing, Vol. 40, No. 7/8, pp. 870–885.

Van Heerden, C. H. and Puth, G. (1995) "Factors that determine the corporate image of South African banking institutions: An explanatory investigation", International Journal of Bank Marketing, Vol. 31, No. 3, pp. 340–355.

Van Riel, C. B. M. (1995) Principles of Corporate Communication, Prentice Hall, London.

Whetten, D. A. and Mackey, A. (2002) "A social actor conception of organisational identity and its implications for the study of organisational reputation", Business and Society, Vol. 41, No. 4, pp. 393–414.

PART III
Corporate architecture design

5
CORPORATE ARCHITECTURE DESIGN MANAGEMENT

Mohammad Mahdi Foroudi, Mohammad Foroud Foroudi, and Pantea Foroudi

Introduction

Chapter 5 offers additional insights into the characteristics and the nature of the management of corporate architecture design by identifying the three main components of the architecture as follows: i) spatial layout and functionality/physical structure; ii) decor and artifacts/symbolic artifacts; and iii) ambient conditions/physical stimuli. These are the most important factors of the physical environment for customer behaviour research in a service context.

Background to corporate architecture design management

Over the past several decades, managers have played a fundamental role in creating and managing architecture, such as physical settings to express the corporate identity of a company and to promote construction of the corporate image and stakeholders' identification through the use of the physical expression of the building (Becker and Steele, 1995), and to influence internal and external stakeholders' identification with the organisation. In a service context, architecture plays an integral role in the behaviours and perceptions of customers, employees, and academics (Han and Ryu, 2009; Sundstrom and Sundstrom, 1986). However, in the marketing literature, there is no systematic investigation of the relationship between the three factors of corporate identity, architecture, and identification.

Architecture and the physical environment are important elements of corporate identity and can influence decision-making (Foroudi et al., 2019; 2020). For example, good architecture will foster a long-term favourable reputation for the company. Consequently, the creation of a favourable corporate image tends to lead to the set of internal and external communicational properties of architecture influencing how an individual understands and interprets it (Bitner, 1992). Studies have shown that there is a complex association among office design, the individual employee, and customer attitudes and behaviours. Additionally, the time individuals spend in the office can be important to creative work/study that has as its foundation face-to-face meetings and that builds on interactions with idea-inspiring artifacts (Elsbach and Bechky, 2007). Architecture and the physical environment can have an impact on the emotional responses and feelings stakeholders have regarding the organisation, where the identification can go beyond simply the design ethos, and employees' individual relationships can lead to their identification with organisational practices, such as corporate branding, which become embodied in the design approach and in the company's reputation (Kioussi, 2008). Furthermore, brands are used as tactical tools that serve to focus on the organisation's products.

Architecture can be defined as the science of designing and constructing a building, which incorporates an aesthetic design (Conway and Roenisch, 1994, p. 21). Architecture is the designing and construction of buildings, which offer human habitation as well as enabling human affairs (p. 36). However, despite the popularity of the concept of architecture, there exists no definite and widely agreed definition of architecture (Unwin, 2009, p. 27), and there is little or no empirical research into how architecture might be defined.

Existing literature has focused on studies that explore the concept of contemporary architecture as an integration of art, industry, and ideas constructed around the concept of social needs. For instance, modern office buildings are complex, and hence they depend on advanced technology (Vischer, 2007). Modern design focuses mainly on the functionality of the different elements of ergonomic design, and there is a tendency to move employees from enclosed and private offices to more open cubicle workspaces. Architecture is not just about buildings, but buildings are a crucial element; the way they are controlled or ordered can convey an emotion or an idea about a company's aim, about its creators, and about its position in time (Vischer, 2007). However, there is a lack of research on consumer and employee perception of contemporary changes in the office environment.

The research in architecture has been driven largely by the disciplines of environmental or architectural psychology (Turner and Myerson, 1998) rather than from the perspective of marketing. Hence, there is a need for a more extensive empirical survey regarding the management of physical settings and architecture in order to create an explanatory model and theory to validate a case study's findings and examining from a multi-disciplinary approach.

Research in the field of architecture shows that it is both a form of art and a significant piece of symbolism, and affects how corporate identity is perceived (Balmer, 2005). The desirable outcomes of a favourable architecture include identification, employee attachment, job satisfaction, well-being, and feelings of comfort (Knight and Haslam, 2010), which affect stakeholders' perceptions of the corporate image (Nguyen, 2006). Other outcomes include customer loyalty and customer satisfaction (Han and Ryu, 2009), motivation and productivity (Davis, 1984; Sundstrom and Sundstrom, 1986), recruiting employees, and improving the company's presence and stature (Melewar et al., 2001). Furthermore, office spaces can have an effect on various elements of the organisational structure, such as formal communication (Moleski and Lang, 1982). Managers need to comprehend the workspace and how it can benefit both employees and employers in enabling them to advance a competitive advantage. Although this issue has been discussed in the literature on design and management (Kirby and Kent, 2010), social identity (Marin and de Maya, 2013), social psychology (Sommer, 1969), and environmental psychology, to date, there has been no comprehensive view that identifies the different types of communication that may affect the formation of a corporate image.

To examine the associations between employees and their physical environment, Davis et al. (2010) state that scholars in physiological standpoints, systems thinking, social relations, symbolism, and cognitive psychology have devised frameworks and theories. However, these lack empirical support, and there is no consistency regarding evaluation of the outcome, which makes assessing their theoretical efficacy and consistency a difficult task (p. 222). Some authors

(Davis et al., 2010) have suggested that there needs to be more direct empirical testing of the competing theories regarding the relationships between employees and the physical environment. The findings of the literature demonstrate the lack of empirical research on relationships between architecture, corporate identity, and the stakeholders' identification traid.

Architecture management construct

The physical environment has an influence on customer behaviour by creating an overall aesthetic impression and corporate image, which is especially pertinent in a service industry (Han and Ryu, 2009). Based on reviewing the previous literature, the three main components of architecture are: i) decor and artifacts/symbolic artifacts; ii) spatial layout and functionality/physical structure; and iii) ambient conditions/physical stimuli. These will be explained in more detail in the following sections. These factors are the main factors of the physical environment for customer behaviour research in a service context (Han and Ryu, 2009; Nguyen and Leblanc, 2002).

Defining the architecture concept

As stated earlier, there is no universally accepted definition of architecture (Unwin, 2009, p. 27). Instead, there is the general comparison of art and buildings. Similar to language, architecture comprises different parts joined together in an artistic manner to give meaning (Unwin, 2009, p. 29). Building architecture is a significant piece of symbolism that functions in a competitive environment (Huppatz, 2005), which is linked with an organisation's image (Hoeken and Ruikes, 2005). In architecture, there is an overlap between the symbolic and the spatial elements (King, 2004). Generally, the term 'architecture' is used to mean the science and the art of designing and erecting physical structures and buildings (Spinellis and Gousios, 2009, p. 7). It helps in solving problems by building houses, networks, and bridges that are distinctive because of their specific characteristics. It is also used to mean the style in which buildings are designed and constructed to give an aesthetic appeal. Specifically in building and construction, the term is used to imply the process of planning, designing, as well as constructing structures to give both aesthetic appeal and functionality (Gruber, 2011, p. 9). Architectural characteristics make a structure fulfil or fit in with the definition of architecture (Unwin 2009, p. 27).

Architecture is a key element of a company's corporate visual identity (Melewar et al., 2006; Otubanjo and Melewar, 2007; Melewar et al., 2006; Van den Bosch et al., 2006). This is because architecture is a sign system, and as the fundamental organisational identity behind the tangible manifestations (Olins, 1989), in enabling employee and consumer-company identification.

In addition, architecture can be defined as the science of designing and constructing a building, which incorporates an aesthetic design into fully developed architecture (Conway and Roenisch, 1994, p. 21). Architecture is the design and construction of buildings, which would offer human habitation as well as accommodation for human affairs. In the process, different materials are used which differentiate one building from another. The exterior and the interior walls of a building define the space which the building occupies (Meiss, 1990, p. 101). The space which the interior of a building encloses defines the space in which the architecture is influential. Architectural space, which emerges as a result of the relationship between planes and boundaries, defines these limits. The limits may be continuous, or they might be bound to a specific boundary. By knowing the space that surrounds a building, either externally or internally, an architect is able to employ architectural methods to produce the required design.

Referring to the discussion on definitions of architecture, 'architect' is derived from a Greek word 'archi', which means a builder or a chef or 'tecton' (Ballantyne, 2002, p. 12). Therefore, architecture can be defined as the art or the process of designing and building houses and other structures. Hays (2000, p. 207) emphasises the element of 'design' to define architecture. The author notes that architecture is no longer viewed, explicitly or implicitly, as the dominant system. Instead, it is viewed in terms of designs. Design from this perspective is seen as a filter which distinguishes abstract from conventional art. Its elaborative nature provides a mechanism in which architecture is designed. Design makes buildings stand squarely on a piece of land.

Johnson (1955) describes architecture as 'a veritable oratory of power made by form' (p. 44). The implication is that gender-neutral language triumph, man's pride, and the will to succeed are applied to realise a visible form. This can be elaborated upon by using examples of the structural and physical construction of cathedrals or other buildings constructed during the Gothic era where solid stones were used (Johnson, 1955). In modern times, the stones used to define space in the structure are hollow. Because of human nature and the will to succeed, in modern structures, architects can create space not only by the use of stones, bricks, and so on, but by means of a range of devices from insulation panels to large open spaces.

Gruber (2011, p. 9) defines architecture as the 'material structure that defines space and enables interactions'. This implies that the built environment is the space used to design a building or related constructions in different scales of architecture. Projects ranging from houses to urban planning are all defined in the context of architecture. In architectural projects, structures of different designs, proportions, heights, and materials are designed, and different elements of architecture are used to create a structure. According to Gruber (2011, p. 12), an architectural project should be designed in such a way that it meets all the conflicting requirements. Thus, the functional levels are not limited to the internal space but also extend to the external space. Intangible aspects, such as geometric order, abstract concept, style, and aesthetic concept, are intertwined with functional relationships of the external environment. The task of the architect is to integrate all the elements to bring a definite meaning to the architecture in the final completed project.

The term 'architecture' is used to refer to 'spatial planning on a larger scale' (Gruber, 2011, p. 8). Physical structures are designed through planning, which may be developed on a large scale. This is achieved through the art of both design and non-design elements. Urbanism and traditional architecture share a symbiotic relationship where structural features are defined by height, size, and functionality emerge. Spatial modulation and structural systems give freedom to modern architecture (Gans, 2000, p. 23).

Although in the modern world, Lee (2010) defines architecture as 'the fundamental organisation of a system in its components, their relationships to each other, and to the environment' (p. 193). In reference to building and construction, this implies that different aspects or elements are incorporated into a system to produce a complete project. The functionality of a system can be described using the works of Nesbitt (1996), who observed that architecture is not limited to the 'superficial styling, applied cosmetically to the outside of buildings' (p. 125). Instead, the focus should be on the enclosed space, which allows inhabitants to carry out or perform different tasks in that particular space. Most of the building construction in the twentieth century is based on the belief that functionalism is best served by a rectangular frame in the form of a concrete and steel frame used to form white stucco, glass, or grey-walled buildings (Nesbitt, 1996, p. 125). The art of developing functionalism through design, space, and structures brings out the meaning in all constructed buildings whether in modern or traditional times.

Nesbitt (1996, p. 132) states that architects like Domingo Alvarez found it hard to describe architecture but instead used a mirror to draw lines to define space. This was symbolic of what architecture was all about. In other words, spatial syntax was used to define architecture. Other architects like Philip Steadman and Lionel March used syntactic terms like 'grids', 'coordinates', and 'lattices' to define architecture (Nesbitt, 1996, p. 132). Thus, rules used in the division of space can be used to define architecture (Nesbitt, 1996). These rules can use size, height, shape, position, aesthetic design, material, and physical structure to extract a meaning in architecture.

Architecture is a reflection the corporal essence of man's habits, which expresses the *lebensfuhl* of an epoch. '*Lebensfuhl*' means some kind of spirit which men seek while instilling an aesthetic interest and its exceptional functionality. Furthermore, it gives an artistic value portrayed through space where new energy is created at that particular time. Therefore, architecture helps human beings to see the world as they want it to be by creating harmony and order. Man's desire is reflected by the way space is divided according to different sizes, heights, and proportions to satisfy the rational nature of human beings. An example of this is the architecture of mediaeval France and Egypt, which was used to show mankind's rationality. A closer look at the Gothic cathedrals and Renaissance churches reveals a sense of divine perfection (Curl, 2002, p. 56). Although a disparity emerges in the styles adopted, the rule of proportionality and the laws of mathematics remain. Laws of proportions, which are major principles of architectural practices, are more important than style. Therefore, contiguous sections and parts combined with mathematical laws bring out the harmony in structural buildings, which predict a degree of aesthetic value or design.

Architecture is formed physical matter. The elements of space and function are widely emphasised in this definition. In the actual stages of design, the building is shaped, and the process of shaping continues to fit functionality. For example, the works of Le Corbusier have contributed significantly to architecture, and some of his architectural worlds have been reshaped to fit the function of a museum of national artifacts. Architecture is a national corporate collective identity (King, 2004). Gans (2000, p. 17), and Le Corbusier (2008, p. 102) note that the writings and the architectural designs of Le Corbusier define architecture as the creation of the human mind, which is expressed in the spirit. During his tours of the Mediterranean, Le Corbusier acknowledged that he saw external monuments that symbolised the human spirit. Similarly, Gans (2000) observed that 'architecture is the coherent construct of the mind' (p. 18). Decorations are symbolic in architecture and are placed in both small and big buildings, in enclosure walls, and in any modest or magnificent structure, founded on the basic principles of geometry and elements of architecture (Gans, 2000, p. 18). To Le Corbusier, architecture cannot be seen as a replica or surrogate of revolution but as a creation of the human mind. In this way, architecture is visual-symbolic and physical-spatial, and it circulates in the discourses of geography and cultural research (King, 2004).

To sum up, architecture has different meanings depending on the time the building was constructed or designed. However, based on this analysis, it could be said that architecture is the art incorporated into a building to give it an aesthetic design and functionality (Gans, 2000). Although some elements, like shape, position, aesthetic design, material, and physical structure, are applied while defining architecture, space and function emerge as the most important elements followed by aesthetic design. These elements differentiate a mere building from a piece of architecture. In this respect, Gans (2000) defined architecture as the work of the mind, and it is not necessarily a surrogate of revolution.

Architecture is a signifier of economic, political, and cultural power (King, 2004). From the ancient times of Gothic buildings, cathedrals, and palaces, to the modern times culminating in the works of Le Corbusier among others, architecture is seen as more of an art combined with science. Other scholars and architects define architecture in the context of culture and the meaning it has to that particular group. Generally, architecture is the artistic and the aesthetic design combined with geometric and architectural laws to bring about a structure. All this is seen by Gans (2000) as the work or the construct of the mind aimed at satisfying inner feelings. Table 5.1 presents a chronology of some of the key definitions of the architecture concept.

A close examination of the definitions of architecture reveals that the definitions support the idea that the relevant literature includes many human aspects, such as identity and character. The complexity of the phenomenon is important to produce the variety of perceptions from different domains of knowledge which have persuaded us all that a possible definition can strip the phenomenon of valuable dimensions. A common treatment can be detected: The main definitions concern the perception and communication of an organisation and its characteristics.

As a review of this literature shows, architecture can be defined as a visual presentation of an organisation, which captures the organisation's identity and purpose (Elsbach and Bechky, 2007) through portraying a specific set of elements that influence the attitudes and behaviour of both employees and consumers (Alessandri, 2001). It can be crucial in assisting employees and consumers identify with the company (Foroudi et al., 2019; 2020).

Architecture and decor and artifacts/symbolic artifacts

Symbolic artifacts are defined as 'aspects of the physical setting that individually or collectively guide the interpretation of the social setting' (Davis, 1984, p. 279); in particular, these enhance the attractiveness of the physical environment (Han and Ryu, 2009). Such artifacts can be linked to the environment's aesthetics, which aim to influence the perceptions of the organisational culture and customer satisfaction (Han and Ryu, 2009). Han and Ryu (2009) have claimed that in addition to their contribution to the attractiveness of the architecture and to customer satisfaction, decor and artifacts/symbolic artifacts also affect customer loyalty. Also, physical artifacts influence professional creative personalities and identities and contribute to the development of a multifaceted demonstration of the identity of the workplace.

Symbolic artifacts include the features of a physical setting, that is, the environment for company's employees (Davis, 1984, p. 278). Elsbach (2004) comments that in corporate settings, 'office decor sits on the front lines of social judgment processes' (p. 119). The artifacts of an organisation are the visible display that may encourage employees to develop an attachment to the organisation; they also influence employee behaviours, thought processes, and feelings and may understand the office decor as cues regarding the identity of the corporation.

TABLE 5.1 Some of the key definitions of architecture concept

Authors	Definitions
Gruber, 2011	Architecture is 'material structure that defines space and enables interactions' (p. 9).
Bitner, 1992; Davis et al., 2010; Leblanc and Nguyen, 1996; Meenaghan, 1995; Saleh, 1998	A favourable design in a space can meet any functional demand.
Knight and Haslam, 2010	Design can be crucial in facilitating customer and client identification.
Han and Rye, 2009	Physical environment can affect customer behaviours by creating an overall corporate image and aesthetic impression, which is particularly pertinent in a service industry.
Vischer, 2007	Architecture is an integration of industry, art, and new social needs.
	Architecture affects people emotionally and indicates a balance between the power, values, and culture of the organisation.
Jun and Lee, 2007	Architecture is the comprehensive visual presentation of the company.
Kent, 2007	Architecture of a location can be comprehended as a 'perception design' whereby designers are appreciative of the consumer's taste and stimulated ideas within signalling in environment.
Elsbach and Bechky, 2007	Architecture involves buildings, which are designed to portray an idea or an emotion of a company's purpose, position in time, and creators. The concept of environment is not only related to the physical part, but also it is related to the social and cultural parts.
Jun and Lee, 2007	Architecture is the comprehensive visual presentation of the company.
Otubanjo and Melewar, 2007; Melewar et al., 2006; Van den Bosch et al., 2006; Balmer, 2005	Architecture is one of the key elements of a corporate visual identity.
Melewar and Jenkins, 2002; Van den Bosch et al., 2006; Yee, 1990	Architecture and landscape together can establish a strong universal corporate identity.
Bitner, 1992; Han and Ryu, 2009	The physical environment is a purposeful environment in which a company can fulfil customers' specific and wants.
He and Balmer, 2005; Otubanjo and Melewar, 2007; Melewar et al., 2006; Van den Bosch et al., 2006	Architecture is one of the key elements of a corporate visual identity.
Jun and Lee, 2007	Architecture is the comprehensive visual presentation of the company.
Rocca, 2007	Architecture has aimed to generate a new association among nature and man by discovering what it means to design with nature in mind.
Kent, 2007	Human perceptions and ideas that are concerned with the physical environment are central to inquiry of architecture.
Foroudi et al., 2020	Architecture of a building can communicate a company's identify and purpose.
Nguyen, 2006	Physical environment as an aesthetic element creates a corporate image which has an impact on the performance of contact personnel.

(continued)

TABLE 5.1 Cont.

Authors	Definitions
Van den Bosch et al., 2006	Architecture supports corporate communication.
Karaosmanoglu and Melewar, 2006	Building architecture is able to present the philosophy and values of a company.
	Architecture has a significant role to play in an organisation as a vehicle for communicating the organisation's image to internal and external stakeholders.
	There are seven components of corporate identity: corporate communication, corporate design, corporate culture, corporate behaviour, corporate structure, corporate strategy, and corporate art.
Balmer, 2005	Building architecture is an art, and it is a significant piece of symbolism that functions in a competitive environment.
Melewar and Karaosmanoglu, 2005	Architecture and interior office design symbolise many aspects of the corporate culture.
Hoeken and Ruikes, 2005	Architecture as an art which could be linked with the image of an organisation.
Balmer, 2005; Huppatz, 2005	Architecture is an art, and it is a significant piece of symbolism that functions in a competitive environment.
Balmer, 2005; Huppatz, 2005	Architecture is an art, and it is a significant piece of symbolism that functions in a competitive environment.
Hoeken and Ruikes, 2005	Architecture is an art which could be linked with the image of the organisation.
King, 2004	Architecture is a signifier of economic, political, and cultural power.
	Architecture is national corporate collective identities.
	Architecture is a sign of modernity in the city, nation, and different discursively constricted worlds.
	Architecture overlaps the symbolic and the spatial.
	Architecture overlaps the symbolic and the spatial.
	Architecture is visually symbolic and physically spatial and it circulates in the discourses of geography of cultural research.
Porter, 2004	'Architecture is an extension; a modification establishing absolute meanings relative to a place' (p. 30).
	'Architecture is the will of the age conceived in spatial terms' (p. 165).
Kornberger and Clegg, 2004	'Architecture is power' (p. 1104).
	'Architecture is a powerful means of directing and redirecting our attention, feelings, and thoughts to certain points through the organisation of spatial structures – shopping centres are, of course, an excellent example of this organisation' (p. 1104).
Melewar, 2003	A company's building architecture, location, and interior decor of offices can help people to recognise the company.
Delanty and Jones, 2002	'Architecture plays an increasingly ambivalent role in the state project today' (p. 457).
	Architecture is a 'quintessentially universalistic expression of civilisation' (p. 452).
	'Architectures create and codify national cultures, which can be recognised as a landmark building, which reflect "national identity and historical narrative of memory"' (p. 457).

TABLE 5.1 Cont.

Authors	Definitions
Ballantyne, 2002	'Architecture is s thing of mind, a dematerialised or conceptual discipline with its typological and morphological variations, and on the other, architecture as an empirical event that concentrates on the senses, on the experience of space' (p. 174).
Melewar and Jenkins, 2002	'Architecture is illustrated by the attention that firms give to the influence of architecture on how their identity is perceived' (p. 82). Architecture is a tangible visual product.
Delanty and Jones, 2002	Architecture is a 'quintessentially universalistic expression of civilisation' (p. 452).
Balmer, 2001	Architecture communicates to people.
Alessandri, 2001	Office layout and architecture of a company should match a company's behaviour and culture. Architecture is both technical and sociological; therefore, the atmosphere of an office is a key expression. Theorists agree that well-designed architecture should be recognised, and it should evoke a positive effect. Architecture design is defined as the preparation of instructions for the manufacturer of artefacts to create an image of corporate identity.
Melewar and Saunders, 2000; Olins, 1990	Architecture is a tangible component of corporate visual identity, but in addition, corporate building architecture can help convey a company's visual identity through fixed assets.
Balmer and Gray, 2000	Architecture is acknowledged to have a positive influence on consumers' awareness of the company and their familiarity with the company. Architecture shows the visibility and recognisability of the company and its products.
Melewar and Saunders, 2000	In architecture, the range of external and internal elements of a building, the overall appearance of the buildings, and the degree of landscaping and gardens surrounding, are the vital factors. Architecture is an important part of communication strategy.
Foroudi et al., 2019; 2020	Architecture is the designing and construction of buildings, which would offer human inhabitation as well as human affairs.
Gans, 2000	'Architecture is the coherent construct of the mind' (p. 18).
Veryzer, 1999	Architecture is the connection between nature and the human perception.
Gray and Balmer, 1998	Architecture is about the design of corporate buildings, and the interior layout of offices and factories. Architecture has become particularly important in service industries. Architecture is probably the most relevant example of design and involves the design of a building or the layout of an area.
Gray and Balmer, 1998	Architecture is the design of buildings and layout of a place to communicate the company's culture to the stakeholders.
Gary and Balmer, 1998	Architecture is probably the most definite example of design. Design of architecture influences the image of the organisation and creates a feeling of recognition to build an image. Architecture is the design of a building and the layout of a place to communicate the company's culture to the stakeholders. Architecture is the design of building and layout of a place.

(*continued*)

TABLE 5.1 Cont.

Authors	Definitions
Saleh, 1998	'Architecture presents an image of the present and future, and not just the past. It should be an architecture that allows for flexibility, the implementation of new ideas, and searches for new outlooks. The new architecture should be considered optional not mandatory, offering flexibility in choice where the client can become a part of the design process' (p. 163).
Becker and Steele, 1995	The aesthetic aspects of architecture are crucial for organisations, since it shows corporate managers' increasing desire to promote the physical expression of the building as a way of constructing and conveying corporate image.
Bloch, 1995	Architecture is an element of corporate visual identity, and it can be a core element in an organisation's visual identity.
	The corporate building of a company may express or emphasise the company's image and can communicate that image to people.
Conway and Roenisch, 1994	Architecture can be defined as the science of designing and constructing a building, which incorporates an aesthetic design to fully develop architecture.
Malaquais, 1994	'Architecture and architect … are linked in a symbiotic relation at whose heart stands one fundamental concern: the acquisition of power. In particular, the link between man and structure hinges on one key concept: a vision of houses as embodiments of the people who construct them' (p. 22).
	'Architecture plays a critical role in the construction of social identity' (p. 21).
Conway and Roenisch, 1994	Architecture is the science of designing and constructing a building, which incorporates an aesthetic design to fully develop architecture.
Bitner, 1992	Architecture can be viewed as the packaging of services with three essential components: ambient conditions, spatial layout, and decor and orientation signals.
	The responses to design of architecture lead in turn to human behavioural responses and attitudes towards corporation.
Bitner, 1992	The responses to design of architecture lead in turn to behavioural responses.
	That human behaviour is influenced by the architecture design and architecture influence on customer and employee behaviours.
	Behaviour is the consequences of the physical environment that create an image which particularly apparent for organisations.
Yee, 1990	Architecture and landscape can establish a strong universal corporate identity.
Tufte, 1990	Architecture is, in many ways, a reflection of the society in which we live, and therefore, we cannot look at it as a profession or as education without considering many different factors influencing it and receiving its influence.
	Architecture is, in different ways, a reflection of the group in where we live, and as a result, we cannot look at it as a profession.

TABLE 5.1 Cont.

Authors	Definitions
Olins, 1990	Architecture is a tangible component of corporate visual identity. Architecture is expressing the corporate identity.
Foroudi et al., 2019; 2020	Architecture is the more important part of a store's image: Its architectural design, exterior design, and interior design.
Abratt, 1989	Architecture and the office layout are the visible artifacts.
Olins, 1989	Architecture is a sign of the fundamental organisational identity behind the tangible manifestations.
Olins, 1989	Architecture is a sign of the fundamental organisational identity behind these tangible manifestations.
Lang, 1987	The physical setting defines human needs, and human behaviour describes the physical environment.
Yee and Gustafson, 1983	'Architecture is an artistic synthesis of economic, political, social and technical circumstances' (p. 20). 'Architecture style is inevitably an arbitrary cultural choice' (p. 24). 'The size of an object comes from relating it to the dimensions of human body, using such indicators as doors, windows and furniture' (p. 229).
Bernard and Bitner, 1982	'Physical evidence: The environment in which the service is assembled and in which seller and customer interact, combined with tangible commodities that facilitate performance or communication of the service' (p. 36).
Krasner, 1980	'Environmental design as nonverbal communication' (p. 9).
Mikellides, 1980	'Architecture is to design things that people get pleasure in making and want to make things that people get pleasure in using' (p. 6).
Oldham and Brass, 1979	'Architecture and physical layout can substantially influence variables such as patterns of communication and social interaction' (p. 24). Architecture is a reflection of man's corporal essence for his habits, which 'expresses the lebensfuhl of an epoch'.
Rapoport, 1977	Architecture expresses cultural values.
Wright, 1970	Architecture is that great living creative spirit which from generation to generation, from age to age, proceeds, persists, creates, according to the nature of man, and his circumstances as they both change. That really is architecture.
Rasmussen, 1964	'Architecture is a very special functional art; it confines space so we can dwell in it, creates the framework around our lives' (p. 10).
Foroudi et al., 2020	Architecture is part of retail identity. Architecture is the way makes up a store's image in the minds of customers.
Johnson, 1955	'Architecture as "a veritable oratory of power made by form"' (p. 44).
Oxford Dictionary	Architecture is the art, the design, or style of a building. Architecture is a general word that is used as the name of a product such as building. Architecture is part of retail identity.

(*continued*)

TABLE 5.1 Cont.

Authors	Definitions
Oxford Dictionary	Pronunciation: /ˈɑːkɪtɛktʃə/noun [mass noun]. 1. The art or practice of designing and constructing buildings: Schools of architecture and design. The style in which a building is designed and constructed, especially with regard to a specific period, place, or culture: Georgian architecture. 2. The complex or carefully designed structure of something: The chemical architecture of the human brain. 3. The conceptual structure and logical organisation of a computer or computer-based system. 1. The surroundings or conditions in which a person, animal, or plant lives or operates: Survival in an often hostile environment (usually with modifier). The setting or conditions in which a particular activity is carried on: A good learning environment (with modifier). Computing the overall structure within which a user, computer, or programme operates: A desktop development environment (the environment) the natural world, as a whole or in a particular geographical area, especially as affected by human activity: The impact of pesticides on the environment (as modifier): A parliamentary environment committee.
Cambridge dictionaries	The art and science of designing and making buildings.

Corporations aim to convey the differentiation in status between employees by giving the higher ranked individuals superior offices compared to those of their colleagues (McElroy and Morrow, 2010, p. 619). However, this can result in employees experiencing a loss of their workplace identity, as their ability to demonstrate their status and uniqueness by displaying their personal artifacts is subsequently restricted (Varlander, 2012). Furthermore, employees can use other physical markers to create an alternative method of conveying status; for instance, the different levels of managers will be able to display different numbers of personal artifacts (Elsbach, 2003, p. 262). Employees can use personal preference to select the artifacts they wish to display; they do not need to be related to work. However, it is the unique nature of such categorisations that make them important to an employee's core sense of self. In addition, 'symbolic artifacts are viewed as aspects of the physical setting that individually or collectively guide the interpretation of the social setting' (Davis, 1984, p. 276); this is relevant mostly to the service industry (Han and Ryu, 2009).

In addition, symbolic artifacts can mean the aesthetics of the office environment: This includes elements such as the colour of the walls, the sort of pictures, the style of furniture, the type of flooring, the presence of flowers, and the overall office décor. All these elements can serve to distinguish one company from its competitors (Han and Ryu, 2009). Davis (1984) states that symbolic artifacts and physical structure 'all tend to communicate information about the organisation and the people who work there' (p. 277). Symbolic artifacts, physical stimuli, and physical structure are all part of the effort to re-design the office space (Davis, 1984). Thus, any changes in the symbolic artifacts can result in a positive reaction; for instance, using bright colours or introducing natural lighting can make the work atmosphere more pleasant in addition to affecting the perceptions of the organisational culture.

Architecture and spatial layout and functionality/physical structure

Spatial layout and functionality/physical structure can be defined as the architectural design, that is, how furnishings are placed in a building, how objects are arranged (e.g., as in the layout of furniture, equipment, and machinery), the spatial relationships among them, as well as the physical appearance, layout of the workplace and location, these aspects are especially pertinent to the service industry (Han and Ryu, 2009; McElroy and Morrow, 2010; Nguyen, 2006). Spatial layout regulates or affects social interaction (Davis, 1984, p. 272) and can influence the perceptions of culture and can affect customer satisfaction, productivity, and motivation. Moreover, the way an organisation is structured can have an impact on the way organisational members behave and can affect employees' comfort. Layout, seating arrangements, tables, and comfort are the major elements of an organisation's physical structure. In addition, managers assume that the physical structure of a workplace will affect how people behave and how they interact. The physical structure is a crucial element in service settings, as it can create the purposeful environment that is necessary to facilitate the employees' work and to fulfil customers' specific wants and needs.

McDonald (2006, p. 1) claims that an exhilarating architectural internal spaces, inspiring, expression, and good functionality are crucial elements of any work-place. For this reason, when designing an office, careful consideration must be given to functionality because there can be significant consequences through a range of functions. An organisation's functional features are based mainly on the work-place in the office. Thus, designers highlight an object's functionality.

The functionality of any spatial layout depends on the ability of some items to assist employees' performance and help them accomplish goals (Bitner, 1992, p. 66). However, although many empirical studies have focused on organisational behaviour and psychology specifically regarding the effects of the functionality and spatial layout dimension from the employees' perspective, to date, scant research has been conducted on how spatial layout and functionality can affect customers in the service sector (Bitner, 1992, p. 66). Bitner (1992) suggests that the efficiency of the layout and the environmental functionality are important especially to customers in environments where they carry out their own functions. For instance, in self-service environments (e.g., ATM), strong directions and a clear layout will help the customer complete the transaction.

Melewar and Jenkins (2002, p. 82) state that the organisation's physical location and structure are an important component of corporate identity. The climate or structure of the organisation is frequently related to the organisation's internal environment (Davis, 1984, p. 271). A company's physical structure conveys a message to employees and outsiders about the company's qualities and capabilities (McElroy and Morrow, 2010 p. 610). Furthermore, it can be used as a symbol (Saleh, 1998, p. 161). The psychological structure is an aspect of a place-belongingness (sense of belonging), which is fundamental for place identity (p. 29). Saleh (1998, p. 153) states that visual image and place identity are not only linked to social and cultural influences, but they are also connected to spatial organisation. In addition, identification with objects can convey the distinctiveness and individuality of places, which, in turn, can be linked to the physical identity along with spatial components (Saleh, 1998, p. 161).

Varlander (2012) claims that the physical structure is crucial for there to be an improved conceptualisation and understanding of an organisation's individuality and flexibility; therefore, top management must design organisational structures so as to increase flexibility (p. 36), which can also be an unintended consequence of planned spatial engagement (p. 35). Furthermore, there is no specific treatment of the function of spatial structure and context for affecting flexibility. Achieving long-term flexibility is 'more costly than delivering short-term functionality, and planners are now more pragmatic, seeking an appropriate balance between cost and adaptability requirements' (McDonald, 2006, p. 4). For instance, designers produce flexible spaces by creating open offices. The layout, which can lead to changes to the size and structure of the organisation as it can be reconfigured more easily at a lower cost to meet customers changing needs.

Architecture and ambient conditions/physical stimuli

The ambient conditions/physical stimuli are those elements of the physical setting that form the intangible characteristics that intrude into the organisation members' or managers' awareness and that can have a widespread influence on how they behave. Physical stimuli include essential factors in the environment of many interpersonal service businesses, such as hotels, hospitals, and banks (Bitner, 1992). Environmental psychologist have conducted research that indicates that it is important for employees to be given the opportunity to control the task-relevant elements of their working environment, as it is where they spend a significant amount of their time. The physical stimuli have a direct impact on employees' behaviours, attitudes, and satisfaction. Consequently, this can lead to improved productivity and better job performance.

In addition, ambient conditions should be an importance for many managers. Managers regularly counteract negative influences by introducing ambient conditions into the workplace environment; this also serves as a reminder 'of what needs to be accomplished' (Davis, 1984, p. 275). The concept of ambient conditions/physical stimuli affect physiological reactions, which can result in feelings of either (dis)comfort during the service encounter. Importantly, managers need to have an awareness of employee's preferences and how this can be balanced against customer needs.

Furthermore, a physical stimulus plays a major role in the formation of customer perceptions of and responses to the environment (Bitner, 1992) by encouraging customers to participate in service consumption. Ambient conditions/physical stimuli generally have a subconscious effect on customer loyalty and customer satisfaction (Han and Ryu, 2009, p. 487). Additionally, they can have an impact on customers' behaviours and attitudes toward the company and can influence consumers' experiences and perceptions (Han and Ryu, 2009). In addition, in service settings, an environment's physical stimuli and stakeholders' subsequent decision to follow service consumption can influence employees' satisfaction, attitudes, behaviours, and performance (Bitner, 1992; Han and Ryu, 2009;) with regard to the service provider. Furthermore, such stimuli affect consumer satisfaction and can predict post-purchase behaviours (Han and Ryu, 2009, p. 494).

In office environments, the psychosocial features of the office and the ambient characteristics include the background characteristics of the environment, which affect the five senses; these encompass a range of elements, for example, noise, music, existence of windows, lighting, temperature, air quality, and scent/aroma/odour (Bitner, 1992), as well as privacy. All of the features acting in conjunction with other elements in a specific location are linked to environmental satisfaction and job satisfaction. Furthermore, physical stimuli in the environment may result in consumers having more favourable perceptions, more favourable behavioural responses, and more favourable experiences (Han and Ryu, 2009). According to Bitner (1992, p. 64), people have emotional reactions to sensory stimuli; for instance, a natural scent such as the aroma of cotton flowers, can increase the 'self-efficacy perceptions, goal setting, use of efficient work strategies, and less confrontational negotiation styles' (Elsbach and Bechky, 2007, p. 203).

The total environment (e.g., noise, lighting, and temperature) can be problematic for office workers; studies have illustrated that having control over these factors is critical (Elsbach and Bechky, 2007) and that they constitute cues to the customer about 'what the service is and what the firm can do' (Bernard and Bitner 1982, p. 39). Noise can be defined as unwanted sound, which affects dissatisfaction of staff regarding the environment (Davis et al., 2010). It is a psychosocial stress, which cannot not be avoided and so should be taken into consideration by the top management of organisations (Davis et al., 2010; Kamarulzaman et al., 2011). Indeed, noise has a direct impact on employees' well-being, performance, efficiency, and productivity; a low degree of noise and distraction shows the importance of architectural privacy. Employees in an open-plan workspace believe that noise is the main source of discomfort and reduced productivity (Bitner, 1992; Vischer, 2007, p. 178).

Another factor of physical stimuli is lighting, which has 'tangible cues' (Leblanc and Nguyen, 1996, p. 48) that tell people 'how to move, how to speak, and how much intimacy is invited (candle light, strobe lights in a club, and brilliant sun on a beautiful beach with beautiful people)' (Kornberger and Clegg, 2004, p. 1107). Modern looking buildings use natural lighting, and the use of bright colours results in a more pleasant work atmosphere, which elicits positive reactions. For example, lighting can create a warm atmosphere in office environments (Han and Ryu, 2009, p. 498). Natural light in a workplace decreases stress and improves productivity (Elsbach and Bechky, 2007, p. 95); it also improves 'comfort and productivity with window size and proximity, as well as with view out, control over blinds and shielding from glare' (Vischer, 2007, p. 178). In contrast, artificial lighting can have a negative impact on people. According to Bitner (1992 p. 64), the glare of lighting can reduce the ability to see and can induce physical pain. For example, 'the lighting in the office gives me headaches' (Knight and Haslam, 2010, p. 723).

Another factor of physical stimuli, which can directly influence employee perception, performance, and job satisfaction, is temperature (Nguyen, 2006). Thus, temperature and air circulation need to be controlled (Davis, 1984; McDonald, 2006; Vischer, 2007); otherwise, it can cause work-related injury or illness from exposure to pollution in the workplace (Davis, 1984, p. 278). For example, the air quality of the workplace can make it hard to breathe, or the temperature of a room can influence people to shiver or perspire. Therefore, office workers prefer to have the ability to change the temperature within their own working area (Knight and Haslam, 2010).

Conclusion

Chapter 5 reviewed the extant literature incorporating views about architecture in this field, while the importance of architecture in achieving business objectives is also examined in this chapter. Based on the review of the literature from different disciplines, such as design, management, organisational, psychology, and social identity, this study found that in recent years, architecture has become particularly significant in service industries to create a sense of attachment for employees and to shape what stakeholders associate with the organisation. Architectural design is defined as the preparation of instructions for the manufacture of artefacts to create images of corporate identity. The chapter demonstrated the significance of designing a building while bearing in mind internal-stakeholders' perceptions along with the interaction and behaviour of human beings with the environment of the organisation. This section dealt with the importance of architecture in maximising the performance of employees. Moreover, the literature review illustrates how architecture influences the human interaction component, which has a significant effect on the stakeholders' perceptions, attitudes, values, and behaviour. In addition, it showed the concern with the role of the physical environment in corporate communication, and its support for corporate culture and values is investigated. The most valuable physical asset of most corporations is the facilities of the corporation; these facilities are functional in operation and are also habitual, symbolic, and environmental. Furthermore, the role of facilities as a means of communicating the organisational culture, values, and policies were acknowledged.

CASE STUDY – SKODAMARIA ANTONELLA FERRI, UNIVERSITAS MERCATORUM, ITALY

Maria Palazzo, University of Salerno, Italy

The case study analyses how the motor manufacturer – Skoda – changed its image.

When it was founded, the Skoda brand was associated with cars such as limousines. However, during the communist era in Czechoslovakia, Skoda decided to produce cars without taking into account consumers' needs. Skoda was then not able to face the new trends set by Western motor manufacturers (Pavlínek and Janák, 2007).

After the 'Velvet Revolution' in the Czech Republic, Skoda became a public company, joining the Global Volkswagen Group, together with Volkswagen, Audi, and Seat. During these years, Skoda's logo was rearranged several times.

Nowadays, Skoda's brand values are based on trustworthiness, good value for money, good technical functionalities, and quality and reliability.

Skoda brand

When a consumer decides to buy a Skoda product, his/her choice is affected by the brand's features and image and by several facets that show the quality of the car.

Taking into account the customer perspective, Skoda was recently considered a better car manufacturer than BMW and Jaguar.

Moreover, Skoda's customer loyalty level, which involves the possibility that consumers make repeated purchases, is second only to that of Mercedes.

Skoda's communication campaigns show the constructive transformations which have changed the organisation and its cars (James, 2002). The relation with Volkswagen is also emphasised. Thanks to all these marketing and branding tactics, research on consumers' perception showed that the brand was associated with positive characteristics: Skoda's brand image achieved quickly enhanced ratings.

Formerly, in fact, the typecast of a Skoda holder was principally retired males. Nowadays, changes in the corporate brand design and other brand features have been able to attract clients from other target populations including wealthy retired individuals, working men, mothers, non-working and working women, married and single women, and younger family individuals.

Future analyses will prove if Skoda will be able to preserve its awareness and reliability as an authentic brand in the automotive sector and whether it will succeed in connecting with other segments of consumers without having to change again its corporate brand design.

Case questions

1. What does the change in the political and social background mean for Skoda's brand personality?
2. How did the Volkswagen Group takeover affect Skoda's brand image?
3. Analyse the corporate brand design of Skoda.

References

James, D. (2002) "Skoda is taken from trash to treasure: TV campaign boosts car's brand mileage", Marketing News, Vol. 36, No. 4, pp. 4–5.

Pavlínek, P. and Janák, L. (2007) "Regional restructuring of the Škoda auto supplier network in the Czech Republic", European Urban and Regional Studies, Vol. 14, No. 2, pp. 133–155.

Key terms and definitions

Ambient conditions/physical stimuli of an environment in service settings can inspire stakeholders to participate in service consumption and subsequently, can influence employees' satisfaction, attitudes, behaviours, and performance regarding the service provider.

Architecture is a visual presentation of a company (Jun and Lee, 2007) that captures the company's identity and purpose, which affects internal-stakeholders' behaviour and attitudes. It can be crucial in promoting employee and internal-stakeholders' identification.

Corporate identity refers to the company's traits, features, attributes, or characteristics, which are presumed to be distinctive, central, and long-lasting; it serves as a vehicle for conveying the philosophy, mission, values, communications; and corporate visual identity of the company to all members of its audience.

Decor and artifacts/symbolic artifacts are the elements of the physical setting; collectively or individually, these can direct the interpretation of the social setting. In addition, they can be linked to the attractiveness and aesthetics of the physical element of the environment and can lead to the development of a complex representation of workplace identity. They are relevant mostly to the service industry.

Identification indicates the degree to which an internal-stakeholder defines him or herself according to the same attributes that he or she considers define the organisation.

Spatial layout and functionality/physical structure can be defined as the architectural design, which includes how furnishings are placed in a building, how objects are arranged (e.g., the layout of furniture, equipment, and machinery), the spatial relationships among them, as well as physical appearance, location, and layout of the workplace; these aspects are especially pertinent to the service industry.

References

Abratt, R. (1989) "A new approach to the corporate image management process", Journal of Marketing Management, Vol. 5, No. 1, pp. 63–76.

Alessandri, S. W. (2001) "Modelling corporate identity: A concept explication and theoretical explanation", Corporate Communications: An International Journal, Vol. 6, No. 4, pp. 173–182.

Ballantyne, A. (2002) What is Architecture? Routledge, London.

Balmer, J. M. T. (2001) "Corporate identity, corporate branding and corporate marketing seeing through the fog", European Journal of Marketing, Vol. 35, Nos. 3/4, pp. 248–291.

Balmer, J. M. T. (2005) "Corporate Brand Cultures and Communities", in Schroeder, J. E. and Salzer-Morling, M. (Eds.), Brand Culture, Routledge, London, pp. 34–49.

Balmer, J. M. T. and Gray, E. R. (2000) "Corporate identity and corporate communications: Creating a competitive advantage", Industrial and Commercial Training, Vol. 32, No. 7, pp. 256–262.

Becker, E. and Steele, E. (1995) Workplace by Design: Mapping the High-Performance Workscape, Jossey-Bass, San Francisco, CA.

Bernard, H. B. and Bitner, M. J. (1982) "Marketing services by managing the environment", Cornell Hotel and Restaurant Administration Quarterly (May), pp. 23–35.

Bitner, M. J. (1992) "Servicescapes: The impact of physical surroundings on customers and employees", Journal of Marketing, Vol. 56, pp. 57–71.

Bloch, P. H. (1995) "Seeking the ideal form: Product design and consumer response", Journal of Marketing, Vol. 59, No. 3, pp. 16–29.

Conway, H. and Roenisch, R. (1994) Understanding Architecture: An Introduction to Architecture and Architectural History, Routledge, London.

Curl, J. S. (2002) Georgian Architecture, David and Charles, Newton Abbot.

Davis, M. C., Leach, D. J., and Clegg, C. W. (2010) "The physical environment of the office: contemporary and emerging issues", International Review of Industrial and Organisational Psychology, Vol. 26, No. 29, pp. 193–237.

Davis, T. R. V. (1984) "The influence of the physical environment in offices", Academy of Management Journal, Vol. 9, No. 2, pp. 271–283.

Delanty, G. and Jones, P. R. (2002) "European identity and architecture", European Journal of Social Theory, Vol. 5, No. 4, pp. 453–466.

Elsbach, K. and Bechky, B. (2007) "It's more than a desk: Working smarter through leveraged office design", California Management Review, Vol. 49, No. 2, pp. 80–101.

Elsbach, K. D. (2003) "Relating physical environment to self-categorizations: Identity threat and affirmation in a non-territorial office space", Administrative Science Quarterly, Vol. 48, pp. 622–654.

Elsbach, K. D. (2004) "Interpreting workplace identities: The role of office décor", Journal of Organisational Behaviour, Vol. 25, No. 1, pp. 99–128.

Foroudi, M. M., Balmer, M. T., Chen, W., and Foroudi, P. (2019) "Corporate identity, place architecture, and identification: An exploratory case study", Qualitative Market Research: An International Journal, Vol. 109 (May), pp. 321–336.

Foroudi, M. M., Balmer, J. M., Chen, W., Foroudi, P., and Patsala, P. (2020) "Explicating place identity attitudes, place architecture attitudes, and identification triad theory", Journal of Business Research, Vol. 109 (March), pp. 321–336.

Gans, D. (2000) The Le Corbusier Guide, Princeton Architectural Press, New York.
Gray, E. R. and Balmer, J. M. T. (1998) "Managing corporate image and corporate reputation", Long Range Planning, Vol. 31, No. 5, pp. 695–702.
Gruber, P. (2011) Biomimetics in Architecture: Architecture of Life and Buildings, Springer Wien, New York.
Han, H. and Ryu, K. (2009) "The roles of the physical environment, price perception, and customer satisfaction in determining customer loyalty in the restaurant industry", Journal of Hospitality and Tourism Research, Vol. 33, No. 4, pp. 487–510.
Hays, K. M. (2000) Architecture Theory Since 1968, The MIT Press, Cambridge.
Hoeken, H. and Ruikes, L. (2005) "Art for art's sake?: An exploratory study of the possibility to align works of art with an organisation's identity", Journal of Business Communication, Vol. 42, pp. 233–246.
Huppatz, D. J. (2005) "Globalising corporate identity in Hong Kong: Rebranding two banks", Journal of Design History, Vol. 18, No. 4, pp. 357–369.
Johnson, P. (1955) "The seven crutches of modern architecture", Perspecta, Vol. 3, pp. 40–45.
Jun, J. W. and Lee, H. S. (2007) "Cultural differences in brand designs and tagline appeals", International Marketing Review, Vol. 24, No. 4, pp. 474–491.
Kamarulzaman, N., Saleh, A. A., Hashim, S. Z., Hashim, H., and Abdul-Ghan, A. A. (2011) "An overview of the influence of physical office environments towards employees", Procedia Engineering, Vol. 20, pp. 262–268.
Karaosmanoglu, E. and Melewar, T. (2006) "Corporate communications, identity and image: A research agenda', Journal of Brand Management, Vol. 14, Nos. 1/2, pp. 196–206.
Kent, T. (2007) "Creative space: Design and the retail environment", International Journal of Retail and Distribution Management, Vol. 35, No. 9, pp. 734–745.
King, A. D. (2004) Spaces of Global Cultures: Architecture Urbanism Identity, Routledge, New York.
Kioussi, S. (2008) Quality Design, Construction and Development Enterprises: Exploring the Model and Marketing Strategies for Integration, Report, UCL, London.
Kirby, A. E. and Kent, A. M. (2010) "Architecture as brand: Store design and brand identity", Journal of Product and Brand Management, Vol. 19, No. 6, pp. 432–439.
Knight, C. and Haslam, S. A. (2010) "Your place or mine? Organisational identification and comfort as mediators of relationships between the managerial control of workspace and employees' satisfaction and well-being", British Journal of Management, Vol. 21, pp. 717–735.
Kornberger, M. and Clegg, S. R. (2004) "Bringing space back in: Organising the generative building", Organisation Studies, Vol. 25, No. 7, pp. 1095–1114.
Krasner, L. (1980) Environmental Design and Human Behaviour: A Psychology of the Individual in Society, Pergamon Press, New York.
Lang, J. (1987) Creating Architectural Theory, the Role of Behavioural Sciences in Environmental Design, Van Nostrand Reinhold Co, New York.
Le Corbusier (2008) Towards Architecture, Frances Lincoln, London.
LeBlanc, G. and Nguyen, N. (1996) "Cues used by customers evaluating corporate image in service firms: An empirical study in financial institutions", International Journal of Service Industry Management, Vol. 7, No. 2, pp. 44–56.
Lee, R. Y. (2010) Computer and Information Science 2010, Springer, Berlin.
Malaquais, D. (1994) "You are what you build: Architecture as identity among the bamileke of west cameroon", Traditional Dwellings and Settlements Review, Vol. 5, No. 11, pp. 21–35.
Marin, L. and de Maya, S. (2013) "The role of affiliation, attractiveness and personal connection in consumer-company identification", European Journal of Marketing, Vol. 47, No 3–4, pp. 655–673.
McDonald, A. (2006) "The Ten Commandments revisited: The qualities of good library space", Liber Quarterly, Vol. 16, No. 2.
McElroy, J. C. and Morrow, P. C. (2010) "Employee reactions to office re-design: A naturally occurring quasi-field experiment in a multi generational setting", Human Relations, Vol. 63, No. 5, pp. 609–636.
Meenaghan, T. (1995) "The role of advertising in brand image development", Journal of Product and Brand Management, Vol. 4, No. 4, pp. 23–34.

Meiss, P. (1990) Elements of Architecture, Taylor and Francis, Hong Kong.
Melewar, T. C. (2003) "Determinants of the corporate identity construct: A review the literature", Journal of Marketing Communications, Vol. 9, No. 4, pp. 195–220.
Melewar, T. C., and Jenkins, E. (2002). "Defining the corporate identity construct", Corporate Reputation Review, Vol. 5, No. 1, pp. 76–90.
Melewar, T. C. and Saunders, J. (2000) "Global corporate visual identity systems: Using an extended marketing mix", European Journal of Marketing, Vol. 34, No. 5, pp. 538–550.
Melewar, T. C., Bassett, K., and Simoes, C. (2006) "The role of communication and visual identity in modern organisations", Corporate Communications: An International Journal, Vol. 11, No. 2, pp. 138–147.
Melewar, T. C., Karaosmanoglu, E., and Paterson, D. (2005) :Corporate identity: Concept, components and contribution", Journal of General Management, Vol. 31, No. 1, 59–81.
Melewar, T. C., Saunders, J., and Balmer, J. M. T. (2001) "Cause, effect and benefits of a standardised corporate visual identity system of UK companies operating in Malaysia", European Journal of Marketing, Vol. 35, Nos. 3/4, pp. 414–427.
Mikellides, B. (1980) Architecture for People: Explorations in a New Humane Environment, Holt, Rinehart, and Winston, New York.
Moleski, W. and Lang, J. (1982) "Organisational needs and human values in office planning", Environment and Behaviour, Vol. 14, No. 3, pp. 319–332.
Nesbitt, K (1996) Theorizing a New Agenda for Architecture: An Anthology of Architectural Theory: 1965–1995, Princeton Architectural Press, New York.
Nguyen, N. (2006) "The perceived image of service cooperatives: An investigation in Canada and Mexico", Corporate Reputation Review, Vol. 9, No. 1, pp. 62–78.
Nguyen, N. and LeBlanc, G. (2002) "Contact personnel, physical environment and the perceived corporate image of intangible services by new clients", International Journal of Service Industry Management, Vol. 13, No. 3/4, pp. 242–262.
Oldham, G. R. and Brass, D. (1979) "Employee reactions to an open-plan office: A naturally occurring quasi-experiment", Administrative Science Quarterly, Vol. 24, No. 2, pp. 267–284.
Olins, W. (1989) Corporate Entity: Making Business Strategy Visible through Design, Thames and Hudson, London.
Olins, W. (1990) "The Wolf Olins Guide to Corporate Identity", Black Bear Press, Cambridge.
Otubanjo, B. O. and Melewar, T. C. (2007) "Understanding the meaning of corporate identity: A conceptual and semiological approach", Corporate Communications: An International Journal, Vol. 12, No. 4, pp. 414–432.
Porter, T. (2004) Archispeak: An Illustrated Guide to Architectural Terms, Routledge, London.
Rapoport, A. (1977) Human Aspects of Urban Form, Pergamon Press, Oxford.
Rasmussen, S. (1964) Experiencing Architecture, M.I.T. Press, Cambridge.
Rocca, A. (2007) Natural Architecture, Design Boom, Princeton Architectural Press, New York.
Saleh, M. A. E. (1998) "Place identity: The visual image of Saudi Arabian cities", HABITATITNL., Vol. 22, No. 2, pp. 149–164.
Sommer, R. (1969) Personal Space: The Behavioural Basis of Design, Engle wood Cliffs, Prentice-Hall, New Jersey.
Spinellis, D. and Gousios, G. (2009) Beautiful Architecture, Sebastopol, O'Reilly.
Sundstrom, E. and Sundstrom, M. G. (1986) Workplaces: The Psychology of the Physical Environment in Office and Factories, Cambridge University Press, Cambridge.
Tufte, E. R. (1990) Envisioning Information, Graphics Press, Connecticut.
Turner, G. and Myerson, J. (1998) New Workspace New Culture: Office Design as a Catalyst for Change, Gower Publishing, Aldershot.
Unwin, S. (2009) Analysing Architecture, Taylor and Francis, London.
Van den Bosch, A. L. M., Elving, W. J. L., and De Jong, M. D. T. (2006) "The impact of organisational characteristics on corporate visual identity", European Journal of Marketing, Vol. 40, Nos. 7/8, pp. 870–885.

Varlander, S. (2012) "Individual flexibility in the workplace: A spatial perspective", The Journal of Applied Behavioural Science, Vol. 48, No. 1, pp. 33–61.

Veryzer, R. W. (1999) "A nonconscious processing explanation of consumer response to product design", Psychology and Marketing, Vol 16, No. 6, pp. 497–522.

Vischer, J. C. (2007) "The effects of the physical environment on job performance: Towards a theoretical model of workplace stress", Stress and Health, Vol. 23, pp. 175–184.

Wright, F. L. (1970) The Future of Architecture, Wright, Penguin Group, London.

Yee, J. (1990) "Landscaping as a marketing tool", The Journal of Property Management, Vol. 55, No. 4, pp. 45–47.

Yee, R. and Gustafson, K. (1983) Corporate Design, Interior Design Books, New York.

6
CORPORATE ARCHITECTURE DESIGN AND HUMAN FACTORS, NEEDS, AND PERFORMANCE

Mohammad Mahdi Foroudi, Mohammad Foroud Foroudi, and Pantea Foroudi

Introduction

Chapter 6 reviews architecture and its relationship with human factors by investigating architecture and its expression of social, economic, and technological realities and also the importance of architecture in today's market. Also, it sheds light on architecture and human performance and the association between architecture and human needs. This chapter explains aesthetics as the creation and appreciation of beauty and its influence on architecture. In addition, it overviews the architectural perception, its assessment and its relation to nature and the human being.

Background to corporate architecture design and human factors, needs, and performance

Architecture and the human factor

Architecture and landscape can establish a strong universal corporate identity (Balmer and Stotvig, 1997; Melewar and Jenkins, 2002; Van den Bosch et al., 2006; Yee, 1990). From a design perspective, 'there are implications for how the design of different working and customer facing environments fits within the firm's wider design strategy' (Moultrie et al., 2007, p. 56). Oldham and Brass (1979) state that design decisions influence the office social environment which is, 'made almost entirely on the basis of expectation or personal prejudice, rather than knowledge' (p. 267). Design is a relationship between people and objects (Jones, 1984). Knight and Haslam (2010) stated that design could be decisive in facilitating customer and client identification with the organisation. Environmental psychology scholars have proposed that human beings design and modify the environment to satisfy their needs and architecture (building environments) integrates elements that are consistent with the occupant's activities (Smith and Bugni, 2002; Sundstrom and Sundstrom, 1986). Place is a product of physical attributes, human conceptions, and activities. A place is 'a unique spot in the universe' and the difference 'between here and there, and it is what allows people to appreciate near and far' (Gieryn, 2000, p. 464). Place is treated as a unifying concept in environmental psychology and human geography theory. Each place should be distinctive (Gieryn, 2000, p. 472) and can be considered to be 'an active part of the construction of a person's identity, representing continuity and change' (Twigger-Ross and Uzzell, 1996, p. 207). Rooney et al. (2010, p. 47) argued that identification with a distinctive place is related to cognitive strategies, which assist in protecting in-group identities.

The association between the environment and an individual can be exclusive if it focused on the interface between environment and people. People view the environment as a social medium and the social and physical has to be bridged. The physical environment is a purposeful environment and should fulfil customers' specific needs and wants (Bitner, 1992; Han and Ryu, 2009).

Architects have to identify users' needs and translate them into the creation of newly built environments. Buildings can be built as aesthetic objects of high commercial and symbolic value. In addition, buildings can function as visible artifacts (Abratt, 1989), photogenic symbols and anonymous functional workplaces (Huppatz, 2005) to expresses users' expectations in spatial form (Groat, 1982; Jencks, 1977). In addition, architecture and the office layout are visible artifacts (Abratt, 1989). An artifact of society is reliant on the spiritual, moral, and temporal well-being of that society. Furthermore, it has been suggested that the architecture of a place can be understood as a 'perception design' where designers include consumers' tastes and thoughts within the symbolism of the environment (Kent, 2007). However, signals in the environment relate to the identity of the occupants, the symbolism of the location, and the function of space (McHarg, 1962). Location and concept creation is a part of architecture (Gray and Balmer, 1998). According to Veryzer (1999), architecture is the connection between nature and human perception. The response to architecture (physical environment) is key to the mission of architecture and environmental planning. The responses to the designs in architecture lead, in turn, to human behavioural responses and attitudes towards the corporation (Bitner, 1992).

Increasing attention has been paid to understanding and measuring the contribution of architecture to identification, and particularly of the office building to identification (Kioussiand Smyth, 2009; Knight and Haslam, 2010). Social identity in 'organisational settings have focused on identification with the organisation or its subunits as the mechanism through which employees exert effort on behalf of the organisation' (Thatcher and Zhu, 2006, p. 1083). A niche market architecture firm has shown a significant yet unarticulated link between design and client identification. Brand management research into niche market architecture organsiations has demonstrated significant yet previously unarticulated links between client identification and the architectural design process (Kioussi and Smyth, 2009).

Architectural design provides an important bridge between customer and client engagement in both product and service markets. Even so, human perceptions and ideas concerning the physical environment are central to the task of architecture (Kent, 2007). Architecture supports the exploration of mankind's desire to reconnect to the earth through the built environment that can be referred as 'natural architecture'. Architecture has aimed to generate a new association between nature and man by discovering what it means to design with nature in mind (Rocca, 2007). According to Knight and Haslam (2010), design can be decisive in facilitating customer and client identification. Social identity theory explains the symbolic meaning of buildings (Sadalla and Sheets, 1993), sense of place, and identification with place (Uzzel et al., 2002) and underplays the significance of identity with place in organisations. However, there has been little examination of how employees establish social identities connected to their workplaces (Rooney et al., 2010, p. 46) except for the authors Elsbach (2003, 2004) and Rooney et al. (2010). Elsbach (2003, 2004) studied physical space and physical markers to discover their relationship with workplace identities in office environments. Rooney et al. (2010) researched the role of employees' identification with place in influencing attitudes toward organisational change. However, little research has been done to explore the connections 'between place and the formation of these identities or how a connection to place influences responses to organisational change' (Rooney et al., 2010, p. 46).

Architecture is not only an art, but it is also an important part of symbolism (Balmer, 2005), which can create visible, and anonymous functional workplaces (Huppatz, 2005) that operate in a competitive environment. Physical structure/spatial layout and functionality should have a primary function to symbolise something and communicate symbolic meaning by creating an overall aesthetic impression (Bitner, 1992, p. 66). The physical environment has an aesthetic element that creates corporate image which impacts on the performance of personnel (Nguyen, 2006). Furthermore, the design principle of interior or exterior space can formulate a visual image. A favourable design for a space can meet any functional demand (Bitner, 1992; Davis et al., 2010; Leblanc and Nguyen, 1996; Meenaghan, 1995; Saleh, 1998) by successfully combining exciting architectural expression, inspiring internal spaces, and good functionality. For example, the height of church spires in a variety of cultures function as symbols of religious power.

The grouping of buildings according to functional elements differentiates them from other buildings. The cathedrals and churches although not designed by architects, as they were built by monks, get classified as architecture. This is because they bring together art and functionality as well as aesthetic value. In most cases, thatched roofed buildings and cottages are not considered to be architecture although it is acknowledged that they have aesthetic value in them. Functionality, which is an important element of architecture, determines how a building is designed and constructed and the main purpose of the building. Buildings like mosques, cathedrals, palaces, castles, and temples, display different meanings through their architecture when compared to mere constructions like garages and cottages (Conway and Roenisch, 2005, p. 9). For instance, the architecture of a mosque is different from that of a cathedral or ancient Gothic buildings. For a physical structure to qualify as architecture it has to be a building that is aesthetically designed (Mitias, 1999, p. 1). However, not all buildings qualify as architecture since the building has also to be well constructed and decorated. The uniqueness of a building makes it fit the definition of architecture in the broad sense that it is well constructed and aesthetically designed. The building embodies particular ideas and designs, which have a monumental appearance giving an aesthetic impression. Some of the early writers and architects like Bernard Rudofsky were mesmerised by traditional architecture (Conway and Roenisch, 2005 p. 8).

However, modern architecture is an integration of industry, art, and new social needs. For instance, modern office buildings are complex and depend on sophisticated technology (Vischer, 2007). Architecture is not just about building, but involves buildings, which are ordered or controlled to communicate an idea or an emotion about a company's purpose, its position in time, and of its creators (Vischer, 2007). According to Saleh (1998) the ideology of contemporary architecture, 'views the person not only as separate and distinct from his physical setting but also as being continually challenged by his environment' (p. 162) and considers, 'the acceleration of social, economic and technological changes, as determinant forces' (p. 163) by presenting an image of 'the present and future, and not just the past' (p. 163). Architecture is, 'quintessentially universalistic expression of civilisation' (Delanty and Jones, 2002, p. 452). Architectures create and codifies national cultures, which can be recognised in landmark buildings, which reflect, 'national identity and historical narrative of memory' (Delanty and Jones, 2002, p. 457). In order to meet this challenge, the physical environment has to be conquered, mastered, and controlled by the continuing efforts of modern science and technology (Proshansky et al., 1983). In the literature modern architecture is defined, however, there is an absence of research on how employees are affected by the move from private, closed offices to the modern environment of open offices (McElroy and Morrow, 2010, p. 615).

In the modern environment architecture has a totally different meaning and so too has architectural theory (Diani and Ingraham, 1988, p. 1). Compared to the ancient styles of the Gothic buildings, it has now become a social art driven by changes in the modern world. With life being flexible, dynamic, and quickly changing, a paradigm shift has led to the construction of buildings which have huge internal spaces and are large enough to allow quick and smooth movements of people coupled with energy and economical progress (Diani and Ingraham, 1988, p. 1). As a result, architecture has become configured more by functional elements to accommodate the changes occurring in the twenty-first century. Modern industry, which was transformed by the industrial revolution, has enabled modern architectural designs. Modern techniques, methods, and materials have changed the purpose of architecture. Space that was formerly enclosed is now treated differently and walls are no longer designed to give just artistic value but also to bring contentment (Conway and Roenisch, 2005, p. 55). However, little is known about the effect of modern changes in office environments (McElroy and Morrow, 2010, p. 612).

Office environments and architecture involves buildings, which are designed to portray an idea or an emotion of a company's purpose, position in time, and of their creators. The concept of environment is not only related to the physical aspect, but it is also related to the social and cultural aspects (Elsbach and Bechky, 2007). The role of architecture should have its place and be understood in society. Nowadays, corporations emphasise human values, customer orientation, business effectiveness, and contemporary designers express transparency, lightness, and authenticity (Elsbach and Bechky, 2007). According to Lang (1987) designers have difficulty in understanding the complexity of people' needs due to lack of education or interest. Architecture is technical and sociological, therefore, the atmosphere of an office is a key result. Theorists agree that well-designed architecture should be recognised and evoke a positive effect. Architectural design is defined as the preparation of instructions for the manufacturer of artefacts to create an image of corporate identity (Alessandri, 2001). Corporate identity is,

> an assembly of visual cues – physical and behavioural by which customers can recognise the company and distinguish it from others'. The power of these visual cues resides in their ability to speak louder than words in forming and reinforcing corporate identity … Other researchers recognise the influence of these visual cues in an organisation's identity formation, but they distinguish visual identity from corporate identity.
>
> *Nguyen, 2006, p. 64*

From the perspective of corporate identity, architects and architectural ideas have a major role in influencing identities, building design and power relations in cities. Corporate architecture and the physical location of a company's buildings is part of corporate identity (Melewar and

Jenkins, 2002). Yee (1990) believes that corporate architecture and its landscape can establish a strong universal corporate identity. In general a company's architecture, location, and the interior decor of its offices can help people to recognise the company (Melewar, 2003). A good location is essential for a successful organisation (Melewar et al., 2006). Furthermore, corporate architecture includes the range of external and internal factors of a building along with the overall appearance of the buildings and the degree of landscaping and gardens surrounding them (Melewar and Saunders, 2000). The layout of a building can create a balance between the private and the public by identifying the public and private realms in space (Melewar and Saunders, 2000, p. 36).

Based on Saleh's (1998) argument, the ideology of the modern physical environment is to view the individual person as separate and distinct from their physical setting so the satisfaction of the ultimate user's requirements are essential. Designers are often unable to understand the complexity of users' needs due to a lack of education or interest. In order to meet this challenge, the physical setting defines human needs, and human behaviour describes the physical environment (Lang, 1987), and functional architecture has to be conquered, mastered, and controlled by the continuing efforts of modern science and technology (Proshansky et al., 1983).

Architecture as an expression of social, economic, and technological realities

The contemporary architecture of the workplace could be explained by the acceleration of socio-economical circumstances and technological changes, based on the assumption of the man-made environment, and the main beliefs of particular societies (Duffy and Tanis, 1993; Saleh, 1998). The concept of environment is not only physical but also social and cultural. Architecture should have its place and understand its role in the society (Davis, 1984). Architecture is technical and sociological. The social, economic, and technological are influenced by the physical appearance of space and image so they are significant. Each of these aspects impacts on the design in a number of ways. According to King (2004), architecture is a signifier of economic, political, and cultural power. The responses to the designs in architecture lead, in turn, to behavioural responses (Bitner, 1992) and the office layout and architecture of a company should match the company's behaviour and the company's culture along with its technological and social parameters. Architecture is about the design of corporate buildings and the interior layout of offices and factories and is a response to a greater demand to accommodate organisational requirements. Architecture has become particularly significant in service industries for improved productivity and efficiency within the current socioeconomic conditions (Sundstrom and Sundstrom, 1986).

Socioeconomic conditions and the quality of materials used in buildings can communicate symbolic meaning and create an overall aesthetic feeling for people (Bitner, 1992, p. 66). Materials used in organisations articulate the culture and values of those organsiations (Schmitt et al., 1995, p. 82). Based on the works of the twentieth century, architecture has been determined by the materials used during the construction process. Ritchie (1994) claims:

> an architecture which uses materials to reflect the conditions of society, where these materials are used in their primary state rather than as products, and engages craftsmen to manipulate them, with or without the use of computers, can represent a late twentieth century evolution of the Arts and Crafts tradition.
>
> p. 52

Using materials from the local area can reflect local society and its characteristics. According to Mostafavi and Leatherbarrow (1993) the

> material selection may precede design development, it may in fact initiate design work. There is no reason to assume that such a selection will be based on the local availability of materials or local technical capacities, often the reverse is true.
>
> *p. 148*

The use of natural materials increases the creative performance of employees' and their positive emotional and cognitive responses.

For instance, architects like Louis Khan defined architecture based on the materials they used. Additionally, materials like clay, steel, stones, and concrete among many others define the strength and the aesthetic design of architecture. Although the aspect of art in architecture cannot be overlapped, it is imperative to note that geometric concepts were, and are, applied in architecture. Both modern and ancients designs have visual architectural elements which define a building. The building's structure is unified by both function and form, which exemplify architecture in a building. Space in buildings has to do with the exterior and the interior of a building, the size of the windows, the ceilings, and antiques define its architecture. The managerial control of space has been a dominant theme in the office management literature since the end of the industrial revolution (Knight and Haslam, 2010). Architectural design helps transcend barriers due to its visual character such as the physical barriers separating office workers after the introduction of air-conditioning which allowed the design of open-plan offices in the 1950s. Organisations spend substantial amounts of money on the construction of an effective building and employees have been given greater authority over the design of their workplace. The space which is organised creates an environment for the users for their various activities and behaviour.

Knight and Haslam (2010) state that there is a strong association between the low levels of privacy afforded by open-plan offices and main components of job dissatisfaction. Open-plan offices impact on employee behaviour at work based on two approaches: i) social relations approach; and ii) sociotechnical approach. The social relations approach 'argues that the absence of interior walls and barriers in open-plan offices facilitates the development of social relationships among employees, which, in turn, positively influence employee motivation and satisfaction'. The interaction between employees increases cohesion, which is a necessary condition for high performance from employees. The socio-technical approach is related to the physical context of an organisation, which impacts on employee work outcomes.

Open-plan offices with informal employee communication and open spatial layout symbolising lack of individual privacy was attractive to organisations as a main preference. For instance, privacy, and open space indicates customer orientation (Gray and Balmer, 1998). Interior design gives the customers a hint of how the organisation will perform (Gray and Balmer, 1998). For example, luxury buildings with expensive interiors can communicate high quality to their target audience (Gray and Balmer, 1998).

The improvement of physical conditions is demanding public taste has shaped the general evolution of architecture (Hassard and Pym, 1990) and created the new architectural style. This architectural style expresses the owner's image in a way that represents all their beliefs and aspirations. Architects build associations to strengthen their designs as a transformational mirror for the client. Buildings reflect the style of the individual companies (Melewar and Akel, 2005).

'Many architects try, in a completely unjustified and facile way, to create their own "styles", as if one man or group of men could overnight replace the action of a whole society over a long period of years' (Constantinos, 1963, p. 2). Each building reflects the style of the building's era as well as its philosophy (Melewar and Akel, 2005). Saleh (1998) documented the relationships between society and architecture as 'the symbolic role of architectonics as symbols to establish and affirm physical identity of place' (p. 161). This links to the specific needs of society and economic performance, which is the purpose of every business enterprise.

In addition, this research has shown an important link between managerial control of space (architecture) and stakeholders' identification with the company (e.g., employees, customers, etc.) and their influence on positive work experience (Knight and Haslam, 2010). The association between the physical environment and the employees' productivity can be traced back to the 1930s (Wilson, 1986). The stronger the architectural design is, the stronger the potential for identification. People often use their work environments to express their uniqueness such as with photographs or sentimental mementos. Design is an expression of employees about who they are and who they aspire to be. According to Knight and Haslam (2010) managerial control of space impacts on the feelings of physical and psychological comfort/discomfort in the office with levels of identification as well as influence upon motivation (Wilson, 1986).

Architecture and human performance

Researchers have shown that architecture, which also consists of noise, furniture arrangement, temperature, and lighting, can influence students' performance (Ahrentzen et al., 1982) and employees' performance (Becker et al., 1983; Brennan et al., 2002; Elsbach and Bechky, 2007; Gray and Balmer, 1998; Kamarulzaman et al., 2011; Knight and Haslam, 2010; McElroy and Morrow, 2010; Varlander, 2012) so it generates new concerns for personnel management (Christie and Gale, 1987) and enhances organisational efficiency (Leaman and Borden, 1993). Moreover, the effects of design yields advantages for operating costs (Maher and von Hippel, 2005) and allows for a flexible use of space (Han and Ryu, 2009), environmental quality, and human well-being (Klitzman and Stellman, 1989). For instance, the open-plan office is normative in most large companies, because it has low operating costs in the minds of organisational decision-makers (Maher and Von Hippel, 2005; Vischer, 1996). According to Kotler and Rath (1984) a good design does not have to be expensive. Designers must limit themselves to what is possible in the company's cost range. A good design creates a positive image for the company (p. 18). For example, modern office designers should provide a mix of workspaces within open-plan offices to provide for workers' diverse needs and reflect their increasingly flexible work patterns (Davis et al., 2010). Open-plan offices enhance employees' satisfaction with their working conditions and allow for flexible use of space as well as increasing employee communication (Boyce, 1974; Canty, 1977; Sundstrom et al., 1980) while also fostering creative interaction and teamwork (Knight and Haslam, 2010).

Industrial psychologists focus on employees and their satisfaction, comfort, and performance (Sundstrom and Sundstrom, 1986). Research by Knight and Haslam (2010) states that organisational outcomes can be enhanced by managerial enrichment of office space. Comfort/discomfort and identification were also found to mediate associations between managerial control and job satisfaction and well-being. Managerial control of office space was connected with feelings of physical and psychological comfort/discomfort in the workplace (Knight and

Haslam, 2010). The consequences of the employees' assessment of the general quality of life in the workplace can lead to job satisfaction (Locke, 1983).

Job satisfaction is also affected by career development activities (such as providing special coaching on the job), social support activities (such as helping with professional goals), and are correlated with higher job satisfaction and lower turnover rates while the physical environment represents a less important parameter (Elsbach and Becky, 2007; Sundstrom and Sundstrom, 1986). Wilson (1985) believes that integrating the physical environment with job design influences employee motivation, satisfaction, and management of the company's culture (Wilson, 1985).

Company culture and symbolic language, and to what extent these reach the audience is part of the remit of architecture. Architects express culture in their design; 'the architect creates the culture image: a physically present human environment that expresses the characteristics rhythmic functional patterns which constitute a culture' (Langer, 1953, p. 96). Architects interpret the cultural characteristics of the society to a physical pattern. They need an understanding of the local culture and its elements and their creative ability enables them to articulate the culture in an appropriate way. Architecture expresses cultural values (Rapoport, 1977). An architect should also understand the local values of any community. Also, global culture is a meaningful idea of national-societal or local culture (King, 2004). In addition, culture is a human and social phenomenon (King, 2004). Moreover, interior design can communicate a company's culture to the stakeholders and if they are in a different line of business, they may be more vital than the others (Gray and Balmer, 1998). The interior office design and office layout can represent the company's culture and any changes can affect the culture of a company (Melewar and Karaosmanoglu, 2006).

According to the authors Elsbach (2003) and Vischer (2005) an important influence on job performance can result from office design and the workspace of the work environment. Vischer's (2007) research findings indicate that the work environment concentrates on psychosocial factors that affect job performance, such as arousal, stress, and distraction. The social psychological and sociological literature investigates employees' reactions to working in spaces which they have developed themselves or that have been imposed upon them by management (Oldham and Brass, 1979; Vischer, 2005). According to Oldham and Brass (1979) 'architecture and physical layout can substantially influence variables such as patterns of communication and social interaction' (p. 24).

King (2004) states that culture is a human and social phenomenon. International culture is a meaningful idea of national-societal or local culture and organisations tended to develop their own architectural expressions as local or national styles. Managers should collaborate with consultants and architects as aesthetic experts, to evaluate the styles (primary attributes, complexity, and representation), themes, and the aesthetic impression of the company. The basic elements for evaluation are sensitivity to the customer; individuality from competition; and expression of corporate mission, values, and culture (Schmitt at al., 1995). Culture is often connected with buildings and the architectural environment (Hankinson, 2004). Architecture can be used for the transformation of productive processes, communicative power, and cultural objects (Huppatz, 2005). Architecture and interior office design symbolise many aspects of corporate culture (Melewar and Karaosmanoglu, 2005). The interior design of an office and its layout can represent the company's culture and any changes can affect the internal culture of the company (Melewar and Karaosmanoglu, 2006). The office layout and architecture of a company should match with company's behaviour and company's culture.

Architecture and human needs

Architects and interior designers are expected to understand human needs and often emphasise the formal, spatial, and visual aspects of their design proposals and develop humanly functional and aesthetically pleasing products. To avoid the risk of early obsolescence, the architectural space should fulfil the expected requirements and be used to judge the degree of success of an architectural work and architecture should try to satisfy human requirements, expectations and needs (Nguyen, 2006). There is a clear interaction between architects and clients. The client is the whole world and represents a mass of people. However, architects think they know more than their clients. Architects should be responsive to public reactions to their work and social and economic changes to the environment. An architect is responsive to human needs by identifying the social structure. Nguyen (2006) states that architecture (physical environment):

> must be designed in response to two types of needs: operations needs expressed by the maximisation of organisational efficiency, and marketing needs to create an environment which influences consumers' attitudes and beliefs toward the organisation and, consequently, its corporate image.
>
> *p. 74*

Knight and Haslam (2010) state that 'office design for non-management staff has tended to focus on issues of job process rather than on the psychological needs and interests of those who carry out particular job functions' (p. 718). Studies of the physical environment in organisations with the reactions toward changes in office design and identify the common efforts to gauge the effects of the physical environment. Indeed there are a number of notable examples of how changes in workplace design resulted in unanticipated consequences for designers (Fayard and Weeks, 2007; Grajewski, 1993; Horgen et al., 1999). Designers try to design the future by employing the very materiality of the office to stimulate organisational change. Modernism is an idea built around the concept of need. Architecture is a song of modernity which projects modernism (Huppatz, 2005). For example, many species of wood express a modern but highly fashionable character (Martineau, 1958). According to King (2004), the root of modernity in architecture starts in the early 1930s and modern science has transformed the nature of architectural creation and adapted its function (Constantinos, 1963). The modern office building's design is dependent on complicated technology and sophisticated techniques (Vischer, 2007). Saleh (1998) declares, 'modernism as an idea was built around the concept of need' (p. 162) and modern management motivates the fulfilment of corporate objectives within the corporation.

According to Barker (1968) the guiding force behind corporate behaviour is the satisfaction of human needs. The physical layout of workplaces can also affect the behaviour of organisational members (Oldham and Rotchford, 1983; Strati, 1990) and show the structure of an organisation (Giddens, 1984; Rosen et al., 1990). An organisation's visual style reflects the behaviour of management and staff at all of the company's levels (Lambert, 1989). Architecture and office layout should match the company's behaviour and company's culture. Architectonic details affect 'emotion-focused' coping behaviour in situations of stress in the workplace (Vischer, 2007). The emotional component is connected with psychological dimensions including feelings and attitudes towards a company (LeBlanc and Nguyen, 1996).

The literature (Baldry, 1997; Elsbach, 2003; Elsbach and Bechky, 2007; Knight and Haslam, 2010; Kotter, 1982; Nguyen, 2006; Oldham and Brass, 1979; Vischer, 2005) confirms that today's employees are concerned with the physical and psychological effects of the office environment and investigate employees' reactions to working in spaces either that they have had imposed upon them by management or developed themselves (Knight and Haslam, 2010; Vischer, 2005). Employees are looking for material and psychological returns, and they have concerns about the quality of work life and the humanisation of the working environment.

Moreover, the failure of facilities to fulfil the employees' needs represents a risk of damaging corporate objectives. This can happen because of concerns with having a healthy workforce, for instance, Vischer (2005) looked at, 'how, when and why the buildings where people work affect their health and morale, so we will be able to help companies make more humane and cost-effective decisions about workspace' (p. 182). For instance, a picture from nature can be an aesthetically uplifting experience which decreases anger and stress in a working environment (Knight and Haslam, 2010). A healthy workforce encourages high quality performance in the organisation. Vischer (2005) states that the term 'work environment' used in stress studies to integrate with psychosocial dimensions such as employee–employer relations, motivation and advancement, job demands and social support. The tangible attributes and the emotional ones are related to psychological dimensions, which are manifested, by feelings and attitudes towards the corporation (Nguyen, 2006).

Poor ambient conditions and physical conditions in the workplace influence physiological reactions, which result in comfort or discomfort (Nguyen, 2006). Comfort is influenced by the psychological parameters and performed activity (e.g., mood, motivation, and stress). The physical comfort in the working environment results in moral, humanitarian, and social pressure. Knight and Haslam (2010) suggest that managerial control of space has a negative influence on staff's experiences at work, which causes psychological discomfort and undermines organisational identification (Briner and Totterdell, 2002; Vischer, 2005) as well as stress and absenteeism (Wegge et al., 2006). According to Elsbach and Bechky (2007) understanding of ergonomics and human factors in workplace design accommodates almost any physical human needs. The design of an office focuses on factors that increase efficiency such as location of supplies (Elsbach and Bechky, 2007).

Additionally, privacy and personalisation of space influence employees' behaviour, which can be controlled (Sommer, 1969). The degree of these behaviours is related to the corporation type and is subject to the social context and organisational culture. Poor physical environmental conditions, people's aspirations, and motivations are the main factors for the acceptance of working conditions (Bitner, 1992) and many employees sacrifice comfort for other gains. Due to their significance for the employees' satisfaction, privacy is a significant factor amongst the features of the physical setting such as spatial layout; office size and location is associated with status; office storage is linked with territoriality and status and partitioning impacts on acoustic as well as visual privacy (Fischer et al., 2004; Vischer, 2007). In work environments, certain cues like desk placement, desk size, computers, and the presence of certificates on the wall symbolise status and influence staff beliefs about the person occupying the office (Bitner, 1992).

Architecture and aesthetic

Marketing professionals take aesthetics and style (as a kind of language in which the architect selects the essential elements to communicate) into account in their work (Weggeman et al., 2007). The concept of aesthetics is, 'closely associated with originality, genius, expressiveness, and the ability of a work of art to appeal beyond rationality to the taste or the senses of the spectator or listener' (Weggeman et al., 2007, p. 347). Aesthetics is part of a deliberate marketing strategy and corporations should be made fashionable and stylish (Dickinson and Svensen, 2000). They defined aesthetic knowledge as the, 'results from this kind of analysis "weak thought" that has the potential to enrich organisational theory based on strong paradigms and the search for universalism and domination' (p. 349). Mitias (1999, p. 1) observes that architecture depends heavily on aesthetic and physical elements. A building, which is aesthetically fitting and physically built, is identified as perfect architecture. This is because the physical structure of a building is defined by its position, shape, and size. Size identifies the space occupied by a building in a particular place (Mitias, 1999).

According to Ballantyne (2002, p. 12), 'the actual fabric of a building is not sufficient to make architecture out of them', instead, the respect accorded to them as buildings make them architecture. This differentiates it from any normal building despite their elegance or appreciation from the on-lookers. The aesthetic design differentiates different buildings of the old and the modern century. For example, architecture embodied in the aesthetic value of walls, roofs, doors, and windows define architectural design. Features like façades, pilasters, and columns bring a different look, which differentiates a building with architecture. Architecture is a well thought out, designed, and constructed building (Conway and Roenisch, 1994, p. 21). The symmetry and static look embodied in buildings like cathedrals and mosques, give a totally different meaning to architecture.

Charles-Édouard Jeanneret-Gris, mostly know as Le Corbusier, is an architect and designer of the twentieth century, defined architecture as 'the masterly, correct magnificent play of masses brought together in light' (Moffett et al., 2003; Le Corbusier, 2008, p. 102). The buildings designed by Le Corbusier were based on aesthetic designs, size, height, and proportion. Using the height of an average man and the golden section as the main proportion (Moffett et al., 2003); this architectural design marked the onset of the modern architecture. In contrast to earlier buildings, the Le Corbusier built houses supported by pillars with 'pilotis' or piers, which supported the building from the ground. The most defined element of the buildings like the Citrohan House was space and size. The points which define Le Corbusier's architecture are pilots which are piers supporting the building from the ground with an elevation and space (Le Corbusier, 2008, p. 103). There was also a roof garden or flat roof for relaxation, which defined space and the aesthetic design. The buildings had interior walls, which were independent and not supported by the support system (Moffett et al., 2003). To ensure illumination of light, Le Corbusier used horizontal windows, which would allow much light into the building. Lastly, there was the facade, which was freely designed, meaning it was independent of the structural supports (Moffett et al., 2003). Architecture is the song of modernity in the city, nation, and different discursively constructed worlds (King, 2004).

Furthermore, architecture is materially or physically built to cast radiance on its surroundings. The positioning of the physical structure, the calculation of the required spaces, and the function of the building portray the architectural elements used in the design and the construction. The crafting of a physical structure on a piece of terrain and the incorporation of other elements like size, height, shape, position, and design, makes complete the definition of the architecture. A building whose exterior attracts the attention of passers-by is regarded as architecture (Mitias 1999, p. 12). This is because the elements, which define a building, are intractably intertwined to form a piece of beautiful work. Unwin (2009, p. 30) notes that architecture has its own conditions, which need to be fulfilled. For example, real materials, which shape a physical structure embodied with aesthetic values, define architecture. Both complex and basic elements of architecture are important in ensuring that a building qualifies as architecture (Unwin, 2009, p. 42).

The architectural shape and design can be defined for that building in that particular form. Different shapes have different meanings, which depend on the architectural design. For example, the shelter given by a particular building either inside or outside defines the particular structure and function of the building. For instance, the Robie House designed and developed by Frank Lloyd was designed in such a way that the relaxation room, the living room, and dining rooms had space at the centre. The terraces, projecting eaves, and the balconies defined and created a transitional space, which was later elongated into the open space adjoining the garden. The architecture of this form can be defined by the space created which involves creative thinking and art. The walls are erected to subdivide or define the experience people derive from the building. A structure erected using glass does not define the space in its architecture as the outside is connected with the inside part of the building (Conway and Roenisch, 1994, pp. 12–15). The connection creates an experience, which has aesthetic beauty, which can help us to appreciate the natural environment. The way buildings enclose space and define it, depend on the materials used and the height of the building.

In the building, the most significant decisions on the specification and characteristics of the corporation's facilities are office location, décor, and the style of office chairs, which are related to the structure of social relations in the place of work and so too are open/enclosed offices, security/access, and furniture setting (Weggeman et al., 2007). According to Vischer (2005) organisations consider the visual aspects of spatial organisation issues (e.g., the height of partitions and the distance between open workstations, resources, such as equipment, technology, and meeting rooms) and architectonic details (e.g., colours, shape, and decoration that have symbolic meaning). These characteristics convey information to the public about the corporation and the public is sensitive to organisations' symbolic quality and the aesthetic of the physical environment (architecture).

Furthermore, architecture affects people emotionally and reflects the balance of culture, power, and values of the organisation (Vischer, 2007). Weggeman et al. (2007) pointed out that for architects beauty is significant, 'which is understandable as it is commonly assumed that the products of their work, architectural designs, should display beauty' but perhaps, 'it appears less obvious at first sight that the products of managerial work can also display beauty, in the sense that they facilitate the origination of aesthetic experiences in work processes in the operational core' (p. 346). An experience with buildings is important. Constantinos (1963) recommended to architects to find a way to bring together the experience and knowledge of the community in order to affect humans, as experiences are perceived by the syntactic and geometrical qualities of the visual part of the environment. According to Weggeman et al. (2007) architects should understand the products of their work, architectural designs, and should display beauty. Beauty is defined by Weggeman et al. (2007) as,

> Something which can and should be universally appreciable through the human faculty of judgement. The experience of beauty has four characteristics: 1) disinterested (we can like an object without wanting to have it); 2) It is universal (objects have the capacity to be found beautiful by any observer); 3) It has purposiveness without purpose (the object displays some reason or function which cannot be completely grasped); 4) It is necessary (if we judge something to be beautiful, we feel as if everyone ought to agree with us.
>
> *Weggeman et al., 2007, p. 355*

The importance of the visual part of the environment and physical setting has been emphasised by some authors (Van Riel and Balmer, 1997). Physical appearance refers to the immediate built environment and the physical setting refers to the exterior and interior design of corporate buildings, which is referred to as the company's architecture (Chesbrough, 2003). Company's architecture is the measure of all the architectonic aspects of the building of the organisation. This extends to aspects of physical setting expressing particular and strategic aspects of the organisation called its profile and those aspects which delineate the organisation as a whole are called corporate identity. An organisation's corporate identity and image are created by the view the organisational members have of the organisation (Kennedy, 1977; Van Riel and Balmer, 1997). The responses to the design in the architecture may lead in turn to behavioural responses (Bitner, 1992). Behavioural studies have shown the significance of the visual quality of the architecture on the well-being of human beings (Ulrich, 1984).

Because of intensive market competition, everything an organisation does should confirm the company's corporate identity (e.g., Borgerson et al., 2009; Olins, 1995). Architecture contributes to overall corporate identity (e.g., Borgerson et al., 2009). Corporate identity requires visibility, tangibility, and consistency with other aspects of corporate activity (Balmer and Gray, 1999) and can be influenced by aesthetic attractiveness. However, the aesthetic aspect of architecture is essential for organsiations, since there is an increase in desire among corporate managers to promote the physical expression of the building as a means of building the corporate image (Becker and Steele, 1995). The structure and design of architecture influences the image of the organisation and creates a feeling of recognition to build an image (Gray and Balmer, 1998). Corporate architectural design is defined as the preparation of instructions for the manufacture of artifacts for creating images of corporate identity. Companies spend enormous amounts of money on designing the locations of a building to project a suitable image (Melewar and Jenkins, 2002) so that people have a good impression of the architecture of their buildings (Schroeder, 2003).

Architectural perception and assessment

Architecture is the connection between nature and the human beings (Veryzer, 1999) and an understanding of the ways humans perceive architecture is a significant issue for both managers and designers. Marketing personnel try to create a favourable image, which is based on perceptions that should be reinforced with visually appealing architecture (Van Heerden and Puth, 1995). Social identity theory can be employed to describe a 'sense of place', attitudes towards environmental sustainability (Carrus et al., 2006), identification with place (Uzzel et al., 2002), and the symbolic meaning of buildings (Sadalla and Sheets, 1993). According to Spencer (2002) the focus on place in environmental perception should be seen as complementary to the environment and place can be seen as a social category to provide identity. The perception of the environment is considered as a participatory experience between the physical setting and people.

The existing theories of social identity as the most significant of the interpersonal identity theories (Tajfel, 1981 and 1982) provides some insight into the increasing potential for better integration between a group of people, a certain lifestyle, and social status. Twigger-Ross et al. (2003) found that social identity theory can easily include the physical environment and the meanings attached to it as well. They defined a place as a social entity or 'membership group' providing identity and people's bonds with residential environments. Social identity theory focuses on the cognitive process of identity (Thatcher and Zhu, 2006) and leads to activities which are congruent with and support institutions that embody their identity (Ashforth et al., 1989).

Architecture, human behaviour, and attitudes towards the corporation

That human behaviour is influenced by architectural design and that architecture influences customer and employee behaviours is undeniable (Bitner, 1992). Numerous studies in social psychology have examined human behaviour and established the impact of architecture and physical layout on social communication (Canter, 1977). The most important concepts used by architecture and environmental psychologies are symbols, interaction, attitude, and socialisation (Lauer and Handel, 1977). However, management has presented architecture (physical settings) as influencing human perception, attitudes, and behaviours (McElroy and Morrow, 2010). Some authors (Han and Ryu, 2009; Mehrabian and Russel, 1974; Russel and Pratt, 1980) have stated that human behaviour is strongly connected with the physical environment.

Human behaviour is a series of 'meant-end actions' (Van Riel and Balmer, 1997, p. 343). According to Lang (1987), behaviour is a function of the people's motivations, which are affected by their perception and meanings of the world and constrains of the physical environment. Literature (Bitner, 1992; Han and Ryu, 2009; Mehrabian and Russell, 1974) states that environmental psychologists believe that people's responses to any environment are in two forms: i) behavioural approach; and ii) behaviour avoidance. Behavioural approach concerns all positive behaviours that are directed at a particular place or workplace (e.g., desire to stay, work, and affiliate). 'Approach behaviour involves such responses as physically moving toward something, exploring an unfamiliar environment, affiliating with others in the environment through verbal communication and eye contact, and the environment' (Booms and Bitner, 1982, p. 38). Behaviour avoidance includes the human beings and their relations with the natural and social environment (Bitner, 1992) and can be described as negative responses such as a desire not to stay, and not to work (Han and Hyu, 2009). Companies try to decrease avoidance behaviours and influence towards individual approach behaviours (Bitner, 1992).

Companies are paying attention to human behaviour and believe that social and architecture can have an effect on stakeholders' performance. Bitner (1992) claims that stakeholders (e.g., employees, customers, etc.) respond to architecture emotionally, cognitively, and physiologically. According to Bitner (1992) companies are concerned with employee and customers behaviours, and the effects of the physical setting on the interactions between employees and customers. A favourable architectural design helps to identify 'desirable customer and/or employee behaviours and the strategic goals that the organisation hopes to advance through its physical facility' (Bitner, 1992, p. 62). According to Van Riel and Balmer (1997) the, 'behaviour of personnel has a direct effect on an organisation's corporate identity and image (Kennedy, 1977) would clearly suggest that personnel should identify with an organisation's ideals and goals' (p. 345). Some studies (Harrison-Walker, 2001; Lau and Ng, 2001) assert that research on stakeholders' behaviour has widely accepted that interpersonal communication (i.e., word-of-mouth in a closed environment) impacts on individuals' behaviours and attitudes. Management, architecture, and environmental psychology shared an attitude among social psychologists. Attitude is defined as, 'certain regularities of an individual's feelings, thoughts, and predisposition to act toward some aspects of his environment' (Secord and Backman, 1964, p. 97).

Environment (architecture) can be defined in terms of its meanings and meanings are the individual's behaviour towards the architecture, and behaviour is the consequence of attitudes. Architects are interested in impacting human behaviour in the workplace environment, such as communication with stakeholders as well as architecture's influence on a customer's ultimate satisfaction (Bitner, 1990), productivity, and motivation (Davis, 1984; Sundstrom and Sundstrom, 1986). The concept of the environmental competence of the users and the complexity of the environmental design should be considered during the first stages of design in order to influence the behaviour and fulfillment of the users' needs. The human ability to deal with the environment is another issue related to human behaviour. Architects need to recognise the environmental competence, physical health, and stress of users at the first stage of design in order to optimise comfort and manage workspace stress successfully (Vischer, 2007). Most people believe in high levels of physiological satisfaction and some seek for decadent comforts (Brebner, 1982).

The physical comfort and the users' control over their workplace can be seen as the result of the implementation of a users' needs approach. A conducive physical environment provides the service and comfort, such as physical movement, which provides high levels of flexibility for the users (Bitner, 1992). For example, the arrangement of seating in airports discourages the travelers from waiting. An ambience of well-appointed comfort as a perception of 'quality' reflects the anxieties, culture and values of developers, designers, and users.

The main role of the designers and architects in organsiations is as a communication conduit of corporate values and the style of the corporation, where style 'encompasses attitudes' and raises the question of how design might translate into values. Design can communicate corporate values as well as corporate strategy (Olins, 1978, 1989, Van Riel, 1995). Style and design are integral aspects of corporate communication and are an integral aspect of corporate communication. The main role of style as a physical expression is to influence attitudes, relationships between employees, and customers. Attitudes toward a design represents a diversity of responses. Organisations are interested to encourage positive attitudes toward an organisation's formal communication (i.e., symbolism, communication, and behaviour), by ensuring that different audiences identify the company and understand the messages that they receive by communicators positively (Balmer, 1995; Van Riel and Balmer, 1997). The positive attitude of an employee towards the corporation is reflected in continued enthusiasm for various types of 'open-plan' office create and interaction between individuals and teamwork as symbols of prevailing equality in the workplace (Knight and Haslam, 2010). On the other hand, a negative attitude may impact the interpretation of the layout and influence on the individual's attitude. Architecture as a physical property has a direct influence on people's attitudes through aesthetics and symbolism.

Architecture and corporate communication

Today there is increasing competition bringing with it highly demanding stakeholders and faster innovation in architecture and office design to meet the varied needs of today's corporate workforce (Elsbach and Bechky, 2007). Corporate communication and marketing are significant for workplace productivity and innovation and organisations need to integrate the latest innovations into workspaces to serve the multiple needs of today's organisations (Elsbach and Bechky, 2007).

Today's organisations can build a building as an aesthetic object of high commercial and symbolic value (Huppatz, 2005) and philosophies (Melewar and Akel, 2005). Buildings can be seen to function as visible, graphical symbols and anonymous functional workplaces The function of workplaces is the sign of specific social activities and behaviours, or as signifiers of the groups of individuals who occupy, work, and own them (Huppatz, 2005). Melewar and Saunders (2000) referring to appearance of buildings proposed that organisations consciously or unconsciously project messages about companies through their built environments, for instance, factories, offices, warehouses, and retail premises. They add that architecture includes the range of external and internal features of a building and overall appearance of the buildings and the design of surrounding landscapes and gardens are also vital factors (Melewar and Saunders, 2000).

However, the new buildings are affected by internal and external customers' perceptions of the organisations, which play a major role in shaping customers' attitudes towards the company (Brown and Dacin, 1997). Some authors (Hankinson, 2004; Huppatz, 2005) have suggested that the company's history, heritage, and cultural background that form the modern world have debilitated people's ability to understand their surroundings (architecture).

Architecture communicates a message to the public (Alessandri, 2001). Some authors (Balmer, 2001; Melewar and Karaosmanoglu, 2006) add that corporate designs communicate the company's identity, internally and externally to people. Furthermore, corporate architecture can be used as a communication asset (Van den Bosch et al., 2006) and for serious business faces (Karaosmanoglo and Melewar, 2006). Discussion of corporate communication usually talks about corporate identity and corporate building architecture as tangible visual products (Christensen and Askegaard, 2001). Moreover, corporate visual identity assists a company to convey the company's visual identity through its buildings (Melewar, 2003). Buildings, interiors, and corporate building architecture can also be an important element in an organisation's visual identity (Van den Bosch et al., 2006). Architecture of a building can communicate the purpose and identity of a company. In addition, architecture as an art which could be associated with the image of an organisation (Hoeken and Ruikes, 2005) communicates the company's identity, internally and externally to people (Melewar and Karaosmanoglu, 2006). According to Balmer (2001) corporate building architecture could communicate to people. Corporate building architecture supports corporate communication and marketing (Melewar and Karaosmanoglu, 2005; Van den Bosch et al., 2006).

Marketing perspectives state that architecture is an important part of communication strategy (Melewar and Saunders, 2000) and covers corporate design (Otubanjo and Melewar, 2007). Architecture, interior design, and location are the determinants of the corporate identity construct (Melewar, 2003). Architecture is the design of a building and the layout of a place which communicates the company's culture to the stakeholders (Gray and Balmer, 1998), for instance, luxury places with expensive interiors can communicate better with their target audience. According to Becker and Steele (1995) there is an increase in desire among corporate managers to promote the physical expression of the building as a means of creating corporate image and corporate reputation.

Architecture and corporate image

Architectures as a graphical element may symbolise many aspects of the corporate culture and become a powerful weapon for the customers. Furthermore, architecture has a significant role in an organisation, internal, external, and stakeholders as a vehicle for communicating image (Melewar and Karaosmanoglu, 2006). Corporate image and corporate identity are often used interchangeably. Corporate image is a global impression formed in the minds of customers, while corporate identity is based in part on the elements that constitute corporate image and corporate identity that is an index of the physical and behavioural (Abratt, 1989). Behaviour is a consequence of the physical environment that creates an image which is particularly apparent for organisations (Bitner, 1992). Organisations use symbols to express the organisational identity that is used by the top managers to develop corporate identity (Hatch and Schultz, 2001). Corporate identity can refer to interior design and architecture (Alessandri and Alessandri, 2004).

Studies by some authors (Canter, 1977; Davis, 1984) show that there is evidence that building design and physical location within a building influence interaction and relationships. The physical location of a building is an important part of corporate identity (Melewar et al., 2006) that can project a positive image (Melewar and Jenkins, 2002), such as the location of offices and shops in city centres, which is related to specific activities (Sundstrom and Sundstrom, 1986). Merging the needs of the settings of specific activities with support for the work needs of office workers is a role of architecture (Duffy and Tanis, 1993; Vischer, 2007).

Architecture can be considered as the packaging of services with three components which are ambient conditions, spatial layout, and décor and orientation signals (Bitner, 1992). i) Ambient conditions (colour, light, temperature, noise, odour, and music) which influence the customers' five senses and their perceptions; ii) spatial layout (design and the arrangement of buildings); and iii) decor and orientation signals (visual symbols used to create an appropriate atmosphere). These three ambient conditions influence corporate image and customer's perceptions (e.g., Bitner, 1990; Nguyen, 2006; Schmitt et al., 1995).

Stakeholders react to architecture on three levels: i) cognitive, customers interpret the physical environment using non-verbal cues that communicate the nature of the service offering and the provider's reputation; ii) physiological, which is a result of the ambient conditions of the setting which can cause comfort or discomfort and encourage the customer to pursue or to interrupt service consumption. It can influence the customer's attitudes and behaviours toward to the service; iii) emotional, which also affects behaviour and attitudes (Bitner, 1992; Nguyen, 2006). Attitudes and behaviour exert a strong impact on customer satisfaction. Moreover, customer satisfaction is described as an important dimension of quality. Accordingly, the quality dimension is a key element that affects customer perceptions of the company, product, and services.

Conclusion

Chapter 6 reviewed architecture and its relationship with human factors. It has investigated architecture and its expression of social, economic, and technological realities and also the importance of architecture in today's market. In addition, it sheds light on architecture and human performance and explained aesthetics as the creation and appreciation of beauty and its influence on architecture. It overviewed the architectural perception, its assessment and its relation to nature and the human being. Architecture, human behaviour, and attitudes towards the corporation were discussed. The relationship between architecture and corporate communication were then addressed. Architecture has a significant role in an organisation, internally, externally, and for stakeholders and its association with corporate image.

CASE STUDY – LOGO DESIGN AND BRAND EXTENSION

Pierluigi Vitale, University of Salerno, Italy

A good brand identity of a company is composed by a good and coherent variation of the visual elements. More and more companies started working in very different areas, so the building of a coherent set of logos is an interesting challenge.

One of the main strategy, as in the case of Amazon, is to keep the company name in the new services and business, such as Amazon Echo, Amazon Music, Amazon Drive, etc. Equally interesting is the case where a product line became a new company: A spin-off.

In this chapter we observed the visual coherency of brand identity, for example, a company such as Xiaomi, a Chinese tech company with a strong growth in the global market, in three variations of its visual identity through the logos.

In its origin area, China and Asia in general, Xiaomi is a manufacturer of a wide range of tech products, from smartphones to smart home devices and, at the same time has a crowdfunding platform, in which examines and brand other companies, in order to let them to promote the launch.

This platform named Xiaomi Youpin and the same Xiaomi are adopting it to test the marketability of the new prototypes.

One of the most engaging product line proposed by Xiaomi in the last years, when the company started to penetrate the European market, was Redmi. 'Xiaomi Redmi' was the mid-range product line, in Xiaomi proposed probably the best smartphones in terms of quality-price rate (150–200€), and for sure this is the best market in which Xiaomi gaining good results. At the beginning of 2019, Redmi became an independent brand (managed by Xiaomi), this operation is not different from the case of Honor (out of Huawei) and Poco (out from the same Xiaomi). In this way the company tries to convert the product line into a brand and to focus them on a specific market target.

Looking at the visual choices, in the case of Xiaomi Youpin, it is clear that there is a similarity with the main one, that it is clearly readable at the bottom of the image, with the same font adopted. Another graphic motif on the top and a different background made the difference between the two logos, without compromising their visual coherence. In the case of Redmi, there is a radical change, with the new logo based on a lettering sans serif, initially followed by the payoff 'by Xiaomi'. This choice underlines the need to distinguish the product-line, after the new brand line, starting by the visual approach. At the same time, this kind of variation is not reflected in the products' design, in which the design of the parent company in all its feature and development. Products by Xiaomi and Redmi also share the operating system named MIUI. Redmi doesn't have an official website, so the process seems far from being concluded. These two different cases tell us two different strategies, in which a company could decide to be present and recognizable, directly from the logo and the naming, or to tell autonomy of a new project, starting by the visual identity.

> **Case questions**
>
> 1. Please explain the choices of Xiaomi about the logo of Xiaomi Youpin.
> 2. Please compare the logo design strategies of Xiaomi Youpin and Redmi.
> 3. Please explain the case of Redmi visual identity.
>
> **References**
>
> www.mi.com/
> www.xiaomiyoupin.com/

References

Abratt, R. (1989) "A new approach to the corporate image management process", Journal of Marketing Management, Vol. 5, No. 1, pp. 63–76.

Ahrentzen, S., Jue, G. M., Skorpanich, M. A., and Evans, G. W. (1982) "School Environments and Stress", in Evans, G. W. (Ed.), Environmental Stress, Cambridge University Press, Cambridge, pp. 224–255.

Alessandri, S. W. and Alessandri, T. M. (2004) "Promoting and protecting corporate identity: The importance of organisational and industry context", Corporate Reputation Review, Vol. 7, No. 3. pp. 252–268.

Alessandrini, S. W. (2001) "Modeling corporate identity: A concept explication and theoretical explanation", Corporate Communications, Vol. 6, No. 4, pp. 173–183.

Ashforth, B. and Mael, F. (1989) "Social identity theory and the organisation", Academy of Management Review, Vol. 14, No. 1, pp. 20–39.

Baldry, C. (1997) "The social construction of office space", International Labour Review, Vol. 136, pp. 365–378.

Ballantyne, A. (2002) What is architecture? Routledge, London.

Balmer, J. M. T. (1995) "Corporate identity: The power and the paradox", Design Management Journal, Vol. 6, No. 1, pp. 39–44.

Balmer, J. M. T. (2001) "Corporate identity, corporate branding and corporate marketing seeing through the fog", European Journal of Marketing, Vol. 35, Nos. 3/4, pp. 248–291.

Balmer, J. M. T. (2005) "Corporate Brand Cultures and Communities", in Schroeder, J. E., Salzer-Morling, M. (Eds.), Brand Culture, Routledge, London, pp. 34–49.

Balmer, J. M. T. and Gray, E. R. (1999) "Corporate identity and corporate communications: creating a competitive advantage", Corporate Communications: An International Journal, Vol. 4, No. 4, pp. 171–176.

Balmer, J. M. T. and Stotvig, S. (1997) "Corporate identity and private banking: A review and case study", International Journal of Banking, Special Edition on Corporate Identity in Financial Services, Vol. 15, No. 5, pp. 169–184.

Barker, R. B. (1968) Ecological Psychology: Concepts and Methods for Studying the Environment Human Behaviour, Stanford University Press, Stanford, CA.

Becker, F. and Steele, F. (1995) Workplace by Design: Mapping the High Performance Workscape, Josey-Bass, San Francisco, CA.

Becker, F. D., Gield, B., Gaylin, K., and Sayer, S. (1983) "Office design in a community college", Environment and Behaviour, Vol. 15, No. 6, pp. 699–726.

Bitner, M. J. (1990) "Evaluating service encounters: The effects of physical surrounding and employee responses", Journal of Marketing, Vol. 54, No. 2, pp. 69–82.

Bitner, M. J. (1992) "Servicescapes: The impact of physical surroundings on customers and employees", Journal of Marketing, Vol. 56, pp. 57–71.

Booms, B. H. and Bitner, M. I. (1982) "Marketing Strategies and Organisation Structures for Service Firms", in Donnelly, J. and George, W. (Eds.), Marketing of Services, American Marketing Association, Chicago, IL.

Borgerson, J. L., Schroeder, J. E., Magnusson, M. E., and Magnussonn, F. (2009) "Corporate communication, ethics, and operational identity: A case study of Benetton", Business Ethics: A European Review, Vol. 18, No. 3.

Boyce, B. R. (1974) "Users: Assessments of a landscaped office". Journal of Architectural Research, Vol. 3, No. 3, pp. 44–62.

Brebner, J. (1982) Environmental Psychology and Building Design, Applied Science Publishers, London.

Brennan, A., Chugh, J., and Kline, T. (2002) "Traditional versus open office design: A longitudinal field study", Environment and Behaviour, Vol. 34, pp. 279–299.

Briner, R. B. and P. Totterdell (2002) "The Experience, Expression and Management of Emotion at Work", in P. Warr (Ed.), Psychology at Work, Penguin, London, pp. 229–252.

Brown, T. J. and Dacin, P. A. (1997) "The company and the product: Corporate associations and consumer product responses", Journal of Marketing, Vol. 61, No. 1, pp. 68–84.

Canter, D. (1977) The Psychology of Place, Architectural Press, London.

Carrus, G., Bonaiuto, M., Bilotta, E., Ceccarelli, M., and Bonnes, M. (2006) *Place-identity process and environmental sustainability: Relations between local identification, support for biodiversity conservation, and use of fresh-water resources*, Paper presented at the 2006 IAPS 19 Conference, Environment, Health and Sustainable Development, Alexandria, Egypt.

Chesbrough, H. W. (2003) "The era of open innovation", Sloan Management Review, Vol. 44, No. 3, pp. 35–41.

Christensen, L. T. and Askegaard, S. (2001) "Corporate identity and corporate image revisited: A semiotic perspective", European Journal of Marketing, Vol. 35, Nos. 3/4, pp. 292–315.

Christie, B. and Gale, A. (1987) Psychophysiology and the Electronic Workplace, Wiley, Chichester.

Constantinos, A. (1963) Architecture in Transition. Oxford University Press, Hutchinson, New York.

Conway, H. and Roenisch, R. (1994) Understanding Architecture: An introduction to Architecture and Architectural History, Routledge, London.

Conway, H. and Roenisch, R. (2005) Understanding Architecture: An Introduction to Architecture and Architectural History, second edition, Routledge, London.

Davis, M. C., Leach, D. J., and Clegg, C. W. (2010) "The physical environment of the office: Contemporary and emerging issues", International Review of Industrial and Organisational Psychology, Vol. 26, No. 29, pp. 193–237.

Davis, T. R. V. (1984) "The influence of the physical environment in offices", Academy of Management Journal, Vol. 9, No. 2, pp. 271–283.

Delanty, G. and Jones, P. R. (2002) "European Identity and Architecture", European Journal of Social Theory, Vol. 5, No. 4, pp. 453–466.

Diani, M. and Ingraham, C. (1988) Restructuring Architectural Theory, Northwestern University Press, Evanston, IL.

Dickinson, P. and Svensen, N. (2000) Beautiful Corporations: Corporate Style in Action, *Financial Times*, Prentice Hall, London.

Duffy, F. and Tanis, J. (1993) "A Vision of the New Workplace", Industrial Development Section, Vol. 162, No. 2, pp. 1–6.

Elsbach, K. and Bechky, B. (2007) "It's more than a desk: Working smarter through leveraged office design", California Management Review, Vol. 49, No. 2, pp. 80–101.

Elsbach, K. D. (2003) "Relating physical environment to self-categorizations: Identity threat and affirmation in a non- territorial office space", Administrative Science Quarterly, Vol. 48, pp. 622–654.

Elsbach, K. D. (2004) "Interpreting workplace identities: The role of office décor", Journal of Organisational Behaviour, Vol. 25, No. 1, pp. 99–128.

Fayard, A. L. and Weeks J. (2007) "Photocopiers and water-coolers: The affordances of informal interaction", Organisation Studies, Vol. 28, No. 5, pp. 605–634.

Fischer, G. N., Tarquinio, C., Vischer, J. C. (2004) "Effects of the self-schema on perception of space at work", Journal of Environmental Psychology, Vol. 24, pp. 131–140.

Giddens, A. (1984) The Constitution of Society, Polity Press, Cambridge.

Gieryn, T. F. (2000) "A space for place in sociology", Annual Review of Sociology, Vol. 26, pp. 463–496.

Grajewski, T. (1993) "The SAS head office: Spatial configuration and interaction patterns", Arkitekturforskning, Vol. 26, No. 2, pp. 3–74.

Gray, E. R. and Balmer, J. M. T. (1998) "Managing corporate image and corporate reputation", Long Range Planning, Vol. 31, No. 5, pp. 695–702.

Groat, L. (1982) "Meaning in Post-Modern architecture: An examination using the multiple sorting task", Journal of Environmental Psychology, No. 2, pp. 3–22.

Han, H. and Ryu, K. (2009) "The roles of the physical environment, price perception, and customer satisfaction in determining customer loyalty in the restaurant industry", Journal of Hospitality and Tourism Research, Vol. 33, No. 4, pp. 487–510.

Hankinson, G. (2004) "The brand images of a tourism destination: A study of the saliency of organic images", Journal of Product and Brand Management, Vol. 13, No. 1, pp. 6–14.

Harrison-Walker, L. J. (2001) "The Measurement of word-of-mouth communication and an investigation of service quality and customer commitment as potential antecedents", Journal of Service Research, Vol. 4, pp. 60–75.

Hassard, J. and Pym, D. (1990) The Theory and Philosophy of Organisations, Routledge, London.

Hatch, M. J. and Schultz, M. (2001) "Are the strategic stars aligned for your corporate brand", *HARVARD BUSINESS REVIEW*, Vol. 69 (February), pp. 128–134.

Hoeken, H. and Ruikes, L. (2005) "Art for art's sake?: An exploratory study of the possibility to align works of art with an organisation's identity", Journal of Business Communication, Vol. 42, pp. 233–246.

Horgen, T. H., Joroff, M. L., Porter, W. L., and Schon, D. A. (1999) Excellence by Design: Transforming Workplace and Work Practice, Wiley, New York.

Huppatz, D. J. (2005) "Globalising corporate identity in Hong Kong: Rebranding two banks", Journal of Design History, Vol. 18, No. 4, pp. 357–369.

Jencks, C. (1977) The Language of Post Modern Architecture, Rizzoli, New York.

Jones, J. C. (1984) "How my thoughts about design methods have changed during the years", in Cross, N. (Ed.), Developments in Design Methodology, John Wiley & Sons Ltd, Bath.

Kamarulzaman, N., Saleh, A. A., Hashim, S. Z., Hashim, H., and Abdul-Ghan, A. A. (2011) "An overview of the influence of physical office environments towards employees", Procedia Engineering, Vol. 20, pp. 262–268.

Kennedy, S. H. (1977) "Nurturing corporate images", European Journal of Marketing, Vol. 11, No. 3, pp. 120–164.

Kent, T. (2007) "Creative space: Design and the retail environment", International Journal of Retail & Distribution Management, Vol. 35, No. 9, pp. 734–745.

King, A. D. (2004) Spaces of Global Cultures: Architecture Urbanism Identity, Routledge, New York.

Kioussi, S. and Smyth, H. (2009) "Client Identification with Design and the Architecture Firm: Scoping Identification through Design-led Visualisation", in Proceedings of International Conference Changing Roles: New Roles; New Challenges, 5–9 October, Delft University of Technology, Rotterdam.

Klitzman, S. and Stellman, J. (1989) "The impact of the physical environment of the psychological well-being of office workers", Social Science and Medicine, Vol. 29, No. 6, pp. 733–742.

Knight, C. and Haslam, S. A. (2010) Your place or mine? Organizational identification and comfort as mediators of relationships between the managerial control of workspace and employees' satisfaction and well-being. British Journal of Management, Vol. 21, No. 3, pp. 717–735.

Kotler, P. and Rath, G. A. (1984) "Design: A powerful but neglected strategic tool", Journal of Business Strategy, Vol. 5, No. 2, pp. 16–21.

Kotter, J. (1982) "What effective general managers really do", Harvard Business Review, Vol. 60, No. 2, pp. 157–169.

Lambert, A. (1989) "Corporate identity and facilities management", *Facilities* (December), pp. 7–12.

Lang, J. (1987) Creating Architectural Theory, the Role of Behavioural Sciences in Environmental Design, Van Nostrand Reinhold Co, New York.

Langer, S. K. (1953) Feeling and Form, Charles Scribner's Sons, New York.

Lau, G. T. and Ng. S. (2001) "Individual and situational factors influencing negative word- of-mouth behaviour", Canadian Journal of Administrative Sciences, Vol. 18, No. 3, pp. 163–178.

Lauer, R. H. and Handel, W. H. (1977) Social Psychology, The Theory and Application of Symbolic Interactionism, Houghton-Mifflin Company, Boston.

Le Corbusier (2008) Towards Architecture, Frances Lincoln, London.

Leaman, A. and Borden, I. (1993) ":The Responsible Work-place: User Expectations", In Duffy, F., C., Laing, A., and Crisp, V. (Eds.), The Responsible Work-place: The Re-design of Work and Offices, DEGW London, Ltd., London, pp. 16–32.

LeBlanc, G. and Nguyen, N. (1996) "Cues used by customers evaluating corporate image in service firms: An empirical study in financial institutions", International Journal of Service Industry Management, Vol. 7, No. 2, pp. 44–56.

Locke, E. (1983) "The Industrial Nature and Causes of Job Satisfaction", in Dunnette, M. (Ed.), Handbook of Organisational Psychology, Wiley, New York, pp. 1297–1349.

Maher, A. and Von Hippel, C. (2005) "Individual differences in employee reactions to open-plan offices", Journal of Environmental Psychology, Vol. 25, No. 2, pp. 219–229.

Martineau, P. (1958) "Sharper focus for the corporate image", Harvard Business Review, Vol. 36 (Nov/Dec), pp. 49–58.

McElroy, J. C. and Morrow, P. C. (2010) "Employee reactions to office re-design: A naturally occurring quasi-field experiment in a multi generational setting", Human Relations, Vol. 63, No. 5, pp. 609–636.

McHarg, I. (1962) "The ecology of the city", American Institute of Architects Journal, Vol. 39, pp. 101–103.

Meenaghan, T. (1995) "The role of advertising in brand image development", Journal of Product and Brand Management, Vol. 4, No. 4, pp. 23–34.

Mehrabian, A. and Russell, J. A. (1974) An Approach to Environmental Psychology, MIT Press, Cambridge, MA.

Melewar, T. C. (2003) "Determinants of the corporate identity construct: A review of literature", Journal of Marketing Communications, Vol. 9, No. 3, pp. 195–220.

Melewar, T. C. and Akel, S. (2005) "Corporate identity in the higher education sector: A case study", Corporate Communications: An International Journal, Vol. 10, No. 1, pp. 41–27.

Melewar, T. C. and Karaosmanoglu, E. (2005) Corporate identity: Concept, components and contribution", Journal of General Management, Vol. 31, No. 1, pp. 59–81.

Melewar, T. C. and Karaosmanoglu, E. (2006) "Seven dimensions of corporate identity: a categorization from the practitioners' perspectives", European Journal of Marketing, Vol 40, Nos. 7/8, pp. 846–869.

Melewar, T. C. and Saunders, J. (2000) "Global corporate visual identity systems: Using an extended marketing mix", European Journal of Marketing, Vol. 34, No. 5, pp. 538–550.

Melewar, T. C., Bassett, K., and Simoes, C. (2006) "The role of communication and visual identity in modern organisations", Corporate Communications: An International Journal, Vol. 11, No. 2, pp. 138–147.

Melewar, T. C. and Jenkins, E. (2002) "Defining the corporate identity construct", Corporate Reputation Review, Vol. 5, No. 1, pp. 76–90.

Mitias, M. H. (1999) Architecture and Civilization, Rodopi, Amsterdam.

Moffett, M., Fazio, M., and Wodehouse, L. (2003) A World History of Architecture, King, London.

Mostafavi, M. and Leatherbarrow, D. (1993) On Weathering: The Life of Buildings in Time. MIT Press, Cambridge, MA.

Moultrie, J., Nilsson, M., Dissel, M., Haner, U., Janssen, S., and Van der Lugt, R. (2007) "Innovation spaces: Towards a framework for understanding the role of the physical environment in innovation", Creativity and Innovation Management, Vol. 16, No. 1, pp. 53–65.

Nguyen, N. (2006) "The perceived image of service cooperatives: An investigation in Canada and Mexico", Corporate Reputation Review, Vol. 9, No. 1, pp. 62–78.

Oldham, G. R. and Brass, D. (1979) "Employee reactions to an open-plan office: A naturally occurring quasi-experiment", Administrative Science Quarterly, Vol. 24, No. 2, pp. 267–284.

Oldham, G. R. and Rotchford, N. L. (1983) "Relationships between office characteristics and employee reactions: A study of the physical environment", Administrative Science Quarterly, Vol. 28, pp. 542–556.

Olins, W. (1978) The Corporate Personality: An Inquiry into The Nature of Corporate Identity, Kynoch Press, Birmingham.

Olins, W. (1989) Corporate Entity: Making Business Strategy Visible through Design, Thames and Hudson, London.

Olins, W. (1995) The New Guide to Corporate Identity, Gower, Aldershot.

Otubanjo, B. O. and Melewar, T. C. (2007) "Understanding the meaning of corporate identity: A conceptual and semiological approach", Corporate Communications: An International Journal, Vol. 12, No. 4, pp. 414–432.

Proshansky, H. M., Fabian, A. K., and Kaminoff, R. (1983) "Place identity: Physical world socialisation of the self", Journal of Environmental Psychology, Vol. 3, No. 1, pp. 57–83.

Rapoport, A. (1977) Human Aspects of Urban Form, Pergamon Press, Oxford.

Ritchie, I. (1994) An Architect's View of Recent Developments in European Museums, the Museum of the Future, Routledge, London.

Rocca, A. (2007) Natural Architecture, Design Boom, Princeton Architectural Press.

Rooney, D., Paulsen, N., Callan, V. J., Brabant, M., Gallois, C., and Jones, E. (2010) "A new role for place identity in managing organisational change", Management Communication Quarterly, Vol. 24, No. 1, pp. 44–73.

Rosen, M., Orlikowski, W. J., and Schmahmann, K. S. (1990) "Building Buildings and Living Lives: A Critique of Bureaucracy, Ideology and Concrete Artifacts", in Gagliardi, P. (Ed.), Symbols and Artifacts: Views of the Corporate Landscape, Walter de Gruyter, Berlin, pp. 69–84.

Russell, J. A. and Pratt, G. (1980) "A description of the affective quality attributed to environments", Journal of Personality and Social Psychology, Vol. 38, pp. 311–322.

Sadalla, E. K. and Sheets, V. L. (1993) "Symbolism in building materials: Self-representational and cognitive components", Environment and Behaviour, Vol. 25, No. 2, pp. 155–180.

Saleh, M. A. E. (1998) "Place IDENTITY: The VISUAL IMAGE OF SAUDI ARABIAN Cities", Habitat International., Vol. 22, No. 2, pp. 149–164.

Schmitt, B. H., Simonson, A., and Marcus, J. (1995) "Managing corporate image and identity", Long Range Planning, Vol. 28, No. 5, pp. 82–92.

Schroeder, J. (2003) "Building brands: Architectural Expression in the electronic age," in L. M. Scott and R. Batra (Eds.), Persuasive Imagery: A Consumer Response Perspective, Lawrence Erlbaum Associates, Mahwah, pp. 355–388.

Secord, P. F. and Backman, C. W. (1964) Social Psychology, McGraw-Hill, New York.

Smith, R. and Bugni, V. (2002) "Designed physical environment as related to selves, symbols, and social reality: A proposal for a paradigm shift for architecture", Humanity and Society, Vol. 26, pp. 293–311.

Sommer, R. (1969) Personal Space: The Behavioural Basis of Design, Engle wood Cliffs, Prentice-Hall, New Jersey.

Spencer, C. (2002) "Arkwright town rebuilt: But a sense of community lost", Social Psychological Review, Vol. 4, No. 2, pp. 23–24.

Strati, A. (1990) "Aesthetics and Organisational Skills", in Turner, B. A. (Ed.), Organisational Symbolism, Walter de Gruyter, New York.

Sundstrom, E. and Sundstrom, M. G. (1986) Workplaces: The Psychology of the Physical Environment in Office and Factories, Cambridge University Press, Cambridge.

Sundstrom, E., Burt, R. E., and Kamp, D. (1980) "Privacy at work: Architectural correlates of job satisfaction and job performance", Academy of Management Journal, Vol. 23, No. 1, pp. 101–117.

Tajfel, H. (1981) Human Groups and Social Categories, Cambridge University Press, Cambridge.

Tajfel, H. (1982) Social Identity and Intergroup Relations, Cambridge University Press, Cambridge.

Thatcher, S. M. B. and Zhu, X. (2006) "Changing identities in a changing workplace: Identification, identity enactment, self-verification, and telecommuting", Academy of Management Review, Vol. 31, pp. 1076–1088.

Twigger-Ross, C. L., Bonaiuto, M., and Breakwell, G. M. (2003) "Identity Theories and Environmental Psychology", in Bonnes, M., Lee, T., and Bonaiuto, M. (Eds.), Psychological Theories for Environmental Issues, Ashgate, Aldershot, pp. 203–234.

Twigger-Ross, C. L. and Uzzell, D. L. (1996) "Place and identity processes", Journal of Environmental Psychology, Vol. 16, pp. 205–220.

Ulrich, R. S. (1984) "View through a window influences recovery from surgery", In Science, No. 224, pp. 420–421.

Unwin, S. (2009) Analysing Architecture, Taylor & Francis, London.

Uzzell, D. L., Pol, E., and Badenas, D. (2002) "Place identification, social cohesion, and environmental sustainability", Environment and Behaviour, Vol. 34, No. 1, pp. 26–53.

Van den Bosch, A. L. M., Elving, W. J. L., and De Jong, M. D. T. (2006) "The impact of organisational characteristics on corporate visual identity", European Journal of Marketing, Vol. 40, Nos. 7/8, pp. 870–885.

Van Heerden, C. H. and Puth, G. (1995) "Factors that determine the corporate image of South African banking institutions: An exploratory investigation", The International Journal of Bank Marketing, Vol. 13, No. 3, pp. 12–17.

Van Riel, C. B. M. (1995) Principles of Corporate Communication, Prentice Hall, London.

Van Riel, C. B. M. and Balmer, J. M. T. (1997) "Corporate identity, concept, its measurement and management", European Journal of Marketing, Vol. 31, Nos. 5/6, pp. 340–355.

Varlander, S. (2012) "Individual flexibility in the workplace: A spatial perspective", The Journal of Applied Behavioural Science, Vol. 48, No. 1, pp. 33–61.

Veryzer, R. W. (1999) "A nonconscious processing explanation of consumer response to product design", Psychology and Marketing, Vol 16, No. 6, pp. 497–522.

Vischer, J. C. (1996) Workplace Strategies: Environment as a Tool for Work, Chapman and Hall, New York.

Vischer, J. C. (2005) Space Meets Status, Routledge, Abingdon.

Vischer, J. C. (2007) The effects of the physical environment on job performance: Towards a theoretical model of workspace stress. Stress and Health: Journal of the International Society for the Investigation of Stress, Vol. 23, No. 3, pp. 175–184.

Wegge, J., Van Dick, R., Fisher, G. K., Wecking, C., and Moltzen, K. (2006) "Work motivation, organisational identification, and well-being in call-centre work", Work and Stress, Vol. 20, pp. 60–83.

Weggeman, M., Lammers, I., and Akkermans, H. (2007) "Aesthetics from a design perspective", Journal of Organisational Change Management, Vol. 20, No. 3, pp. 346–358.

Wilson, S. (1985) "Premises of excellence", Facilities, Vol. 4, No. 1, pp. 11–14.

Wilson, S. (1986) "Conditions of office", In Design Journal, pp. 98–100.

Yee, J. (1990) "Landscaping as a marketing tool", The Journal of Property Management, Vol. 55, No. 4, pp. 45–47.

7
CORPORATE ARCHITECTURE DESIGN, CORPORATE IDENTITY, AND IDENTIFICATION

Mohammad Mahdi Foroudi, John M. T. Balmer, and Pantea Foroudi

Introduction

Chapter 7 explains the key elements of corporate identity which are an influence on corporate architecture design: i) philosophy, mission, and value; ii) communication; and iii) visual identity, and how these factors could be implemented in the design of a favourable architecture. In addition, this chapter describes how a favourable architecture design could improve customer/company identification.

Background to corporate architecture design, corporate identity, and identification

Architecture as a substantial piece of symbolism can be viewed as the guidelines for the manufacturer of artefacts to devise an image of corporate identity. For instance, a company's architecture plays a crucial role in how the business presents itself. This process plays a main role in shaping customers' respondents towards the company (Brown and Dacin, 1997). Architecture helps consumers to concentrate on the business, what it communicates or delivers, what it represents, and it permits the organisation to send a consistent messages to stakeholders (Duncan and Moriarty, 1998). The marketing literature confirmed that managers focus on the company's architecture to create a strong corporate identity. The development of a corporate identity programme and its journey requires adopting a new visual identity for British universities, in their corporate architecture. In addition, a company's architecture and landscape often enhance a strong universal corporate identity (Balmer and Stotvig, 1997; Kennedy, 1977). Knight and Haslam (2010) state that managerial control of space directly affects consumers' and employees' identification with the corporate personality.

Nevertheless, based on the assumption of Elsbach (2003) that a relationship exists between architecture and corporate identity, this relationship has yet to be tested and validated. Nevertheless, empirical research related to the corporate identity and its relationship to architecture at a stakeholders' level remains scarce. Due to the lack of understanding of the subject 'architecture' from a multi-disciplinary approach made the researcher think about a pluralistic

DOI: 10.4324/9781003054153-8

study where qualitative methods are used in conjunction with quantitative methods to inspect a domain that, to date, has received little or no attention (Deshpande, 1983; Zinkhan and Hirschheim, 1992). This research builds a conceptual model from the internal-stakeholders' perceptional view and attempts to clarify these causal associations among the diverse variables and the role of various factors affecting corporate identity and architecture, therefore, to conceptually illuminate ambiguities that exist in the related studies.

Corporate identity and architecture relationships

Recent research (Balmer, 2001; 2005; 2006; Foroudi et al., 2019; 2020) has discussed the importance for decision makers to focus on the company's architecture to create a strong corporate identity. For example, architecture, location, and the interior decor of offices play a crucial role in how companies illustrate themselves to stakeholders.

The marketing literature confirmed that managers should focus on architecture to create a strong corporate identity. Olins (1995) and Melewar et al. (2006) claim that an organisation's architecture is a major part of corporate identity. It is recommended that a successful organisation must have a favourable location, and therefore, firms spend huge amounts of money to acquire key sites to convey the appropriate corporate identity and image. Corporate identity can be viewed as the sum of all the factors which, when integrated, form a presentation of what a company is and how it is different from other companies (Downey, 1986, p. 7).

In addition, architecture is considered to be the expression of a company's internal creativity which communicates the company's corporate essence to the internal and external stakeholders. Therefore, this sense of corporate identity communicates the company's personality (Downey, 1986) and the impression that the public has of the organisation is also constructed at the same time. Schmitt at al. (1995) recommended that managers collaborate with consultants and architects to evaluate the styles (primary attributes, complexity, and representation), themes, and the aesthetic impression of the company as the basic elements for evaluation which are sensitivity to the customer; individuality from rival firms and the expression of the company's values and corporate mission. To provide the value and mission of a company, the management of an organisation's aesthetics must go beyond a statement of one's 'corporate identity'. Corporate aesthetics must be managed and planned to provide clear guidelines on how to enhance a company's, and its products' appeal (Schmitt et al., 1995). Corporate identity comes from the services or products a company offers, its management, its employees, its work climate and attitude, and is originated in the positive and negative influences of communication between planned and perceived image (Northart, 1980, p. 29).

The development of a corporate identity programme and its journey requires adopting a new visual identity such as a favourable company's architecture. For example, company's architecture and landscape often enhance a strong universal corporate identity (Kennedy, 1977). In fact, visual dimensions are carefully re-designed and transmitted to internal and external audiences especially when companies need to alter their visual identity to achieve a higher market profile or to convey new organisational forms such as mergers and acquisitions. For example, Peugeot's headquarters are located just off the Champs Elysees in Paris, which is one of the most expensive and prestigious roads in the world. Melewar et al. (2006) recommended that it is vital for a successful company to have a favourable location, and therefore, companies are willing to spend large sums of money to obtain key sites to transmit the desired image and a main location which has a significant element of visual identity (Kirby and Kent, 2010) provides the organisation with continual exposure to the general public.

The general public recognises the company and differentiates it from others by the company's visual cues, such as building design. The power of visual cues lies in their ability to speak louder than words in establishing and strengthening corporate identity (Nguyen, 2006). The non-verbal cues convey the nature of the offered service and give an indication of the reliability of the service provider's reputation (Nguyen, 2006). For instance, when a customer first visits a lawyer's office, the architecture, the décor, and the quality of the furniture can create an impression of the firm's prestige and level of success (p. 67). The importance of architecture is shown by how firms pay attention to the affect architecture has on how consumers perceive their identity. In addition, from an architectural perspective the environment of architecture and buildings have been considered to signify good taste, status, and power due to the attention paid to the identity of the architect and it can influence a company's prestige (Brauer, 2002; Kirby and Kent, 2010). Furthermore, a favourable architecture can have an influence on the rise of consumption. The way environmental elements can create and convey corporate image is well-recognised for companies, particularly in service sectors such as the financial, corporate headquarters, and public institutional realms. Hence, despite the clear rationale that corporate identity has an affect on architecture, and architecture has an affect on corporate identity, there is scant research into the contribution architecture makes to identity and how identity contributes to architecture (Kirby and Kent, 2010).

Corporate identity and identification relationships

Corporate identity and identification are powerful terms as both concepts contribute to the very definition of the identity of a person, a group, or an organisation. Corporate identity and corporate identification are root concepts in organisation and behaviours in contemporary organisations (Albert et al., 2000). Based on the social identity theory, people consider themselves to belong to specific social groups or certain categories, for instance, ethnicity, political affiliation, gender, and so on, and people wish to differentiate themselves from others in social contexts (Marin and de Maya, 2013). Identity and identification explain the means by which individuals act as members of the group or the organisation. Internal-stakeholders' identification with a company that has a favourable identity allows them to see themselves in a way which reflects favourably on the company and which enhances their sense of self-worth. Thus, the uniqueness of an organisation's identity can be partly determined due to the perception of others.

The organisational identification literature has assumed that greater attractiveness of an organisation's perceived identity will lead to consumers developing a strong identification with the organisation. For instance, a company's internal-stakeholders, who believe their organisation has a particular culture, structure, or some other characteristic that differentiates it from other groups, are likely to experience strong levels of organisational identification. Some authors (Bhattacharya and Sen, 2003) found that consumers who viewed their university as unique in its attitudes, practices, and values had high levels of organisational identification. In addition, Dutton et al. (1994) state that those employees and customer's beliefs about the distinguishing, chief, and enduring attributes of an organisation can provide an influential corporate image and have an impact on the degree to which internal-stakeholders identify with the company.

Following on from the discussion above, this chapter claims that a strong identity will have a positive impact on organisational identification. Based on this argument, we suggest that corporate identity, which is an organisation's uniqueness, is expressed in a set of distinctive attributes, which could affect internal-stakeholders' identification. Thus, this research has identified a strong, direct association among corporate identity and identification.

Architecture and identification relationships

The association among the concept of architecture and identification has been recognised by previous scholars (Knight and Haslam, 2010; Nguyen, 2006; Thatcher and Xhu, 2006). Scholars (Rooney et al., 2010) state that different employees and consumers can give different meanings to architecture, and the significance of these meanings will result in different groups within a place having a variety of responses to changes to that place. The results show that place identity is an essential and different mode of place identification that leads different groups to have a different awareness of the values, possibilities, and efficiency of places. People have different ideas of how a place can help them construct or defend their identities and self-esteem. Place identity theory argues that the way employees identify with their workplace affects how they perceive major organisational change. Physical changes in the environment have an effect on stakeholders' feelings about, and emotional responses to, the organisation, which become deeper as the relationship develops. There are two ways this can happen. First is the clients' sense of identification with the employees with whom they have direct contact (Kioussi, 2008). Second is the identification developed beyond the attitudes and sets of individual relations with multiple internal stakeholders to identify within the company's practices as a component of corporate branding, which is embodied in a variety of designs.

Based on social identity theory, which explains the buildings' symbolic meaning, as well as the sense of, and identification with, a place, the stakeholders of an organisation define themselves in relation to their own places of work/study. According to Spencer (2002) the emphasis on place in the environmental perception should be viewed as complementary, and place can be seen as a social category to provide identity. A perception of the environment is considered as a participatory experience between the physical setting and people.

In order to understand customers, managers should focus on the language of client identification at the client–architecture interface and emphasise how communication from the architectural practice both influences and is influenced by clients. Clients and end-users identify not only with the buildings themselves but also with those responsible for the design. Design can be seen by the clients as an expression of themselves, who they are, and who they aspire to be. Brand management research into firms offering niche market architecture established important associations between the architectural process and client identification. In addition, it also assists with client identification via the design of the building, which in some cases supports and develops client corporate branding. Archistars and architects may assign most promotional resources to the visual language of an organisation. Organisations appreciate design quality in advertising and are aware of how it helps the sale of their services and products. Visual imagery is the gateway to inspiring corporate identification, originally on the merit of the design, yet then via the development of relationships. In addition, favourable service and design practices increase most in the context of brand management language, describing up-to-date design and a robust professional image.

In addition, for employees and customers, place identification can influence employee's and customers' attitudes toward organisational change (Rooney et al., 2010). However, there is scant information regarding how place is connected to the formation of client identification and the way a connection to a place influences how employees respond to organisational change. Organisational change occurs in places that have a dynamic connection to social action and interaction. Based on place identity theory, stakeholders respond to physical modifications in the place in order to protect their sense of self-efficacy and connectedness in their place, particularly when such changes are considered to threaten their identity. Furthermore, organisational change should be more alert to the role of place identification in employee's and customer's responses to change in their places. Major organisational change often entails altering places in psychologically important ways. Organisational changes, such as implementing new working methods or relocating to a new building, change how employees identify with, and relate to, each other and with the workplace. Managerial control of the workplace can have a negative effect on employees' organisational identification and so can result in suboptimal work experiences.

Place identity can be defined as a potpourri of conceptions, memories, interpretations, ideas, or any feelings related to the particular place settings. This association among the setting and the self can actively construct the individual's own positioning in his or her environment. As people form emotional attachments to places, research shows that it is more likely that they will be resistant to any changes to those places. Positive and negative experiences in a place give rise to specific attitudes, beliefs, feelings, and values about the physical world, and these can form an individual's place identity. The concept of a place identity is created through physical setting experience, how they communicate with each other, it is a function of what people do and what they consider to be good or bad about a place. Place identification can indicate membership of a group of people who are defined by a specific place. If this position is taken, then place identification is a type of social identification (Twigger-Ross and Uzzell, 1996). The identification objects portray the places' distinctiveness and individuality and becomes its physical identity along with other spatial components. Their ties, connections, and affiliations with the place and the larger culture are aspects of space identity (Saleh, 1998). Customer perceptions and meanings strongly resonate and align with not only the architecture but also with the aims of the architects. Personal identification and social identification are strengthened amongst those who represent the client organisation and the end-users.

Corporate identity dimensions and architecture dimensions relationships

Architecture can establish a strong corporate identity. Discussion in the literature about the components of corporate identity is widespread. A number of studies in marketing and corporate identity usually assume that corporate identity management as a multifaceted phenomenon and also requires a holistic and multi-disciplinary as well as an integrated approach (Bernstein, 1986). Corporate identity management constructs aim to recognise aspects of identity that are manageable and used to develop corporate identity.

The company's products and services transmit the aggregate of message to a group or groups over a certain period, which have influence in forming the company's corporate identity (Balmer, 1998). In addition, corporate identity refers to a company's traits, features, attributes, or characteristics that are presumed to be essential, unique, and enduring. Corporate identity comprises core values (operating philosophy, leadership, mission, and vision) and demographics (location, country of origin, size, age, competitive position, and business) of the organisation.

Corporate identity comprises the soul (culture, values), voice (communication), and mind (e.g., vision and philosophy). In addition, corporate identity reflects the three major dimensions, namely, values, mission, and philosophy; communications; and corporate visual identity. Managers play a significant role in the development and management of corporate identity as it is inextricably associated with, 'understanding how and why various constituents form corporate associations and the specific corporate associations that they hold' (Dacin and Brown, 2002, pp. 254–255). A well-organised corporate identity is one of a company's most precious marketing assets and as an explicit combination of all the methods the organisation uses to presents itself to all of its audiences via perceptions and experiences in order to generate a favourable associations with the groups upon which the corporation depends.

In order to account for the relationship, which seems to exist between architecture and the antecedent factors of interest (i.e., ambient conditions/physical stimuli and functionality/physical structure, spatial layout, and decor and artifacts/symbolic artifacts), social identity theory which has been used extensively in marketing studies is applied. Due to the lack of research reported in the marketing and design literature, there is a significant gap concerning the relationship between functionality/physical structure and spatial layout and architecture chiefly with regard to the service industry. According to this theory, members define the organisation by the same criteria that they think define themselves. A favourable architectural and design-led research study investigating engaging end users in, and giving them a certain amount of control over, the design process is beneficial for workplace design and for helping employee recognition as part of working practices (Davis et al., 2010). Also, the impact of new working practices may be part of re-designed or very flexible open-plan office space (Davis et al., 2010). Office space re-design is frequently based upon managers' own experiences and interpretations of employee work patterns, mainly without any professional input or specific research. In addition, the office design can be key in influencing decision-making processes, and some significant decisions may not be given the thoughtfulness it deserves as a consequence.

With regard to spatial layout and functionality remarkably little research has been published about how functionality and spatial layout can affect customers in commercial service settings. The physical structure and spatial layout of companies symbolise something (Saleh, 1998) and provides messages regarding the companies' capabilities and qualities for employees and outsiders alike and influence how people interact and also how they behave.

Studies show the multifaceted association among office design and employee attitudes and behaviours as well as how time spent in the office can be crucial to creative work that builds on face-to-face meetings and interactions with idea-inducing artifacts (Elsbach and Bechky, 2007). Architecture (physical environment) is thought to be the packaging of services. There are three components: physical structure/spatial layout and functionality; ambient conditions/physical stimuli; and symbolic artifacts/decor and artifacts. The major antecedents of corporate identity are those factors that predict, nurture, or undermine the perceived corporate identity during consumption. Based on the review of the related literature, three main factors in creating a favourable corporate identity were revealed. These factors are usually used by customers as cues to predict their impression of corporate identity such as: visual identity; philosophy, mission, and values; and communication. The relationship between the antecedents' factors of corporate identity and the antecedents' factors of architecture (physical structure/spatial layout and functionality, and decor and artifacts/symbolic artifacts) will be discussed in this section.

Corporate visual identity and architecture

Management of corporate visual identity is based on the principle that a company can use visual cues to transmit its quality, style, and prestige to internal and external stakeholders (Melewar and Saunders, 1999). Corporate identity is the company' visual statement to the world of what and who the company is, of the way the company views itself, and so it is closely linked with the way the world views the corporation and how it influences held views of companies. Furthermore, corporate identity is the degree to which it is conceptualised as a function of leadership and by its emphasis on the visual elements.

Visual identity management has significant implications in the field of business. Conceptualising the management of corporate visual identity in terms of precise dimensions is crucial, as it involves creating and implementing instructions for how symbolism is used within the company. The internal purpose of corporate visual identity relates to employees' identification with the organisation through the ambient conditions/physical stimuli of an environment in service context that inspire consumers and employees to follow service consumption and consequently, influence employees' behaviours, performance, attitudes, and satisfaction and toward the service provider.

Ambient conditions/physical stimuli, such as visual openness, light, and sound, in addition to thermal comfort and ventilation are all crucial to employee productivity (e.g., hospitals, hotels, and banks). Furthermore, a balance must be established between the customer needs and the employee preferences. Ambient conditions/physical stimuli usually have a subconscious impact on customer loyalty and on customer satisfaction. Furthermore, it has an impact on the attitudes of stakeholders and on how stakeholders behave with regard to the company. In addition, they can affect consumers' experiences and perceptions. During the service encounter, the outcome of the ambient conditions/physical stimuli present in the setting may result in (dis)comfort which in turn will encourage the customer to pursue or to interrupt the service consumption. Consequently, this can affect their behaviours and attitudes toward the service provider. In addition, the effect on stakeholders' behaviours and their attitudes toward the company can influence consumers' experiences and perceptions.

Stakeholders' perceptions of ambient conditions/physical stimuli and human responses to the environment have been studied by some authors. Physical stimuli in the environment can activate behaviour and need to be considered in theories of organisational behaviour, especially in models of motivation and goal setting. Stimulus cues frequently influence behaviour in unintended ways and directly affect apparently unconnected feelings and beliefs about the place and the people. People respond to their environments holistically. Thus, managers must ensure that they create a reliable belief to communicate in the market.

Companies' corporate identity field are most concerned with visual representations of the corporation emphasised through planned cues which constitute the organisation's visual identity, that is, the graphics and designs associated with an organisation's elements of self-expression and symbols to generate physical recognition for the organisation and distinguish the firm from all others through the company's physical structure/spatial layout and functionality. A company's physical structure/spatial layout and functionality of the physical setting are especially significant components of visual identity and influence social interaction. A corporate visual identity consists of an interior and exterior of buildings (offices, headquarters, retail stores, plants, etc.), corporate symbol/logo, corporate name, colour, typeface, symbolism understanding, and staff appearance which convey organisational characteristics, printed material e.g., stationery, promotional literature, etc. Corporate visual identity delivers recognisability and result in an emotional reaction to the corporation.

Today's efforts at office re-design are more purposeful, with changes in physical structures and decor and artifacts/symbolic artifacts, and they can be linked to the beauty/aesthetics of a place, as well as influencing perceptions of customers. Architecture and office layout are considered to be a visible symbolic artifact. Symbolic artifacts/decor and artifacts and orientation signals are visual symbols, which can generate a suitable place and direct consumers throughout the service encounter. Architectonic details, which include design details, signage, colours and decor, artwork, transmit senses and can have a symbolic importance which can evokes emotions in an audience.

In the current value-image era, researchers have emphasised the extremely important role played by symbolic artifacts/decor and artifacts in architecture in the process of managing the corporate image. From the consumer's point of view, decor and artifacts are the degree of overall customer satisfaction and subsequent customer behaviour. Behaviour and the distinctiveness of territoriality can be demonstrated by the relatively frequent occurrence of individuals who demonstrate territorial behaviour with regard to objects whose value are only symbolic or subjective. For example, university students may expend effort to support a specific seat in the lecture hall as their own, and similarly they feel emotional indignation or a sense of loss if another student uses 'their' seat simply because of a sense of ownership, irrespective of any strategic or material value it may have compared to any other carrel or seat. It can emphasise and explain some forms of behaviour by consumers and employees, while simultaneously exploring and explaining what a distinct phenomenon is. The changes in the symbolic artifacts, such as an increase in natural lighting and the use of bright colours produce a more pleasing work atmosphere, which evokes optimistic reactions.

The visual identity paradigm focuses on organisational nomenclature, company name, logos, buildings, company's architecture, and the design and decor of corporate retail outlets' architecture and exterior design, interior design, or anything that can be related to design. For instance, architecture (physical evidence, environmental design, and décor) helps to convey tangible hints that affect customer behaviour. The visual identity of an organisation can be viewed as identification. Furthermore, the design components indicate the company's culture and values and should be recognised by the organisation's consumers and employees. In the context of a service encounter, the physical environment can affect the way consumers view service failure and should be used to distinguish a company's services from those of rival companies. Corporate visual identity assists a company to convey the company's visual identity through its buildings. Decor and orientation are visual symbols used to produce an appropriate atmosphere. Buildings, interiors, and corporate building architecture can also be a crucial component in a company's visual identity.

To conclude, it is proposed that the corporate visual identity, as a main element of corporate identity, will influence architecture (components of architecture: physical structure/spatial layout and functionality, ambient conditions/physical stimuli, and symbolic artifacts/decor and artifacts).

Philosophy, mission, value, and architecture

Philosophy, mission, values, and architecture are presented to the outside world through corporate identity. In the marketing literature, there is widespread acceptance of the idea that corporate identity refers to the characteristics, features, attributes, and traits of a company that are assumed to be crucial, unique, and long-lasting.

Corporate identity management is concerned with conception and development, and serves to communicate the expression of an organisation's philosophy, mission, and ethos which managers and employees associate with the company as well as reference to external constituencies. Furthermore, environmental psychology and marketing research suggest that the physical environment can serve as a marketing tool to communicate the main tangible cues and to communicate the company's philosophy, mission, and values to the consumers. Since first impressions really count, physical structure/spatial layout and functionality can communicate information to the customer about how the firm sees itself and about how it wishes its customers to behave. It has also been suggested that corporate identity is eclectic in that it draws on a wide range of management and non-management disciplines and hence it might be viewed as an emerging philosophy or approach. The management of a corporate identity involves the dynamic interplay among the company's corporate culture, the philosophy of its key executives, its business strategy, and its organisational design.

In service marketing, the first impressions which can describe the 'right thing' in the minds of employees and consumers that really count are the company's physical structure/spatial layout and functionality (Bernard and Bitner, 1982). Favourable architectural designs are a highly regarded aesthetic element (Bateson, 1989; Bitner, 1992; Nguyen, 2006) in the creation of the corporate image. However, there needs to be careful consideration of functionality of the corporate image, as there are many consequences through a range of functions. It should communicate the company's philosophy, the reason for its existence and may have a strong impact on how contact personnel perform. It must be designed taking into consideration two types of need: operational needs, which are expressed by the maximisation of organisational efficiency; and marketing needs, the aim being to create an environment that has an impact on consumers' beliefs about and attitudes toward the organisation and, consequently, its corporate image in the minds of customers and employees (Bateson, 1989; Bitner, 1992; Nguyen, 2006). Customers and employees form their expectations about services through tangible cues, such as architecture, furnishings, parking facilities temperature, lighting, colour, and layout and interactive quality relates to the interactions that take place between the customer and the contact personnel during the service encounter (Leblanc and Nguyen, 1996).

The mission statement can be used to express the corporate philosophy to convey a sense of purpose and commonality. A corporate mission is a corporation's purpose and the reason the company exists. Therefore, it is the most important part of the corporate philosophy. Thus, an organisation's mission provides the foundation for its identity and establishes core directions for employee conduct. Mission statements vary significantly, but they tend to emphasise the value, guiding principles, and positive behaviour within the company's ideology and belief system in order to promote the company's philosophy and culture. A company's mission statement acts as a principle of order and organises the company's principles (Fritz et al., 1999).

There is often some confusion between corporate mission and vision. De Witt and Meyer (1998) confirmed that the corporate mission is the basic point of departure, whereas a corporate vision is the desired future towards which the company travels (Melewar, 2003). Levin (2000) explains vision as 'a high lucid story of an organisation's preferred future in action. A future that describes what life will be like for employees, customers, and other key stakeholders' (p. 93). Cummings and Davies (1994) elucidate that, 'the value of any statement of corporate mission or vision lies in fusing together a corporation's many elements by providing some commonality of purpose' (p. 150).

There is a relationship between corporate vision and the values embedded in the organisational culture. Those values are central to the process of identity formation. The starting point for a company's philosophy is the company's vision and values, which play a major role how its corporate identity is formed. They are the ethical principles and beliefs that underpin the company's culture, and are a major belief system within a company, which encompasses daily language and ideologies. Organisational values are crucial to organisational culture, and it is important that such values be understood; therefore, they should be actively shaped. A corporate value belief system within the organisation includes rituals, ideologies, and language that guide the culture of the company and shape the corporate identity. Furthermore, it is espoused by the managers or the founder. A corporate value, mission, and philosophy should impact on the design of ambient conditions/physical stimuli. The ambient conditions/physical stimuli include a wide range of background characteristics of the environment such as temperature, colour, lighting, music, noise, and scent. All can influence the customers' and employees' five senses and affect their perceptions of, as well as their responses to, the environment (Nguyen, 2006).

Architecture, workspace design, and ambient conditions/physical stimuli assume more significance since employees and consumers tend to spend long periods in the servicescape (Bitner, 1992). Their physical comfort (lighting, temperature) and responses to noise levels and/or music have an impact on productivity and overall satisfaction. The ambient conditions are mainly vital in forming first impressions, for communicating corporate values, mission and philosophy, service concepts, reasons for repositioning a service, and in highly competitive industries where consumers seeks cues for differentiation and recognition of the organisation (Bitner, 1992; Parish et al., 2008).

Customers recognise architecture, location, and the interior decor of offices (Balmer and Stotvig, 1997; Melewar et al., 2006), banks, hospitals, and retail stores. The office decor or the location and style of office chairs is the main element of architecture and as a means of understanding the structuring of social relations within the workplace. Workplace identity refers to the symbolic self-categorisations individuals employ to convey their identities in a specific workplace (Elsbach and Bechky, 2007). Employees can feel a loss of workplace identity if there is a limited ability to demonstrate uniqueness and organisation by displaying their personal artifacts.

A symbolic artifact is the aspect of the physical setting that collectively or individually direct the clarification of the social setting which is mostly pertinent to the service industry. In addition, decor and artifacts influence the degree of overall customer satisfaction and subsequent customer behaviour. Customers act differently in different places because of the effect of symbolic artifacts; therefore, a company should have distinctive mission, values, and philosophy. Symbolic artifacts refer to the aesthetics of the office of environment: the type of flooring, colours of the walls, flowers, pictures, style of furniture, and overall office decor which differentiate the company and place from its rivals.

The philosophy, mission, and values dimension attempts to bring a strategic basis to the corporate identity construct and helps channel employee attention in a particular direction, shared goals and expectations, in order to understand how their individual roles fit within a larger picture (Ledford et al., 1995) as well as being articulated by the company's audiences and employees. Corporate value, mission, and philosophy have influence on architecture and its elements including physical structure/spatial layout and functionality, ambient conditions/physical stimuli, and decor and artifacts/symbolic artifacts. Therefore, based on the discussion that highlights the importance of the philosophy, mission, and value, its ambiguous relationship within marketing research, and finally, its relevance to the context of the current research.

Communication and architecture

An organisation's communication refers to the corporate identity can not only influence the strategy content as well but can also provide stakeholders with a corporate communication system. Corporate identity is the signature that is visible in everything a corporation does and communicates. The notion of corporate identity is generally seen as belonging to the sender side of the communication process. Moreover, corporate identity is self-presentation via communication. For instance, the physical structure/spatial layout and functionality are indispensable in service settings, which is the purposeful environment that helps to fulfil employees' and customers' specific wants and needs and which affects the customers' and employees' comfort.

Employees and customers experience their jobs differently in different environments. Architecture can provide spaces with a range of functionality which all workers and consumers can access as and when they need to (Davis et al., 2010). Physical space can be arranged to assist the communication and work patterns required by the job (Allen and Henn, 2007). Modern design focuses mainly on the functionality of features of ergonomic design; these offer workers a range of different types of workspace, in accordance with the characteristics of their job and work styles. For example, overall layout, comfort, and seating/table organisations are the key components of physical structure. In self-service environments, such as Automated Teller Machines (ATM), the simple layout and clear directions assist the customer in completing the transaction easily (Bitner, 1992, p. 67).

Based on the environmental psychology research into workspace and architecture, which has focused on floor arrangement and furniture layouts, the height and the density of workstation partitions, the amount and convenience of file and work storage space, and dimensions of office furniture, for example, work surfaces, are the elements of furniture and spatial layout that have the most impact on individual workers and users (Vischer, 2007). The physical structure and physical layouts and proximity to employees and consumers influence patterns of social interaction and thus shape the social and relational aspects of work and people may configure their jobs to change and shape the place. According to McDonald (2006), successfully combining good functionality, exciting inspiring internal spaces, and architectural manifestation are essential. Physical structure/spatial layout and the functionality of design affects the accessibility of resources that organisations would like employees and consumers to rely upon when making important decisions. Furthermore, architecture, as a major element of corporate identity, is a tangible representation and is manifest in the way the organisation behaves and communicates.

Markwick and Fill (1997) claim that corporate identity is an important factor determining whether communication is effective and in identifying which form of communication best conveys an image, and it seeks an integrated approach to transmit identity in harmonised and coherent messages through both internal and external forms of communication. Furthermore, corporate identity as one-way management harmonises all consciously-used forms of internal and external communication as effectively and efficiently as possible. In this way, management creates a favourable basis for relationships with the groups upon which the company depends. Marketing communication is the type of communication aimed to support the services and products offered by the corporation.

Corporate identity has many ways to communicate to make the organisation distinctive. Thus, in addition to products and services, advertising, sales promotion, sponsorship and direct selling, corporate advertising, and public relations activities, are aimed to improve recognition of and familiarity with the company in preference to using individual advertising to convey the company's identity. Marketing communication activities aim not only to position a company's services in the market but also to promote the company itself as well.

Service providers are concerned about the relationship between architecture and the ambient conditions/physical stimuli in the workplace environment that counteract negative influences as well as to serve as a reminder 'of what needs to be accomplished' which is a major priority for many managers. Managers constantly plan, build, control, and change the physical environment of an organisation, but often, there is only partial understanding of the way a particular design or a change in design affects the ultimate users of the facility. Furthermore, managers, in essence, are ordering the information cues that influence or control their behaviours through architecture (Davis, 1984). In addition, managers have to be able to differentiate among those aspects of the stimulus in the environment and architecture that can be ordered in advance; those stimuli that enter the office and that can be channelled (i.e., either to the waste basket, filing cabinet, tickler file, or other people); and those aspects of the stimulus environment that have to be responded to, acted on, or lived with (Davis, 1984). However, in some cases managers simply have to adapt to the architecture and physical environment, mentally block out irrelevant cues, and concentrate on their own work schedule of priorities. Significantly, the managers must be aware of the need to balance employee preferences with customer needs, and typically they remove people's rights to personalise their workspace. Instead, they dictate how architecture should be used, and this can have a direct contribution to employees' emotions in the workplace (Knight and Haslam, 2010).

The stakeholders' feelings at work and changes in the symbolic artifacts can produce a positive reaction, for instance, natural lighting and the use of bright colours make a more pleasant work atmosphere as well as affecting the perceptions of culture. The office has developed into an important location for creative, learning, and symbolic interactions. Because of this trend, the décor and the design of offices has assumed a renewed significance for corporate managers (Elsbach and Bechky, 2007). Service business managers constantly plan, build, control, and change an organisation's architecture design such as physical surroundings to influence behaviours, to create an image, and to have an effect on stakeholders' perceptions and satisfaction. In addition, managers need to be aware of the impressions they create and avoid presenting physical cues that can have negative or contradictory connotations (Davis, 1984). It is concluded that the favourability of stakeholders' perception of a company will be improved by their perceptions of the extent to which the marketing communication activities reflect the identity a company intends to create in stakeholders' minds. Therefore, based on previous research, which suggests that corporate identity is made manifest in communication of the organisation and everything that is pertinent to a company is communication and exerts an extensive range of influence.

Conclusion

This chapter provides an in-depth detailed investigation of the association among architecture, corporate identity, and stakeholders' identification. In this regard, the researcher has developed a conceptual framework, which is based on different theories such as social identity and attribution. Corporate identity and the antecedents of corporate identity (philosophy, values, and mission; communication and corporate visual identity) and architecture as well as the main underlying dimensions that constitute the construct of architecture (physical structure/spatial layout and functionality, ambient conditions/physical stimuli, and symbolic artifacts/decor and artifacts) were identified.

CASE STUDY – QUIKSILVER

Maria Palazzo, University of Salerno, Italy

Quiksilver Inc. was born in Australia in 1969. The company is now one of the leading sports and lifestyle companies in the world, linked with the areas of surf, snowboard, and skateboard (Ind and Watt, 2004).

> Since its beginnings in 1969, Quiksilver has combined function, fit, art and fashion to develop boardshorts and clothing for mountain and ocean lovers across the globe. While still sticking to the core roots of the mountain and the wave, Quiksilver has become recognized as the premium youth lifestyle and culture clothing brand within the action sports market. Quiksilver has an ever-changing array of materials, prints, and technologies. In addition to boardshorts, Quiksilver designs and produces an entire line of lifestyle apparel, wetsuits, and snow outerwear available across the globe. Our elite team of athletes have become icons throughout the world. Our mission is to inspire the youth and progress as the world around us evolves.
> www.quiksilver.com/customer-service-corporate-information-about-us.html

Today the company is focused on product design, manufacturing, and distribution of different brands. The product portfolio is based on surfing, skateboarding, and snowboarding items.

When compared to sports (i.e., rugby and football), surf is a small niche market. Nevertheless, thanks to communication campaigns, athlete endorsements, and other branding strategies, the small niche sector became a huge industry. During the 2000s, the sector grew due to the fact that it gained more appeal thanks to movies such as: 'Blue Crush', 'Lords of Dogtown', and 'Step into Liquid'.

In the same year, direct competitors of the company were Billabong, Rip Curl, Oakley, Volcom, Reef, Vans, etc. while indirect competitors were Levi Strauss, Abercombie & Fitch, Nike, and Target (Djaballah, 2017).

Quiksilver issues

Quiksilver Inc. had to face several issues in 2000. First, the company's strategy started to focus on acquisitions. Quiksilver, in fact, decided to diversify its business adding unrelated sports such as golf and skiing. This was seen as a problem by loyal customer who thought that the organisation was losing its core features, its corporate personality, and damaging the key elements used to create its unique corporate design, identified by the wave and the mountain.

Moreover, Quiksilver had financial problems, as it had to recall products that didn't meet industry quality norms. In 2008, actually, it had to recall children's clothes as they showed risk of burn injury due to potential ignition of the garment. Therefore, consumers' confidence and trust in the organisation suffered from these negative circumstances.

Brand differentiation

Brands linked with specific sports have been involved in communication campaigns promoting the lifestyle associated with these sports (Bouchet et al., 2013). Thus, two main target audiences are selected by sports marketers:

- Opinion leaders (called 'cool kid's'). They live and enjoy all facets of the sport lifestyle and buy certain brands as they think these make them cool.
- The 'other kids'. They buy the brands to be similar to the 'cool kid's'.

In order to reach both target audiences, companies try to combine events, sponsorships, athlete-endorsements and many other communication and branding strategies.

The most well-known event in the surfing sector is the ASP World Tour, that celebrate the world's best surfers. Moreover, sport brands usually invest in sponsoring World Tour events and smaller events such as the World Qualifying Series. These events offer companies different branding opportunities and reinforce identification as they give media coverage on communication channels, such as: TV, radio, life-webcasts on corporate website, etc. In fact, Quiksilver decided to be the sponsor of three events linked with the surfing world in Australia, France, and New York.

Besides, the company also created good relationships with several brand ambassadors and journalists of sport magazines who were experts of surf, skate, or snowboard trips. These relationship with the surf, skate, and snowboard magazines boosted the brand image and reinforced the identification with the company (Anderson, 2016).

Future analyses will prove if Quiksilver will be able to preserve its image and reliability as a genuine brand related to surf, skateboard, and the snowboard field and whether it will succeed in connecting with consumers without having to change the corporate design and other elements of corporate identity, in order to not alienate the main market segment.

Case questions

1. After the financial crisis, what can Quiksilver do to restructure its image and reach consumer loyalty?
2. How can Quiksilver build a good corporate architecture design and differentiate itself from direct and indirect competitors without alienating the core audience?
3. What should Quiksilver do to reinvent and reinforce its corporate identity?

References

Anderson, J. (2016) "On trend and on the wave: Carving cultural identity through active surf dress", Annals of Leisure Research, Vol. 19, No. 2, pp. 212–234.

Bouchet, P., Hillairet, D., and Bodet, G. (2013) Sport Brands, London, Routledge.

Djaballah, M. (2017) "Giving Sense to Corporate Social Responsibility in Sporting Events: A Case Study of the Quiksilver Pro France", in Contemporary Sport Marketing, London, Routledge, pp. 55–71.

Ind, N. and Watt, C. (2004) "Quiksilver", in Inspiration, Palgrave Macmillan, London, pp. 119–120.

Key terms and definitions

Ambient conditions/physical stimuli of an environment in service settings encourage stakeholders to pursue the service consumptions and subsequent effect on employees' behaviours, attitudes, satisfaction, and performance toward the service provider.

Architecture is a visual presentation of a company and encapsulate the company's purpose and identity, set of elements (physical structure/spatial layout and functionality, ambient conditions/physical stimuli of an environment, and symbolic artifacts/decor and artifacts) which influence on internal-stakeholders' attitude, and behaviour. It can be decisive in facilitating employee, internal-stakeholders' identification.

Communication is the aggregate of messages from both official and informal sources, through a variety of media, by which a company conveys its identity to its multiple audiences or stakeholders.

Corporate identity is the features, characteristics, traits, or attributes of a company that are presumed to be central, distinctive and enduring and serves as a vehicle for expression of the company's philosophy, values, mission, and communications; and corporate visual identity to all its audience.

Corporate visual identity is an assembly of visual cues to make an expression of the organisation by which an audience can recognise the company and distinguish it from others in serving to remind the corporate real purpose in serving to remind the corporate real purpose.

Identification is the degree to which internal-stakeholders defines him or herself by the same attributes that he or she believes define the organisation.

Mission is the company purpose, the reason for which a company exists.

Philosophy is the core values and assumptions that constitute the corporate culture, business mission, and values espoused by the management board or founder of the company.

Physical structure/spatial layout and functionality is the architectural design and physical placement of furnishings in a building, the arrangement of objects (e.g., arrangement of buildings, machinery, furniture, and equipment), the spatial relationships among them, physical location, and physical layout of the workplace which particularly pertinent to the service industry and can symbolise something.

Symbolic artifacts/decor and artifacts is aspects of the physical setting that individually or collectively guide the interpretation of the social setting, can be related to the aesthetics and attractiveness of the physical of the environment, develop a complex representation of workplace identity and is mainly relevant to the service industry.

Value is the dominant system of beliefs and moral principles that lie within the organisation that comprise everyday language, ideologies, rituals, and beliefs of personnel.

References

Albert, A., Ashforth, B. E., and Dutton, J. E. (2000) "Organisational identity and identification: Charting new waters and building new bridges", Academy of Management Review, Vol. 25. No. 1, pp. 13–17.

Allen, T. J. and Henn, G. W. (2007) The Organisation and Architecture of Innovation: Managing the Flow of Technology, Butterworth-Heinemann, Oxford.

Balmer, J. M. T. (1998) "Corporate identity and the advent of corporate marketing", Journal of Marketing Management, Vol. 14, No. 8, pp. 963–996.

Balmer, J. M. T. (2001) "Corporate identity, corporate branding and corporate marketing seeing through the fog", European Journal of Marketing, Vol. 35, Nos. 3/4, pp. 248–291.

Balmer, J. M. T. (2005) "Corporate Brand Cultures and Communities", in Schroeder, J. E. and Salzer-Morling, M. (Eds.), Brand Culture, Routledge, London, pp. 34–49.

Balmer, J. M. T. (2006) "Comprehending corporate marketing and the corporate marketing mix", working paper, Bradford School of Management, Bradford.

Balmer, J. M. T. and Stotvig, S. (1997) "Corporate identity and private banking: A review and case study", International Journal of Banking, Special Edition on Corporate Identity in Financial Services, Vol. 15, No. 5, pp. 169–184.

Bernard, H. B. and Bitner, M. J. (1982) "Marketing Services by Managing the Environment", Cornell Hotel and Restaurant Administration Quarterly, (May), pp. 23–35.

Bernstein, D. J. (1986) Company Image and Reality: A Critique of Corporate Communications, Cassell Educational Ltd, London.

Bhattacharya, C. B. and Sen, S. (2003) "Consumer-company identification: A framework for understanding consumers' relationships with companies", Journal of Marketing, Vol. 67, No. 2, pp. 76–88.

Bitner, M. J. (1992) "Servicescapes: The impact of physical surroundings on customers and employees", Journal of Marketing, Vol. 56, pp. 57–71.

Brauer, G. (2002) Architecture as Brand Communication, Birkhauser, Basel.

Brown, T. J. and Dacin, P. A. (1997) "The company and the product: Corporate associations and consumer product responses", Journal of Marketing, Vol. 61, No. 1, pp. 68–84.

Cummings, E. M. and Davies, P. T. (1994) Children and Marital Conflict: The Impact of Family Dispute and Resolution, Guilford, New York.

Dacin, P. and Brown, T. (2002) "Corporate Identity and Corporate Associations: A Framework for Future Research", Corporate Reputation Review, Vol. 5, Nos. 2/3, pp. 254–253.

Davis, M. C., Leach, D. J., and Clegg, C. W. (2010) "The physical environment of the office: contemporary and emerging issues", International Review of Industrial and Organisational Psychology, Vol. 26, No. 29, pp. 193–237.

Davis, T. R. V. (1984) "The influence of the physical environment in offices", Academy of Management Journal, Vol. 9, No. 2, pp. 271–283.

De Wit, B., and Meyer, R. (1998) Strategy, Process, Content and Context, 2nd ed. Thomson Learning, London.

Deshpande, R. (1983) "Paradigms lost: On Theory and method in research in marketing", The Journal of Marketing, Vol. 47 (Fall), pp. 101–110.

Downey, S. M. (1986) "The relationship between corporate culture and corporate identity", Public Relations Quarterly, Vol. 31, No. 4, pp. 7–12.

Duncan, T. and Moriarty, S. E. (1998) "A communication-based marketing model for managing relationships", Journal of Marketing, Vol. 62 (April), pp. 1–13.

Elsbach, K. and Bechky, B. (2007) "It's More than a desk: Working smarter through leveraged office design", California Management Review, Vol. 49, No. 2, pp. 80–101.

Elsbach, K. D. (2003) "Relating physical environment to self-categorizations: Identity threat and affirmation in a non-territorial office space", Administrative Science Quarterly, Vol. 48, pp. 622–654.

Fishbein, M. and Ajzen, I. (1975) Belief, Attitude, Intention, and Behavior, Addison-Wesley, Reading, MA.

Foroudi, M. M., Balmer, M. T., Chen, W., and Foroudi, P. (2019) "Corporate identity, place architecture, and identification: An exploratory case study", Qualitative Market Research: An International Journal, Vol. 109 (May), pp. 321–336.

Foroudi, M. M., Balmer, J. M., Chen, W., Foroudi, P., and Patsala, P. (2020) "Explicating place identity attitudes, place architecture attitudes, and identification triad theory", Journal of Business Research, Vol. 109 (March), pp. 321–336.

Fritz, J. M. H., Arnett, R. C., and Conkel, M. (1999) "Organisational ethical standards and organisational commitment", Journal of Business Ethics, Vol. 20, No. 4, pp. 289–299.

Kennedy, S. H. (1977) "Nurturing corporate images", European Journal of Marketing, Vol. 11, No. 3, pp. 120–164.

Kioussi, S. (2008) Quality Design, Construction and Development Enterprises: Exploring the Model and Marketing Strategies for Integration, Report, UCL, London.

Kirby, A. E. and Kent, A. M. (2010) "Architecture as brand: Store design and brand identity", Journal of Product & Brand Management, Vol. 19, No. 6, pp. 432–439.

Knight, C. and Haslam, S. A. (2010) "Your place or mine? Organisational identification and comfort as mediators of relationships between the managerial control of workspace and employees' satisfaction and well-being", British Journal of Management, Vol. 21, pp. 717–735.

LeBlanc, G. and Nguyen, N. (1996) "Cues used by customers evaluating corporate image in service firms: An empirical study in financial institutions", International Journal of Service Industry Management, Vol. 7, No. 2, pp. 44–56.

Ledford, J., Wendenhof, J., and Strahley, J. (1995) "Realising a corporate philosophy", Organisational Dynamics, Vol. 23, pp. 5–19.

Levin, M. L. (2000) "Vision revisited", The Journal of Applied Behavioural Science, Vol. 36, No. 1, pp. 91–107.

Marin, L. and Riuz de Maya, S. (2013) "The role of affiliation, attractiveness and personal connection in consumer-company identification", European Journal of Marketing, Vol. 47, No 3–4, pp. 655–673.

Markwick, N. and Fill, C. (1997) "Towards a framework for managing corporate identity", European Journal of Marketing, Vol. 31, Nos. 5/6, pp. 396–409.

McDonald, A. (2006) "The Ten Commandments revisited: The qualities of good library space", Liber Quarterly, Vol. 16, No. 2.

Melewar, T. C. and Karaosmanglu, E. (2006) "Seven dimensions of corporate identity: A categorisation from the practitioners' perspectives", European Journal of Marketing, Vol. 40, Nos. 7/8, pp. 846–869.

Melewar, T. C. (2003) "Determinants of the corporate identity construct: A review the literature", Journal of Marketing Communications, Vol. 9, No. 4, pp. 195–220.

Melewar, T. C. and Saunders, J. (1999) "International corporate visual identity: Standardisation or localisation?", Journal of International Business Studies, Vol. 30, No. 3, pp. 583–598.

Melewar, T. C., Bassett, K., and Simoes, C. (2006) "The role of communication and visual identity in modern organisations", Corporate Communications: An International Journal, Vol. 11, No. 2, pp. 138–147.

Nguyen, N. (2006) "The perceived image of service cooperatives: An investigation in Canada and Mexico", Corporate Reputation Review, Vol. 9, No. 1, pp. 62–78.

Northart, L. J. (1980) "Corporate identity is not a design problem", Public Relations Journal (November), pp. 28–36.

Parish, J. T., Berry, L. L., and Lam, S. Y. (2008) "The effect of the servicescape on service workers", Journal of Service Research, Vol. 10, No. 2, pp. 220–238.

Rooney, D., Paulsen, N., Callan, V. J., Brabant, M., Gallois, C., and Jones, E. (2010) "A new role for place identity in managing organisational change", Management Communication Quarterly, Vol. 24, No. 1, pp. 44–73.

Saleh, M. A. E. (1998) "Place identity: The visual image of Saudi Arabian cities", Habitat International, Vol. 22, No. 2, pp. 149–164.

Schmitt, B. H., Simonson, A., and Marcus, J. (1995) "Managing corporate image and identity", Long Range Planning, Vol. 28, No. 5, pp. 82–92.

Spencer, C. (2002) "Arkwright town rebuilt: But a sense of community lost", Social Psychological Review, Vol. 4, No. 2, pp. 23–24.

Thatcher, S. M. B. and Zhu, X. (2006) "Changing identities in a changing workplace: Identification, identity enactment, self-verification, and telecommuting", Academy of Management Review, Vol. 31, pp. 1076–1088.

Twigger-Ross, C. L., danUzzell, D. L. (1996) "Place and identity processes", Journal of Environmental Psychology, Vol. 16, pp. 205–220.

Vischer, J. C. (2007) "The effects of the physical environment on job performance: Towards a theoretical model of workplace stress", Stress and Health, Vol. 23, pp. 175–184.

Zinkhan, G. M. and Hirschheim, R. (1992) "Truth in marketing theory and research: An alternative perspective", Journal of Marketing, Vol. 56, No. 2, pp. 80–88.

PART IV
Corporate brand website design

8
CORPORATE BRAND WEBSITE DESIGN MANAGEMENT

Pantea Foroudi, Mohammad Mahdi Foroudi, and Elena Ageeva

Introduction

Chapter 8 explains the philosophical understanding of corporate brand website design management, the key components, and antecedents. From the research into corporate brand website designs and corporate image sense that a favourable corporate brand website design has desirable organisational outcomes. A favourable corporate brand website design is a strong company tool to show its corporate identity, an avenue to improve the company's image and reputation, leading to the enhancement of company identification, as well as to create consumer's loyalty. Thus, corporate brand website design represents a key segment in corporate identity management.

Background to corporate brand website design management

Corporate brand website design is a part of the corporate identity, and is fundamental to corporate visual identity (Ageeva and Foroudi, 2019; Ageeva et al., 2019) and its effect on the economic performance of companies. The website, by showing the personality of the organisation, can impact viewers' opinions of the organisation and promote a positive image (Ageeva et al., 2019).

Marketing scholars (Ageeva and Foroudi, 2019; Ageeva et al., 2019; Gwinner and Swanson, 2003) claim that based on the notion of social identity, the organisation paradigm views an organisation as a social actor with enduring qualities, being distinctive and diverse to differentiate the company and the product to competitors. Well-organised corporate identity management improves a favourable attitude between companies' stakeholders (Ageeva and Foroudi, 2019; Ageeva et al., 2019; Foroudi et al., 2018). This paradigm focuses on the association between the organisation and stakeholders (corporate image) which can create reputation, loyalty, and identification. Exceptional corporate brand website design became very popular in order to receive competitive advantage, improve corporate image, increase reputation, enhance marketing communication, gain consumers' identification and loyalty, as well as to enable innovation (Ageeva and Foroudi, 2019; Ageeva et al., 2019; Foroudi et al., 2018).

Marketing research highlighted corporate brand website design as a valuable device to create more efficient cognitive responses. Marketing scholars (Alhudaithy and Kitchen, 2009) have divided website characteristics into two comprehensive groups: 'those that contribute to attractiveness, pleasure or fun (termed hedonic features) and those that contribute to usefulness or ease of use (termed utilitarian features)' (Alhudaithy and Kitchen, 2009, p. 59). These two broad categories can be explained as the features people desire to gain experiential benefits that contribute to pleasure (hedonic website use/features) or obtain functional benefits that contribute to ease of use (utility website use/features) (Alhudaithy and Kitchen, 2009).

Utilitarian features focus on the task, whereas hedonic features focus on the stimulation of sensory attributes (Cotte et al., 2006). Utilitarian and hedonic features come from marketing science where hedonic consumption represents consumer behaviour that is connected to fantasy and is multisensory, while utilitarian consumption is connected to practical human needs. Furthermore, utilitarian consumption focuses on the accomplishment of a determined result, which is normal in cognitive consumer behaviour. The combination of a website's features is based on the type of website and the goal for which it was created. In e-commerce, elements of hedonic and utilitarian consumption should both be adopted (Ageeva et al., 2019; Voss et al., 2003). However, in the banking industry it is believed that utility features are more important than hedonic features and should be kept to a minimum (Alhudaithy and Kitchen, 2009; Ndubisi and Sinti, 2006; Pollach, 2005), as 'hedonism is not a salient usage factor' (Ndubisi and Sinti, 2006, p. 24).

Corporate brand website design is a way for a company to transmit a reliable image to consumers (Ageeva and Foroudi, 2019; Ageeva et al., 2019; Foroudi et al., 2018). Also, a corporate brand website design forms a first impression that evokes positive and negative emotional reactions (Bruner and Kumar, 2000; Coyle and Thorson, 2001). Moreover, corporate brand website design can help the firm to create differentiation and gain competitive advantage (Brown, 1998), and contribute to improving customer relationships. According to Beatty et al. (2001), the website is recognised as a key point of contact between users and companies, without the need for a formal business relationship. The website is built to present the objectives and principles of the company and its activities and plays a crucial role in the organisation's representation to internal and external stakeholders.

The two main levels of studies on corporate identity and corporate image are recognised by Brown et al. (2006) as: (i) the organisation level, related to 'how an organisation creates enduring identity, distinctive to communicate to its stakeholders'; (ii) individual level examination which is related to how the organisation's stakeholders view the organisation. The second level is employed in the current research. According to Dowling (2001), communication activities of the company can be an effective tool to convey their corporate identity. As a means of corporate communication, a website should be built with care, as it constitutes a powerful interface for promoting corporate identity (Topalian, 2003) and for building relationships with its audience (Booth and Matic, 2011; Pollach, 2005). Companies spend significant time and money to design favourable visual identities (e.g., a website) that communicate the companies' identity, which impacts on stakeholders' perception (Olins, 1989).

Corporate identity refers to a company's marketing, behaviour, psychology, and sociology (Palmer and Bejou, 2006). The multi-disciplinary approach views corporate identity as obtained by companies. It is based on the policy or decision makers who decide how to communicate to the company's stakeholders and supports the company's uniqueness. The website of company, the core aspect of the company's corporate identity, should be managed by a multidisciplinary process in order to achieve a desirable and favourable image.

Several studies have focused on corporate brand website designs as an aspect to translate corporate identity, and its components have been the subject of enquiry, providing a significant domain of the literature (Ageeva and Foroudi, 2019; Ageeva et al., 2019; Foroudi et al., 2018; Pollach, 2003).

An internet revolution brought a phenomenon of corporate brand website designs as an effective tool to advance with corporate identity and create a relationship with the respective audience (Booth and Matic, 2011; Pollach, 2005). The literature discusses various consequences of corporate brand website designs, such as enhancing corporate images (Okazaki, 2006) and improving reputation (De Chernatony, 1999). In addition, a number of studies were conducted in this area regarding internet banking (Ageeva et al., 2019; Bravo et al., 2012). Based on the studies on marketing, there is limited comprehensive analysis on the impacts of corporate brand website design on users' perception towards the company website (image and reputation of the company), consumer identification, and loyalty (Ageeva and Foroudi, 2019; Ageeva et al., 2019; Foroudi et al., 2018; Hendricks, 2007; Tarafdar and Zhang, 2008).

Hong and Kim (2004) proposed to view the website as a building, as an artefact that people build in cyber space, instead of real space. They have common goals to provide consumers with appropriate interactions and user expectations are relevant for both. Ganguly et al. (2010) viewed websites in a similar way as Hong and Kim (2004), from the architecture perspective and divided it grouped into four design elements: content, structure, interaction, and presentation. 'This is analogous to the architecture perspective of website design' (Ganguly et al., 2010, p. 305).

Based on the definition by Dacin and Brown (2002), corporate image is the conceptual image people hold of the company (actual identity). Can a company's corporate brand website design communicate a corporate image? A company's corporate brand website design can communicate in a very subtle way. Websites are found to be an increasingly significant element of a company's integrated marketing communication (IMC) plans (Bellman and Rossiter, 2004). Corporate brand website design can also enhance the company's image (Bravo et al., 2009). Companies should realise the importance of the company website to control their stakeholders' perceptions. Corporate brand website designs have emerged as a crucial way for the company to show itself to all stakeholders, as a core aspect of the corporate visual identity (CVI) (Ageeva and Foroudi, 2019; Ageeva et al., 2019; Foroudi et al., 2018), and also a source of sharing information inter-organisationally and intra-organisationally (Tarafdar and Zhang, 2008). In addition, websites enable an organisation to create a mental picture in consumers' minds (Ageeva et al., 2019).

Graphic design scholars believe that a company's mission and values should reflect on the company's visual identity after special merger or acquisition. They have identified the significant responses to the visual characteristics of the website which will give the stakeholders a positive picture in order to show the individuality of the company (AbuGhazaleh et al., 2012). Scholars (Ageeva and Foroudi, 2019; Ageeva et al., 2019; Foroudi et al., 2018) recommended that the corporation's visual identity should be contemporary, fashionable, and modern.

Companies' brand websites allow businesses to express their companies socially desirable and control perception of their enterprise to customers. According to Osorio (2001), a website should be a more visible artefact for communicating with users. A corporate brand web design can generate diverse responses from its users and can generate reputation and image.

Businesses use websites along with other communication channels in order to establish their reputation. In the next sections, corporate brand website design and its elements are defined. The definition of corporate image, reputation, consumer–company identification, and loyalty are then illustrated.

Corporate brand website design favourability concept

To explore the phenomenon and evaluate the concept, the formation of relevant terminology is needed. Scholars (Beatty et al., 2001) have interchangeably adapted a variety of different terminologies as their meanings have overlapped, such as 'web site', 'site', 'web pages', 'website', 'brand website', 'corporate brand website design'. In this thesis the phrases 'corporate brand website design' and 'corporate brand website design favourability' are adopted and their application is the root of this thesis.

Researchers (Alhudaithy and Kitchen, 2009; Alsajjan and Dennis, 2010; Kesharwani and Bisht, 2012) have used different approaches to investigate corporate brand website designs. Some scholars (Alsajjan and Dennis, 2010; Kesharwani and Bisht, 2012) have used the information technology literature (IT), in particular, the technology acceptance model (TAM) or a defined version of TAM, to study corporate brand website designs due to the acceptance that new information technology remains a challenge for users. Davis (1989) established TAM as addition to the theory of reasoned action (TRA), grounded in the attitude–behaviour theory within cognitive psychology (Alsajjan and Dennis, 2010). According to Davis (1989), centered on TAM, the use of computer technologies by consumers is dependent on their psychological desire to utilise, which relies on their attitude; incorporating two values, such as perceived ease of use (PEOU) and perceived usefulness. Particularly in respect of internet banking, TAM has been used to construct models, such as the internet banking acceptance model (IBAM), which contends that perceived usefulness and perceived manageability influence attitudinal intention through subject norms and trust.

Another area of research into website characteristics can broadly be distinguished into people's desire to gain experiential benefits that contribute to pleasure (hedonic website use/ features) or obtain functional benefits that contribute to ease of use (utility website use/ features) (Alhudaithy and Kitchen, 2009). The concepts of utilitarianism and hedonism 'originate from the marketing field', whereby hedonic is described as 'those facets of consumer behaviour that relate to the multisensory, fantasy and emotive aspects of one's experience with products' (p. 30) and utilitarian consumption 'is driven by functional requirements and usually includes goods which are either functional or essential'. Therefore, utilitarian features focus on the task, whereas hedonic features are defined through individuals' desire for sensory stimulation (Cotte et al., 2006).

Furthermore, utilitarian consumption focuses on the accomplishment of defined results characteristic of cognitive customer behaviour. To review the studies on website features, according to the e-commerce literature, internet shopping combines utilitarian and hedonic elements (Babin et al., 1994; Voss et al., 2003). George and Kumar (2014) stated that internet banking is a result of e-commerce in the context of banking, where an attractive website is not the only requirement that is essential for success, but that electronic service quality is also a significant issue. However, several studies in the banking sector stated that utility features are more important than hedonic features (Alhudaithy and Kitchen, 2009; Pollach, 2005). This is supported by the study of Ndubisi and Sinti (2006), who found that banks should limit the hedonistic functionality of their internet banking (Alhudaithy and Kitchen, 2009), as 'hedonism is not a salient usage factor' (Ndubisi and Sinti, 2006, p. 24).

The preferred website management and formation is thus a crucial approach for the company's market performance (Foroudi et al., 2016). The company's website reflects the objectives and beliefs of the corporation and its activities and plays an integral role in introducing itself to internal and external stakeholders. The website design of the corporate brand is a core aspect of the corporate identity and therefore should be properly maintained (Opoku et al., 2006). While designing a website, organisations have some key challenges (Lin, 2013) to design and develop an efficient website to fulfil their customers' needs. A logical and easy-to-use website will decrease customers' likelihood of causing errors, while giving them a pleasing experience. Alhudaithy and Kitchen (2009) observed that 'websites offer the opportunity for marketers to utilise a wide assortment of cues, such as colours, images and sounds to attract consumers' (p. 58) and 'generate favourable attitudes', and that 'consumers linger on their favourite websites' (Koiso-Kanttila, 2005, p. 63).

A favourable website has to be practical while providing beneficial and useful data. Favourability reflects the optimistic overview of a customer towards the business and is linked to the audience's preferences. The favourability of a website for corporations giving them a pleasing experience customers favour the design of a corporate brand's website.

The elements of corporate brand website design favourability

There is a growing tendency for consumers to build a customised corporate website design to achieve a competitive advantage (Brown, 1998), enhance advanced marketing communication techniques, enhance customer relationships, lower expenses, innovate in terms of the company's corporate identity strategy reputation management, financial reporting, and increase loyalty and satisfaction (Santouridis et al., 2009). Findings have investigated website quality/dimensions/elements (Cyr, 2008), while others have looked at the adoption of technology, in particular, internet banking. The fundamentals are: (i) the degree of ease of use; (ii) reliability; (iii) appearance; (iv) communication; (v) incentive aspects; and (vi) customization, which can determine customer outcomes in terms of e-services and the implementation towards internet banking.

There are a large number of publications about information systems and websites that would enable users to define the potential factors of corporate brand website design. First, a number of publications discuss the notion of website characteristics. This body of work recognises a range of factors that result in effective website performance, positive attitudes towards the website, trust, satisfaction, and loyalty. This body of research identifies a variety of aspects that leads to successful website efficiency, positive attitudes concerning websites, trust, satisfaction, and loyalty. Tarafdar and Zhang (2008) have observed the most significant aspects of corporate brand website designs entail organising the information and data, accessibility of the website and technological characteristics (access speed, security, and availability). Cyr and Head (2013) researched the nature of website functionality and included aspects such as content, graphic design, and navigational design. In addition, researchers investigated the features of various websites, namely, customer satisfaction (Muylle et al., 2004), website consistency, convenience of use (Gefen and Straub, 2000), and content quality (Alba et al., 1997). The key features entail data and content of the organisation, website accessibility and its technical features (Ageeva et al., 2019a; 2019b; 2019c).

Database processing relates to an arrangement of the information on the website (Ganguly et al., 2010). According to Abels et al. (1997), the organisation of information entails of the general layout and the number of live hyperlinks. The information needs to be recent, easy to comprehend (McKinney et al., 2002), beneficial, and relevant for the website's content (Bruce, 1998; Davis et al., 1989). The home page should be the baseline to conduct the data analysis in order to investigate the availability of resources (Osorio, 2001). Another important characteristic of the website is ease of use (Foroudi et al., 2018; Ageeva and Foroudi, 2019). This, sometimes known as 'usability', can be described as the convenience with which the website is accessible (Doll et al., 1994; Nielsen, 2000). It can help users to accomplish their goal on the website (Agarwal and Venkatesh, 2002). Other essential characteristics of the website are its technical properties, which consist of security, availability, and speed of access (Tarafdar and Zhang, 2008). According to Keeney (1999), the continued use of websites by browsers depends on website availability. Security is guaranteed by validated and secure transactions. Speed of access, according to Rose et al. (1999), indicates how quickly the website can provide and show web pages. The argument here is that the website's characteristics are key factors in affecting the perception of the users, their experience, feelings, and attitudinal behaviour.

Second, a large body of research focuses on the adoption of technology, in particular with respect to adoption/online capabilities of internet banking. It was found that the design characteristics of internet banking sites impact on adoption. The results of this study suggest that attitudinal influences play an important part in the development of internet banking. Similarly, by examining the IBAM model, Alsajjan and Dennis (2010) found that the intention towards internet banking adoption is attitudinal. In addition, a connection has been found between website features and positive attitudes. Investigations that sought to identify the scope to CWF's design of a favourable corporate brand website established the value of variables, such as perceived usefulness and perceived ease of use, focused on TAM (and linked to satisfaction (Casalo et al., 2008; Santouridis et al., 2009). In addition, security has been highlighted as a key factor in internet banking.

Third, researchers have focused on the website as a part of the service quality, which indicates website quality as a multidimensional construct from a user perspective. According to Kim and Stoel (2004), 'every study assessing website quality that we have located provides some empirical evidence that website quality is a multidimensional construct. This is true whether website users or website designers evaluated the website or whether the site was selling or not' (p. 620). Scholars (Foroudi et al., 2018; Zhang and Von Dran, 2002) have documented many aspects of website quality. For instance: i) Aladwani and Palvia (2002) have established four categories of website quality: technological adequacy, information quality, personal content, and presentation; ii) Zhang and Von Dran (2002) explored website quality using 11 dimensions: cognitive outcomes, information content, enjoyment, privacy, visual appearance, user empowerment, technical support, navigation, organisation of information, impartiality, and credibility; iii) Barnes and Vigden (2001) have explored three categories of website quality: usability, information, and interaction; iv) Lin and Lu (2000) operationalised website quality into three dimensions: response time, system accessibility, and information quality; v) Liu and Arnett (2002) found four categories of website quality: quality of information and service, system use, playfulness, and system design quality; and vi) Lociano (2000) uncovered 12 categories of website quality for websites selling goods and services: tailored communication, informational fit-to-task, intuitive operations, trust, visual appeal, ease of understanding, response time, emotional appeal, innovativeness, relative advantage, consistent image, and online completeness.

O'Cass and Carlson (2012) defined website service quality 'as the evaluation process of the characteristics experienced by the consumer during the interaction between the firm and the customer via the web site interface' (p. 430).

The literature review of this study has led to the establishment of a conceptual framework which starts with a series of variables preceding the design of corporate brand websites and at the same time explains their findings. The constructs that are considered in this study are visual, navigation, usability, information, customisation, availability, security, customer service, perceived corporate social responsibility, website credibility, perceived corporate culture, corporate image, corporate brand website design favourability, corporate reputation, consumer–company identification, and loyalty. The next section covers the conceptual framework of the research and a number of hypotheses for further examination. These fundamental elements help to establish the brand identity by being converted into a physical result.

Navigation

Navigation of the website is a common construct mentioned by many scholars to link pages without misleading the user (Ageeva et al., 2018; Foroudi et al., 2016; Schoon and Cafolla, 2002). The navigation scheme that supports or prevents access to various sections on a website is identified by Gefen et al. (2000). Sundar et al. (2003) found that visitors' perspectives on the website correspond favourably to the number of connections and the design of navigation. According to Tarafdar and Zhang (2008), navigation design consists of the layout of the website elements (hyperlinks and tabs) and the way they are positioned. It is crucial for the website to have consistent navigation with appropriate labelling that clearly shows the destination of the user (Tovey, 1998).

The navigation construct was found to be an important element of website success and a core factor of website design (Sterne, 1995). Pollach (2005) concluded that: i) company managers should pay careful attention to the navigation on the website; ii) in particular, if a company 'wants to be associated with care for the environment, employee diversity, or cutting-edge research and development, it is well advised to make the corresponding sections accessible from the global menu or at least the home page'; iii) 'contextual navigation can be extremely useful, because it draws users' attention to related pages that may be buried somewhere in the web site'; and iv) 'the more pages a user sees the better for the company image, as they expose a user to a variety of topics, potentially ranging from social affairs and global citizenship to financial success, innovation, or quality' (p. 298). Similarly, the well-designed website that offers a strong navigation is highly linked to the overall perceptions about the organisation (Braddy et al., 2003; 2008).

Thus, if the navigation on the website is difficult to manage, it generates a negative impression towards the organisation as it is perceived that it shows how other practices and policies at the organisation are conducted. Drawing on this discussion, the focus is on how users can access the website and how these features can help users to navigate the website.

Visual

According to the literature, the visual aspects of the website, as a powerful force, are counted as fundamentals to a favourable corporate brand website design. According to Ganguly et al. (2010) and Garrett (2003), the visual elements of the website concern the graphical aspects (graphics, colours, pictures, and several font modes), which advance with the website's appearance and sensation. The visual design of the website is an important part of building a favourable corporate brand website design (Foroudi and Marvi, 2020). Scholars (Ekhaml, 1996; Nicotera, 1999) have emphasised the importance of elements of the visual design, such as colours, that are based on the function of the website (Nicotera, 1999), consistent typography and quality of images (Ekhaml, 1996). Correspondingly, elements, such as logo, colour, typeface, slogan, and name, are frequently stated by scholars (Bartholme and Melewar, 2011; Dowling, 1994) as corporate visual identity factors. Visual identity allows an organisation to be identifiable and noticeable by offering additional indicators for individuals to recognise an organisation. The visual identity elements are often tied to the uniformity of the overall vision and emotional response of the website (Garrett, 2003).

Indeed, the website's visual design covers the 'aesthetic beauty and the emotional appeal of the website' (Ganguly et al., 2010, p. 310). Cyr (2008) connected the visual design of the website to the 'overall enjoyment' of the user. According to researchers, the website's visual design concerns the culture and can result in trust (Cyr, 2008; Ganguly et al., 2010), and satisfaction (Cyr, 2008; Cyr and Head, 2013). Culture affects the website design choices (Ageeva et al., 2019a; 2019b), in particular, the colour is a common distinction among culture and implies different meanings (Cyr and Trevor-Smith, 2004). For example, Sun (2001) claimed that collectivist visitors (e.g., those from China) have a genuine passion for visuals whereas individualistic visitors favour a rational and systematic format of website pages. According to Cyr (2008), visual design is related to satisfaction and trust throughout all cultures (Canada, China, and Germany). The visual aspects of a website can be found in the way that the enterprise employs its 'visual art' and 'structural design' to build a website with the general look and feel of its customers (Cyr, 2008; Foroudi, 2019; 2020; Foroudi et al., 2016; 2020; Melewar et al., 2016)

Information

The design of information is among the crucial features of the website. The content design concerns both the knowledge which is provided on the web as well as how the material is structured (Ganguly et al., 2010; Foroudi et al., 2016; Melewar et al., 2016). It addresses the aspects of the web site and provides the user with correct or incorrect details regarding services or goods (Cyr, 2008). In addition, website information is associated with the assessment of alternatives with the business of interest (Ranganathan and Ganapathy, 2002).

From simple web browsers to interactive audio and video content, the collection of information has expanded dramatically and should be structured according to users' satisfaction. The concept of information can be a useful part of the design process of websites to instil trust amongst its users. Indeed, according to scholars (Ageeva and Foroudi, 2019; Cyr, 2008), information is characterised as a crucial move towards satisfaction. Likewise, Kim and Eom (2002) observed that information on the company website as well as goods and services would have a significant impact on the company's satisfaction. Researchers (Park and Stoel, 2005) indicated that additional information could contribute to greater purchase intention on the website. Additionally, Mithas et al. (2006) discovered that information on the website can lead to customer loyalty if information is relevant, current, and accurate. Moreover, in relation to culture and information on the website, 'a customer from a masculine culture will pay more importance to information design' (Ganguly et al., 2010, p. 310). In brief, information design is an essential aspect of a website, and therefore, it can constructively affect the design of a corporate brand website. The information reflects the nature of the content, its structure, and its importance to the website's objective.

Usability

Usability is another significant aspect of the website (Foroudi et al., 2016; Melewar et al., 2016). Usability is the key point that users use to determine their online environment. Donnelly (2001) claims that usability is the most critical consideration in the assessment of the website by its users. In fact, usability is crucial in reaching customers' satisfaction. In addition, the usability of the website will allow users to effectively accomplish their aim of accessing the website (Kim and Eom, 2002). Usability (Doll et al., 1994; Nielsen, 2000) or ease of use should be clarified with easier use of the website. In general, usability is related to ease use of the website, hence is considered to be a key factor in improving electronic commerce. Usability refers to the ease of the web, to the degree that it is intimidating, desirable, and enjoyable and to the effective use of multimedia. Basically, usability ensures that the website is intuitive and helps its users to easily locate what they are searching for (Lin, 2013). According to Casalo et al. (2008), usability includes: i) 'the ease of understanding the structure of a website, its functions, interface and the contents that can be observed by the user'; ii) 'simplicity of use of the website in its initial stages'; iii) 'the speed with which the users can find what they are looking for'; iv) 'the perceived ease of site navigation in terms of time required and action necessary in order to obtain the desired results'; and v) 'the ability of the users to control what they are doing, and where they are, at any given moment' (p. 326).

In addition, website usability would allow users to achieve their website related goals (Agarwal and Venkatesh, 2002). Moreover, usability will enhance the degree of trust as 'the ease of use of a computer system favours more complete learning and a greater capacity to infer how the system will act' and 'greater usability favours a better comprehension of the contents and tasks that the consumer must realise to achieve an objective (e.g., make an order)' (p. 2). Centered upon the above argument, in this research usability refers to the attempts necessary for using the website that helps the user to effectively control the system (Davis, 1989; Nielsen, 1994).

Customisation

The web is experiencing a transition whereby the value proposition rests on how customisable it is. The relevance of personalisation in the layout of the corporate brand website has been addressed. Researchers (Foroudi et al., 2016; Melewar et al., 2016; Srinivasan et al., 2002) widely adopted customisation constructs in their studies. Customisation is a company's desire to individualise its customer services and products. Customisation of the product and service will offer the business a market edge as a differentiation factor for greater customer satisfaction, although it affects the user's decisions as it makes it very challenging and too colloquial for enterprises to perform (Arora et al., 2008).

Tarafdar and Zhang (2008) identified the customisation of a website as one that is effectively tailored based on its users' need. Similarly, according to Fan et al. (2013), customisation is 'the ability of a web site to tailor products, services, and the transactional environment to individual customers' (p. 372). An updated and personalised website design, with successful use of visual elements, will result in greater loyalty and more positive attitudes toward the organisation. Moreover, specific attributes, such as personalised websites, have been found to favourably impact both customer reputations (Srinivasan et al., 2002) and e-loyalty.

Chang and Chen (2009) used customisation as a dimension of website quality, in line with convenience, character, and interactivity. Srinivasan et al. (2002), based on in-depth interviews, identified the '8Cs – customisation, contact interactivity, care, community, convenience, cultivation, choice, and character – that potentially impact e-loyalty' (p. 41). It was found by these authors that all the 8Cs, with the exception of convenience, have a major influence on e-loyalty. According to Srinivasan et al. (2002), customisation affects e-loyalty as 'customisation increases the probability that customers will find something that they wish to buy' and 'individuals are able to complete their transactions more efficiently when the site is customised' (p. 42). Next, these authors concluded that if a company can effectively narrow the choice for the individual by using customisation, it can make it appealing for the customer to visit the website again. Schrage (1999) pointed out that customisation provides an advantage for retailers as 'the web has clearly entered the phase where its value proposition is as contingent upon its abilities to permit customisation as it is upon the variety of content it offers' (p. 20). Also, Ostrom and Iacobucci (1995) stated that customisation can signal high quality. Therefore, the capability of a website to customise the goods, services and transaction environment for particular user is customisation.

Security

As access to the internet becomes easier, our society is gradually becoming dependant on the internet. In particular, consumers are concerned regarding their online security whilst accessing the internet to make a transaction. As a consequence, security is among the major features for users to evaluate the website in terms of the website being secure to use. According to Ranganathan and Ganapathy (2002) and Yoon (2010), due to the perceptions about financial online transactions and privacy risks, users remain cautious about online security despite the existence of technical advances (e.g., digital signature, cryptography, authentication). Findings on the notion of internet banking have highlighted the significance of security features. Security is implemented by offering authenticated and secure transactions to users (Ageeva et al., 2019a; Foroudi et al., 2018), and indicating the degree to which the website may be defined as 'secure' while meeting requirements for users to execute protected transactions.

A number of studies on internet banking mentioned that security is an important determinant, for example, the security of financial transactions and personal data (Durkin et al., 2008; Liao and Cheung, 2008). Yoon (2010) has studied the antecedents of customer satisfaction for the Chinese internet banking setting and discovered that security, design, speed, detailed information, and customer service have a major effect on customer satisfaction. This author noted that the more customers use internet banking, the less they are concerned about the issues of security and privacy. Wolfinbarger and Gilly (2003) implied that 'four factors – website design, fulfillment/reliability, privacy/security and customer service – are strongly predictive of customer judgments of quality and satisfaction, customer loyalty and attitudes toward the website' (p. 183). This is consistent with Szymanski and Hise (2000), who claimed that convenience, merchandising, website design, and financial stability will influence consumers' satisfaction. Based on the discussion above, security reflects the extent to which the website can be seen as secure and has the required provisions for the operation of secure transactions.

Availability

It has become essential for users to be in charge on the website, therefore, making availability one of the main considerations. The significance of the availability feature on the website was addressed by Tarafdar and Zhang (2008). System availability is defined as 'the correct technical functioning of the site' (Alwi and Ismail, 2013, p. 562). Additionally, authors (Foroudi and Marvi, 2020; Tarafdar and Zhang, 2008) have also identified availability as how conveniently a website can be accessed by its users. Accessibility or availability to the website is critical for users to continue to use the site.

Website designers should consider that 'adding a lot of active elements to the website, for example, can affect the speed and influence website performance' and 'inadequate infrastructure in terms of server capacity can impair the availability of the website' (Tarafdar and Zhang, 2008, p. 22); this can irritate consumers and they might leave the website. The website transaction speed or response time is widely discussed as a significant factor for commercial website evaluations (Aladwani and Palvia, 2002) and customer satisfaction with information systems (Yoon, 2010). According to Liao and Cheung (2002), consumers are highly sensitive to the speed of service delivery. Based on the aforementioned statement, availability is the right technical output of the website.

Website credibility

The credibility of the website is how customers perceive the expertise and trustworthiness of the website. The credibility of online communication and information has been a big concern since the advent of the internet. The need for a comprehensive understanding of online credibility is growing throughout social media and user generated content. The credibility of the website is seen by users as a significant factor in the quality and information provided on the website. The credibility of websites will therefore impact the opinions, perceptions, and behaviour of users.

The concept of credibility can be defined as the extent to which users believe that the website is reliable and trustworthy (Metzger et al., 2003). Scholars (Metzger et al., 2003; Stamm and Dube, 1994) have argued that the aspects of credibility can vary depending on the choice of source and the context. The term credibility comes from the credibility of public speakers based on the skills and trustworthiness of the speakers (Lowery and DeFleur, 1995). Rhetoricians (Boyd, 2008; Warnick, 2004) employed the 'ethos' terminology to clarify the way the subjective quality of credibility evaluation (also known as trustworthiness) is mainly created by the message receiver. While the question of credibility has been a concern since the period of Aristotle, recent technical advancement has drawn new attention to this issue, particular with regards to website credibility.

Credibility of the website is the extent to which users perceive the website's trustworthiness and expertise. It is of paramount importance for consumers to believe that the website is credible. Investigating the credibility of a website is crucial for users, especially for information seekers. As Fogg et al. (2001) pointed out, the website should mention the credentials of the owners and team. Pollach (2005) stated that by implementing multiple persuasive appeals such as evidence from third parties, numbers and humanisation, the credibility of company communications can be improved; moreover, firms can substantiate their statements. Rains and Karmikel (2009) considered that the following features on the website constitute the credibility of the website: i) stable structural characteristics (privacy policy, third-party endorsements); and ii) information (external references, statistics, testimonials).

Customer service

Customers are at the centre of academia and practice, especially in today's technology-driven environment. It is important to define and satisfy the needs and desires of the customer in order to create a company–customer partnership. In an online world, consumers prioritise convenience (Meuter et al., 2000), and expect more productivity and power. Parasuraman et al. (2005) claimed that website administrators have to determine the user's online customer service experience in order to be able to deliver greater service levels.

In the website quality literature, the notion of customer service is considered to be a part of service quality. Indeed, 'customer support services can be regarded as the responsiveness dimension of service quality' (Yoon, 2010, p. 1298). Scholars (Jun and Cai, 2001; Liao and Cheung, 2008) have empirically investigated responsiveness as a determining factor of the quality of internet banking services. Parasuraman et al. (2005) expressed customer service in terms of the contact, responsiveness, and compensation dimensions. Customer service can be referred to as the level of efficiency of the service offered to users online and offline. Joseph and Stone (2003) have defined customer service as the willingness of the customer to provide input and to address issues and complaints in order to resolve them.

A number of scholars (Francis and White, 2002; Vila and Kuster, 2011; Yoon, 2010) have used the term 'customer service' in their studies. Francis and White (2002) used the customer service construct as one of the dimensions to measure 'perceived internet retailing quality (PIRQUAL)', together with website store functionality, product attribute description, ownership conditions, delivery, and security. Yoon (2010) analysed the context of customer satisfaction in China regarding internet banking and found that customer services have a major effect on customer satisfaction, in accordance with security design, speed, and information quality. Vila and Kuster (2011) regarded customer service, website security, information content, and usability as the four concepts to evaluate the impact on purchase intention and the effectiveness of the website. According to Parasuraman et al. (2005), online self-service and associated face-to-face services are likely to be linked to the basis of the service effectiveness by users. Based on the discussion above, customer service is the degree to which the service provided to customers is efficient, helpful, and willing.

Perceived corporate social responsibility

Corporate social responsibility (CSR) is fundamental in the current business environment. Across the world, companies employ their websites to display their CSR activities (Maignan and Ralston, 2002). Websites are an official means for businesses to introduce themselves as they wish to be perceived by an extensive number of stakeholders (Bondy et al., 2004), and thus, the distribution of information has become a particular process. CSR is a consumer understanding of corporate environmental responsibility, where business is involved, towards others in the society (Holloway, 2004; Klein and Dawar, 2004). CSR activities show the identity of the company, which enables stakeholders to identify with the company due to the intercept of their own identities with that of the company (Maignan and Ferrell, 2004; Sen and Bhattacharya, 2001). Chapple and Moon (2005) stated that:

CSR as a component of business–society relations is manifest in a variety of indicators within companies (e.g., staff, processes, codes and budgets devoted to CSR); corporate communications (e.g., Web site reporting, free–standing CSR reports, corporate branding); core stakeholder demands from consumers, employees, and investors; and wider stakeholder demands and pressure from nongovernmental organisations (NGOs), the media, and governmental organisations.

p. 417

The notion of CSR goes back to at least the 1930s. According to Glavas and Kelley (2014), CSR holds meaning around the 'societal norms and expectations of corporations'.

A number of studies (e.g., Basil and Erlandson, 2008) highlighted the importance of consumers' perception of the CSR activities of companies. CSR is a crucial prerequisite in the business environment which consumers support and demand. Basil and Erlandson (2008) emphasised that it is no longer sufficient for companies to just act in a socially responsible manner, and that it is crucial to communicate the social responsibility activities of companies to the stakeholders in order that they are recognised for them accordingly. According to Basil and Erlandson (2008), in their study of CSR activities on companies' websites, 'websites can contain both what the company is actually doing in terms of CSR, and what the company wants the public to perceive it is doing in terms of CSR' (p. 130). In addition, they noted that 'publicly presenting socially responsible internal policies enhances success' (p. 135). To communicate social responsibility activities, it is best to employ the company's website, as it is targeted at a wide variety of stakeholders (Esrock and Leichty, 2000). Therefore, in this research, the understanding of CSR by consumers is the perception of corporate environmental responsibility, social engagement, responsiveness, and accountability of corporations.

Perceived corporate culture

Corporate culture is regularly expressed throughout the corporation's website. The nature and details of the website concerning organisational values, strategies, rewards, and priorities does have an impact on users' expectations. According to Overbeeke and Snizek (2005), 'the information found in corporate websites enables one to unmask important differences and similarities in corporate culture across industries and geopolitical boundaries' (p. 349). They conducted a study of 'website and corporate culture' across the websites of 12 multinational corporations in two distinct industry sectors: i) food services; and ii) pharmaceuticals and concluded that all 12 companies portray themselves as informed and responsible business owners on their websites.

Perceived organisational culture is a user's understanding of a corporation's values, attitudes, and actions based on corporate identity (Foroudi and Foroudi, 2020; Foroudi et al., 2017; 2020; Melewar et al., 2018; 2020). The corporate culture is the organisation's core values and a part of corporate identity (Bernstein, 1986; Melewar, 2003). Similarly, Dowling (1986) defines corporate culture as a corporation's shared values, behaviour, beliefs, labelled as the 'what' of a company (Melewar, 2003). Furthermore, culture plays a key role in improving corporate identity (Kiriakidou and Millward, 2000; Melewar, 2003). In addition, corporate identity is the source of corporate culture and identity is the 'why' of a company (Dowling, 1986; Melewar, 2003). In addition, corporate culture relates to the values and the vision of the company's founder and management board.

Overbeeke and Snizek (2005) stated that:

> by studying the externally communicated culture of a company, researchers are no longer dependent on access to employee feedback or company documents to analyse a company's culture. Rather, researchers may now access corporate web sites with impunity, making whatever comparisons across or within companies they deem worthwhile or interesting.
>
> *p. 347*

Nowadays companies often use corporate brand website designs to communicate their company's culture (Ageeva and Foroudi, 2019).

Drawing on the discussion above, perceived corporate culture is the understanding of customers regarding corporate values, the founder of the company, corporate history, corporate philosophy, corporate mission, country of origin, corporate principles, and the company's subdivisions running and developing through corporate identity. The components of the perceived corporate culture are defined as follows: i) corporate values is represented by the values of an organisation, which can be defined as a core system of convictions within an organisation that forms the identity of the company; ii) corporate philosophy is a synthesis of the basic beliefs and norms of an enterprise that forms the corporate culture, which reflects the organisation's objectives to establish further strong relationships; iii) corporate mission is the reason why the organisation exists and the purpose that differentiates it from its competitors; iv) corporate principles outline and clarify the organisation's ideals, goals, and purpose which form the basis of all corporate activities; v) corporate history is a retrospective record of the company's formation and commercial activities which shapes corporate identity by its relation with corporate culture; vi) the company's founder is an individual who founded the company, making it indistinguishable from the company's identity; vii) the country of origin is identified as the country where the company headquarters is based, which can affect the quality of the product or brand, brand loyalty, brand choice, brand preference perceived by users and which has a close bond with the company's corporate identity (Foroudi et al., 2019); and viii) the company's subculture refers to a particular group within the organisation, comprising of subsets of organisational participants who communicate frequently with each other, using a shared form of thought that is exclusive to the group.

Conclusion

Chapter 8 provides the significant body of literature focusing attention on favourable corporate brand website design. Current theoretical investigation of corporate brand website designs refers to this phenomenon as a powerful way for organisations to communicate with consumers and represents an important element of corporate identity management that helps to develop an image of itself in the user's mind. Grounded in the literature review, this research developed the notion of corporate brand website design favourability as the degree to which an organisation develops its corporate identity through corporate brand website design, as a fundamental of corporate visual identity, to gain positive attitudes from the users, by diffusing consistent images and messages regarding the environment of the organisation to an organisation's potential users by enabling the organisation to create a positive image of itself in the user's mind.

CASE STUDY – E-COMMERCE AND DISCOUNTING DYNAMICS DESIGN

Pierluigi Vitale, University of Salerno, Italy

One of the main promotion strategies for online stores is the coupon code application. Almost all the e-commerce websites provide this function, with different web-design strategies. The route to order placing is quite different and it tells us about stores' different approaches. In this case study, we observe a comparison between two Chinese e-commerce websites compared with the top one: Amazon.

In the last five years, the Chinese tech market has increased in volume more and more and e-commerce sites have adapted their structure and their contents very rapidly. Translations are more efficient and web design is more similar to that of occidental online stores. For sure, they apply a price competition strategy. On one hand, they push their affiliate programmes, with interesting commissions for the users and networks that offer their products (5% to 10% according to the sector). On the other hand, they have several agreements with many *deals* publishers, which circulate their competitive prices online through coupon codes with short expiry dates. Observing the cart functions of three emblematic e-commerce sites – Gearbest, Edwaybuy, and Amazon – it is possible to read their needs and design strategy to gain sales. Amazon is a leader in this market, with 280.5 billion dollars in revenue; Gearbest is one of the main Chinese e-commerce sites, part of the holding Global Top E-Commerce Co Ltd, in the tech field, with 3,892.07 billion dollars in revenue; Edwaybuy is an emerging Chinese online store.

In the buying process, observing the three interfaces, it is possible to notice that the box: *Apply the coupon* is positioned at different stages. On Amazon, entry of the code comes at the final stage, after the selection of the payment method and before the last action: *Place the order*. On Gearbest, it is possible to apply the code only after the login step, so the subscription (and the data release and treatment) is mandatory.

On Edwaybuy it is possible to apply the code directly in the cart, with the chance to place the order without any registration to the platform. These three circumstances are readable as the three different stages of maturity of the three stores and their relevance in the market. Amazon is a top leader and has a huge reputation, that leads users to prefer the platform for the quality of the service, from the speed of the delivery to the customer relationship management. Prices are not always the cheapest online, and the interface suggests that the discount is not a key choice for purchases on Amazon.

In the comparison between Gearbest and Edwaybuy, it is possible to read the different stages of maturity in the same market: Chinese stores for occidental customers. Gearbest has a long tradition and several advertising strategies founded on data management. The store applies retargeting strategies through the main advertising platforms: Google and Facebook. To do this, it is necessary to collect a huge amount of data, letting the people receive a discount in change. Edwaybuy is certainly the smallest in this benchmarking. The store provides a good service and good prices (faster than Gearbest in terms of delivery, cheaper than Amazon) but in its launch phase, sales seems to be more fundamental than the data, so they decided to reduce the purchase path through coupons in order to conclude the transaction.

Finally, we can assume that in the lifecycle of the stores, from the introduction to maturity, the discount dynamics in the interface are directly related to the stage, with the secondary observation that this should also be related to the data relevance in the platform's strategies.

Case questions

1. Explain the purchase process of the three stores.
2. Compare the web design of Amazon and Gearbest.

References

www.amazon.it/
www.edwaybuy.com/
https://it.gearbest.com/

Key terms and definitions

Availability is the correct technical performance of the website.

Company's subculture refers to the distinct group within that company, which consists of the subsets of organisational members who interact regularly with one another employing a common way of thinking that is unique to the group.

Corporate brand website design favourability is the extent to which a company projects its corporate identity, through corporate brand website design, as a primary vehicle of corporate visual identity, to gain positive attitudes from the consumers by transmitting consistent images and messages about the nature of the organisation to a company's audience, which enables a company to build a positive image of itself in the consumer's mind.

Corporate history represents a chronological account of a company's creation and business activities, which influences corporate identity through its connection with the corporate culture.

Corporate mission is the reason why the organisation exists and the purpose that differentiates it from its competitors.

Corporate philosophy is a combination of the main values and norms of the organisation that form its corporate culture, which represents the intention of the company to help to build more meaningful relationships.

Corporate principles represent the materialisation and clarification of the values, targets, and mission of the organisation, which construct the foundation for all corporate activities.

Corporate social responsibility is the consumers' perceptions of corporate environmental responsibility, which includes the social involvement, responsiveness, and accountability of companies, and consumers' expectations of corporations.

Corporate values are characterised by the values of the company that can be identified as a central system of beliefs inside the company, which shape the corporate identity.

Country of origin is defined as the country where the corporate headquarters of the company marketing the product or brand is located, which can influence the quality of the brand perceived by customers, brand loyalty, brand choice, brand preference perceived by customers, and has a strong link with the corporate identity of the company.

Customer service is the degree to which the service provided to customers is efficient, helpful, and willing.

Customisation is the ability of a website to tailor products, services, and the transactional environment to individual customers.

Founder of the company represents the person who brought the company into existence, which makes them inseparable from the identity of the company.

Information on the website refers to the quality of the content, the way it is arranged, and how relevant it is to the purpose of the website.

Navigation is the extent to which users can navigate the website and represents those characteristics that help users navigate the website better.

Perceived corporate culture is the consumers' perceptions about the corporate values, corporate philosophy, corporate mission, corporate principles, corporate history, founder of the company, country of origin, and company's subculture running and resulting from the corporate identity.

Security refers to the degree to which the website can be perceived as safe and has the necessary provisions for executing secure transactions.

Usability refers to the effort required to use the website, with which the user is capable of learning to manage the system with ease.

Visual impact is the extent to which the company uses their 'graphic design' and 'structure design' to create the overall look and feel of the website for users.

Website credibility is the degree to which consumers believe in the website's expertise and trustworthiness.

Acknowledgement

Many thanks to Helnaz Ahmadi Lari for editing the chapter.

References

Abels, E. G., Domas White, M., and Hahn, K. (1997). Identifying user-based criteria for Web pages. Internet Research, 7(4), 252–262.

AbuGhazaleh, N. M., Al-Hares, O. M., and Haddad, A. E. (2012). The value relevance of goodwill impairments: UK evidence. International Journal of Economics and Finance, 4(4).

Agarwal, R. and Venkatesh, V. (2002). Assessing a firm's web presence: A heuristic evaluation procedure for the measurement of usability. Information Systems Research, 13(2), 168–186.

Ageeva, E. and Foroudi, P. (2019). Examining the destination website: A case of Visit Tatarstan, Place Branding: Connecting Tourist Experiences to Places, Edited by Foroudi, P., Mauri, C., Dennis, C., and Melewar, T. C., Routledge, London.

Ageeva, E., Foroudi, P., Melewar, T. C., Nguyen, B., and Dennis, C. (2019a). A holistic framework of corporate website favourability. Corporate Reputation Review, 21 (Sep), 1–14.

Ageeva, E., Melewar, T. C., Foroudi, P., and Dennis, C. (2019b). Evaluating the factors of corporate website favorability: A case of UK and Russia. Qualitative Market Research: An International Journal. 22(5), 687–715.

Ageeva, E., Melewar, T. C., Foroudi, P., and Dennis, C. (2019c). Cues adopted by consumers in examining corporate website favorability: An empirical study of financial institutions in the UK and Russia. Journal of Business Research, 98 (May), 15–32.

Ageeva, E., Melewar, T. C., Foroudi, P., Dennis, C., and Jin, Z. (2018). Examining the influence of corporate website favorability on corporate image and corporate reputation: Findings from fsQCA. Journal of Business Research, 89 (Aug), 287–304.

Aladwani, A. M. and Palvia, P. C. (2002). Developing and validating an instrument for measuring user-perceived web quality. Information and Management, 39(6), 467–476.

Alhudaithy, A. I. and Kitchen, P. J. (2009). Rethinking models of technology adoption for internet banking: The role of website features. Journal of Financial Services Marketing, 14(1), 56–69.

Alsajjan, B. and Dennis, C. (2010). Internet banking acceptance model: Cross-market examination. Journal of Business Research, 63(9), 957–963.

Alwi, S. and Ismail, S. (2013). A framework to attain brand promise in an online setting. Marketing Intelligence and Planning, 31(5), 557–578.

Arora, N., Dreze, X., Ghose, A., Hess, J. D., Iyengar, R., Jing, B., … and Sajeesh, S. (2008). Putting one-to-one marketing to work: Personalization, customization, and choice. Marketing Letters, 19(3–4), 305–321.

Babin, B. J., Darden, W. R., and Griffin, M. (1994). Work and/or fun: Measuring hedonic and utilitarian shopping value. Journal of Consumer Research, 20(4), 644–656.

Barnes, S. J., and Vidgen, R. (2001). An evaluation of cyber-bookshops: The WebQual method. International Journal of Electronic Commerce, 6(1), 11–30.

Bartholme, R. H. and Melewar, T. C. (2011). Remodelling the corporate visual identity construct: A reference to the sensory and auditory dimension. Corporate Communications: An International Journal, 16(1), 53–64.

Basil, D. Z. and Erlandson, J. (2008). Corporate social responsibility website representations: A longitudinal study of internal and external self-presentations. Journal of Marketing Communications, 14(2), 125–137.

Beatty, R. C., Shim, J. P., and Jones, M. C. (2001). Factors influencing corporate web site adoption: A time-based assessment. Information and management, 38(6), 337–354.

Bellman, S. and Rossiter, J. R. (2004). The website schema. Journal of Interactive Advertising, 4(2), 38–48.

Bernstein, D. (1986). Company Image and Reality: A Critique of Corporate Communications. Cassell Educational Ltd, London.

Bondy, K., Matten, D., and Moon, J. (2004). The adoption of voluntary codes of conduct in MNCs: A three-country comparative study. Business and Society Review, 109(4), 449–477.

Booth, N. and Matic, J. A. (2011). Mapping and leveraging influencers in social media to shape corporate brand perceptions. Corporate Communications: An International Journal, 16(3), 184–191.

Boyd, D. M. (2008). Taken Out of Context: American Teen Sociality in Networked Publics. ProQuest, Ann Arbor, MI.

Braddy, P. W., Meade, A. W., and Kroustalis, C. M. (2008). Online recruiting: The effects of organisational familiarity, website usability, and website attractiveness on viewers' impressions of organisations. Computers in Human Behavior, 24(6), 2992–3001.

Braddy, P. W., Thompson, L. F., Wuensch, K. L., and Grossnickle, W. F. (2003). Internet recruiting: The effects of web page design features. Social Science Computer Review, 21(3), 374–385.

Bravo, R., Matute, J., and Pina, J. M. (2012). Corporate social responsibility as a vehicle to reveal the corporate identity: A study focused on the websites of Spanish financial entities. Journal of Business Ethics, 107(2), 129–146.

Bravo, R., Montaner, T., and Pina, J. M. (2009). The role of bank image for customers versus non-customers. International Journal of Bank Marketing, 27(4), 315–334.

Brown, T. J. (1998). Corporate associations in marketing: Antecedents and consequences. Corporate Reputation Review, 1(3), 215–233.

Brown, T. J., Dacin, P. A., Pratt, M. G., and Whetten, D. A. (2006). Identity, intended image, construed image, and reputation: An interdisciplinary framework and suggested terminology. Journal of the Academy of Marketing Science, 34(2), 99–106.

Bruce, H. (1998). User satisfaction with information seeking on the internet. Journal of the American Society for Information Science, 49(6), 541–556.

Bruner, G. C. and Kumar, A. (2000). Web commercials and advertising hierarchy-of-effects. Journal of Advertising Research, 40(1–2), 35–42.
Casalo, L. V., Flavian, C., and Guinaliu, M. (2008). The role of satisfaction and website usability in developing customer loyalty and positive word-of-mouth in the e-banking services. International Journal of Bank Marketing, 26(6), 399–417.
Chang, H. H. and Chen, S. W. (2009). Consumer perception of interface quality, security, and loyalty in electronic commerce. Information and Management, 46(7), 411–417.
Chapple, W. and Moon, J. (2005). Corporate social responsibility (CSR) in Asia: A seven-country study of CSR web site reporting. Business and society, 44(4), 415–441.
Cotte, P. and Dupraz, D. (2006, January). Spectral imaging of Leonardo Da Vinci's Mona Lisa: A true color smile without the influence of aged varnish. In Conference on Colour in Graphics, Imaging, and Vision (Vol. 2006, No. 1, pp. 311–317). Society for Imaging Science and Technology.
Coyle, J. R. and Thorson, E. (2001). The effects of progressive levels of interactivity and vividness in web marketing sites. Journal of Advertising, 30(3), 65–77.
Cyr, D. (2008). Modeling web site design across cultures: relationships to trust, satisfaction, and e-loyalty. Journal of Management Information Systems, 24(4), 47–72.
Cyr, D. and Head, M. (2013). Website design in an international context: The role of gender in masculine versus feminine oriented countries. Computers in Human Behavior, 29(4), 1358–1367.
Cyr, D. and Trevor-Smith, H. (2004). Localization of web design: An empirical comparison of German, Japanese, and United States web site characteristics. Journal of the American Society for Information Science and Technology, 55(13), 1199–1208.
Dacin, P. A. and Brown, T. J. (2002). Corporate identity and corporate associations: A framework for future research. Corporate Reputation Review, 5(2–3), 254–263.
Davis, F. D. (1989). Perceived usefulness, perceived ease of use, and user acceptance of information technology. MIS Quarterly, 319–340.
Davis, F. D., Bagozzi, R. P., and Warshaw, P. R. (1989). User acceptance of computer technology: A comparison of two theoretical models. Management Science, 35(8), 982–1003.
De Chernatony, L. (1999). Brand management through narrowing the gap between brand identity and brand reputation. Journal of Marketing Management, 15(1–3), 157–179.
Doll, W. J., Xia, W., and Torkzadeh, G. (1994). A confirmatory factor analysis of the end-user computing satisfaction instrument. MIS Quarterly, 453–461.
Donnelly, V. (2001). Designing easy-to-use websites: A hands-on approach to structuring successful websites. Addison-Wesley Longman Publishing Co., Inc, London.
Dowling, G. R. (1986). Managing your corporate images. Industrial Marketing Management, 15(2), 109–115.
Dowling, G. R. (1994). Corporate Reputations: Strategies for Developing the Corporate Brand. Kogan Page, London.
Dowling, G. R. (2001). Creating Corporate Reputations. Oxford University Press, Oxford.
Durkin, M., Jennings, D., Mulholland, G., and Worthington, S. (2008). Key influencers and inhibitors on adoption of the internet for banking. Journal of Retailing and Consumer Services, 15(5), 348–357.
Ekhaml, L. T. (1996). Make your presence known on the web! Tips for writing and publishing web documents. School Library Media Activities Monthly, 12(10), 33–35.
Esrock, S. L. and Leichty, G. B. (2000). Organisation of corporate web pages: Publics and functions. Public Relations Review, 26(3), 327–344.
Fan, Q., Yul Lee, J., and Kim, J. (2013). The impact of web site quality on flow-related online shopping behaviors in C2C e-marketplaces: A cross-national study. Managing Service Quality: An International Journal, 23(5), 364–387.
Fogg, B. J., Marshall, J., Kameda, T., Solomon, J., Rangnekar, A., Boyd, J., and Brown, B. (2001). Web credibility research: a method for online experiments and early study results. In CHI'01 extended abstracts on Human factors in computing systems (pp. 295–296). ACM.
Foroudi, M. M. and Foroudi, P. (2020). Corporate Identity: Definition and Component, Building Corporate Identity, Image and Reputation in the Digital Era, edited by Melewar, T. C., Dennis, C., and Foroudi, P. Routledge, London.

Foroudi, P. (2019). Influence of brand signature, brand awareness, brand attitude, brand reputation on hotel industry's brand performance. International Journal of Hospitality Management, 76 (Jan), 271–285.

Foroudi, P. (2020). Corporate brand strategy: Drivers and outcomes of corporate brand orientation. International Marketing, International Journal of Hospitality Management, 88 (July), 1–14.

Foroudi, P. and Marvi, R. (2020). Some like it hot: The role of identity, website, co-creation behavior on identification and love. European Journal of International Management.

Foroudi, P., Akarsu, T. N., Ageeva, E., Foroudi, M. M., Dennis, C., and Melewar, T. C. (2018). Promising the dream: Changing destination image of London through the effect of website place. Journal of Business Research, 83, 97–110.

Foroudi, P., Cuomo, M. T., Foroudi, M. M., Katsikeas, C. S., and Gupta, S. (2020). Linking identity and heritage with image and a reputation for competition. Journal of Business Research, 113 (May), 317–325.

Foroudi, P., Dinnie, K., Kitchen, P. J., Melewar, T. C., and Foroudi, M. M. (2016). IMC antecedents and the consequences of planned brand identity in higher education. European Journal of Marketing, 51(3), 528–550.

Foroudi, P., Gupta, S., and Melewar, T. C. (2017). Corporate logo. History, Definition, and Component, International Studies of Management and Organization, 47(2), 176–196.

Foroudi, P., Marvi, R., and Amiri, N. S. (2019). Love is the Bridge Between You and Everything: Relationships of Identity, Experience, and Benevolence to Travelers' Loyalty and Willingness to Purchase, Strategizing in the Fourth Industrial Revolution: Transforming hospitality and tourism, edited by Tajeddini, K., Ratten, V., and Merkle, T., Routledge, London.

Francis, J. E. and White, L. (2002). PIRQUAL: A scale for measuring customer expectations and perceptions of quality in Internet retailing, edited by Evans, K. and Scheer, L., 263–270.

Ganguly, B., Dash, S. B., Cyr, D., and Head, M. (2010). The effects of website design on purchase intention in online shopping: The mediating role of trust and the moderating role of culture. International Journal of Electronic Business, 8(4–5), 302–330.

Garrett, J. J. (2003). The Elements of user Experience: User-Centered Design for the Web, New Riders, Indianapolis, IN.

Gefen, D. and Straub, D. W. (2000). The relative importance of perceived ease of use in IS adoption: A study of e-commerce adoption. Journal of the Association for Information Systems, 1(1), 8.

George, A. and Kumar, G. G. (2014). Impact of service quality dimensions in internet banking on customer satisfaction. Decision, 41(1), 73–85.

Glavas, A. and Kelley, K. (2014). The effects of perceived corporate social responsibility on employee attitudes. Business Ethics Quarterly, 24(2), 165–202.

Gwinner, K. and Swanson, S. R. (2003). A model of fan identification: Antecedents and sponsorship outcomes. Journal of Services Marketing, 17(3), 275–294.

Hendricks, A. (2007). Webmasters, web policies, and academic libraries: A survey. Library Hi Tech, 25(1), 136–146.

Holloway, J. C. (2004). Marketing for Tourism. Pearson Education, London.

Hong, S., and Kim, J. (2004). Architectural criteria for website evaluation–conceptual framework and empirical validation. Behaviour and Information Technology, 23(5), 337–357.

Joseph, M. and Stone, G. (2003). An empirical evaluation of US bank customer perceptions of the impact of technology on service delivery in the banking sector. International Journal of Retail and Distribution Management, 31(4), 190–202.

Jun, M. and Cai, S. (2001). The key determinants of internet banking service quality: A content analysis. International Journal of Bank Marketing, 19(7), 276–291.

Keeney, R. L. (1999). The value of internet commerce to the customer. Management Science, 45(4), 533–542.

Kesharwani, A. and Singh Bisht, S. (2012). The impact of trust and perceived risk on internet banking adoption in India: An extension of technology acceptance model. International Journal of Bank Marketing, 30(4), 303–322.

Kim, E. B. and Eom, S. B. (2002). Designing effective cyber store user interface. Industrial Management and Data Systems, 102(5), 241–251.

Kim, S. and Stoel, L. (2004). Dimensional hierarchy of retail website quality. Information and Management, 41(5), 619–633.

Koiso-Kanttila, N. (2005). Time, attention, authenticity and consumer benefits of the Web. Business Horizons, 48(1), 63–70.

Kiriakidou, O. and Millward, L. J. (2000). Corporate identity: External reality or internal fit? Corporate Communications: An International Journal, 5(1), 49–58.

Klein, J. and Dawar, N. (2004). Corporate social responsibility and consumers' attributions and brand evaluations in a product–harm crisis. International Journal of Research in Marketing, 21(3), 203–217.

Lacobucci, D., Ostrom, A., and Grayson, K. (1995). Distinguishing service quality and customer satisfaction: The voice of the consumer. Journal of Consumer Psychology, 4(3), 277–303.

Liao, Z. and Cheung, M. T. (2002). Internet-based e-banking and consumer attitudes: An empirical study. Information and Management, 39(4), 283–295.

Liao, Z. and Cheung, M. T. (2008). Measuring consumer satisfaction in internet banking: A core framework. Communications of the ACM, 51(4), 47–51.

Lin, J. C. C. and Lu, H. (2000). Towards an understanding of the behavioural intention to use a web site. International Journal of Information Management, 20(3), 197–208.

Lin, Y. J. (2013). Evaluation factors influencing corporate website effectiveness. Journal of Global Business Management, 9(3), 42.

Liu, C. and Arnett, K. P. (2002). An examination of privacy policies in Fortune 500 web sites. American Journal of Business, 17(1), 13–22.

Loiacono, E. T. (2000). Webqual(tm): A Web Site Quality Instrument. University of Georgia.

Lowery, S. A. and DeFleur, M. L. (1995). Milestones in Mass Communication Research: Media Effects (3rd ed.), Longman, White Plains, New York.

Maignan, I. and Ferrell, O. C. (2004). Corporate social responsibility and marketing: An integrative framework. Journal of the Academy of Marketing Science, 32(1), 3–19.

Maignan, I. and Ralston, D. A. (2002). Corporate social responsibility in Europe and the US: Insights from businesses' self-presentations. Journal of International Business Studies, 33(3), 497–514.

McKinney, V., Yoon, K., and Zahedi, F. M. (2002). The measurement of web-customer satisfaction: An expectation and disconfirmation approach. Information systems research, 13(3), 296–315.

Melewar, T. C. (2003). Determinants of the corporate identity construct: A review of the literature. Journal of marketing Communications, 9(4), 195–220.

Melewar, T. C., Foroudi, P., Dinnie, K., and Nguyen, B. (2018). The role of corporate identity management in the higher education sector: an exploratory case study. Journal of Marketing Communications, 24(4), 337–359.

Melewar, T. C., Foroudi, P., Gupta, S., Kitchen, P. J., and Foroudi, M. M. (2016). Integrating identity, strategy and communications for trust, loyalty and commitment. European Journal of Marketing, 51(3), 572–604.

Melewar, T. C., Foroudi, P., and Jin, Z. (2020). Corporate branding, identity, image and reputation: Current and future trends, developments and challenges (editorial notes), Journal of Business Research.

Metzger, M. J., Flanagin, A. J., Eyal, K., Lemus, D. R., and McCann, R. M. (2003). Credibility for the 21st century: Integrating perspectives on source, message, and media credibility in the contemporary media environment. Annals of the International Communication Association, 27(1), 293–335.

Meuter, M. L., Ostrom, A. L., Roundtree, R. I., and Bitner, M. J. (2000). Self-service technologies: Understanding customer satisfaction with technology-based service encounters. Journal of Marketing, 64(3), 50–64.

Mithas, S., Ramasubbu, N., Krishnan, M. S., and Fornell, C. (2006). Designing web sites for customer loyalty across business domains: A multilevel analysis. Journal of Management Information Systems, 23(3), 97–127.

Muylle, S., Moenaert, R., and Despontin, M. (2004). The conceptualization and empirical validation of web site user satisfaction. Information and Management, 41(5), 543–560.

Ndubisi, N. and Sinti, Q. (2006). Consumer attitudes, system's characteristics and internet banking adoption in Malaysia. Management Research News, 29(1/2), 16–27.

Nicotera, C. L. (1999). Information access by design: Electronic guidelines for librarians. Information Technology and Libraries, 18(2), 104.

Nielsen, J. (1994). Usability Engineering. Elsevier, Amsterdam.

Nielsen, J. (2000). Designing Web Usability. New Riders Publishing, Indianapolis.

O'Cass, A. and Carlson, J. (2012). An e-retailing assessment of perceived website-service innovativeness: Implications for website quality evaluations, trust, loyalty and word of mouth. Australasian Marketing Journal (AMJ), 20(1), 28–36.

Okazaki, S. (2006). Excitement or sophistication? A preliminary exploration of online brand personality. International Marketing Review, 23(3), 279–303.

Olins, W. (1989). Corporate Identity: Making Business Strategy Visible Through Design. Thames and Hudson, London.

Opoku, R., Abratt, R., and Pitt, L. (2006). Communicating brand personality: Are the websites doing the talking for the top South African business schools? Journal of Brand Management, 14(1), 20–39.

Osorio, N. L. (2001). Web sites of science–engineering libraries: An analysis of content and design. Issues in Science and Technology Librarianship, 29(2).

Overbeeke, M. and Snizek, W. E. (2005). Web sites and corporate culture: A research note. Business and Society, 44(3), 346–356.

Palmer, A. and Bejou, D. (2006). The future of relationship marketing. Journal of Relationship Marketing, 4(3–4), 1–10.

Parasuraman, A., Zeithaml, V. A., and Malhotra, A. (2005). ES-QUAL a multiple-item scale for assessing electronic service quality. Journal of Service Research, 7(3), 213–233.

Park, J. and Stoel, L. (2005). Effect of brand familiarity, experience and information on online apparel purchase. International Journal of Retail and Distribution Management, 33(2), 148–160.

Pollach, I. (2003). Communicating corporate ethics on the world wide web a discourse analysis of selected company web sites. Business and Society, 42(2), 277–287.

Pollach, I. (2005). Corporate self-presentation on the WWW: Strategies for enhancing usability, credibility and utility. Corporate Communications: An International Journal, 10(4), 285–301.

Rains, S. A. and Karmikel, C. D. (2009). Health information-seeking and perceptions of website credibility: Examining Web-use orientation, message characteristics, and structural features of websites. Computers in Human Behavior, 25(2), 544–553.

Ranganathan, C. and Ganapathy, S. (2002). Key dimensions of business-to-consumer web sites. Information and Management, 39(6), 457–465.

Rose, G., Khoo, H., and Straub, D. W. (1999). Current technological impediments to business-to-consumer electronic commerce. Communications of the AIS, 1(5es), 1.

Santouridis, I., Trivellas, P., and Reklitis, P. (2009). Internet service quality and customer satisfaction: Examining internet banking in Greece. Total Quality Management, 20(2), 223–239.

Schoon, P. and Cafolla, R. (2002). World Wide Web hypertext linkage patterns. Journal of Educational Multimedia and Hypermedia, 11(2), 117–140.

Schrage, M. (1999). The next step in customization. MC Technology Marketing Intelligence, 8, 20–21.

Sen, S. and Bhattacharya, C. B. (2001). Does doing good always lead to doing better? Consumer reactions to corporate social responsibility. Journal of Marketing Research, 38(2), 225–243.

Srinivasan, S. S., Anderson, R., and Ponnavolu, K. (2002). Customer loyalty in e-commerce: An exploration of its antecedents and consequences. Journal of Retailing, 78(1), 41–50.

Stamm, K. and Dube, R. (1994). The relationship of attitudinal components to trust in media. Communication Research, 21(1), 105–123.

Sterne, J. (1995). World Wide Web Marketing: Integrating the Internet into Your Marketing Strategy. John Wiley & Sons, Inc, New York.

Sun, H. (2001). Building a culturally-competent corporate web site: An exploratory study of cultural markers in multilingual web design. In Proceedings of the 19th Annual International Conference on Computer Documentation (pp. 95–102). ACM.

Sundar, S. S., Kalyanaraman, S., and Brown, J. (2003). Explicating web site interactivity impression formation effects in political campaign sites. Communication Research, 30(1), 30–59.

Szymanski, D. M. and Hise, R. T. (2000). E-satisfaction: An initial examination. Journal of Retailing, 76(3), 309–322.

Tarafdar, M. and Zhang, J. (2008). Determinants of reach and loyalty—A study of website performance and implications for website design. Journal of Computer Information Systems, 48(2), 16–24.

Topalian, A. (2003). Experienced reality: The development of corporate identity in the digital era. European Journal of Marketing, 37(7/8), 1119–1132.

Tovey, J. (1998). Organising features of hypertext. Journal of Business and Technical Communication, 12(3), 371–380.

Vila, N. and Kuster, I. (2011). Consumer feelings and behaviours towards well designed websites. Information and Management, 48(4), 166–177.

Voss, K. E., Spangenberg, E. R., and Grohmann, B. (2003). Measuring the hedonic and utilitarian dimensions of consumer attitude. Journal of Marketing Research, 40(3), 310–320.

Warnick, B. (2004). Online ethos source credibility in an "authorless" environment. American Behavioral Scientist, 48(2), 256–265.

Wolfinbarger, M. and Gilly, M. C. (2003). eTailQ: Dimensionalizing, measuring and predicting etail quality. Journal of retailing, 79(3), 183–198.

Yoon, C. (2010). Antecedents of customer satisfaction with online banking in China: The effects of experience. Computers in Human Behavior, 26(6), 1296–1304.

Zhang, P. and Von Dran, G. M. (2002). User expectations and rankings of quality factors in different website domains. International Journal of Electronic Commerce, 6 (2), 9–33.

9
CORPORATE BRAND WEBSITE DESIGN, IMAGE, IDENTIFICATION, AND LOYALTY

Pantea Foroudi, Mohammad Mahdi Foroudi, and Elena Ageeva

Introduction

Chapter 9 examines how the design of a favourable corporate brand website design could influence a company's image, identification, and loyalty. The chapter discusses companies' corporate websites and how to communicate and distinguish themselves to their consumers and audience to create favourable images and reputation. A well-designed company's corporate website impacts on company's corporate image. The next section clarifies the notion of corporate image as an important consequence of corporate website favourability. Additionally, corporate website favourability will also be explained as a consequence of the corporate image, corporate reputation, consumer–company identification, and loyalty.

Background to corporate brand website design, image, identification, and loyalty

Today's world is becoming increasingly online and visually focused. Website use is becoming second nature and its patterns, governed by the rapid pace of the resources becoming available and the growing number of information elements on offer, are changing. A website as an integral aspect of corporate identity management would allow companies to communicate with potential consumers in today's world (Bravo et al., 2012; Foroudi et al., 2016; Opoku et al., 2006). The corporation's website is a key tool for corporate visual identity while playing a major role in highlighting the extent to which an organisation represents itself to its external and internal stakeholders (Foroudi, 2019; 2020; Schlosser, 2003). Corporate visual identity management is associated with the terminology of graphic design, which is a major part of the corporate identity that a corporation could use to establish its own quality, prestige, and style to stakeholders (Olins, 1991; Stuart, 1999; Tagiuri, 1982) and offers firms a dimension of differentiation that is challenging for rivals to replicate (Melewar et al., 2001). Developing a corporate website as being among the primary aspects of corporate visual identity, in accordance with the symbol, logo, name, typography, slogan or colour, is a means of presenting corporate identity visually. The construction of an organisation's visual identity, such as website, is a dynamic and expensive process (Henderson and Cote, 1998); as a result, managers take enormous interest in creating a favourable corporate website to generate a constructive image of the business. The significance of websites has attracted considerable attention from marketing scholars and practitioners (Foroudi et al., 2016; Melewar et al., 2016; Pollach, 2005; Wheeler, 2012). In addition, company managers face issues when building the website according to consumers' and companies' needs. Moreover, a website can provide certain operational advantages, such as reduced opportunities for clerical errors, lower overhead costs, and a quicker response to new market opportunities (Beatty et al., 2001). A corporate website allows a corporation to create an impression of itself in the mind of the customer (Foroudi et al., 2016). The effective management of a company website generates a favourable corporate image. A well-constructed corporate website will consequently lead to a positive corporate image and corporate reputation, strengthen user identification with an organisation, build loyalty, as well as ultimately increasing profits.

There is increasing pressure on organisations to create their corporate website based on the company's corporate identity (Ageeva et al., 2019a; 2019b) and plan their communication strategies carefully. According to Rahimnia and Hassanzadeh (2013), 'only a handful of studies in academic literature have specifically examined corporate website issues', and 'website content has naturally become one of the most important issues for companies that want to maximise profits by promoting their services or products in a competitive and limited market' (pp. 240–241).

Marketing managers in corporations have been striving to attract target customers for many years. Thus, they have offered a high-quality website to satisfy their users in order to maintain brand loyalty. Consumers can be loyal because they value social interaction and because the company's way of doing business is supported by their own values. However, businesses are failing to establish long-term partnerships with clients; in particular, decent quality is not adequate to successfully distinguish competitive businesses (Foroudi et al., 2020ab). In addition, the company website is almost an ideal market due to its up-to-date information which allows customers to evaluate the offering of vendors all around the world (Srinivasan et al., 2002). Website quality is by far the most relevant, as it depicts the dominant or perhaps the only interaction with consumers for e-retailers (Palmer and Griffith, 1998)

Company websites should be a more visible artefact for interacting with consumers. The home page should be the baseline for research users to explore the access to its services. A website that is practical and easy to use will reduce the risk to visitors while making their experience more enjoyable. These outcomes will probably enhance consumers' perception (image and reputation); in addition, consumers will feel that the company's success is their success (identification). These associations are essential influences that foster very deep consumer loyalty. As a result, interest in business websites has grown at a remarkable pace (Foroudi et al., 2016; Melewar et al., 2016; Pollach, 2005). Even so, insufficient scientific research has so far been undertaken in this field in order to achieve a true sense of the definition. This research is primarily aimed at delivering the true and accurate scale for 'corporate website favourability', as, to the best scholars, none has been available to date. In this context, the current study aims to explore the concept of corporate website favourability in the financial sense in the United Kingdom and Russia, as resources offered to scholars and professionals in the global economy are growing significantly. The other aims at investigating the antecedents and consequences of corporate website favourability, with regard specifically to corporate image, corporate reputation, consumer–company identification, and loyalty. Alternatively, the key question is: What are the characteristics, antecedents, and consequences of corporate website favourability as a domain-specific construct?

Corporate website favourability and corporate image

Corporate image is a frequently researched term through psychological and marketing studies. In the marketing literature, corporate image indicates the connection, beliefs, and attitudes towards the organisation held in the consumer's mind (Barich and Kotler, 1991). Corporate image is nonetheless generated by the corporation, as well as by other sources, including the media, labour unions, environmental organisations, etc. Corporate image depicts attitudes, beliefs, impressions, and associations formed by customers regarding the business. Corporate image is developed through a communication process by which the organisation develops and transmits the meaning of the brand. A company's image impacts attitudes toward its products (Foroudi et al., 2014). Since the image denotes how an audience perceives the company, as well as its elements, it holds an external foundation. Corporate identity is developed into the corporate image and, through time, corporate reputation via corporate communication practices.

Corporate websites are an effective tool to reinforce corporate identity, as a means of corporate communication (Topalian, 2003). As a major aspect of corporate identity management, managers should aim to improve the organisation's website in order to build or preserve a positive image in the user's mind. The ultimate purpose of the corporate website is to spread the business image, hence the website is used as the company's virtual storefront (Pantano et al., 2019; Pitt and Papania, 2007). Thus, a website allows an organisation to create its own image in the mind of the customer (Tarafdar and Zhang, 2008). Therefore, once consumers develop a positive perspective towards corporate website favourability, their perception about the organisation is more desirable and favourable. This research refers to the corporate image as the consumer's initial impression compared with its competitors and constitutes an advantage enabling businesses to discern and improve the likelihood of success (Foroudi and Marvi, 2020).

Corporate image and corporate reputation

Corporate reputation is the concept that forms the corporate image through time. By other means, a positive corporate reputation would be established with the aid of a consistent perception by the positive corporate image. Additionally, the positive perception of users has an effect on their attitudes and behaviours concerning an organisation (Sen and Bhattacharya, 2001). Besides, corporate image affects the reputation of an organisation, and it can also be inferred that corporate reputation is the company's ultimate perception of stakeholders over time. As a result, corporations can enhance organisational reputation by creating and promoting their identity to their core stakeholders (Dowling, 2004). According to Neil (1998), a favourable reputation can be established and improved by a website.

Scholars (Foroudi et al., 2014; Melewar et al., 2017) noted that corporate image and corporate reputation are two separate terms linked to each other. Consequently, the favourable perception that customers have about the business would have a positive effect on the judgement and feelings of consumers regarding the company. On the basis of prior studies, customers who have positive opinion about a company can contribute to a positive assessment of the company's reputation (Walsh et al., 2009). This study has identified that corporate reputation concerns an assessment that creates strong direct and indirect information and knowledge from an organisation over time (Hussain et al., 2020).

Corporate reputation and consumer–company identification

Reputation is therefore characterised as the nature in which corporations are regarded externally (Foorudi et al., 2020; Ind, 1992; Selame and Selame, 1988). Researchers (Bhattarcharya and Elsbach, 2002; Hong and Yang, 2009; Reade, 2001) have illustrated the relationship between favourable reputation of the organisation and identification with the organisation. In particular, Hong and Yang (2009) found that favourable company reputation positively influences consumer–company identification. A favourable reputation can be accrued via personalised and original website design (Srinivasan et al., 2002). Thus, reputation can be strengthened by websites (Neil, 1998). Cox and Emmott (2007) observed that reputation is one of the determinants for the website provision. Similarly, a case study of library websites by Srinivasan et al. (2002) showed that websites can positively affect reputation.

The reputation of the organisation is an indication of a company's achievement, since the well-regarded organisation is perceived to be a success. If individuals perceive the company's reputation as efficient, their positive brand association may also be improved. Previous studies (Bhattacharya et al., 1995) have shown that a strong reputation corresponds to positive company identification. The notion of customer–business identity reflects a close social connection between the consumer and the corporation, in such a manner that customers are regarded by the same qualities as they characterise in the corporation. The consumer–company identification' reflects the social ties between the consumer and the firm, such that the consumer distinguishes themselves in line with the same features that they classify the company with (Einwiller et al., 2006).

Consumer–company identification and loyalty

Consumers who associate with an organisation are psychologically attached to that organisation, which leads them to believe that the company's achievements and goals are their own (Bhattacharya and Sen, 2003). Consumers who are affiliated with an enterprise appear to be more loyal to it and establish a coherent social identity. When consumers associate themselves with a company, they are more likely to recommend the product. According to Foroudi et al. (2020d), the identity commitment indicates a more stable and enduring desire in the sense of customer–company partnerships, so that loyalty is a natural product of consumer company identification. Martinez and Del Bosque (2013), observed the lack of information on the notion of identity as well as the importance of consumer–company identification towards loyalty. Researchers have found that customer identity affects consumer loyalty.

A loyal customer brings more substantial advantages to a company than a new customer, as she/he is far less affected by price fluctuations. The direct impact of loyalty on the profit and revenue of a company is examined by Reichheld et al. (2000), who noted that a rise in user retention rates may increase profits. Businesses are often preoccupied on their website with building customer loyalty.

Consumers who are committed to a company are unlikely to switch to an alternative brand. Such consumers would benefit an organisation far beyond the new ones, as the former are less affected by price fluctuations. Reichheld et al. (2000) examined the direct relationship of loyalty with the profit and revenue of a company, noting that a rise in the user retention rate may increase profits. This study investigated loyalty as the psychological commitment and desire of the customer to maintain business with the company, manifested over time, where there are many accessible substitutes (Liang et al., 2008; Melewar et al., 2016).

Corporate website favourability, satisfaction, and image

Satisfaction is extensively studied throughout the marketing literature (Foroudi et al., 2020e; Oliver, 1980; 1981). Additionally, in addition, the value of satisfaction has been underlined throughout both traditional service quality studies, as well as the online context in particular (Santouridis, 2009). Some studies consider (Yoon, 2002) that recurrent satisfaction with a vendor leads to loyalty. The connection between satisfaction and willingness to buy is examined by Cronin and Taylor (1992), who points out that customer satisfaction is a result of quality of service. According to Anderson et al. (1994) and Gronroos (1984, 1990, 2001), service quality precedes the satisfaction of customers. Flavian et al. (2006) have indicated that positive emotional components emerge from a worldwide assessment of factors contributing to consumers' experiences. Satisfaction reflects the consumer's favourable disposition.

Satisfaction is among the core priorities of user experience. Customer satisfaction relies on the structure of the application through the website. Furthermore, Yoon (2002) proposed that navigation design may necessarily lead to satisfaction. Similarly, Cyr (2008) noted that satisfaction can be affected by the navigation design of the website. In fact, information per se is characterised as a crucial step towards satisfaction (Flavian et al., 2006; Szymanski et al., 2000) and trust (Flavian et al., 2006). The images and visual design of the website are nearly correlated with satisfaction (Vance et al., 2008). The findings from Cyr (2008) have confirmed that the aesthetics of websites contribute to morale and satisfaction in several regions.

Hu et al. (2009) has scientifically observed how customer loyalty would improve the company image by stating that 'the results confirm that high service quality leads to superior perceived value, customer satisfaction, and favourable perceptions of corporate image' (p. 121). The ultimate perception about the service company is impacted by perceived service quality and service value, as well as customer satisfaction, which has a positive impact on consumer perception about the business. Customer satisfaction can act as the user's evaluation about a product or service according to the user's demands and desires (Oliver, 1980).

Corporate website favourability, attractiveness, and image

The attractiveness of an organisation is extensively studied through the recruitment literature. Businesses that employ more skilled workers have a wider range of career applicants. With technical growth, internet recruitment has been the most convenient means of hiring new employees over the past decade. Companies wishing to recruit the finest employees must introduce themselves as effectively as possible on the company website. In addition, the concept of attractiveness throughout recruitment research was widely discussed in terms of website colours, fonts, images, and bulleted versus texts (Braddy et al., 2008; Cober et al., 2003). The understanding of organisational attractiveness is affected by the exposure of corporate recruitment websites (Braddy et al., 2008). These authors have found that the company website can and do influence the viewers' impression of the organisation by psychological processes based on signalling theory. They clarified that signalling theory suggests that any material that a person encounters will direct his or her opinion of the company, meaning that websites can become the indicator to what it will be like to function throughout the company and hence have an effect on the individual's attraction to the company (Turban, 2001). This happens since entities believe that the details (the website and materials displayed on the website) and features (the quality of the website) define the entire organisation. Similarly, Williamson et al. (2003) stated that the website has an effect on organisation attractiveness. This confirms the notion presented throughout the prior studies (Gatewood et al.,1993) whereby career applicants are much more responsive to organisations which they regard favourably. This could therefore lead towards a better view of the organisation by maintaining a well-designed website which attracts consumers (Braddy et al., 2008). The concept of attraction is the way the business is thrilling, attractive, enjoyable, and subjectively pleasing in the consumer's mind.

Conclusion

Chapter 9 presents an approach that has significant implications for a company by investigating the significance of the favourable corporate website for achieving consumer objectives. A company website will affect and generate a positive user perception by offering insights into the essence of the organisation. Hence, for developing a positive reputation and prevent misunderstanding, company websites must be incorporated into the current consistent branding strategy.

CASE STUDY – DELL AND WEBSITE DEVELOPMENT

Maria Palazzo, University of Salerno, Italy

The focus on websites in marketing does not have a very long history, as the concept of the website is relatively new in itself. Websites started from the creation of the internet, which drastically changed the world forever. The concept can be better understood through looking at the major milestones of the internet and website creation.

A web/website can be explained as a system of interconnected hypertext documents accessed through the internet with the use of a computer or mobile/table/watch device. The word website was born from the word 'web', which is derived from the 'world wide web', which was the first ever website built. The term 'world wide web'/'web' represents the combination of the webpages on the internet (network of computers).

Website development

The history of the website started with the idea of the world wide web (or web) in 1989 by Tim Berners-Lee, followed by the first website (world wide web) created in 1990 and finally going live in 1991 in Switzerland (w3.org). Since then there have been major developments and advances in the way websites are built and how they are perceived. The changes in the web are conventionally marked by the names Web 1.0, Web 2.0, Web

3.0, Wed 4.0 developments, however there is no clear agreement between the website development period dates, as they tend to overlap each other.

The era of information consumption and the first stage of website development began with the world wide web's first ever website gaining free world wide public access in 1993 and which lasted until the dot com crash in 2000. This period is called 'Web 1.0', in which websites were represented as static pages with flat data and limited interaction. In other words, the websites were mainly for 'read' information purposes.

The next era of website development was social media interaction, conventionally called Web 2.0. The major shifts were the change from the 'advertising' approach to 'word of mouth', which shifted the focus from companies to communities, as well as marking the change from owning information to sharing it. This period marks the creation of the world's most famous social media platforms LinkedIn (in 2003), Facebook (in 2004), YouTube (in 2005), and Twitter (in 2006).

The third period is the era of cooperation known as Web 3.0, and represents the semantic web. The major shift from Web 2.0 to Web 3.0 is represented by the shift of focus from communities to individuals. In respect of website studies, this period is marked by the holistic view of the website and the importance of aligning the strategy of the company to the website strategy. To summarise, websites are still in the development stage and constantly evolving. There is a need for better understanding of websites as a holistic concept that drives companies' success. The next sections therefore provide an enhanced understanding of the topic, in the case of Dell.

Dell

Dell is an international information technology company that creates, sells, and distributes computers and associated products/services. Dell highlights in its corporate website that:

> Our story began with two technology companies and one shared vision: to provide greater access to technology for people around the world. Dell Technologies is instrumental in changing the digital landscape the world over, fueled by the desire to drive human progress through technology.
> *https://corporate.delltechnologies.com/en-gb/about-us/who-we-are.htm*

The CEO, Michael Dell, set up Dell in 1984. Over the last 30 years, the direct selling strategy implemented by the company has strengthened its positioning in the PC sector. Actually, Dell's direct selling strategy allows it to create a personalised products offer able to meet customers' needs. In fact, the direct selling strategy gave Dell a competitive advantage: To be capable of customizing computers leveraging on high technology (Lawton and Michaels, 2001).

Nevertheless, with the rapid changes of high technology, the competition has become very strong. Many other companies are present in the market, such as: HP, Acer, Apple, Sony, Lenovo (IBM), Toshiba, etc. It must be said that they are compatible with each other, even if they are focused on different actions: Marketing, logistics, R&D, customer service. To succeed in this battle, time seems to be a decisive factor. Besides, a strong brand name with good reputation as well as inventiveness and technology enhancement are all fundamental items for Dell to achieve market leadership.

Direct selling strategy of Dell: Corporate brand website

Compared with the common selling strategy chosen by other PC companies, Dell's direct selling strategy, developed thanks to its corporate website and on the build-to-order business model, has its advantages (Kraemer et al., 2000). The key success factor of Dell's direct selling strategy is linked with the fact that Dell succeeded in simplifying its supply chain and in selecting useful communication channels. Choosing not to rely on intermediaries, Dell reduced the risk of relying on market forecasts to find the right production strategy. Besides, the direct selling business model, developed through the corporate website, gave Dell the chance to understand customers and meet their need thanks to customization. Another advantage of direct selling is the build-to-order strategy. This strategy allows Dell to combine the latest technology with customers' requests to generate high technology computers for the consumer market.

An additional benefit is achieved thanks to the use of the internet as a direct selling channel. In comparison with other distribution tactics (i.e., retailers, wholesalers), Dell's corporate website is able not only to reduce the operational cost and increase efficiency but also to aid the organisation in reaching customers with less expensive products (Lawton and Michaels, 2001). In sum, the direct selling strategy, developed thanks to the web, reinforces Dell's reaction to market needs, reduces its operation costs, strengthens its brand image, and customer loyalty which helps Dell create a high return on investment.

Case questions

1. Can Dell sustain its success in the future by meaning its corporate brand website?
2. Can the corporate brand website limit Dell's success?
3. Analyse the key components of a successful corporate brand website design.

References

Kraemer, K. L., Dedrick, J., and Yamashiro, S. (2000). Refining and extending the business model with information technology: Dell Computer Corporation. The Information Society, 16(1), 5–21.

Kumar, S. and Craig, S. (2007). Dell, Inc.'s closed loop supply chain for computer assembly plants. Information Knowledge Systems Management, 6(3), 197–214.

Lawton, T. C. and Michaels, K. P. (2001). Advancing to the virtual value chain: Learning from the Dell model. Irish Journal of Management, 22(1), 91.

Key terms and definitions

Attractiveness is how exciting, attractive, appealing, fun, and subjectively pleasing the company is in the minds of consumers.

Consumer–company identification represents the strong social relationships between the consumer and the company, such that consumers perceive themselves by the same attributes that they believe define the company.

Corporate identity is what the company is in regard to the entity's distinctive and enduring traits.

Corporate image is the overall immediate impression left in the minds of customers in comparison to its competitors and represents an asset, which allows companies to differentiate and increase the chances of success.

Corporate reputation concerns judgement that results from the reception of direct and indirect experiences and information of a company over time.

Corporate visual identity is the combination of visual cues by which an audience can recognise the company and differentiate it from others.

Corporate website favourability is the extent to which a company projects their corporate identity through the corporate website, as a primary vehicle of corporate visual identity, to gain positive attitudes from the consumers by transmitting consistent images and messages about the nature of the organisation to a company's audience to enable a company to build a positive image of itself in the consumer's mind.

Loyalty is the consumer's psychological attachment and intention to continue doing business with the company, expressed over time, where several alternatives are available.

Satisfaction is the consumer's evaluation of a product or service with regard to their needs and expectations.

Acknowledgement

Many thanks to Helnaz Ahmadi Lari for editing the chapter.

References

Ageeva, E., Melewar, T. C., Foroudi, P., and Dennis, C. (2019a). Cues adopted by consumers in examining corporate website favorability: An empirical study of financial institutions in the UK and Russia. Journal of Business Research, 98 (May), 15–32.

Ageeva, E., Foroudi, P., Melewar, T. C., Nguyen, B., and Dennis, C. (2019b). A holistic framework of corporate website favourability. Corporate Reputation Review, 21 (Sep), 1–14.

Anderson, E. W. and Fornell, C. (1994). A customer satisfaction research prospectus. Service quality: New directions in theory and practice, 14(1), 239–266.

Barich, H. and Kotler, P. (1991). A framework for marketing image management. Sloan Management Review, 32(2), 94–104.

Beatty, R. C., Shim, J. P., and Jones, M. C. (2001). Factors influencing corporate web site adoption: A time-based assessment. Information and Management, 38(6), 337–354.

Bhattacharya, C. B. and Elsbach, K. D. (2002). Us versus them: The roles of organizational identification and disidentification in social marketing initiatives. Journal of Public Policy and Marketing, 21(1), 26–36.

Bhattacharya, C. B. and Sen, S. (2003). Consumer-company identification: A framework for understanding consumers' relationships with companies. Journal of Marketing, 67(2), 76–88.

Bhattacharya, C. B., Rao, H., and Glynn, M. A. (1995). Understanding the bond of identification: An investigation of its correlates among art museum members. Journal of Marketing, 46–57.

Braddy, P. W., Meade, A. W., and Kroustalis, C. M. (2008). Online recruiting: The effects of organisational familiarity, website usability, and website attractiveness on viewers' impressions of organisations. Computers in Human Behavior, 24(6), 2992–3001.

Bravo, R., Matute, J., and Pina, J. M. (2012). Corporate social responsibility as a vehicle to reveal the corporate identity: A study focused on the websites of Spanish financial entities. Journal of Business Ethics, 107(2), 129–146.

Cox, A. and Emmott, S. (2007). A survey of UK university web management: Staffing, systems and issues. Campus-Wide Information Systems, 24(5), 308–330.

Cronin Jr, J. J. and Taylor, S. A. (1992). Measuring service quality: A reexamination and extension. Journal of Marketing, 55–68.

Cyr, D. (2008). Modeling web site design across cultures: relationships to trust, satisfaction, and e-loyalty. Journal of Management Information Systems, 24(4), 47–72.

Dowling, G. R. (2004). Corporate reputations: Should you compete on yours? California Management Review, 46(3), 19–36.

Einwiller, S. A., Fedorikhin, A., Johnson, A. R., and Kamins, M. A. (2006). Enough is enough! When identification no longer prevents negative corporate associations. Journal of the Academy of Marketing Science, 34(2), 185–194.

Flavian, C., Guinaliu, M., and Gurrea, R. (2006). The role played by perceived usability, satisfaction and consumer trust on website loyalty. Information and Management, 43(1), 1–14.

Foroudi, M. M., Balmer, J. M., Chen, W., Foroudi, P., and Patsala, P. (2020d). Explicating place identity attitudes, place architecture attitudes, and identification triad theory. Journal of Business Research, 109 (March), 321–336.

Foroudi, P. (2019) Influence of brand signature, brand awareness, brand attitude, brand reputation on hotel industry's brand performance, International Journal of Hospitality Management, 76 (Jan), 271–285.

Foroudi, P. (2020) Corporate Brand Strategy: Drivers and Outcomes of Corporate Brand Orientation in International Marketing. International Journal of Hospitality Management, 88 (July), 1–14.

Foroudi, P. and Marvi, R. (2020). Some like it hot: The role of identity, website, co-creation behavior on identification and love. European Journal of International Management.

Foroudi, P., Dinnie, K., Kitchen, P. J., Melewar, T. C., and Foroudi, M. M. (2016). IMC antecedents and the consequences of planned brand identity in higher education. European Journal of Marketing, 51(3), 528–550.

Foroudi, P., Marvi, R., and Imani, S. (2020b). The impact of internal marketing on knowledge sharing capability. European Journal of International Management.

Foroudi, P., Marvi, R., and Kizgin, H. (2020e). The others: The role of individual personality, cultural acculturation, and perceived value on self-esteem, satisfaction, and performance proficiency. International Journal of Information Management, 52(June).

Foroudi, P., Melewar, T. C., and Gupta, S. (2014). Linking corporate logo, corporate image, and reputation: An examination of consumer perceptions in the financial setting. Journal of Business Research, 67(11), 2269–2281.

Foroudi, P., Tabaghdehi, S. A. H., and Marvi, R. (2020a). The gloom of the COVID-19 shock in the hospitality industry: Study of consumer risk perception and adaptive belief in dark cloud of pandemic. International Journal of Hospitality Management, 92 (Jan).

Gatewood, R. D., Gowan, M. A., and Lautenschlager, G. J. (1993). Corporate image, recruitment image and initial job choice decisions. Academy of Management Journal, 36(2), 414–427.

Gronroos, C. (1984). A service quality model and its marketing implications. European Journal of Marketing, 18(4), 36–44.

Gronroos, C. (1990). Relationship approach to marketing in service contexts: The marketing and organisational behavior interface. Journal of Business Research, 20(1), 3–11.

Gronroos, C. (2001). The perceived service quality concept – a mistake? Managing Service Quality: An International Journal, 11(3), 150–152.

Henderson, P. W. and Cote, J. A. (1998). Guidelines for selecting or modifying logos. Journal of Marketing, 62(2), 14–30.

Hong, S. Y. and Yang, S. U. (2009). Effects of reputation, relational satisfaction, and customer–company identification on positive word-of-mouth intentions. Journal of Public Relations Research, 21(4), 381–403.

Hu, H. H., Kandampully, J., and Juwaheer, T. D. (2009). Relationships and impacts of service quality, perceived value, customer satisfaction, and image: An empirical study. The Service Industries Journal, 29(2), 111–125.

Hussain, S., Melewar, T. C., Priporas, C., Foroudi, P., and Yousef, W. (2020). Understanding celebrity trust and its effects on other credibility and image constructs: A qualitative approach. Corporate Reputation Review.

Ind, N. (1992). The Corporate Image: Strategies for Effective Identity Programmes. Kogan Page, London.

Liang, C. J. and Wang, W. H. (2008). Do loyal and more involved customers reciprocate retailer's relationship efforts? Journal of Services Research, 8(1), 63.

Martinez, P. and Del Bosque, I. R. (2013). CSR and customer loyalty: The roles of trust, customer identification with the company and satisfaction. International Journal of Hospitality Management, 35, 89–99.

Melewar, T. C., Foroudi, P., Gupta, S., Kitchen, P. J., and Foroudi, M. M. (2016). Integrating identity, strategy and communications for trust, loyalty and commitment. European Journal of Marketing, 51(3), 572–604.

Melewar, T. C., Foroudi, P., Kitchen, P., Gupta, S., and Foroudi, M. M. (2017). Integrating Identity, strategy and communications for trust, loyalty and commitment. European Journal of Marketing, 51(3), 572–604.

Melewar, T. C., Saunders, J., and Balmer, J. M. (2001). Cause, effect and benefits of a standardised corporate visual identity system of UK companies operating in Malaysia. European Journal of Marketing, 35(3/4), 414–427.

Neil, S. (1998). Web site images a cut above. PC Week (Nov), 23, 25–26.

Olins, W. (1991). Corporate Identity. Thames and Hudson, Toledo, Spain.

Oliver, R. L. (1980). A cognitive model of the antecedents and consequences of satisfaction decisions. Journal of Marketing Research, 460–469.

Oliver, R. L. (1981). Measurement and evaluation of satisfaction processes in retail settings. Journal of Retailing, 57(3), 25–48.

Opoku, R., Abratt, R., and Pitt, L. (2006). Communicating brand personality: Are the websites doing the talking for the top South African business schools? Journal of Brand Management, 14(1), 20–39.

Palmer, J. W. and Griffith, D. A. (1998). An emerging model of web site design for marketing. Communications of the ACM, 41(3), 44–51.

Pantano, E., Priporas, C. V., and Foroudi, P. (2019). Innovation starts at the storefront: Modelling consumer behaviour towards storefront windows enriched with innovative technologies. International Journal of Retail and Distribution Management, 47(2), 202–219.

Pitt, L. F. and Papania, L. (2007). In the words: Managerial approaches to exploring corporate intended image through content analysis. Journal of General Management, 32(4), 1–16.

Pollach, I. (2005). Corporate self-presentation on the WWW: Strategies for enhancing usability, credibility and utility. Corporate Communications: An International Journal, 10(4), 285–301.

Rahimnia, F. and Hassanzadeh, J. F. (2013). The impact of website content dimension and e-trust on e-marketing effectiveness: The case of Iranian commercial saffron corporations. Information and Management, 50(5), 240–247.

Reade, C. (2001). Antecedents of organisational identification in multinational corporations: Fostering psychological attachment to the local subsidiary and the global organisation. International Journal of Human Resource Management, 12(8), 1269–1291.

Reichheld, F. F., Markey Jr, R. G., and Hopton, C. (2000). The loyalty effect-the relationship between loyalty and profits. European Business Journal, 12(3), 134.

Santouridis, I., Trivellas, P., and Reklitis, P. (2009). Internet service quality and customer satisfaction: Examining internet banking in Greece. Total Quality Management, 20(2), 223–239.

Schlosser, A. E. (2003). Computers as situational cues: Implications for consumers product cognitions and attitudes. Journal of Consumer Psychology, 13(1), 103–112.

Selame, E., and Selame, J. (1988). The Company Image: Building Your Identity and Influence in the Marketplace. Wiley, Chichester.

Sen, S. and Bhattacharya, C. B. (2001). Does doing good always lead to doing better? Consumer reactions to corporate social responsibility. Journal of Marketing Research, 38(2), 225–243.

Srinivasan, S. S., Anderson, R., and Ponnavolu, K. (2002). Customer loyalty in e-commerce: an exploration of its antecedents and consequences. Journal of Retailing, 78(1), 41–50.

Stuart, H. (1999). Towards a definitive model of the corporate identity management process. Corporate Communications: An International Journal, 4(4), 200–207.

Szymanski, D. M. and Hise, R. T. (2000). E-satisfaction: An initial examination. Journal of retailing, 76(3), 309–322.

Tagiuri, R. (1982). Managing Corporate Identity: The Role of Top Management. Division of Research, Graduate School of Business Administration, Harvard University.

Tarafdar, M. and Zhang, J. (2008). Determinants of reach and loyalty—A study of website performance and implications for website design. Journal of Computer Information Systems, 48(2), 16–24.

Topalian, A. (2003). Experienced reality: The development of corporate identity in the digital era. European Journal of Marketing, 37(7/8), 1119–1132.

Turban, D. B. (2001). Organisational attractiveness as an employer on college campuses: An examination of the applicant population. Journal of Vocational Behavior, 58(2), 293–312.

Vance, A., Elie-Dit-Cosaque, C., and Straub, D. W. (2008). Examining trust in information technology artifacts: the effects of system quality and culture. Journal of Management Information Systems, 24(4), 73–100.

Walsh, G., Mitchell, V. W., Jackson, P. R., and Beatty, S. E. (2009). Examining the antecedents and consequences of corporate reputation: A customer perspective. British Journal of Management, 20(2), 187–203.

Wheeler, A. (2012). Designing Brand Identity: An Essential Guide for the Whole Branding Team. John Wiley & Sons, New York.

Williamson, I. O., Lepak, D. P., and King, J. (2003). The effect of company recruitment web site orientation on individuals' perceptions of organisational attractiveness. Journal of Vocational Behavior, 63(2), 242–263.

Yoon, S. J. (2002). The antecedents and consequences of trust in online-purchase decisions. Journal of Interactive Marketing, 16(2), 47–63.

PART V
Corporate brand sensuality

10

EVOLUTION OF BRANDING

Towards an historical understanding of the concept branding, experience, and senses

Tugra Nazli Akarsu

Introduction

This chapter aims to shed light to the concept of branding, as well as to the scrutiny of concept of 'experience' within the marketing discipline. As the concept of 'senses' are being interchangeably used with 'experience', this chapter attempts to illustrate how the concept of 'experience' paved way to the introduction of 'senses' throughout the literature.

Background

The concept of *branding* was first addressed in the literature in 1942, when an article published in the Journal of Marketing, 'Techniques of Appraising Brand Preference and Brand Consciousness by Consumer Interviewing' by H. D. Wolfe, referred to increased brand usage due to the increased brand consciousness of consumers. However, it would be a mistake to think that this marked the start of the idea of branding: The phenomenon can be traced back to 2250–2000 BCE in the Indus Valley, where craftsmen marked their goods and artefacts with unique seals for informational purposes in trade, for industrialists, resellers, and government experts (Moore and Reid, 2008; Wolpert, 2000).

Other examples of symbols and pictures being used in the name of branding are found in the Greek, Roman, and Egyptian civilisations, when merchants preferred to use visual signs and pictures in order to both make their shops more eye-catching and maintain their trade (Moore and Lewis, 2005). Papyrus was first used by the early Egyptians more than 3,000 years ago, later leading to the development of paper which, in turn, led to the early stages of mass communication. Early societies were largely illiterate; hence archaeologists studying civilisations until the thirteenth century have traced visual labels, signs, and pictures reflecting different societies and different market regions (Osborne, 1996). In the thirteenth century, the revival of craftsmanship, the creation of a middle class, and better conditions for individuals enabled a smooth transition from visual signs and pictures to handwritten leaflets, which were handed out to attract and advertise to consumers. After this period, the practice of legal protection also began, with the use of proprietary marks by guilds, large quantities

DOI: 10.4324/9781003054153-11

of printed advertisements, the standardisation of trademarks and stamps, and the appearance of newspaper advertisements developing over the period from the fourteenth to the seventeenth century (Osborne, 1996).

The dawn of the Industrial Revolution encouraged the growth of mass production accompanied by modernism and industrialisation, which would eventually bring early forms of advertising and branding phenomena aimed both at identifying goods with assured quality and at stimulating demand for maximum profit. The concept of brand names did not exist until the American Civil War (1861–1865), when products were monopolised by the government (Landa, 2005). By this time, huge demand for packaged goods had driven industry to switch from the use of barrels and open containers to packaged goods with the promise of sealed freshness. Before this transformation to sealed and packaged goods, almost all products – except tobacco, wine, and ale, which had to be *branded* with their trademarks because they were considered 'commodities' – were sold from barrels without the use of any kind of manufacture (ibid.).

However, with the emergence of packaged goods, manufacturers had to come up with some sort of 'name' to promote their products and attract customers; it can therefore be said that the rise of the packaged product phenomenon led the way to the 'golden years' of advertising, mostly through print-orientated advertisements such as newspapers, local periodicals, and booklets (Gross and Sheth, 1989). During this period, the transition from barrels to packaged goods led to whole industries seeking desirable and attractive images for their products, which brought new concepts to the basic perception of trade which had been progressing since 2250–2000 BCE (Gross and Sheth, 1989).

The emergence of 'branding': A snapshot from 1920s to 1960s

In this regard, the evolution of branding cannot be divorced from the modernised world: It has been improving and developing throughout the centuries, having significant impacts at both societal and individual level, such as the invention of photography, improvements in transportation, and the invention of the telephone (Landa, 2005): All these creations of the modern world enable brands to stimulate consumers and enhance the products' value. Besides modernisation, ignoring radical changes in economic systems and their side-effects as regards both brands and their strategies would not be prudent in terms of branding practices. Therefore, priority can be given to war economies and economic policy transitions in terms of understanding the concept of brand management.

In terms of changing economic policies, a significant milestone occurred between the 1920s and the 1980s, after the end of the 'golden age' of capitalism in 1970s. The beginning of considerable stagnation in the demand for financial capital and a tendency towards a decrease in profit rates drove the United States and the United Kingdom to abandon Keynesian economic policy in favour of an open and free market policy, which also led most other countries in the same direction. The Keynesian principles of a protectionist economic system controlled by government therefore gave way to a new economic policy, giving sudden momentum to world trade and its sphere of influence (Ongun, 2012). Therefore, the 1980s mark a milestone in terms of the branding context, as the world economy shifted from a *Keynesian economy* to *a free market economy*.

Kapferer (2004) also highlights that, by the 1980s, managers had realised that their brands represented an asset. Previously, the value of a company had been measured in terms of its tangible assets, which had evolved from land and buildings to equipment and plants. However, it emerged that company value now meant significantly more than just financial value and tangible assets, and also encompassed *brands*.

As the meaning and concept of brands has evolved and improved, many definitions have been proposed over the years from different academic backgrounds, and the way that brands are perceived in each study needs to be defined. However, the most commonly used concept of brand was proposed by the American Marketing Association (AMA) in 1960 as follows:

> a name, term, sign, symbol or design, or a combination of them which is intended to identify the goods and services of one seller or a group of sellers and to differentiate them from those of competitors.

The emergence of 'experience' in marketing[1]

Background

With the realisation of the notion of 'brands' as well as its value by the 1980s, the historical timeline of the evolution of branding intersects with an increasing attention to the notion of 'experience', where corporations sought to achieve a competitive edge over their rivals by providing their customers with a more *pleasurable* experience (Pine and Gilmore, 1998).

Looking to this intersection, one can comment that it is definitely not a coincidence. With the increasing attention to brands and having a transformation from 'commodities' to 'services', companies realised that from the consumer's point of view, there is a transformational shift from satisfying one's needs to fulfilling one's desires and having fun and engaging with an experience one is demanding. From a managerial point of view, to sustain this demand companies should deliver a value in order to create an 'experience' by means of its brands. In this case, by delivering a value to consumers, companies have to provide benefits not only through *tangible goods or services*, but also by means of their customers' interactions with places and people for the purpose of shaping and engaging the experiences (Foroudi et al., 2018; Akarsu et al., 2019)

As a first step towards this new and challenging phenomenon, Pine and Gilmore (1998) proposed a new compelling model to show what companies need in order to satisfy the needs of consumers in the sphere of changing needs, values, and experience circle. With this in mind, Pine and Gilmore (1998) presented 'the progression of economic value model'. The progression of the economic value model presents a curve for companies to show them how they need to evolve, as companies to evolve their commodities into goods, then customise those goods in order to transform them into services, and to customise services into experiences – which will be, for them, the highest value offered by companies.

An introduction to the concept of 'experience'

By looking the historical timeline within the marketing domain, even though the recognition towards experience occurred in 1980s, due to its multifaceted nature, the experience concept has been studied in different disciplines, and has been incorporated from philosophy and social sciences where it is defined as 'a subjective episode in the construction/transformation of the individual, with, however, an emphasis on emotions and sense lived during immersion at the expense of the cognitive dimension' (Caru and Cova, 2003, p. 273).

Even though the concept of experience emerged in its full strength at the beginning of the 1980s, the root of the experience concept can be traced back to the eighteenth century and the European Romanticism movement (Caru and Cova, 2003), when marketers were inspired by the period's ideas of heightened, emotionally driven subjective experiences, as articulated within society, the arts, politics, and written works (Buswell et al., 2016). Later, in 1925, an American philosopher John Dewey proposed the four main aspects of experience, which are action, emotion, cognition, and communication.

It can be said Dewey's proposition of experience led marketers and scholars to invent a new definitions of experience with significantly different dimensions from those which can be empirically measured and it has been absorbed into the marketing discipline with different terms, such as product experience (Hoch, 2002), shopping experience (Kerin et al., 1992), customer experience (Gentile et al., 2007), consumer experience (Tsai, 2005), service experience (Hui and Bateson, 1991), Airbnb experience (Akarsu et al., 2020), consumption experience (Holbrook and Hirschman, 1982), and brand experience (Brakus et al., 2009). Even though the terminologies seem different from one another, the differences in conceptualising 'experience' could be the result of investigating the notion in different contexts. Table 10.1 aims to present the various definitions of 'experience' found in the marketing domain.

The emergence of 'experience' in marketing

Although the literature offers different definitions of experience, the first conceptualisation belongs to Holbrook and Hirschman (1982), who highlight that, rather than purchasing to meet functional needs, consumers are indicating a need to integrate their lifestyle into the products that they buy for their symbolic meanings, in other words seeking 'fun, amusement, fantasy' (ibid., p. 135). It can be said that this is a breakout from traditional marketing, which put limitations and boundaries on consumers by casting them as 'rational decision makers who base their purchasing choice on functional features' (Cleff and Walter, 2014, p. 8).

With the acknowledgement of the experience concept, it can be used to describe consumers who are emotionally driven and seeking a pleasurable experience through the products or services that companies provide (Cleff and Walter, 2014).

Schmitt (1999) also emphasises the importance of experience, as consumers no longer demand functional values, but rather are looking for products and services which offers cognitive, behavioural, sensorial, and emotional values, describing experience as:

> the private events that occur in response to stimulation and often result from direct observation and/or participation in events, whether real, virtual, or in dreams providing sensory, emotional, cognitive, behavioural, and relational value that replaces functional values.
>
> *p. 60*

Throughout the years, the literature has offered different definitions of experience, as it has been evident that interest in experience is gradually increasing (Groeppel-Klein, 2005; Gulas and Bloch, 1995; Krishna, 2011a: Krishna, 2011b; Morrin and Ratneshwar, 2003).

Solutions and recommendations

There are various definitions of 'experience', which fall into different categories. The word 'experience' is derived from the Latin *experiential* and means:

TABLE 10.1 The various concept of 'experience' defined by scholars in marketing literature

Author	Year	Construct	Definition
Holbrook and Hirschman	1982	Customer experience	"A phenomenon directed toward the pursuit of fantasies, feelings and fun' (p. 132).
Hui and Bateson	1991	Service experience	'The consumer's emotional feelings during the service encounter' (p. 33).
Arnould and Price	1993	Service experience	'Experience is characterized by high levels of emotional intensity and is triggered by unusual event' (p. 26).
Carbone and Haeckel	1994	Customer experience	'The takeaway impression formed by people's encounters with products, services, and businesses – a perception produced when humans consolidate sensory information' (p. 8).
Pine and Gilmore	1998	Customer experience	'An experience occurs when a company intentionally uses services as the stage, and goods as props, to engage individual customer in a way that creates a memorable event. Commodities are fungible, goods tangible, services intangible, and experiences memorable' (p. 98).
Gupta and Vajic	2000	Service experience	'Experience is an emergent phenomenon. It is the outcome of participation in a set of activities within a social context. (…) An experience occurs when a customer has any sensation or knowledge acquisition resulting from some level of interaction with different elements of a context created by a service provider' (p. 33).
Shaw and Ivens	2002	Customer experience	'An interaction between an organisation and a customer. It is a blend of an organisation's physical performance, the senses stimulated, and emotions evoked each intuitively against customer experience across all moments of contact' (p. 6).
Poulsson and Kale	2004	Commercial experience	'An engaging act of co-creation between a provider and a consumer wherein the consumer perceives value in the encounter and in the subsequent memory of that encounter' (p. 270).
Berry et al.	2006	Service experience	'What is an experience clue? It is anything in the service experience the customer perceives by its presence – or absence. If the customer can see, hear, taste, or smell it, it is a clue' (p. 44).

(*continued*)

TABLE 10.1 Cont.

Author	Year	Construct	Definition
Mascarenhas	2006	Customer experience	'A totally positive, engaging, enduring, and socially fulfilling physical and emotional consumer experience across all major levels of consumer consumption chain and one that is brought about by a distinct market offering that calls for active interaction between consumers and providers' (p. 399).
Meyer and Schwager	2007	Customer experience	'The internal and subjective response customers have to any direct or indirect contact with a company' (p. 2).
Gentile et al.	2007	Customer experience	'A set of interactions between a customer and a product, a company, or part of its organisation, which provoke a reaction. This experience is strictly personal and implies the customer's involvement at different levels (rational, emotional, sensorial, physical and spiritual. Its evaluation depends on the comparison between a customer's expectations and the stimuli coming from the interaction with the company and its offering in correspondence of the different moments of contact or touch-points' (p. 397).
Sandstom et al.	2008	Service experience	'A service experience is the sum total of the functional and emotional outcome dimensions of any kind of service ... intangible services or tangible products. The service experience is always individual and unique to every single customer and every single occasion of consumption, and it assumes that the customer is an active co-creating part of the service consumption process' (p. 118).
Brakus et al.	2009	Brand experience	'The subjective, internal consumer responses (sensations, feelings, and cognitions) and behavioural responses evoked by brand-related stimuli' (p. 53).
Walter et al.	2010	Customer experience	'Customer's direct and indirect experience of the service process, the organisation, and the facilities and how the customer interacts with the service firm's representatives and other customers' (p. 238).

TABLE 10.1 Cont.

Author	Year	Construct	Definition
Klaus and Maklan	2011	Service experience	'Service experience is the customer's assessment of all attributes of their direct and indirect dealings with a service provider that explains their behavioural loyalty through repeat purchasing' (p. 21).

the state, extent, duration, or result of being engaged in a particular activity or in affairs, something approved by or made on the basis of such experience' or 'something personally encountered, undergone or lived through, as an event.

Gove, 1976, p. 800

Even though the history and definitions of experience have been provided in the sections above, in order to differentiate experience from other brand-related concepts, the next sections will provide further explanation on how experience diverges from other similar constructs such as satisfaction, attitude, and emotion (Brakus et al., 2009; Fishbein and Ajzen, 1975). Even though experience can be seen as converging to similar concepts, it is better to clarify the precise differences between experience and other-related constructs. The next sections will provide more clarity by reviewing the literature on experience and its differences from other-related constructs.

Experience versus satisfaction

Even though satisfaction is considered as one of the most important issues for business organisations of all types, there is little empirical evidence in the literature providing the conceptual differences between experience and satisfaction. According to the literature, one of the most-cited definitions refers to satisfaction as 'a customer's post-consumption evaluation of a product or services' (Mittal and Frennea, 2010, p. 3). From this definition, it can be noted that satisfaction is an outcome-orientated construct, which generally occurs when the perceived performance of a service or product matches the actual performance, or exceeds customers' expectations (Bearden and Teel, 1983). However, experience is a process-orientated construct: It can occur spontaneously, and can be short-term or long-term.

According to Brakus et al. (2009), 'over time, these long-lasting brand experiences, stored in consumer memory, should affect consumer satisfaction and loyalty' (p. 6). In the same vein, it is generally accepted by scholars (Heiens and Pleshko, 1996; Meyer and Schwager, 2007) that satisfaction can be a psychological phenomenon as a result of series of experiences, where the intensity of satisfaction can be calculated as the subtraction of good experiences from bad experiences.

Experience versus attitude

Attitudes refers to a 'learned predisposition to respond in a consistently favourable or unfavourable manner with respect to a given object' (Fishbein and Ajzen, 1975, p. 6). Another generally accepted conceptualisation of attitude refers to 'general evaluations based on beliefs or automatic affective reactions' (Brakus et al., 2009, p. 7). From the brand perspective, therefore, it can be said that brand attitude can be defined as a positive or negative general evaluation of a brand. Unlike brand attitude, brand experience, for example, cannot be considered as 'general evaluative judgements' towards a brand: Brand experience consists of specific feelings coming from sensations, emotions, cognitions, and behavioural responses (Brakus et al., 2009).

Even though brand experience consists of specific dimensions rather than general evaluations, a small fraction of brand experience comprises the general evaluations in which consumers express their experience of a brand. Nevertheless, the precise difference between brand attitude and brand experience lies in 'learned predispositions' (Fishbein and Ajzen, 1975, p. 6) versus 'specific sensations, feelings, cognitions and behavioural responses triggered by specific brand related stimuli' (Brakus et al., 2009, p. 7). Therefore, it can be clearly said that attitude differs from experience, as discussed above (Palmer, 2010).

Experience versus emotion

According to Park et al. (2010), attachment can be explained as the strong emotional bond evoked towards a brand, characterised by three important emotional elements: Affection, passion, and connection. Regarding the conceptualisation of the differences between experience and brand attachment, Brakus et al. (2009) note that 'over time, experiences may result in emotional bonds, but emotions are only one internal outcome of the situation that evokes experiences' (p. 54).

'Experience' in marketing: How to conceptualise it?

From the definitions proposed in Table 10.1, it can be seen that there is a recognition of companies going beyond the functional value of products or services they provide, and creating value by provoking emotions. The early definitions could lead scholars to understand that experience can be conceptualised with emotions and feelings (Arnould and Price, 1993; Holbrook and Hirschman, 1982; Hui and Bateson, 1991); however, this is not the case. Experience has been conceptualised by scholars with different dimensions, and, as can be seen in Table 10.2, since it encapsulates not merely emotions and feelings, but also affective, cognitive and behavioural layers, it should be explored with a holistic approach (Brakus et al., 2009; Gentile et al., 2007).

Table 10.2 presents the studies which have provided the dimensions of experience in different contexts, and demonstrates that these are varied. A search of the literature reveals 180 different studies exploring experience in different contexts and industries, of which 113 present dimensions of the concept in different contexts. Looking at these different definitions, it can be seen that the dimensions of experience have evolved and have started to focus on different aspects such as physical (Gentile et al., 2007; Mascarenhas et al., 2006) and sensory (Brakus et al., 2009).

Looking at the different interpretations and dimensions of experience, it can be acknowledged that many of these are represented in narrow concepts. Zarantonello and Schmitt (2010) argue that, even though the definitions can vary, the concept of brand experience has the broadest conceptual notion in the marketing context. They further explain that the other experience concepts are limited either to specific industrial contexts (i.e., service

TABLE 10.2 Experience and its dimensions in the marketing literature

Author	Year	Type of study	Context	Dimensions
Holbrook and Hirschman	1982	Conceptual	–	Fun, feelings, fantasies
Hirschman	1984	Empirical	Consumer	Cognition seekers, sensation seekers, novelty seekers
Alba and Hutchinson	1987	Conceptual	–	Cognitive effort, cognitive structure, analysis, elaboration, memory
Fournier	1991	Conceptual	–	Functional, experiential, identity roles
Hui and Bateson	1991	Empirical	–	Emotions
Arnould and Price	1993	Empirical	Leisure	Harmony with nature, communities, personal growth, self-renewal
Otto and Ritchie	1996	Empirical	Tourism	Hedonic, novelty, stimulation, safety, comfort, interactive
Grove and Fisk	1997	Empirical	Retail	Social interaction, presence of others, servicescape, waiting lines, demographic variables
Pine and Gilmore	1998	Conceptual	–	Entertainment, education, aestheticism, escape
Hoeffler and Ariely	1999	Empirical	–	Effort, choice, experience
McIntosh	1999	Empirical	Heritage	Environment, presence of other visitors
Schmitt	1999	Conceptual	–	Sense (sensory experiences), feel (affective experiences), think (cognitive experiences), act (physical experiences), relate (social identity experiences)
Holbrook	2000	Review	–	Experience, entertainment, exhibitionism, evangelizing
Grenwell et al.	2002	Empirical	Sports	Core product, service personnel, physical facility
Poulsson and Kale	2004	Empirical	Leisure	Personal, relevance, novelty, surprise, learning, engagement
O'Cass and Grace	2004	Empirical	Bank	Core service, interpersonal service, advertising servicescape, self-image congruence, publicity, word of mouth, brand name, brand aroused feelings, country of origin
Chang and Chieng	2006	Empirical	Service brands	Individual experience (sense, feel, think), shared experience (act, relate)
Rahman	2006	Empirical	Bank	Cognitive, emotional, physical
Mascarenhas	2006	Empirical	–	Social, physical, emotional

(*continued*)

TABLE 10.2 Cont.

Author	Year	Type of study	Context	Dimensions
Gentile et al.	2007	Empirical	–	Sensorial, emotional, cognitive, pragmatic, lifestyle, relational component
Knutson et al.	2007	Empirical	Hospitality	Incentive, benefit, convenience, utility, trust, environment, accessibility
Tynan and McKechnie	2008	Conceptual	–	Enjoyment, entertainment, learning, skills, nostalgia, fantasising, evangelising
Wirtz and Mattilla	2009	Empirical	–	Objective knowledge, subjective knowledge
Grewal et al.	2009	Empirical	Retail	Political, economic, promotion, price, merchandise, supply chain, location
Verhoef et al.	2009	Empirical	Retail	Social environment, service interface, atmosphere, price, assortment, channel, past customer experience
Brakus	2009	Empirical	Consumer brands	Sensory, emotional, intellectual, behavioural
Slatten et al.	2009	Empirical	Winter park	Ambience, interaction, design
Jain and Bagdare	2011	Empirical	Retail	Emotional, cognitive, physiological, behavioural, social
Zarantonello and Schmitt	2010	Empirical	Brand	Sensory, affective, behavioural, intellectual
Kaplandiou and Vogt	2010	Empirical	Sports	Emotional, organisational, social, physical, environmental
Walls et al.	2011	Empirical	Luxury hotels	Physical environment (ambience, sensorial, functional, symbolic), human interaction (employees and fellow guests)
Kim et al.	2012	Empirical	Tourism	Hedonism, refreshment, local culture, meaningfulness, knowledge, involvement, novelty
Brocato et al.	2012	Empirical	Retail	Similarity, physical appearance, suitable behaviour

experience) or to a certain timeframe of consumers' behaviour (i.e., shopping experience) (Zarantonello and Schmitt, 2010). According to Skaard et al. (2011),

> as for brand experience, we consider customer experience to span the context-specific experience terms such as shopping experience and service experience. However, if one assumes that both customers and non-customers may have experiences with a brand, brand experience remains the conceptually broadest experience construct.
>
> p. 2

TABLE 10.3 Experience and identification of common dimensions.

	Other names used	Authors and years
Sensory	Sense, sensorial, aesthetic, physiological	Holbrook and Hirschman (1982); Arnould and Price (1993); Pine and Gilmore (1998); Schmitt (1999); Goulding (2000); Dubé and Le Bel (2003); Poulsson and Kale (2004); Shaw and Ivens (2005); Berry et al. (2006); Gentile et al. (2007); Jain and Bagdare (2009); Hosany and Witham (2009); Verhoef (2009); Brakus et al. (2009); Klaus and Maklan (2011); Brocato et al. (2012); Klaus and Maklan (2012)
Emotional	Affective, feel, entertainment	Holbrook and Hirschman (1982); Pine and Gilmore (1998); Schmitt (1999); McIntosh and Prentice (1999); Goulding (2000); Dube and Le Bel (2003); Poulsson and Kale (2004); Shaw and Ivens (2005); Mascarenhas et al. (2006); Ralston et al. (2007); Gentile et al. (2007); Hosany and Witham (2009); Verhoef et al. (2009); Jain and Bagdare (2011); Brakus et al. (2009); Klaus and Maklan (2012)
Intellectual	Cognitive, functional, educational, stimulation	Holbrook and Hirschman (1982); Fournier (1991); Arnould and Price (1993); Mano and Oliver (1993); Otto and Ritchie (1996); Pine and Gilmore (1998); Schmitt (1999); Poulsson and Kale (2004); Ralston et al. (2007); Gentile et al. (2007); Verhoef et al. (2009); Hosany and Witham (2009); Brakus et al. (2009)
Behavioural	Physical, physical experiences, escapist, physical presence	Unger and Kernan (1983); Fournier (1991); Arnould and Price (1993); Pine and Gilmore (1998); Schmitt (1999); Poulsson and Kale (2004); Shaw and Ivens (2002); Hansen et al (2005); Mascarenhas et al. (2006); Gentile et al. (2007); Nagasawa (2008); Hosany and Witham (2010); Verhoef et al. (2009); Verhoef (2009); Jain and Bagdare (2011); Brakus et al. (2009)

In the same vein, Duncan and Moriarty (2006) further argue that in the experience concept, brand should be the 'touchpoint' where a company provides the experience. It has also been noted that a brand 'touchpoint' is created when a customer, prospect, or other stakeholder is exposed, in some manner, to a brand and consequently has 'a brand experience' (Duncan and Moriarty, 2006, p. 237). In the light of the discussion presented above, it can be said that brand experience promotes the idea of the multidimensionality of experience and also encapsulates the main themes, which are the sensory, behavioural, affective, and intellectual dimensions. Table 10.3 presents the four dimensions of brand experience and the intersections of dimensions with other studies.

Future research directions

According to Achrol and Kotler (2012), the core of marketing – which itself is carried out to enable companies to better compete with one another in order to survive – is consumption. In traditional marketing, consumer satisfaction was considered key, with products being described in terms of utility; however, marketers in the twenty-first century primarily focus on experience and the human senses, and on how these can benefit from the growth of technology and the age of information (Achrol and Kotler, 2012; Brakus et al., 2009; Gentile et al.,

2007). Many prominent studies posit that, in experiential marketing, consumer experience is formed by consumer responses (i.e., sensations, feelings, and cognition), which are themselves triggered by brand-related stimuli; thus, consumer experience is filtered through the human senses (Achrol and Kotler, 2012; Brakus et al., 2009; Krishna, 2012; Lindstrom, 2006).

In this vein, if we look at the practical applications, it is evident to see that companies have tried to employ multisensorial branding strategies to deliver more effective brand experiences so as to interact with consumers in multisensory and hedonic ways (Helmefalk and Hulten, 2017; Pine and Gilmore, 1998; Pralahad and Ramaswamy, 2004; Schmitt, 1999). As Lindstrom (2006) notes, the leading service brands thought to deliver the most influential branding experiences, such as *Disney*, *Starbucks Coffee*, and *Singapore Airlines*, embed their brand features into the experience that they promise to deliver to their consumers (Ding and Tseng, 2015; Tynan and McKechnie, 2009).

The literature pertinent to experience and the senses has drawn much attention to psychology and sociology, since postmodern consumers have been seeking both individual and collective brand experiences (Wright, et al., 2006; Ding and Tseng, 2015; Simmons, 2008). Thus, the human senses are considered to be the determining phenomenon for delivering an effective *experience* to gain a competitive edge for companies (Tynan and McKechnie, 2009).

Conclusion

The definitions of experience in the literature suggest understanding has evolved from 'fantasies, feeling and fun' (Hirschman and Holbrook, 1982, p. 132) to the 'subjective, internal consumer responses (sensations, feelings and cognitions) and behavioural responses evoked by brand-related stimuli' (Brakus et al., 2009, p. 53). The reasons for this transition are threefold:

1. Consumers used to be bombarded with 3,000 advertising messages in 1970s, and now consumers are bombarded with 10,000 messages by marketers a day (Lindstrom, 2005; Pentz and Gerber, 2013; Vinnikova, 2016). The traditional communication channels used by marketers no longer satisfy consumers, therefore this challenge has forced marketers to change their communication strategies (Cleff and Walter, 2014).
2. With the advent of heavy dependence on technology, there is a reciprocal relationship, whereby on the one hand companies deliver their services and products by using technological advances in the production, promotion, distribution, and consumption of goods (Hracs et al., 2013, p. 1144); while on the other hand, the challenging yet attainable opportunities afforded by technology to bring down the entry barriers to the market create fierce competition for companies wishing to increase their market share (Cleff and Walter, 2014). In the same vein, according to Brown (2017):

> now consumers are in a state of permanent connectivity, even when hundreds of feet below ground on the tube or thousands of feet above ground in the air. The expectation is a seamless, frictionless experience with businesses irrespective of the channel or combination of channels.
>
> *p. 1*

This discussion highlights that providing experiences to consumers will become more and more important for companies wishing to position themselves in the competitive

market, since as 'goods and services become commoditised, the customer experiences that companies create will matter most' (Pine and Gilmore, 1998, p. 97). Therefore, the need can be seen to investigate experience and its outcomes so that companies can provide a more sophisticated experience through their brands.
3. As consumers are seeking pleasure and trying to fit brands and products to their lifestyles (Cleff and Walter, 2014; Fransen and Lodder, 2010), the experience that a company provides through its brands and services can be considered as becoming a core concept for consumers (O'Shaughnessy and O'Shaughnessy, 2002).

CASE STUDY – AVON COSMETICS AND BRAND SENSUALITY

Maria Palazzo, University of Salerno, Italy

Tugra Nazli Akarsu, University of Southampton, United Kingdom

The literature reveals that there are various definitions of brand sensuality. The definition of senses can be traced back to Aristotle, who defined them as *tactus* (touch), *odoratus* (smell), *auditus* (hearing), *gustus* (taste), and *visus* (sight).

In the marketing discipline, there is a common supposition that 'sense' and 'experience' are synonyms, however, they are not. Sensory marketing deals with how consumers engage with the sensory aspects of products that appeal to the human senses; while experience involves a broader perspective, embodying the whole experience of a consumer, including not just the senses but also events, advertisements, employees, etc. Therefore, it is logical to say that the use of sensory marketing, i.e., the use of sensorial stimuli in connection with a company's services or products, can lead a consumer to have a positive attitude, which, in turn, enables him or her to have a pleasurable experience with the company's services or products by virtue of sensorial gratification. The next sections, therefore, provide an enhanced understanding of the evolution of sensory marketing, in the case of Avon.

Introduction

According to the information provided on the corporate website, Avon

> is the leading social selling beauty company in North America, and Avon's North American business includes independent sales Representatives across the United States, Puerto Rico, and Canada. (…) It's been over 60 years since Avon launched in the UK, growing to become a household name that everyone knows and loves. From 'ding-dong' deliveries of our beloved brochures to sharing stories on Instagram, we've grown to become a beauty brand people connect with.
>
> *www.avon.uk.com/About-Avon/*

Avon, the biggest directly selling company is present in more than 150 nations. The organisation was born with a quite radical business model in 1886, when David H. McConnell decided to sell perfumes door-to-door in the US. Avon has nowadays developed a bigger portfolio which involves many beauty, home, and fashion products (i.e., cleansers and toners, makeup, fragrances, skin care products, hair care products, watches, bath and body products, toys, children wear, etc.) (Klepacki, 2010; Chelekis and Mudambi, 2010).

Brand sensuality as a base for brand value

During its early years, in addition to first-of-its-kind business model, McConnell realised that in his door-to-door business model, the most efficient way to reach out to its target market (females) was to hire women as sales representatives (Avon Representatives, 2020). This led him to recruit a team of women to be sales representatives, aligned with his passion on empowering women by giving them their economic freedom (Avon Worldwide, 2020). With its increasing presence of female salesperson team in the US, the term 'Avon Lady' was born – to identify the elegant female salespeople of Avon. In early 1950s, Avon launched its revolutionary and considered to be the one of the longest-running advertising campaigns: 'Ding Dong, Avon calling' – showing an elegant 'Avon Lady' aligned with a catchy jingle. This iconic ad has been used by Avon from 1954 to 1967, where different variations of its iconic hook: 'Ding Dong' has been latter used on many other Avon ad campaigns throughout the years. In addition to its iconic advertising campaigns, Avon started to publish 'Avon brochures' and used one of the popular gimmicks: offered free samples in the brochures for the advertised products.

Avon has created a strong brand value becoming the 'most trusted brand' in different countries and 'the top 100 brands of America' according with the opinion of several experts of the sector. The confidence that Avon induced in its clients has created a brand image which use brand sensuality's features to promote the overall companies' characteristics and its products while setting the basis for a strong customer bond.

Through its foundation, with a slogan of 'Avon for Women: We believe in a better world for women, which is a better world for all' (Avon Worldwide, 2020), Avon Foundation is investing in supporting several philanthropic causes devoted to increase awareness of breast cancer prevention, end domestic violence against women, and support economic freedom of women: This helped to link the company brand with positive feelings and emotions in the mind of customers (Racolta-Paina and Luncasu, 2014).

What has made Avon able to reach this goal is the way it deals with clients: It does not offer just products but well-being and self-esteem that associate the brand with the progressive empowerment of women in everyday life. Besides, Avon has been able to leverage on a successful way of getting in contact with customers: Its unique strategy of increasing sales has made Avon capable of reaching its clients directly and attaining immediate feedback. This not only helps in defining its brand value but also develops an original customer–company relationship.

Brand sensuality as a base for brand image

Avon has always presented its brand sensuality as the key component to develop a brand of woman. The brand image of Avon is reinforced not only on the fact that the brand offers good products to the customers but also as it is active in creating job opportunities to woman who can choose how to work for the company and be more independent. Actually, while the cost of many products is under $10, the organisation provides financial help to sale representatives to get almost 40% of the achieved profit: This is an encouragement for the employees to join the corporation (Dolan and Scott, 2009).

The Avon brand image is reinforced due to the fact that the company has been working not only following utilitarian purposes but also has chosen to pay attention to several philanthropic causes: This has added a positive side to its corporate reputation. Philanthropist brand image is expressed also by the fact that Avon has decided not to conduct any animal testing for its products.

Case questions

1. Please explain how Avon can use brand sensuality to strengthen its brand image and reputation.
2. Please analyse the brand sensuality in Avon.
3. Please explore how sales representatives can rise the sensorial cues of the Avon products and brand.

References

Avon Corporate Website (2020). www.avon.com/
Avon Representatives (2020). www.reps-r-us.co.uk/
Avon Worldwide Foundation (2020). www.avonworldwide.com/about-us/our-story
Chelekis, J. and Mudambi, S. M. (2010). MNCs and micro-entrepreneurship in emerging economies: The case of Avon in the Amazon. Journal of International Management, 16(4), 412–424.
Dolan, C. and Scott, L. (2009). Lipstick evangelism: Avon trading circles and gender empowerment in South Africa. Gender and Development, 17(2), 203–218.
Klepacki, L. (2010). Avon: Building the world's premier company for women. John Wiley & Sons, New York.
Racolta-Paina, N. D. and Luncasu, A. (2014). The sales force of multi-level marketing companies in the context of the marketing communications mix. Case study: Avon Cosmetics Romania. In the Proceedings of the International Conference "Marketing- from Information to Decision" (p. 185). Babes Bolyai University, Romania.

Key terms and definitions

Brand attachment is the strong emotional bond evoked towards a brand, characterised by three emotional components: Affection, passion, and connection.
Brand attitude is the consumers' positive or negative general evaluation of a brand.
Brand experience is a sum of all engaging interactions between brand and consumer, where the brand tries to connect with the consumer by creating a memorable, sensorial, emotional,

and spiritual level of involvement via the brand's products, goods, services, and atmospheric cues.

Branding is the process of creating an identification and differentiation through name, symbol, design, which gives a unique holistic representation of an entity, which in turn becomes the most valuable asset.

Satisfaction is a psychological and an outcome-orientated phenomenon, which generally occurs when the perceived performance of a service or product matches the actual performance, or exceeds customers' expectations

The progression of the economic value allows companies to evolve their commodities into goods, then customise those goods in order to transform them into services, and to customise services into experiences – which will be, for them, the highest value offered by companies.

Note

1 Please note that the title/subtitles of this section should be content specific.

References

Achrol, R. S. and Kotler, P. (2012). Frontiers of the marketing paradigm in the third millennium. Journal of the Academy of Marketing Science, 40(1), 35–52.

Akarsu, T. N., Foroudi, P., and Melewar, T. C. (2020). What makes Airbnb likeable? Exploring the nexus between service attractiveness, country image, perceived authenticity and experience from a social exchange theory perspective within an emerging economy context. International Journal of Hospitality Management, 91, 1–14.

Akarsu, T. N., Melewar, T. C., and Foroudi, P. (2019). Sensory Branding: What it is, why it matters, and how to use it. In, Foroudi, P. and Palazzo, M. (Eds.), Contemporary Issues in Branding. 1st ed., pp. 131–152 London: Routledge.

Alba, J. W. and Hutchinson, J. W. (1987). Dimensions of consumer expertise. Journal of Consumer Research, 13(4), 411–454.

Arnould, E. J. and Price, L. L. (1993). River magic: Extraordinary experience and the extended service encounter. Journal of Consumer Research, 20(1), 24–45.

Bearden, W. O., and Teel, J. E. (1983). Selected determinants of consumer satisfaction and complaint reports. Journal of Marketing Research, 20(1), 21–28.

Berry, L. L., Wall, E. A., and Carbone, L. P. (2006). Service clues and customer assessment of the service experience: Lessons from marketing. Academy of Management Perspectives, 20(2), 43–57.

Brakus, J. J., Schmitt, B. H., and Zarantonello, L. (2009). Brand experience: What is it? How is it measured? Does it affect loyalty? Journal of Marketing, 73(3), 52–68.

Brocato, E. D., Voorhees, C. M., and Baker, J. (2012). Understanding the influence of cues from other customers in the service experience: A scale development and validation. Journal of Retailing, 88(3), 384–398.

Brown, T. (2017). Why consumers are now dependent on digital? Raconteur. Available at: www.raconteur.net/why-consumers-are-now-dependent-on-digital/

Buswell, J., Williams, C., Donne, K., and Sutton, C. (2016). Service Quality in Leisure, Events, Tourism and Sport (2nd ed.). Oxford: CABI Tourism Texts.

Carbone, L. and Haeckel, S. H. (1994). Engineering customer experiences. Journal of Marketing Management, 3(3), 8–19.

Caru, A. and Cova, B. (2003). Revisiting consumption experience: A more humble but complete view of the concept. Marketing Theory, 3(2), 267–286.

Chang, P. and Chieng, M. (2006). Building consumer–brand relationship: A crosscultural experiential view. Psychology and Marketing, 23(11), 927–959.

Cleff, T., Lin, I. C. and Walter, N. (2014). Can you feel it? The effect of brand experience on brand equity. Journal of Brand Management, 11(2), 7–27.

Ding, C. G. and Tseng, T. H. (2015). On the relationships among brand experience, hedonic emotions, and brand equity. European Journal of Marketing, 49(7/8), 994–1015.

Dubé, L. and Le Bel, J. (2003). The content and structure of laypeople's concept of pleasure. Cognition and Emotion, 17(2), 263–295.

Duncan, T. and Moriarty, S. (2006). How integrated marketing communication's 'touchpoints' can operationalize the service-dominant logic? In Vargo, S. L. and Lusch, R. F. (Eds.), The Service-Dominant Logic of Marketing: Dialog, Debate and Directions (pp. 236–249). Armonk, NY: M. E. Sharpe.

Fishbein, M. and Ajzen, I. (1975). Belief, Attitude, Intention, and Behavior: An Introduction to Theory and Research. Reading, MA: Addison-Wesley.

Foroudi, P., Akarsu, T. N., Ageeva, E., Foroudi, M. M., Dennis, C., and Melewar, T. C. (2018). Promising the dream: Changing destination image of London through the effect of website place. Journal of Business Research, 83, 97–110.

Fournier, S. (1991). Meaning-based framework for the study of consumer-object relations. Association for Consumer Research, 18, 736–742.

Fransen, M. L. and Lodder, P. (2010). The effects of experience-based marketing communication on brand relation and hedonic brand attitudes: The moderating role of affective orientation. Advances in Consumer Research, 37, 801–802.

Gentile, C., Spiller, N., and Noci, G. (2007). How to sustain the customer experience: An overview of experience components that co-create value with the customer. European Management Journal, 25(5), 395–410.

Goulding, C. (2000). The museum environment and the visitor experience. European Journal of marketing, 34(3/4), 261–278.

Gove, P. B. (ed.) (1976). Webster's Third New International Dictionary. Massachusettes, MA: G. and C. Merriam Company.

Greenwell, T. C., Fink, J. S., and Pastore, D. L. (2002). Assessing the influence of the physical sports facility on customer satisfaction within the context of the service experience. Sport Management Review, 5(2), 129–148.

Grewal, D., Levy, M., and Kumar, V. (2009). Customer experience management in retailing: An organizing framework. Journal of Retailing, 85(1), 1–14.

Groeppel-Klein, A. (2005). Arousal and consumer in-store behaviour. Brain Research Bulletin, 67(5), 428–437.

Gross, B. L. and Sheth, J. N. (1989). Time-oriented advertising: A content analysis of United States magazine advertising, 1890–1988. Journal of Marketing, 53(4), 76–84.

Grove, S. J., and Fisk, R. P. (1997). The impact of other customers on service experiences: A critical incident examination of 'getting along'. Journal of Retailing, 73(1), 63–85.

Gulas, C. S. and Bloch, P. H. (1995). Right under our noses: Ambient scent and consumer responses. Journal of Business and Psychology, 10(1), 87–98.

Gupta, S. and Vajic, M. (2000). The contextual and dialectical nature of experiences. In Fitzsimmons, J. A. and Fitzsimmons, M. J. (Eds.), New Service Development: Creating Memorable Experiences (pp. 33–51). Thousand Oaks, CA: Sage Publications.

Heiens, R. A. and Pleshko, L. P. (1996). Categories of customer loyalty: An application of the customer loyalty classification framework in the fast food market. Journal of Food Products Marketing, 3(1), 1–12.

Helmefalk, M., and Hultén, B. (2017). Multi-sensory congruent cues in designing retail store atmosphere: Effects on shoppers' emotions and purchase behavior. Journal of Retailing and Consumer Services, 38, 1–11.

Hirschman, E. C. (1984). Experience seeking: A subjectivist perspective of consumption. Journal of Business Research, 12(1), 115–136.

Hirschman, E. C. and Holbrook, M. B. (1982). Hedonic consumption: Emerging concepts, methods and propositions. Journal of Marketing, 46(3), 92–101.

Hoch, S. (2002). Product Experience Is Seductive. Journal of Consumer Research, 29 (December), 448–454.
Hoeffler, S. and Ariely, D. (1999). Constructing stable preferences: A look into dimensions of experience and their impact on preference stability. Journal of Consumer Psychology, 8(2), 113–139.
Holbrook, M. B. (2000). The millennial consumer in the texts of our times: Experience and entertainment. Journal of Macromarketing, 20(2), 178–192.
Hosany, S. and Witham, M. (2010). Dimensions of cruisers' experiences, satisfaction, and intention to recommend. Journal of Travel Research, 49(3), 351–364.
Hracs, B. J., Jakob, D., and Hauge, A. (2013). Standing out in the crowd: The rise of exclusivity-based strategies to compete in the contemporary marketplace for music and fashion. Environment and Planning A, 45(5), 1144–1161.
Hui, M. K. and Bateson, J. E. (1991). Perceived control and the effects of crowding and consumer choice on the service experience. Journal of Consumer Research, 18(2), 174–184.
Jain, R. and Bagdare, S. (2011). Music and consumption experience: A review. International Journal of Retail and Distribution Management, 39(4), 289–302.
Kapferer, J. N. (2004). The New Strategic Brand Management: Creating and Sustaining Brand Equity Long Term. London: Kogan Page.
Kaplanidou, K. and Vogt, C. (2010). The meaning and measurement of a sport event experience among active sport tourists. Journal of sport management, 24(5), 544–566.
Kerin, R. A., Jain, A., and Howard, D. J. (1992). Store shopping experience and consumer price-quality-value perceptions. Journal of Retailing, 68(4), 376–397.
Kim, J. H., Ritchie, J. B., and McCormick, B. (2012). Development of a scale to measure memorable tourism experiences. Journal of Travel research, 51(1), 12–25.
Klaus, P. and Maklan, S. (2011). Bridging the gap for destination extreme sports – a model of sports tourism customer experience. Journal of Marketing Management, 27(13–14), 1341–1365.
Knutson, B. J., Beck, J. A., Kim, S. H., and Cha, J. (2007). Identifying the dimensions of the experience construct. Journal of Hospitality and Leisure Marketing, 15(3), 31–47.
Krishna, A. (2011a). An integrative review of sensory marketing: Engaging the senses to affect perception, judgment and behaviour. Journal of Consumer Psychology, 22(3), 332–351.
Krishna, A. (2011b). Sensory marketing: Research on the sensuality of products. Hoboken, NY: Taylor and Francis Group.
Krishna, A. (2012). An integrative review of sensory marketing: Engaging the senses to affect perception, judgment and behavior. Journal of Consumer Psychology, 22(3), 332–351.
Landa, R. (2005). Designing Brand Experience: Creating Powerful Integrated Brand Solutions. New York: Delmar Cengage Learning.
Lindstrom, M. (2005). Brand Sense: build Powerful Brands Through Touch, Taste, Smell, Sight and Sound. New York: Simon & Schuster Adult Publishing Group.
Lindstrom, M. (2006). Brand sense: How to build powerful brands through touch, taste, smell, sight and sound. Strategic Direction, 22(2).
Mano, H. and Oliver, R. L. (1993). Assessing the dimensionality and structure of the consumption experience: Evaluation, feeling, and satisfaction. Journal of Consumer Research, 20, 451–466.
Mascarenhas, O. A., Kesavan, R., and Bernacchi, M. (2006). Lasting customer loyalty: A total customer experience approach. Journal of Consumer Marketing, 23(7), 397–405.
McIntosh, A. J. and Prentice, R. C. (1999). Affirming authenticity: Consuming cultural heritage. Annals of Tourism Research, 26(3), 589–612.
Meyer, C. and Schwagner, A. (2007). Understanding Customer Experience. Zurich: Harvard Business Review.
Mittal, V. and Frennea, C. (2010). Customer satisfaction: A strategic review and guidelines for managers. MSI Fast Forward Series, Marketing Science Institute, Cambridge, MA.
Moore, K. and Lewis, L. (2005). Birth the Multinational II. Copenhagen: Copenhagen Business School Press.

Moore, K. and Reid, S. (2008). The birth of brand: 4000 years of branding. Business History, 50(4), 419–432.

Morrin, M. and Ratneshwar, S. (2003). Does it make sense to use scents to enhance brand memory? Journal of Marketing Research, 40(1), 10–25.

Nagasawa, S. Y. (2008). Customer experience management: Influencing on human Kansei to management of technology. The TQM Journal, 20(4), 312–323.

O'Cass, A. and Grace, D. (2004). Exploring consumer experiences with a service brand. Journal of Product and Brand Management, 13(4), 257–268.

Ongun, M. T. (2012). '1980'lerden Küresel Krize Dünya Ekonomisi', Ekonomik Yaklaşım, 23, 39–76.

O'Shaughnessy, J. and Jackson O'Shaughnessy, N. (2002). Marketing, the consumer society and hedonism. European Journal of Marketing, 36(5/6), 524–547.

Osborne, R. (1996). Greece in the making, 1200–479 BCE. London: Routledge.

Otto, J. E. and Ritchie, J. (1996). The service experience in tourism. Tourism Management, 17(3), 165–174.

Palmer, A. (2010). Customer experience management: A critical review of an emerging idea. Journal of Services Marketing, 24(3), 196–208.

Park, C. W., MacInnis, D. J., Priester, J., Eisingerich, A. B., and Iacobucci, D. (2010). Brand attachment and brand attitude strength: Conceptual and empirical differentiation of two critical brand equity drivers. Journal of Marketing, 74(6), 1–17.

Pentz, C. and Gerber, C. (2013). The influence of selected senses on consumer experience: A brandy case. Acta Commercii, 13(1), 1–7.

Pine, B. J. and Gilmore, J. H. (1998). The experience economy. Harvard Business Review, 76(6), 18–23.

Pine, B. J., Gilmore, J. H., and Joseph, I. B. (1998). Welcome to the experience economy. Harvard Business Review, 97–107.

Poulsson, S. H. and Kale, S. H. (2004). The experience economy and commercial experiences. The Marketing Review, 4(3), 267–277.

Prahalad, C. K. and Ramaswamy, V. (2004). Co-creation experiences: The next practice in value creation. Journal of Interactive Marketing, 18(3), 5–14.

Rahman, Z. (2006). Customer experience management—A case study of an Indian bank. Journal of Database Marketing and Customer Strategy Management, 13(3), 203–221.

Ralston, L. S., Ellis, G. D., Compton, D. M., and Lee, J. (2007). Staging memorable events and festivals: An integrated model of service and experience factors. International Journal of Event Management Research, 3(2), 24–38.

Sandström, S., Edvardsson, B., Kristensson, P., and Magnusson, P. (2008). Value in use through service experience. Managing Service Quality: An International Journal, 18(2), 112–126.

Schmitt, B. H. (1999). Experiential Marketing: How to get Customers to Sense, Feel, Think, Act and Relate to Your Company and Brands. New York: Free Press.

Shaw, C. and Ivens, J. (2002). Building Great Customer Experiences. New York: Palgrave MacMillan.

Simmons, G. (2008). Marketing to postmodern consumers: Introducing the internet chameleon. European Journal of Marketing, 42(3/4), 299–310.

Skard, S., Nysveen, H., and Pedersen, P. E. (2011). Brand and customer experience in service organizations: Literature review and brand experience construct validation, SNF Working Paper No. 9033. Available at: http://brage.bibsys.no/xmlui/bitstream/handle/11250/166668/ SNF_WP09_11.pdf?sequence1

Slåtten, T., Mehmetoglu, M., Svensson, G., and Sværi, S. (2009). Atmospheric experiences that emotionally touch customers. Managing Service Quality: An International Journal, 19(6), 721–746.

Tsai, S. P. (2005). Integrated marketing as management of holistic consumer experience. Business Horizons, 48(5), 431–441.

Tynan, C. and McKechnie, S. (2009). Experience marketing: A review and reassessment. Journal of Marketing Management, 25(5–6), 501–517.

Unger, L. S. and Kernan, J. B. (1983). On the meaning of leisure: An investigation of some determinants of the subjective experience. Journal of Consumer Research, 9(4), 381–392.

Verhoef, P. C., Lemon, K. N., Parasuraman, A., Roggeveen, A., Tsiros, M., and Schlesinger, L. A. (2009). Customer experience creation: Determinants, dynamics and management strategies. Journal of Retailing, 85(1), 31–41.

Vinnikova, A. (2016). A case of hedonic perception of foreigners towards Chinese culture-specific odours from scent marketing perspective. Archives of Business Research, 4(3), 21–44.

Walls, A., Okumus, F., Wang, Y., and Kwun, D. J. W. (2011). Understanding the consumer experience: An exploratory study of luxury hotels. Journal of Hospitality Marketing and Management, 20(2), 166–197.

Walter, U., Edvardsson, B., and Öström, Å. (2010). Drivers of customers' service experiences: A study in the restaurant industry. Managing Service Quality: An International Journal, 20(3), 236–258.

Wirtz, J. and Mattila, A. S. (2000). The moderating role of target-arousal on the impact of effect on satisfaction—an examination in the context of service experiences. Journal of Retailing, 76(3), 347–365.

Wolpert, S. A. (2000). A New History of India (6th ed.). New York: Oxford University Press.

Wright, L. T., Cova, B., and Pace, S. (2006). Brand community of convenience products: New forms of customer empowerment–the case 'my Nutella The Community'. European Journal of Marketing, 40(9–10), 1087–1105.

Zarantonello, L. and Schmitt, B. H. (2010). Using the brand experience scale to profile consumers and predict consumer behaviour. Journal of Brand Management, 17(7), 532–540

11

EVOLUTION OF SENSES

From no-nonsense era to the rise of sensory marketing

Tugra Nazli Akarsu

Introduction

This chapter aims to scrutinise the emergence of 'senses' for the last three decades by categorising it into three main eras: i) 1929–1970 – no-nonsense era; ii) 1970–1990 – the rise of advertisements; and iii) 1990 to date – the rise of sensory marketing.

Background

Even though marketing practices can be traced back to 2000–2500 BCE (Sheth and Parvatiyar, 1995; Moore and Reid, 2008; Wolpert, 2000), the domain of theories regarding the idea of creating *value and relationships* with consumers rather than traditional marketing logic has emerged since the 1980s (Achrol and Kotler, 2012; Holbrook and Hirschman, 1982). It can be said that the development of paradigms in marketing has been influenced by the recognition of the senses, cognition, emotion, and perception of consumers which were seen as incidental in traditional strategies (Rajput and Dhillon, 2013).

With the rising importance of understanding the scope of providing consumers with an experience in order to differentiate a brand from its competitors, and getting rid of conventional marketing strategies (Usunier and Lee, 2012) has led the evolving marketing pattern to understand the emotional and sensational standpoints of multisensorial strategies. Therefore, more recently, a holistic approach to brands has been implemented, and *sensual and emotional* content has been recognised in order to generate a favourable experience, where experiences are delivered through *senses, feelings,* and *cognitive and behavioural responses* (Brakus et al., 2009, Doyle, 1994). This paradigm shift has forced the current market to acknowledge the transformation in the field of marketing and to analyse consumers' perceptions of brands which evoke their senses and emotions (Hulten et al., 2009; Rajput and Dhillon, 2013).

From the managerial perspective, it may be expected that companies need to keep pace with the paradigm shifts and to take action towards the ongoing changing environment in order to retain existing customers and gain new ones. Therefore, there is a no longer a need for companies to concentrate on their own needs: Instead, they need to focus on customers' needs in order to provide them with a personal experience while altering their perceptions.

In order to make the shift from a linear buyer–seller approach to creating an emotional relationship between consumer and brand, the minds of consumers and human behavioural differences in decision-making processes need to be understood from the perspective of a sensorial approach. From the viewpoint of marketing executives, it is of the utmost importance to embrace paradigm shifts to be able to quickly respond to changing circumstances (Penaloza and Venkatesh, 2006).

The literature uncovers that there are various definitions of 'senses' in different studies (Hulten, 2013; Morrin and Ratneshwar, 2003; Peck and Childers, 2003; Raghubir and Krishna, 1999). Even though the conceptualisation varies, the definition of senses is coming through the same root: *Aristotle*. The definition of senses can be traced back to Aristotle, who defined them as *visus* (sight), *auditus* (hearing), *odoratus* (smell), *tactus* (touch), and *gustus* (taste) (Achrol and Kotler, 2003). The word sensory is rooted directly from Medieval Latin word '*sensationem*', and from Late Latin '*sensatus*' and finally, Latin '*sensus*' which implies '*pertaining to sense or sensations*' (Etymology Dictionary, 2020). Scrutiny of the marketing literature regarding the emergence of senses reveals that in terms of its conceptualisation, the phenomenon has existed only in the past three decades. Three main eras can be identified that are relevant in this context: i) 1929–1970 ('no-nonsense' era); ii) 1970–1990s (the rise of advertisements); and iii) 1990 to date (the rise of sensory marketing). Therefore, this chapter attempts to illustrate these three main eras to give an enhanced background towards an understanding of sensory marketing.

From no-nonsense era to the rise of sensory marketing

1929–1970: No-nonsense era

When the Great Depression (1929–1939) brought the US to a standstill, it created a domino effect in most markets, driving consumers to reduce their spending and live frugally (Flatters and Willmort, 2009). From the end of the Great Depression to the beginning of the 1970s, consumers continued to be motivated to live frugally, considered to be the source of significant economic downturn (Birkner, 2013; Lastovicka et al., 1999; Yeniaras and Akarsu, 2017). This whole period, including the Great Depression itself, is presented as the 'no-nonsense' era in terms of branding by Krishna (2011, p. 3). With the emergence of the popularity of branded goods in the 1970s, companies started to embed the sensorial aspects of the products in their advertising campaigns to appeal to consumers and create an interaction between consumers and the product (Krishna, 2011; Puccinelli et al., 2009).

1970–1990: The rise of advertisements

It is evident in the pertinent literature that from the 1970s to the 1980s, advertising was perceived as the best way to communicate with consumers. Companies tried to use sensorial stimuli in their advertising since TV and major magazines were the most available and common media to reach out to consumers (Bagwell, 2007; Teixeira, 2014). The first academic articles grasping the importance of store environment in affecting consumer behaviour can be traced back to the 1950s and 1960s (Cox, 1964; Martineau, 1958; Smith and Currow, 1966), but the milestone for this stream of thought can be considered 1970s, when Kotler's article 'Atmospherics as a marketing tool' was published in the *Journal of Retailing*. Kotler (1973) coined the term 'store environment', emphasising that atmosphere should not be neglected and store atmosphere should be conceived as the 'silent language' of communication with customers. Kotler (1973) also emphasises that atmosphere is:

> apprehended though sense. Therefore, an atmosphere of a particular set of surroundings is describable in sensory terms. The main sensory channels for atmosphere are sight, sound, scent and touch.
>
> *pp. 50–51*

Kotler's description of the store atmosphere as needing to be consciously designed to create certain impacts on consumers, such as enhancing the probability of purchasing behaviour, has been acknowledged by other scholars, as he is a pioneer on this intriguing subject (Turley and Milliman, 2000). Bitner (1992) later advocated the idea that the store atmosphere should be carefully designed and controlled by managers and practitioners, who could use these settings to change consumers' perceptions, stating:

> in marketing there is a surprising lack of empirical research or theoretically based framework addressing the role of physical surroundings in consumption settings. Managers continually plan, build and change an organisation's physical surroundings in an attempt to control its influence on patrons, without really knowing the impact of a specific design and atmospheric change on its users.
>
> *p. 57*

Even though the concept of atmosphere and its effects was proposed by Cox (1964) and Kotler more than 50 years ago, the mainstream retail environment and the building of sensorial cues into the retail atmospheric were not sufficiently captured until the beginning of the 1990s (Baker et al., 1992; Gulas and Schewe, 1994; Turley and Milliman, 2000). This is because at the end of the 1980s, with the emergence of the new perspective of hedonism in consumer behaviour, the concept of consumption underwent a breakthrough, switching away from being a functional and rational concept that fulfilled a need, and becoming something fun and with the need or desire for something different such as experiences and sensations (Berner and Van Tonder, 2003) or seeking pleasure (Malina and Schmidt, 1997).

1990 to date: The rise of sensory marketing

By the end of the 1980s, there was increased attention on traditional marketing's stance against consumer perceptions, and it was facing growing accusations of being too rational (Holbrook and Hirschman, 1982; Daucé and Rieunier, 2002; Schmitt, 1999; Solomon 2008). According to the empirical research, it is agreed that several factors have an impact on buying behaviour, which means consumers can no longer be seen in purely rational terms: these factors include 'hedonism, fantasies, feelings and fun (Holbrook and Hirschman, 1982); the moods of consumers

(Hill and Gardner, 1987), and consumption rituals (Rook, 1985)' (Farias et al., 2014, p. 87). This revolutionary shift from the rational paved the way to considering a new aspect in consumption, 'the influence of experiential', as discussed by Holbrook and Hirschman (1982). From the 1980s to the present day, different aspects of experience have been reviewed and investigated by scholars (Donovan and Rossiter, 1982; Pullman and Gross, 2004; Schmitt, 1999); and with the transformation of marketing and the increased recognition of experience, it has been agreed that in order to create positive experiences, sensorial strategies and different cues should be investigated, as it is 'the creation of a consumption environment that produces specific emotional effects on the person, like pleasure or excitation that can increase his possibility of buying' (Kotler, 1973, p. 49).

From this perspective, Kotler's (1973) emphasis on creating a controlled store atmosphere should matter more to retail managers and brand practitioners, as shops are the most convenient location for consumer-brand interaction and for using consumers' senses to give them an enhanced positive experience by manipulating their perceptions towards the brand (Donovan and Rossiter, 1982; Farias et al., 2014). For many marketers, managers, and practitioners, finding an ideal strategy to generate positive responses from consumers is critical; for retailers, it should be more important to embrace sensory strategies, since a larger set of consumers' behavioural outcomes are connected to the sensorial strategies a brand can implement by using different dimensions.

From one of the earlier studies belonging to this era, Turley and Milliman (2000) emphasises the effect of atmospherics on shopping behaviour by reviewing the pertinent literature to expand both theoretical and empirical understanding for further studies. They conceptualise atmospherics as stimuli which lead to a cognitive effect within individuals and, in turn, lead individuals to behavioural responses.

As Turley and Milliman (2000) state:

> the physical environment interacts with the characteristics of individuals to determine their response. Therefore, an atmosphere that produces a certain response in one individual or group of people at a given point in time may produce an entirely different response in another individual or group. For example, an atmosphere that produces a positive response in teenagers may produce a negative response in older shoppers. Second, the store's atmosphere influences both the customers and the store's employees, who, in turn, through their interactions, influence each other.
>
> p. 194

Another approach presented by Bonnin (2006) proposes a conceptual framework for the environment–customer relationship in service organisations. What Bonnin (2006) offers can be considered quite different from the other literature, since the study investigates the dimensions of the physical environment that create possible positive responses for service organisations, where different physical environments can lead customers to avoid the company or the services it provides. It proposes the ideal physical variables for a positively perceived servicescape that managers and practitioners might want to implement in their service settings.

Another influential study in terms of highlighting the literature gap and being a research motivator is Lin's (2004) 'consumer's evaluation process of a servicescape'. The study proposes a conceptual model as an extension of the *Gestalt approach* and principles of perception, where the Gestalt approach serves as a guide to understand and explain how an individual forms an impression or a perceptual image of a servicescape, how the image formation then leads to an emotional response, and finally, the actual appraisal or evaluation of a specific service environment.

Lin, 2004, p. 163

By proposing the often-ignored Gestalt concept, Lin (2004) underlines that perception plays a vital role in individuals' way of seeing the world, since it has a function of collecting cues and sources from both the environment and from 'one's own predisposition, expectations, motives, and knowledge gleaned from past learning experiences' (p. 164). Therefore, Lin (2004) articulates that little research has been conducted and not enough attention has yet been paid to consumers' perceptions and evaluations related to the servicescape.

The study notes that there are individual-level variables (micro-variables), and those which are outside the individual (macro-variables) that can influence an individual's way of mental image formation. Micro-variables can be pre-consumption expectations, goal behaviours, personality traits and cognitive style. Macro-variables, on the other hand, can be aesthetic effects (such as interior décor and design), and socio-cultural influences (e.g., *feng shui* principles, individualism vs. collectivism).

Lin (2004) uses the hotel industry to give an example of how individuals' perceptions are based on various stimuli they receive from the environment, or servicescape, which lead them to form a mental image, then to an evaluation stage and as a result, make a behavioural response. Lin takes a hotel lobby as a demonstration of a situation involving many different stimuli and variables, such as interior décor, colours, scents, music, or employees, that can all be evaluated and, in turn, lead individuals to demonstrate approach or avoidance behaviour. Therefore, the front desk alone can affect individuals, a fact which can be overlooked when assessing the main factors influencing customers' evaluation of a product or service. Table 11.1 presents the literature review conducted on the physical environment/servicescape/atmospherics and their dimensions in the relevant literature in a chronological order.

When it comes to Krishna's (2011) proposition of sensory marketing, she conceptualises perception and sensation as the stages of processing the senses. From the psychology perspective, perception can be defined as 'the active process of selecting, organising, and interpreting the information brought to the brain by senses' (Shergill, 2012, p. 81). Therefore, it is logical to say that while sensorial stimuli are collected from the environment, like data, perception refers to the interpretation of the data collected from the environment. Even though sensorial stimuli are collected and interpreted to create perception, it has been assumed that perception is not solely determined by the sensorial stimuli from the environment (Shergill, 2012). As Shergill (2012) highlights,

> perceptions are influenced by a whole range of factors relative to the individual. These include cultural background and experience, individual differences in personality or intelligence, values, past experience, motivations (both intrinsic and extrinsic), cognitive styles, emotional states, attention, perceptual set or readiness, prejudices, the context in which something is perceived and the individual's expectations.
>
> *p. 89*

Table 11.2 presents definitions of 'senses' in marketing literature proposed by scholars.

TABLE 11.1 Important terms and their dimensions introduced by researchers

Author	Year	Terms introduced	Dimensions of the term
Kotler	1973	Atmospherics	Visual, aural, olfactory, tactile
Baker	1986	Atmospherics	Ambient factors, design factors (aesthetics and functional), social factors
Parasumaran et al.	1988	Servqual	Reliability, responsiveness, empathy, assurance, tangibility
Bitner	1992	Servicescape	Ambient conditions, spatial layout and functionality, sign, symbols and artefacts
Baker et al.	1994	Store Atmospherics	Ambient factors, social factors, design factors
Berman and Evans	1995	Atmospherics	External variables, general interior variables, layout design variables, point of purchase and decoration variables
Wakefield and Blodgett	1996	Servicescape	Layout accessibility, facility aesthetics, facility cleanliness, seating comfort, electronic equipment and displays
Wakefield and Baker	1998	Tangible service factors	Building design, ambience, décor and equipment
Turley and Milliman	2000	Atmospherics	Human variables, external variables, general interior variables, layout design variables, point of purchase and decoration variables
Brady and Cronin	2001	Service quality	Quality of physical environment, interaction quality, outcome quality
Lin	2004	Servicescape	visual cues, audial cues, olfactory cues, emotional response, behavioural response
Venkatraman and Nelson	2008	Consumption space	Photo-elicitation built environment

Future research directions

According to the Sensory Retail Design Report (2016), 'retail spaces today are far more than mere locations where customers buy or compare products. They've become a place where consumers experience the brand, discover what it stands for and how it relates to their identity and lifestyle' (p. 10). With the increased significance of technology, changing lifestyles, and evolving customer needs (Rafaeli and Vinai-Yavetz, 2004), different visual technologies, such as virtual reality, are being used as a part of the servicescape, where consumers can have positive responses by experiencing a hint of future technology (Hyslop, 2015).

According to Villiers (2016), 'we (practitioners) acknowledge that marketing is the management and manipulation of sensory perception. Marketing establishes a connection or communication between the external (a brand, a product, a service) and the internal (the consumer; their needs, desires and sensory perception' (p. 2). As Villiers (2016) also highlights, for many

TABLE 11.2 Sensory marketing introduced by researchers

Author	Year	Terms introduced	Dimensions of the term
Raz et al.	2008	Sensory marketing	'Can be defined as a group of key levers which are controlled by the producer and/or by the distributor to create a specific multi-sensory atmosphere around the product or the service either by focusing on sale outlet environment or product environment, and the communication or characteristics of the product itself' (p. 719).
Krishna	2012	Sensory marketing	'The word of sensory means relating to sensation or the senses and the word sensual is similar in meaning, relating to a gratification of senses, as is the word sensuous. I define sensory marketing that engages the consumer senses and affects their behaviour … affect our emotions, memories, perceptions, preferences, choices, and consumption of products' (p. 1).
Hulten	2011	Multi-sensory brand experience	'Concept in relation to the human mind and senses – smell, sound, sight, taste, and touch – in generating customer value, experiences, and image' (p. 257).
Haase et al.	2018	Sensory perception	'The capture of the magnitude of each sensory dimension (i.e., visual, acoustic, haptic, olfactory, and gustatory), for example, to what degree the object of investigation is seen as visually appealing. As the presented approach comprises all five senses, all possible use cases are addressed, and the respective senses can be examined in a consistent manner' (p. 727).
Petit et al.	2019	Digital sensory marketing	'Digital interactive technologies (which enable the creation and/or manipulation of products on the screen), especially sensory-enabling technologies (i.e., SETs, those that can deliver sensory inputs), can be helpful when, for instance, it comes to creating a "webmosphere" (i.e., the conscious designing of web environments to create positive effects). These technologies can also help inform the consumer about those other sensory properties of a product (e.g., its texture, smell, and possibly even taste) that are simply not available currently in most (primarily visual) online environments' (pp. 42–43).

marketers, managers, and practitioners, finding an ideal strategy to generate positive responses for consumers may be critical: For retailers, it should be more important to embrace multi-sensorial strategies, since a larger set of consumers' behavioural outcomes are connected to the sensorial strategies a brand can implement using different dimensions.

According to Lindstrom (2007), sensorial strategies are 'incredibly important when you sell a brand, that you are leveraging the senses as much as you possibly can. The more emotional engagement you create between the consumer and the product, really the more the consumer is prepared to pay for it' (p. 3). It is evident that what the context is, brands are heavily implementing the sensory marketing strategies into the consumption-spaces, whether it is physical or online spaces. With the increasing integration of technology in the last decade, consumers started to observe and experience technological integrations in sensory marketing strategies of brands. According to Hemsley (2016), one of the biggest trends

> will be the increased use of virtual reality technology, including those with added sensory experiences involving taste and smell. The number of virtual reality shopping experiences will also increase as online users move around the store, try products and then describe and review the items online using filmed live reviews.
>
> *p. 1*

Another interesting fact revealed through Galvanic Skin Response (GSR) research investigating the comfort levels of consumers in consumption spaces found that 17% consumers were uncomfortable in stimulant-free environments (Retail Experience, 2019). To take these into consideration, there are numerous examples of brands that are blending sensory cues with the advanced technology in the consumption space to make consumers feel 'engaged' and 'having personal experience'. For example, Zara, one of the leading fashion brands, started to change its mannequins with augmented reality experience (Street, 2018). Burberry, Rimmel, and Gap are also among the brands working on augmented virtual reality applications rather than simply using traditional visual cues, in order to deliver a more enhanced experience to their consumers (Street, 2018),

Neuromarketing consultant and Professor Gemma Calvert has also stated the importance of investing in those cues, by noting,

> every day is a multi-sensory opportunity for brands and in a crowded marketing environment, marketers must go beyond the visual. In fashion, for instance, there is so much emphasis on how clothes look but much less on how they smell and feel, which would really engage consumers.
>
> *Hemsley, 2016, p. 2*

According to Jansson-Boyd, also as emphasised in Hemsley's (2016) article, 'some consumers are more tactile than others. These people tend to be more conscious about what they are touching and more aware of the weight or texture of specific items they are considering buying' (p. 1). Additionally, along with the 'touchpoints', brand manager should keep in mind that products need to be accessible in fashion retail settings, so that brands can communicate with consumers in the appropriate way to increase their in-store experience.

One of the most prominent examples of invested the unexpected cues in a traditional message can be Pernod Ricard UK's sensory campaign which has implemented as scented posters throughout Oxford Underground Station in London (French, 2019) with the idea of their marketing campaign to be 'playful, fresh, and as disruptive as possible' (OutdoorGlobal, 2019, nd). In the same line, by investing olfaction and vision, Hendrich Gin attempted to use a 'scented tunnel' in different underground stations in London to promote their rose-cucumber flavoured gin (French, 2019).

Another unconventional approach to sensory marketing can be Marriott International's in order to promote different destinations where Marriott is being located by using augmented reality and virtual reality. To allowing potential visitors to 'virtually' feel and experience different destinations, as well as presenting them with smell and sound, Marriott Hotel can be considered one of the brands in hospitality industry that moves sensory marketing strategies one step further (Marriott, 2015).

The bottom line? We now know that sensory marketing can be a powerful tool, especially with the unconventional strategies, by thinking out of the box, when it comes to its applications. Any investigation of sensory marketing requires a study of the notion of human senses, which are the primary drivers of any experiences that use sensorial human cognition (Hulten, 2011). As Pine and Gilmore (1998) emphasise, 'the more senses engage with [an experience], the more effective and memorable it can be' (p. 4).

As it is being highlighted from the practical examples, using multi-sensory cues have an undeniable impact on consumers' emotion, attitude, and behaviour (Helmefalk and Hulten, 2017). Due to its impact on consumers emotion as well as the time they spend in the retail settings, Helmefalk and Hulten (2017) suggest that the consumption spaces should be curated more in line with multi-sensory cues to deliver pleasurable experience to consumers. When it comes to the situation of COVID-19 and the post-lockdown strategies of brands, according to Retail Week (2021), in order to encourage consumers to come back to the retail setting, it is expected to see a drastic acceleration in implementation of sensory strategies – to ensure the safety of customers during COVID-19 such as touchless augmented reality systems to provide a virtual try-on for consumers (MKTG, 2020).

CASE STUDY – GAP LOGO REDESIGN FAILURE

Maria Palazzo, University of Salerno, Italy

Tugra Nazli Akarsu, University of Southampton, United Kingdom

Lessons to be learned

The concept of the corporate logo has been defined differently in diverse studies and several meanings have been assigned by different authors. The majority of these meanings have merged from marketing. From sensory marketing perspective, design elements, characters, logos, slogans are the major components of visual stimuli, which in fact are a part of brand design and identity as well as marketing communication (Brakus et al., 2009; Moreria et al., 2017). The visual stimuli thus in turn evoke positive and negative emotional reactions and therefore to create positive associations of the company and brand to various stakeholders, lead consumers to have positive brand experience (Brakus et al., 2009, Krishna, 2010). Besides, design literature refers to the corporate logo as a set of elements (colour, typeface, name, and design).

Taking these two approaches into account, the concept of the corporate logo can be defined as follows: Corporate logo is the signature of a company with an essential communication, distinctiveness, which can reflect a company's image. The next sections illustrate the importance of the visual stimuli through the case of Gap: Lessons to be learned.

Introduction

Gap is a global clothing retailer born in 1969 in San Francisco, United States, with a simple value proposition: To facilitate the search of a pair of jeans that fit (Gap Inc Newsroom, 2020). In early years, Levi's jeans and records are the only items on sale, yet with its increasing popularity, Gap started its own production with Gap label in its third anniversary (Gap Inc Newsroom, 2020). Especially with the launch of its iconic Pocket-T, in the very first decade of its foundation, the brand name Gap became synonymous with American style clothing: Jeans and T-shirts (Biron, 2019). Thus, Gap's clothes are available for all kind of people who are not too much involved with fashion style's trends and that want to wear casual clothes at school, workplaces, or at leisure time.

As a substantial part of its growth strategy, Gap started to grow its business into new apparel categories such as: Aaccessories, clothes for men, women, kids, and personal care goods. The brand in fact comprises Gap Body, Gap Baby, and Gap outlets. The company had a quick development in a small period of time. To elevate its brand, Gap opened its first overseas store in London in 1987. In 1988, Gap introduced its iconic blue square Gap logo, after using lowercase letters since its foundation. It has nowadays more than 3,000 retail stores over 130,000 employees in the US, the UK, Japan, France, Canada, and Ireland and in fact with its acquisitions over time, Gap Inc is running five brands: Athleta, Old Navy, Intermix, Banana Republic, including the Gap brand.

In 1998, to promote its new Khaki line of trousers, Gap has aired its iconic 30 seconds long *Khaki Swing* television commercial in the prime time. The ad was inspired from the 1920s Harlem Swing Era, where dancers were doing Lindy Hoop. In such a short time, the ad became viral (Biron, 2019; Gap Inc Newsroom, 2020). To increase its effect on consumers, Gap came up with an ad series as a continuation of Khaki Swing: *Khaki Country*, *Khaki Soul*, and *Khaki Rock*.

As being the largest specialty retail company in the US (Biron, 2019), Gap has amplified the civic engagement through different campaigns and collaborations with organisations for different causes in recent years. In 2020, Gap Kids introduced its 'Be the Future' campaign as a collective call-to-action for young generations to tackle important issues such as sustainability, activism, and climate justice, where Gap collaborated with inspirational young activists (Gap Inc Newsroom, 2020a; Trendhunter, 2020).

Aligned with the brand image, Banana Republic announced 'Will Work for a Better Republic' campaign in partnering with non-profit organisations: Rock the Vote and Delivering Good to appreciate and recognise the new working environments –homes – of individuals, as well as motivating individuals to vote for the 2020 US presidential election (Fashion United, 2020; Gap Inc Newsroom, 2020b).

The reason for the initiatives that Gap is recently taking is considered as getting back its 'American optimism for change' association in a modern way linked to the brand since its founding year: 1969 – which has been also considered as another defining milestone of 'American optimism for change' (PR Newswire, 2020).

Gap's rebranding attempt that lasted six days

In 2010, Gap unveiled its new logo – the first redesign attempt in 24 years. The original Gap logo – showing the 'GAP' in capital letters inside a blue square was replaced with a logo where there was a blue square sitting on the letter 'p'. The reason of this redesigning attempt has explained as company wanted to take more contemporary and current approach while 'honouring the heritage through the blue box while still taking it forward' (BBC News, 2010).

However, it backfired. The rebranding attempt initiated a public protest, where the new logo received a massive criticism on social media even the consumers created a 'Make your own Gap logo' website, which imminently went viral (Halliday, 2010).

This created a huge level of customers confusion and several loyal clients said to be not satisfied with the new logo and the new brand identity. The result of this dissatisfaction was a decrease of sales of 10% compared with the previous year. Gap answered to these critiques taking into account the customers' point of view and going back to the old logo and brand identity (Morris, 1992).

To find out what went wrong in Gap's rebranding attempt, a neuromarketing company, Neurofocus conducted a neuro-study to discover consumers' subconscious response towards Gap's old and new logo. The study results showed that while the original blue squared logo leads consumers to have heightened perception with a registration of 'active', 'stylish', and 'authentic' attributes, the new logo failed to register all these attributes (PR Newswire, 2010).

Gap also decided to modify the management team in the same year. The president of Gap North America, in fact, was substituted by Art Peck who formerly was the president of Gap's outlet. Moreover, the Gap's international marketing manager was substituted. These changes in the management showed to customers that the company was really interested in facing their complaints and that it was taking care of them (Weitzman, 2002). The organisation also planned to build a new international creative centre in New York so that communication, graphic design, and fabrication could be centralised and managed by Pam Wallack, president of Gap North America.

Case questions

1. What kind of strategies does Gap decide to implement in order to face the new logo issue as well as to restructure the brand?
2. Explain how visual cues can help Gap to reposition itself in the mind of customers.

References

BBC News. (2010). www.bbc.co.uk/news/magazine-11517129
Brakus, J. J., Schmitt, B. H., and Zarantonello, L. (2009). Brand experience: What is it? How is it measured? Does it affect loyalty? Journal of Marketing, 73(3), 52–68.
Cohen, B. and Ciampi, T. (1991). "The Gap prepares to cut Levi's brand from its herd", Women's Wear Daily, July 31
FashionUnited. (2020). https://fashionunited.uk/news/fashion/banana-republic-in-partnership-with-delivering-good-and-rock-the-vote/2020090250694
Frazier. M. (2007). "Experts to ailing Gap: Stand for something or be history", Advertising Age, January 15.
Gap Inc Newsroom. (2020a). www.gapinc.com/en-us/articles/2020/08/gap-celebrates-the-changemakers-of-tomorrow-in-%E2%80%98be

Gap Inc Newsroom. (2020b). www.gapinc.com/en-us/articles/2020/09/banana-republic-will-work-for-a-better-republic%E2%80%9D-i http://247wallst (2010).

Krishna, A. (2010). Sensory Marketing. Research on the Sensuality of Products. New York: Routledge.

Marriott International. (2015). Marriott Hotels introduces the first ever in-room virtual reality experience. Available at: https://news.marriott.com/news/2015/09/09/marriott-hotels-introduces-the-first-ever-in-room-virtual-reality-travel-experience [Accessed 27 September 2020]

Moreira, A. C., Fortes, N., and Santiago, R. (2017). Influence of sensory stimuli on brand experience, brand equity and purchase intention. Journal of Business Economics and Management, 18(1), 68–83.

Morris, K. (1992). "The thrill is gone: The Gap searches for ways to become airborne again", Financial World, December 8.

Newsbreak. (2020). www.newsbreak.com/news/1612962643541/gap-celebrates-the-changemakers-of-tomorrow-in-be-the-future-gapkids-campaign-featuring-youth-activists

PR Newswire. (2010). www.prnewswire.com/news-releases/brain-gap-neurofocus-study-reveals-what-went-wrong-with-the-gaps-new-brand-logo-105165954.html

PR Newswire. (2020). www.prnewswire.com/news-releases/gap-launches-fall-stand-united-campaign--a-tribute-to-individuals-united-by-humanity-for-equality-301125451.html

The Guardian. (2010). www.theguardian.com/media/2010/oct/12/gap-logo-redesign

Trendhunter. (2020). www.trendhunter.com/trends/be-the-future-gapkids

Weitzman, J. (2002). "Gap's woes deepen as credit rating hits rock-bottom level", Women's Wear Daily, February 15.

Key terms and definitions

Atmospheric is the deliberate design of a dedicated space to create positive buying environment that lead consumers to trigger emotional influences in order to increase their purchase probability.

Hedonism is an intention to experience fun, sensory stimulation and to seek excitement in the shopping process.

Perception is the interpretation of the data collected from the environment.

Sensory marketing is the ability to interact with consumers by engaging any of their five senses (sight, hearing, smell, touch, and taste) in order to affect their emotions and perceptions, and deliver more meaningful and memorable experiences.

Servicescape is the physical environment created by managers and practitioners, encapsulating three dimensions: i) ambient conditions; ii) spatial layout and functionality; and iii) signs, symbols, and artefacts.

References

Achrol, R. S. and Kotler, P. (2012). Frontiers of the marketing paradigm in the third millennium. Journal of the Academy of Marketing Science, 40(1), 35–52.

Bagwell, K. (2007). The Economic Analysis of Advertising. In Handbook of Industrial Organization (pp. 1701–1784). Amsterdam: Elsevier.

Baker, J. (1986). The role of the environment in marketing services: The consumer perspective. The Services Challenge: Integrating for Competitive Advantage, 1(1), 79–84.

Baker, J., Grewal, D., and Parasuraman, A. (1994). The influence of store environment on quality inferences and store image. Journal of the Academy of Marketing Science, 22(4), 328–339.

Baker, J., Levy, M., and Grewal, D. (1992). An experimental approach to making retail store environmental decisions. Journal of Retailing, 68(4), 445–460.

Berman, B., and Evans, J. R. (1995). Retail Management: A Strategic Approach (6th ed.). Princeton, NJ: Pearson Education Limited.

Birkner, C. (2013), "Thrifty brits: Economic austerity in the UK has given rise to a more frugal British consumer", Marketing News, 8 August.

Biron, B. (2019). The rise and fall of Gap, one of the most iconic and beloved American retailers. Business Insider. Available at: www.businessinsider.com/gap-company-history-rise-and-fall-pictures-2019-11?r=USandIR=T [Accessed 27 September 2020]

Bitner, M. J. (1992). Servicescapes: The impact of physical surroundings on customers and employees. Journal of Marketing, 56(2), 57–71.

Brady, M. K. and Cronin Jr, J. J. (2001). Some new thoughts on conceptualizing perceived service quality: A hierarchical approach. Journal of Marketing, 65(3), 34–49.

Brakus, J. J., Schmitt, B. H., and Zarantonello, L. (2009). Brand experience: What is it? How is it measured? Does it affect loyalty? Journal of Marketing, 73(3), 52–68.

Cox, K. (1964). The responsiveness of food sales to shelf space changes in supermarkets. Journal of Marketing Research, 1(2), 63–67.

Daucé, B. and Rieunier, S. (2002). Le marketing sensoriel du point de vente. Recherche et Applications en Marketing (French Edition), 17(4), 45–65.

Donovan, R. and Rossiter, J. (1982). Store atmosphere: An environmental psychology approach. Journal of Retailing, 58(1), 34–57.

Doyle, P. (1994). Marketing Management and Strategy. Harlow: Financial Times/Prentice Hall.

Etymology Dictionary. Available at: http://etymonline.com/index.php?allowed_in_frame=0&search=tornado [Accessed 27 September 2020]

Farias, S. A., Aguiar, E. C., and Melo, F. V. (2014). Store atmospherics and experiential marketing: A conceptual framework and research propositions for an extraordinary customer experience. International Business Research, 7(2), 87–99.

Flatters, P. and Willmott, M. (2009). Understanding the post-recession consumer. Harvard Business Review, 87(7–8), 106–112.

French, P. (2019). Hendrick's Gin unveils scented London underground ad campaign, The Drinks Business. Available at: www.thedrinksbusiness.com/2019/07/hendricks-gin-unveils-scented-london-underground-ad-campaign [Accessed 27 September 2020]

Gulas, C. S. and Schewe, C. D. (1994). Atmospheric Segmentation: Managing Store Image with Background Music, Enhancing Knowledge Development in Marketing. Chicago, IL: American Marketing Association.

Haase, J. and Wiedmann, K. P. (2018). The sensory perception item set (SPI): An exploratory effort to develop a holistic scale for sensory marketing. Psychology and Marketing, 35(10), 727–739.

Halliday, J. (2010). Gap scraps logo redesign after protests on Facebook and Twitter. *The Guardian*. Available at: www.theguardian.com/media/2010/oct/12/gap-logo-redesign [Accessed 27 September 2020]

Helmefalk, M. and Hultén, B. (2017). Multi-sensory congruent cues in designing retail store atmosphere: Effects on shoppers' emotions and purchase behavior. Journal of Retailing and Consumer Services, 38, 1–11.

Hemsley, S. (2016). Top sensory marketing trends for 2016. Available at: om/top-sensory-marketing-trends-for-2016/ [Accessed 27 September 2020]

Hill, R. P. and Gardner, M. P. (1987). The buying process: Effects of and on consumer mood states", in Wallendorf, M. and Anderson, P. (Eds.), NA – Advances in Consumer Research, Volume 14. Provo, UT: Association for Consumer Research, pp. 408–410.

Holbrook, M. B. and Hirschman, E. C. (1982). The experiential aspects of consumption: Consumer fantasies, feelings, and fun. Journal of Consumer Research, 9(2), 132–140.

Hulten, B. (2011). Sensory marketing: The multi-sensory brand-experience concept. European Business Review, 23(3), 256–273.

Hulten, B. (2013). Sensory cues as in-store innovations: Their impact on shopper approaches and touch behaviour. Journal of Innovation Management: The International Journal of Multidisciplinary Approaches to Innovation, 1(1), 17–37.

Hulten, B., Broweus, N., and Dijk, M. V. (2009). What is Sensory Marketing? In Sensory Marketing. London: Palgrave MacMillan.

Hyslop, J. (2015). Oceanic mobility and settler-colonial power: Policing the global maritime labour force in durban harbour c. 1890–1910. The Journal of Transport History, 36(2), 248–262.

Kotler, P. (1973). Atmospherics as a marketing tool. Journal of Retailing, 49(4), 48–64.

Krishna, A. (2011). An integrative review of sensory marketing: Engaging the senses to affect perception, judgment and behaviour. Journal of Consumer Psychology, 22(3), 332–351.

Krishna, A. (2012). An integrative review of sensory marketing: Engaging the senses to affect perception, judgment and behavior. Journal of Consumer Psychology, 22(3), 332–351.

Lastovicka, J. L., Bettencourt, L. A., Hughner, R. S., and Kuntze, R. J. (1999). Lifestyle of the tight and frugal: Theory and measurement. Journal of Consumer Research, 26(1), 85–98.

Lin, I. Y. (2004). Evaluating a servicescape: The effect of cognition and emotion. International Journal of Hospitality Management, 23(2), 163–178.

Lindstrom, M. (2007). Brand Sense: Sensory Secrets Behind the Stuff We Buy. London: Kogan Page.

Malina, D. and Schmidt, R. A. (1997). It's business doing pleasure with you: Sh! A women's sex shop case. Marketing Intelligence and Planning, 15(7), 352–360.

Martineau, P. (1958). The personality of the retail store. Harvard Business Review, 36(1), 47–55.

Moore, K. and Reid, S. (2008). The birth of brand: 4000 years of branding. Business History, 50(4), 419–432.

Morrin, M. and Ratneshwar, S. (2003). Does it make sense to use scents to enhance brand memory? Journal of Marketing Research, 40(1), 10–25.

Parasuraman, A., Zeithaml, V. A., and Berry, L. L. (1988). SERVQUAL: A multiple-item scale for measuring consumer perceptions of service QUALITY. Journal of Retailing, 64(1), 12–40.

Peck, J. and Childers, T. L. (2003). Individual differences in haptic information processing: The need for touch scale. Journal of Consumer Research, 30(3), 430–442.

Penaloza, L. and Venkatesh, A. (2006). Further evolving the new dominant logic of marketing: From services to the social construction of markets. Marketing Theory, 6(3), 299–316.

Petit, O., Velasco, C., and Spence, C. (2019). Digital sensory marketing: Integrating new technologies into multisensory online experience. Journal of Interactive Marketing, 45, 42–61.

Pine, B. J. and Gilmore, J. H. (1998). Welcome to the experience economy. Harvard Business Review, 76(4), 97–105.

Puccinelli, N. M., Goodstein, R. C., Grewal, D., Price, R., Raghubir, P., and Stewart, D. (2009). Customer experience management in retailing: Understanding the buying process. Journal of Retailing, 85(1), 15–30.

Pullman, M. E. and Gross, M. A. (2004). Ability of experience design elements to elicit emotions and loyalty behaviors. Decision Sciences, 35(3), 551–578.

Rafaeli, A. and Vilnai-Yavetz, I. (2004). Emotion as a connection of physical artifacts and organizations. Organization Science, 15(6), 671–686.

Raghubir, P. and Krishna, A. (1999). Vital dimensions in volume perception: Can the eye fool the stomach? Journal of Marketing Research, 36(3), 313–326.

Rajput, N. and Dhillon, R. (2013). Frontiers of the marketing paradigm for the third millennium: Experiential marketing. Global Journal of Management and Business Studies, 3(7), 711–724.

Raz, C., Piper, D., Haller, R., Nicod, H., Dusart, N., and Giboreau, A. (2008). From sensory marketing to sensory design: How to drive formulation using consumers' input? Food Quality and Preference, 19(8), 719–726.

Retail Experience. (2019). Sensory experiences boost sales by 10%. Available at: www.retailcustomerexperience.com/news/sensory-experiences-boost-sales-by-10/ [Accessed 27 September 2020]

Retail Week (2021). Available at: www.retail-week.com/retail-voice/three-strategies-retail-brands-should-adopt-now-for-success/7036815.article [Accessed 27 September 2020]

Rook, D. W. (1985). The ritual dimension of consumer behavior. Journal of Consumer Research, 12(3), 251–264.

Schmitt, B. H. (1999). Experiential Marketing: How to get Customers to Sense, Feel, Think, Act and Relate to Your Company and Brands. New York: Free Press.

Sensory Retail Design Report. (2016). Available at: www.stylepsychology.co.uk/sensoryretaildesign. [Accessed 27 September 2020]

Shergill, H. K. (2012). Experimental Psychology. Delhi: PHI Learning Private. Ltd.

Sheth, J. N. and Parvatiyar, A. (1995). The evolution of relationship marketing. International Business Review, 4(4), 397–418.

Smith, P. C. and Curnow, R. (1966). "Arousal hypothesis" and the effects of music on purchasing behavior. Journal of Applied Psychology, 50(3), 255–256.

Solomon, M. R. (2008). Consumer Behavior: Buying, Having, and Being (8th ed.). New York: Prentice Hall.

Street, C. (2018). Zara to launch an Augmented Reality app in its stores. *Evening Standard*. Available at: www.standard.co.uk/insider/fashion/zara-to-launch-an-augmented-reality-app-in-its-stores-a3789441.html [Accessed 27 September 2020]

Teixeira, T. T. (2014). The rising cost of consumer attention: Why you should care and what you can do about it (Working Paper 14–055). Harvard Business School.

Turley, L. and Milliman, R. E. (2000). Atmospheric effects on shopping behaviour. Journal of Business Research, 49(2), 193–211.

Usunier, J.-C. and Lee, J. A. (2012). Marketing Across Cultures. Harlow: Prentice Hall/Financial Times.

Van Tonder, C. L. and Berner, A. (2003). The postmodern consumer: Implications of changing customer expectations for organisation development in service organisations. SA Journal of Industrial Psychology, 29(3), 1–10.

Venkatraman, M. and Nelson, T. (2008). From servicescape to consumptionscape: A photo-elicitation study of Starbucks in the New China. Journal of International Business Studies, 39(6), 1010–1026.

Villiers, M. (2016). Sensory marketing – What is it, which brands are successful at it? Available at: www.bizcommunity.com/Article/196/423/155281.html [Accessed 27 September 2020]

Wakefield, K. L. and Baker, J. (1998). Excitement at the mall: Determinants and effects on shopping response. Journal of Retailing, 74(4), 515–539.

Wakefield, K. L. and Blodgett, J. G. (1996). The effect of the servicescape on customers' behavioural intentions in leisure service settings. Journal of Services Marketing, 10(6), 45–61.

Wolpert, S. A. (2000). A New History of India (6th ed.). New York: Oxford University Press.

Yeniaras, V. and Akarsu, T. N. (2017). Frugal doesn't mean ordinary: A religious perspective. Journal of Islamic Marketing, 8(2), 204–217.

12
SENSORY MARKETING
Environmental psychology theory approach

Tugra Nazli Akarsu

Introduction

This chapter aims to present environmental psychology theory (EPT), the widely use theory adopted into the sensory marketing studies. The chapter also illustrates Mehrabian and Russel's (1974) stimulus–organism–response (S-O-R), which is widely applied by scholars as a framework.

Background

Looking at the shifting trend in marketing throughout the years, because of advancement in technology, increasing knowledge, awareness, and the way in which societies apprehend these factors, consumers wish to be informed and smarter (Cooper, 2014; Cruz, 2017). Thus, today's consumers are forcing marketers to alter their strategies where the physical connection between brand and consumers is mundane (Cruz, 2017). Although marketing practitioners introduced sensory marketing earlier than marketing scholars explored it, because practitioners observe consumers' needs, desires, and demands, Achrol and Kotler (2012) have discussed the emergence of this marketing trend, the reasons why businesses should implement it, and how to do so (Achrol and Kotler, 2012; Hulten, 2015).

According to these authors (Achrol and Kotler, 2012; Hulten, 2015), the consumer experience should be fundamental to marketing, as experience is filtered through the human senses. They argue further that there is little understanding of the way in which the human senses influence consumer experience, or of the implications. Therefore, they urge scholars to obtain a better understanding of the five senses and consumer experience, as well as of the consumer perceptions and emotions elicited through the interaction of the senses with sensory stimuli. Since postmodern consumers seek both collective and individual brand experiences (Cova and Pace, 2006; Ding and Tseng, 2015; Simmons, 2008), the human senses are considered as important phenomena for delivering positive brand experiences (Tynan and McKechnie, 2009). It is evident that the interest in sensory and experiential marketing research has been

DOI: 10.4324/9781003054153-13

gradually increasing (Groeppel-Klein, 2005; Gulas and Bloch, 1995; Krishna, 2011; Morrin and Ratneshwar, 2003).

With regard to the empirically investigate the influence of sensory stimuli/cues on consumers affective and cognitive attributes, which in turn determine whether consumer will either have approach/avoidance behaviour, environmental psychology theory (EPT), and stimulus–organism–response (S-O-R) framework is one of the most dominant theories/frameworks applied in various influential empirical studies (Chebat and Michon, 2003; Chen and Hsieh, 2011; Helmefalk, 2019; Hulten, 2013; Kim et al., 2020; Kumar and Kim, 2014). Therefore, this chapter aims to offer the insights on the theory and framework, also present a snapshot on the empirical studies those applied EPT and S-O-R.

Environmental pyschology theory and S-O-R framework

Mehrabian and Russell's (1974) EPT and their suggested S-O-R model fundamentally propose that stimuli from atmospheric surroundings have an influence on individuals' cognitive and affective reactions which, in turn, shape whether an individual will either approach or avoid that atmosphere (ibid.). This theory has been widely used to understand consumer behaviour and has been employed in many studies in the marketing domain (Arora, 1982; Chang et al., 2011; Davis et al., 2008; Donovan and Rossiter, 1982). Moreover, it has been adapted to understand the effect of environmental surroundings on consumer behaviour in the retail context in the past decade (Chebat and Michon, 2003; Chen and Hsieh, 2011; Kumar and Kim, 2014).

In the S-O-R model conceptualised by Mehrabian and Russell, stimulus refers to the environmental inputs or environmental characteristics which affect consumer emotional responses, such as colour, scent, ambience, etc. (Chang et al., 2011; Eroglu et al., 2001); organism refers to individuals' emotional states; and response refers to individuals' positive or negative behavioural responses, such as purchase intention, recommendations, and complaining behaviours (Donovan and Rossiter, 1982). Stimulus describes the environmental inputs that lead consumers to a certain emotional state, which, in turn, lead them to a positive or behavioural outcome as a response to the 'internal processes and structures intervening between stimuli external to the person and the final actions, reactions or responses emitted. The intervening processes and structures consist of perceptual, physiological feeling and thinking activities' (Bagozzi, 1986, p. 46).

Mehrabian and Russell's (1974) environmental psychology theory has been extensively accepted and has become dominant in different studies researching the retailing and service industries (Baker et al., 1992; Lin, 2004; Vinnikova, 2016), virtual stores (Eroglu et al., 2001; Manganari et al., 2011; Yun and Good, 2007), and service stores (Foxall and Greenley, 1999; Jang and Namkung, 2009). It has been suggested by researchers (Diener et al., 1985; Diener and Emmons, 1986; Wakefield and Baker, 1998) that this theory should be adopted for the purpose of understanding the effect of sensorial cues in an atmosphere on consumers, with one researcher going so far as to say that 'the generalisability of […] Mehrabian and Russell's environmental theory [confirms] that stimulus, emotion and response are strongly associated' (Vieira, 2013, p. 1425). For this particular research, the S-O-R model can be considered as the backbone of the conceptual framework, which was constructed on the environmental psychology theory and uses the S-O-R model to explain the mechanism of individuals' internal states and behavioural responses triggered by exposure to a physical environment.

Issues, controversies, problems

In order to trace the origin of environmental psychology theory, it is necessary to look at 'the situational theorists' (Lutz and Kakkar, 1975), who note that:

> situation relevant for the understanding of consumer behaviour is the psychological situation, which may be defined as an individual's internal responses to, or interpretations of, all factors particular to a time and place of observation which are not stable intra-individual characteristics or stable environmental characteristics, and which have a demonstrable and systematic effect on the individual's psychological processes and/or his overt behaviour.
>
> *p. 440*

As highlighted by Lutz and Kakkar (1975), 'the effects on behaviour of the situation in which that behaviour occurs have long been recognized, but seldom systematically investigated' (p. 439). Empirical research conducted by Belk (1974) brings a new perspective by drawing a distinction between 'situation' and 'environment', noting that 'situation and environment […] represent distinct sources of influence on consumer behaviour and should not be used synonymously. Environment is the broader construct and represents a general milieu of behaviour, whereas situation is a more momentary concept' (pp. 1–2). As a complementary perspective, Wright (1974) also argue that situation could affect overt behavioural outcomes, and the effect of situation could 'gain meaning and effect only though the perception of the individual' (p. 5).

In this sense, situational theorists have recognised the need for a taxonomy of situations or situational components, to enable researchers to generalise the examination of situational influence. In creating this taxonomy, in order to explain consumer behaviour which is affected by various situational components, scholars have started to identify and categorise different situational components, for example, physical surroundings (Barker, 1968; Belk, 1974, Toffler, 1970), group opinion (Gorden, 1952), and goal structure (Belk, 1974). As part of the creation of a taxonomy allowing situational variables to 'become meaningful in the explanation of consumer behaviour' (Lutz and Kakkar, 1975, p. 441), Mehrabian and Russell's (1974) environmental psychology theory notes, 'the impact of the situation on behaviour is mediated by emotional responses, so that any set of conditions initially generates an emotional (affective, connotative, feeling) reaction, which in turn leads to a behavioural response' (ibid.).

A study by Parboteeah et al. (2009) conceptualises perceived enjoyment as the organism, which could be considered as an affective reaction. In the same vein, Chui et al. (2016) also utilises hedonism as the organism, as it is supported that hedonic perception indicates the affective state of mind of a consumer. In addition to hedonism, brand experience can also be considered as an organism, where emotional states can be achieved through it.

According to Kumar and Kim (2014):

> When the S-O-R model is applied in the retail context, stimuli are the store atmospheric cues that affect the internal states of the consumer. A cue is defined as a characteristic, event, or object, external to a person that can be predetermined and used to

categorize a stimulus object (Schellinck, 1980). Specifically, stimuli (S) in the retailing context refer to all the physical and nonphysical elements of a store, which are within the retailer's control to enhance customers' shopping experience (Eroglu and Machleit, 1990; Turley and Chebat, 2002).

p. 688

According to Donovan and Rossiter (1982), emotions that customers experience in retail environments lead them to either approach or avoid the store as an outcome behaviour. Therefore, this research theorises brand experience as organism, where 'it can mediate the relationship between store environment and shopping behaviour' (Kumar and Kim, 2014, p. 688).

In terms of the response component of the S-O-R model, this study utilises repurchase intention, which refers to the consumer's willingness to make another purchase from the same company for the service or product based on his/her previous experience and desire to experience the same circumstances (Andriopoulos and Gotsi, 2001; Wakefield and Baker, 1998). According to Chui and Lai's (2013) empirical study, customers' hedonic perceptions influence their revisit intentions for auction websites.

The 'situation relevant for the understanding of consumer behaviour is the psychological situation, which may be defined as an individual's internal responses to, or interpretations' (Lutz and Kakkar, 1975, p. 440); and, as Hansen (1972) agrees, 'altogether, how the actor perceives the situation is as important as the actual elements found in the physical environment' (p. 47).

Future research directions

Even though Mehrabian and Russell's (1974) theory and model dominate the literature, the results of empirical studies have diversified and have generally consisted of independent variables (as stimuli), mediators (as organism), and dependent variable (as response) (Lin, 2004; Turley and Milliman, 2000; Vieira, 2013). It has been strongly suggested in the literature that when consumers interact with sensorial cues in the environment, they begin to construct an unconscious mental image based on these cues, which, in turn, affects their cognitive, affective, and behavioural responses where these depend on consumer-related variables (Eroglu et al., 2003; Kim and Moon, 2009; Koo and Ju, 2010; Lin, 2004).

In the past decade, many studies, especially those which have applied environmental psychology theory have highlighted that the store environment (i.e., sensorial cues) has an undeniable effect on consumers' attitudes, leading to an emotional and behavioural outcome based on consumers' identity (Eroglu et al., 2003; Koo and Ju, 2010). When it comes to sensorial marketing and the influence of individual related variables on sensory cues, the importance of individual-level consumer characteristics has not been appreciated, yet, some scholars (Bone and Ellen, 1999; Koelega, 1994) have been pioneers by examining different individual-level characteristics and urging scholars to bring new insights by investigating the topic further.

The literature (Jacoby, 2002; Markus and Kitayama, 1991; Mathras et al., 2016; Lin, 2004; Yoon and Park, 2012) notes that determining specific sensorial stimuli for effective marketing strategies cannot be fully reliable without understanding the effect of individual-level consumer characteristics. Endogenous or internal factors, such as values, expectations, or needs (Bruner, 1957; Jacoby, 2002; Markus and Kitiyama, 1991) should be taken into account when investigating how sensorial inputs (i.e., colour, scent, and sound) interact with consumers and affect the outcomes. For example, according to Bone and Ellen (1999), when investigating the influence of olfaction cues on consumer responses, the importance of moderated effects such as context effects (e.g., a stressful task) and individual characteristics (e.g., gender) should be acknowledged and should not be ignored where these have been identified by previous researchers. Moreover, according to Koelega's (1994) study on the impact of gender on the relationship between olfactory cues and sensitivity, women are more prone than men to be sensitive to olfactory cues.

Another study, carried out by Eroglu et al. (2003), scrutinized the moderating role of two individual traits, atmospheric responsiveness and involvement on the relationship between atmospheric cues in the online environment and consumers' emotional and cognitive states, which, in turn, influence consumers' shopping behaviours (such as satisfaction, approach, and avoidance behaviour). According to the results, for consumers who have a low involvement in visiting the website and those with high atmospheric responsiveness, the atmosphere of a website influences perceived pleasure. Overall, the two individual traits, involvement and atmospheric responsiveness, were found to have a moderating effect on the website atmospherics (stimulus), and pleasure (organism), which influenced shopping behaviour (response).

Another pioneering study conducted by Koo and Ju (2010) also used the S-O-R model to examine the influence of the atmospheric cues of online stores on the affective emotional states of consumers, which, in turn, lead consumers to positive behavioural outcomes. More interestingly, by extending the model, they investigated the moderating effect of perceptual curiosity on the relationship between online atmospheric cues and consumers' emotional affective states, where perceptual curiosity refers to the personal tendency to investigate and be curious about the surrounding environment. Atmospheric cues (stimulus) were found to influence consumers with high perceptual curiosity, who were found to be more pleased and aroused (organism), leading them, in turn, to have positive behavioural intentions (response), compared with consumers with low perceptual curiosity.

As such, as highlighted by Helmefalk and Hulten (2017), 'although retailers have acknowledged the importance of scents and their effects on consumer behaviour, it remains difficult to establish the appropriateness of scents in retail settings in relation to age, culture and other personal attributes (Morrin and Chebat, 2005; Möller and Herm, 2013).' (p. 3). In the same vein, Elder et al. (2010) further addresses the questions for scholars to investigate 'For example, do individuals differ in motivation to touch by demographics such as gender and age? What impact does culture have on motivation to touch? How does the ability to differentiate haptic attributes vary across individuals? We do know that sensitivity to touch declines with age (Stevens & Patterson, 1995; Thornbury & Mistretta, 1981), but what are the implications for marketing?', where Elder et al. (2011) emphasizes that to extend the knowledge on individual characteristics and specifically, investigating their moderating effects 'would provide more information to the marketer about the relative importance of different modalities of cues in designing an offer or in formulating communication.' (p. 14). Table 12.1 presents the scrutiny of the empirical literature that has applied S-O-R model.

TABLE 12.1 Research implemented S-O-R model

Authors	Year	Industry	Stimulus	Organism	Response	Moderator
Yoo et al.	1998	Retailing	Store location, atmosphere, facilities	Positive emotions, negative emotions	Store attitudes	–
Eroglu et al.	2003	Online store	Online environment cues	Pleasure, arousal	Satisfaction, avoid behaviour, approach behaviour	Consumers' involvement, atmospheric responsiveness
Davis et al.	2008	Online hypermarket	High task cues, low task cues	Pleasure, arousal, satisfaction	Avoid behaviour, approach behaviour	Customer cultural orientation
Liu and Jang	2009	Restaurant	Dining atmospherics	Emotional responses, perceived value	Behavioural intentions	–
Kang et al.	2011	Spa	Environmental sensory components	Consumer emotions	Behavioural intentions	–
Lam et al.	2011	Casino	Ambience, navigation, seating comfort, interior décor, cleanliness	Customer satisfaction, cognitive, affective	Desire to stay, intention to revisit	–
Walsh et al.	2011	Coffee shops	In-store music, in-store aroma, price, service quality, price	Emotions	Store satisfaction Store loyalty	–
Chen and Hsieh	2011	Chain store supermarkets	Store atmospheric factors	Cognitive valuation, emotional responses	Approach behaviours	–
Wong et al.	2012	Shopping mall	Mall/store quality, quality of merchandise, convenience, enhancements, price orientation	–	Shopping enjoyment	–
Cui and Lai	2013	Online auction website	Effectiveness of bidding agent, network effect, product diversity	Utilitarian perception, hedonic perception	E-loyalty	–

(continued)

TABLE 12.1 Cont.

Authors	Year	Industry	Stimulus	Organism	Response	Moderator
Osman et al.	2014	Shopping mall	In-store atmospherics	Mood	Time spent, money spent, repatronage intention	–
The	2014	Coffee shops	Exterior, general interior, store layout, interior displays, human variable	Experience, mood, emotion	Cognitive affective behaviour	Personality
Jalil et al.	2015	–	Facility aesthetics, ambience, spatial layout, employee factor	Customer satisfaction	Return intentions, positive word of mouth	–
Vinnikova	2016	Lab experiment	Odour	Emotional state	Approach or avoidance response	Gender, age, education, culture, ethnic origin, smoking habits, duration of stay in China association with Chinese culture

CASE STUDY – NESCAFÉ GOLD BLEND

Maria Palazzo, University of Salerno, Italy

Tugra Nazli Akarsu, University of Southampton, United Kingdom

Introduction

The story of Nescafé started in 1929 with a challenging but yet strategic mission given by Nestlé chairman Louis Dapples to its employers: To come up with 'soluble coffee cubes' in order to decrease the surplus of coffee stocks that Nescafé had due to the Wall Street Crash and the collapse of coffee prices (Nestle, 2020a). In 1938, the answer was found and by using first three letters of Nestlé and suffixing it with 'café', Nescafé brand was born.

The increasing popularity of Nescafé coincided with World War II, where it was consumed in the US, the UK, and Switzerland, even delivered to the US army forces in their food rations. Having a long shelf life, and keeping its taste longer under a massive war brought an unprecedented success in terms of Nescafé's popularity and sales (Nescafe, 2020), such that Nescafé joined the crew of important missions and moments: Record-breaking expedition to Mount Everest in 1953 and crew of Apollo 11 in 1969, which made Nescafé as the first coffee brand and product who landed on Moon (Nescafé, 2020).

One of the major breakthroughs of Nescafé was Nescafé Gold Blend, introduced in 1965, which was made of freeze-dried soluble coffee (Golding & Peattie, 2005). The company communicated Gold Blend leveraging on product superiority: .Nothing is as good as gold (…) Gold Blend'. The name 'Gold Blend' has been promoted to link the product to a premium segment, such that 'golden-roasted coffee beans' are being used for this premium product (Nestlé, 2020b). The issue was that, even though Gold Blend was a successful product and was sold with a premium price strategy, it was not easily reached by many customers. The brand and product request were consequently partial (Neacsu, 2018).

Nestlé promoted its product with different communication plan highlighting that:

> Nestlé is the world's favourite coffee brand, enjoyed in over 180 countries worldwide. With over 80 years of experience in selecting, roasting and blending the very best coffee, it's no surprise that over 5,500 cups of Nestlé coffee are drunk every second! Discover all the different kinds of coffee beans and the various ways to roast them. In the middle of a busy day, it's important to have some time for yourself and appreciate the moment. So, take a break and focus on the now with Nescafé Gold Blend.
>
> *www.nescafe.com/gb/our-coffees/gold/nescafe-gold-blend*

The aim of this effort was to appeal consumers who want a premium coffee experience at home, anytime. Therefore, since its introduction in market, Nestlé put a considerable effort to improve the product. All product changes were analysed with blind product tests before being launched in the market. Moreover, the company decide also to improve the packaging, leveraging on tactile/haptic cues of the packaging. The pot/jar that holds a product can differentiate it from the competitors and create a competitive advantage.

Gold Blend changed its packaging, as follows:

- During the sixties: The jar was curled.
- During the seventies: A smooth-sided jar was presented with a new Gold Blend logo.
- During the eighties: A cubic jar was proposed with new labelling.
- During the nineties: An exclusive 'waisted' jar design was showed.

One of the major improvements was specially designed glass-jar for Nescafé Gold Blend, where Nestlé formulated an 'aroma-lock lid', that preserves taste and the aroma even longer (Nescafé, 2020) so that consumers get 'fresh coffee aroma' every time they open the jar. Several customer researches highlighted that the new features and design of the jar, improved thanks to tactile/haptic cues, has set the basis for the strengthening the brand and product image of Nescafé Gold Blend (Khamis, 2009).

Case questions

1. After you have written down what corporate brand sensuality is, analyse the relationship between what this feature has to offer to brands and which company might be interested in it.
2. After you have written down what tactile/haptic cues are, including all of their benefits, analyse the relationship between what they can offer to brands and which company might be interested in developing them.
3. List the reasons why Nescafé use tactile/haptic cues.

References

Golding, K. and Peattie, K. (2005). In search of a golden blend: Perspectives on the marketing of fair-trade coffee. Sustainable Development, 13(3), 154–165.

Khamis, S. (2009). 'It Only Takes a Jiffy to Make' Nestlé, Australia and the Convenience of Instant Coffee. Food, Culture & Society, 12(2), 217–233.

Neacsu, A. N. (2018). Quality management on the coffee market. Bulletin of the Transilvania University of Brasov. Economic Sciences. Series V, 11(1), 109–118.

Nescafé. (2020). www.nescafe.com/gb/about-us

Nestlé. (2020a). www.nestle.com/aboutus/history/nestle-company-history/nescafe-75-years

Nestlé. (2020b). www.nestle.com/brands/allbrands/nescafe-gold

Key terms and definitions

Environmental psychology theory concerns the stimuli from atmospheric surroundings which have an effect on individuals' affective and cognitive reactions which, in turn, determine whether an individual will approach or avoid that atmosphere.

Moderating variable is a variable that can 'strengthen' or 'weakening' the relationship between dependent and independent variables with its nature, where a moderating variable can change the direction of the relationship between dependent and independent variables.

S-O-R (stimulus-organism-response) is a stimulus that refers to environmental inputs or characteristics such as colour, scent, and ambience, which affect consumers' emotional responses; organism refers to individuals' emotional states; and response refers to positive or negative behavioural responses, such as purchase intention, recommendations, and complaining behaviours

Taxonomy is a specific classification or organisation of an entity to divide it into groups.

References

Achrol, R. S. and Kotler, P. (2012). Frontiers of the marketing paradigm in the third millennium. Journal of the Academy of Marketing Science, 40(1), 35–52.

Andriopoulos, C. and Gotsi, M. (2001). Living' the corporate identity: Case studies from the creative industry. Corporate Reputation Review, 4(2), 144–154.

Arora, R. (1982). Validation of an S-O-R model for situation, enduring, and response components of involvement. Journal of Marketing Research, 19(4), 505.

Bagozzi, R. P. (1986). Attitude formation under the theory of reasoned action and a purposeful behaviour reformulation. British Journal of Social Psychology, 25(2), 95–107.

Baker, J., Levy, M., and Grewal, D. (1992). An experimental approach to making retail store environmental decisions. Journal of Retailing, 68(4), 445.

Barker, R. G. (1968). Ecological Psychology: Concepts and Methods for Studying the Environment of Human Behavior. Stanford, CA: Stanford University Press.

Belk, R. W. (1974). An exploratory assessment of situational effects in buyer behavior. Journal of Marketing Research, 11(2), 156–163.

Bone, P. F. and Ellen, P. S. (1999). Scents in the marketplace: Explaining a fraction of olfaction. Journal of Retailing, 75(2), 243–262.

Bruner, J. S. (1957). On perceptual readiness. Psychological Review, 64(2), 123–152.

Chang, H., Eckman, M., and Yan, R. (2011). Application of the stimulus-organism-response model to the retail environment: The role of hedonic motivation in impulse buying behaviour. The International Review of Retail, Distribution and Consumer Research, 21(3), 233–249.

Chebat, J. and Michon, R. (2003). Impact of ambient odours on mall shoppers' emotions, cognition, and spending. Journal of Business Research, 56(7), 529–539.

Chen, H. S. and Hsieh, T. (2011). The effect of atmosphere on customer perception and customer behaviour responses in chain store supermarkets. African Journal of Business Management, 5(24), 10054–10066.

Cooper, L. (2014, October 17). Sensory marketing – Could it be worth $100m to brands? Marketing Week. www.marketingweek.com/2013/10/30/sensory-marketing-could-it-be-worth-100m-to-brands/

Cova, B. and Pace, S. (2006). Brand community of convenience products: new forms of customer empowerment – the case "my Nutella The Community". European Journal of Marketing, 40(9/10), 1087–1105.

Cruz, A. (2017). How to engage your customers with sensory branding – Online marketing institute. Available at: www.onlinemarketinginstitute.org/blog/2017/03/engage-customerssensory-branding/ [Accessed 29 January 2018]

Cui, X. and Lai, V. S. (2013). E-Loyalty to online auction websites: A Stimulus-Organism-Response model. The Pacific Asia Conference on Information Systems (PACIS), PACIS 2013, 126.

Cui, X., Lai, V. S., and Lowry, P. B. (2016). How do bidders' organism reactions mediate auction stimuli and bidder loyalty in online auctions? The case of Taobao in China. Information and Management, 53(5), 609–624.

Davis, L., Wang, S., and Lindridge, A. (2008). Culture influences on emotional responses to on-line store atmospheric cues. Journal of Business Research, 61(8), 806–812.

Diener, E. and Emmons, R. A. (1986). Influence of impulsivity and sociability on subjective well-being. Journal of Personality and Social Psychology, 50(6), 1211–1215.

Diener, E. D., Emmons, R. A., Larsen, R. J., and Griffin, S. (1985). The satisfaction with life scale. Journal of Personality Assessment, 49(1), 71–75.

Ding, C. G. and Tseng, T. H. (2015). On the relationships among brand experience, hedonic emotions, and brand equity. European Journal of Marketing, 49(7/8), 994–1015.

Donovan, R. and Rossiter, J. (1982). Store atmosphere: An environmental psychology approach. Journal of Retailing, 58(1), 34–57.

Elder, R. S., Aydinoglu, N. Z., Barger, V., Caldara, C., Chun, H., Lee, C. J., and Stamatogiannakis, A. (2011). A sense of things to come: Future research directions in sensory marketing. In Sensory Marketing (pp. 391–406). London: Routledge.

Eroglu, S. A. and Machleit, K. A. (1990). An Empirical study of retail crowding antecedents and consequences. Journal of Retailing, 66, 201–221.

Eroglu, S. A., Machleit, K. A., and Davis, L. M. (2001). Atmospheric qualities of online retailing: A conceptual model and implications. Journal of Business Research, 54(2), 177–184.

Eroglu, S. A., Machleit, K. A., and Davis, L. M. (2003). Empirical testing of a model of online store atmospherics and shopper responses. Psychology and Marketing, 20(2), 139–150.

Foxall, G. R. and Greenley, G. E. (2000). Predicting and explaining responses to consumer environments: An empirical test and theoretical extension of the behavioural perspective model. The Service Industries Journal, 20(2), 39–63.

Gorden, R. L. (1952). Interaction between attitude and the definition of the situation in the expression of opinion. American Sociological Review, 17(1), 50–58.

Groeppel-Klein, A. (2005). Arousal and consumer in-store behaviour. Brain Research Bulletin, 67(5), 428–437.

Gulas, C. S. and Bloch, P. H. (1995). Right under our noses: Ambient scent and consumer responses. Journal of Business and Psychology, 10(1), 87–98.

Hansen, F. (1972). Consumer Choice Behavior: A Cognitive Theory. New York: The Free Press.

Helmefalk, M. (2019). Browsing behaviour as a mediator: The impact of multi-sensory cues on purchasing. Journal of Consumer Marketing, 36(2), 253–263.

Helmefalk, M. and Hultén, B. (2017). Multi-sensory congruent cues in designing retail store atmosphere: Effects on shoppers' emotions and purchase behavior. Journal of Retailing and Consumer Services, 38, 1–11.

Hult, B. M. (2015). The impact of sound experiences on the shopping behaviour of children and their parents. Marketing Intelligence and Planning, 33(2), 197–215.

Hultén, B. (2013). Sensory cues as in-store innovations: Their impact on shopper approaches and touch behavior. Journal of Innovation Management, 1(1), 17–37.

Jacoby, J. (2002). Stimulus-Organism-Response reconsidered: An evolutionary step in modeling (consumer) behaviour. Journal of Consumer Psychology, 12(1), 51–57.

Jalil, N. A. A., Fikry, A., and Zainuddin, A. (2016). The impact of store atmospherics, perceived value, and customer satisfaction on behavioural intention. Procedia Economics and Finance, 37, 538–544.

Jang, S. and Namkung, Y. (2009). Perceived quality, emotions, and behavioural intentions: Application of an extended Mehrabian–Russell model to restaurants. Journal of Business Research, 62(4), 451–460.

Kang E., Boger C. A., Back K.-J., and Madera J. (2011). The impact of sensory environments on Spagoers' emotion and behavioural intention. 16th Graduate Students Research Conference. Available at: http://scholarworks.umass.edu/gradconf_hospitality/2011/Presentation/77/Google Scholar

Kim, W. G. and Moon, Y. J. (2009). Customers' cognitive, emotional, and actionable response to the servicescape: A test of the moderating effect of the restaurant type. International Journal of Hospitality Management, 28(1), 144–156.

Koelega, H. S. (1994). Sex differences in olfactory sensitivity and the problem of the generality of smell acuity. Perceptual and Motor Skills, 78(1), 203–213.

Koo, D. and Ju, S. (2010). The interactional effects of atmospherics and perceptual curiosity on emotions and online shopping intention. Computers in Human Behaviour, 26(3), 377–388.

Krishna, A. (2011). An integrative review of sensory marketing: Engaging the senses to affect perception, judgment and behaviour. Journal of Consumer Psychology, 22(3), 332–351.

Kumar, A. and Kim, Y. (2014). The store-as-a-brand strategy: The effect of store environment on customer responses. Journal of Retailing and Consumer Services, 21(5), 685–695.

Lam, L. W., Chan, K. W., Fong, D., and Lo, F., (2011). Does the look matter? The impact of casino servicescape on gaming customer satisfaction, intention to revisit, and desire to stay. International Journal of Hospitality Management, 30(2011), 558–567.

Lin, I. Y. (2004). Evaluating a servicescape: The effect of cognition and emotion. International Journal of Hospitality Management, 23(2), 163–178.

Liu, Y. and Jang, S. (2009). Perceptions of Chinese restaurants in the U.S.: What affects customer satisfaction and behavioral intentions? International Journal of Hospitality Management, 28, 338–348.

Lutz, R. J. and Kakkar, P. (1975). The psychological situation as a determinant of consumer behaviour. Advances in Consumer Research, 2, 439–454.

Manganari, E. E., Siomkos, G. J., Rigopoulou, I. D., and Vrechopoulos, A. P. (2011). Virtual store layout effects on consumer behaviour: Applying an environmental psychology approach in the online travel industry. Internet Research, 21(3), 326–346.

Markus, H. R. and Kitayama, S. (1991). Culture and the self: Implications for cognition, emotion, and motivation. Psychological Review, 98(2), 224–253.

Mathras, D., Cohen, A. B., Mandel, N., and Mick, D. G. (2016). The effects of religion on consumer behaviour: A conceptual framework and research agenda. Journal of Consumer Psychology, 26(2), 298–311.

Mehrabian, A. and Russell, J. A. (1974). The basic emotional impact of environments. Perceptual and Motor Skills, 38(1), 283–301.

Möller, J. and Herm, S. (2013). Shaping retail brand personality perceptions by bodily experiences. Journal of Retailing, 89, 438–446.

Morrin, M. and Chebat, J. C. (2005). Person-place congruency: The interactive effects of shopper style and atmospherics on consumer expenditures. Journal of Service Research, 8(2), 181–191.

Morrin, M. and Ratneshwar, S. (2003). Does it make sense to use scents to enhance brand memory? Journal of Marketing Research, 40(1), 10–25.

Myung Ja, K. Lee, C.-K., and Jung, T. (2020). Exploring consumer behavior in virtual reality tourism using an extended stimulus-organism-response model. Journal of Travel Research, 59(1), 69–89.

Osman, S., Sim Ong, F., Nor Othman, M., and Wei Khong, K. (2014). The mediating effect of mood on in-store behaviour among Muslim shoppers. Journal of Islamic Marketing, 5(2), 178–197.

Parboteeah, D. V., Valacich, J. S., and Wells, J. D. (2009). The influence of website characteristics on a consumer's urge to buy impulsively. Information Systems Research, 20(1), 60–78.

Schellinck, D. A. (1980). Determinants of cue choice behavior (Doctoral dissertation (8108653). ProQuest Dissertations and Theses Global.

Simmons, G. (2008). Marketing to postmodern consumers: Introducing the internet chameleon. European Journal of Marketing, 42(3/4), 299–310.

Stevens, J. C. and Patterson, M. Q. (1995). Dimensions of spatial acuity in the touch sense: Changes over the life span. Somatosensory and Motor Research, 12, 29–47.

Teh, G. M., Kalidas, V., and Zeeshan, M. (2014). Personality as a moderator of SOR model. Review of Integrative Business and Economics Research, 3(2), 67.

Thornbury, J. M., and Mistretta, C. M. (1981). Tactile sensitivity as a function of age. Journal of Gerontology, 36(1), 34–39.

Toffler, A. (1970). Future shock. Toronto: Bantam Books.

Turley, L. W. and Chebat, J. C. (2002). Linking retail strategy, atmospheric design and shopping behaviour. Journal of Marketing Management, 18(1–2), 125–144.

Turley, L. and Milliman, R. E. (2000). Atmospheric effects on shopping behaviour. Journal of Business Research, 49(2), 193–211.

Tynan, C. and McKechnie, S. (2009). Experience marketing: A review and reassessment. Journal of Marketing Management, 25(5–6), 501–517.

Vieira, V. A. (2013). Stimuli–organism-response framework: A meta-analytic review in the store environment. Journal of Business Research, 66(9), 1420–1426.

Vinnikova, A. (2016). A case of hedonic perception of foreigners towards Chinese culture-specific odours from scent marketing perspective. Archives of Business Research, 4(3), 21–44.

Wakefield, K. L. and Baker, J. (1998). Excitement at the mall: Determinants and effects on shopping response. Journal of Retailing, 74(4), 515–539.

Walsh, G., Shiu, E., Hassan, L. M., Michaelidou, N., and Beatty, S. E. (2011). Emotions, store-environmental cues, store-choice criteria, and marketing outcomes. Journal of Business Research, 64(7), 737–744.

Wong, Y. T., Osman, S., Jamaluddin, A., and Chan, Y. F. B. (2012). Shopping motives, store attributes and shopping enjoyment among Malaysian youth. Journal of Retailing and Consumer Services, 19(2), 240–248.

Wright, P. (1974). The harassed decision maker: Time pressures, distractions, and the use of evidence. Journal of Applied Psychology, 59(5), 555–561.

Yoo, C., Park, J., and Maclinnis, D. J. (1998). Effects of store characteristics and instore emotional experiences on store attitude. Journal of Business Research, 42, 253–263.

Yoon, S. and Park, J. E. (2012). Do sensory ad appeals influence brand attitude? Journal of Business Research, 65(11), 1534–1542.

Yun, Z. and Good, L. K. (2007). Developing customer loyalty from e-tail store image attributes. Managing service quality. An International Journal, 17(1), 4–22.

13
SENSORY MARKETING

Visual cues and audial cues

Tugra Nazli Akarsu

Introduction

This chapter aims to present an overview to visual and audial cues from sensory marketing literature, where the different elements of those cues and how those cues engage consumers and influence on consumers cognitive, affective attitudes, as well as judgements are also discussed via the chapter.

Visual cues: Background

Vision is the most dominant sensory system belonging to human beings, since it is used and encountered more than any other sensory cue (Biswas et al., 2014; Hulten, 2013; Schiffman, 2001). From a marketing perspective, it is logical to state that visual cues are the first sensorial cue noticeable by consumers and comprise the biggest part of branding strategies in environmental settings (Biswas et al., 2014; Hulten, 2013). However, this becomes a problem. According to the *Forbes*, consumers are being exposed to around 4,000–10,000 visual ads each day (Simpson, 2017).

In the conceptualisation of visual cues, colour, logos, lighting, fixtures, graphics, signage, and even mannequins can be examples of visual cues used by companies to influence consumers' behaviour and possible purchases (Hulten, 2013; Kahn and Deng, 2010; Krishna, 2008; Seock and Lee, 2013). According to Helmefalk and Berndt (2018), visual cues can be simple physical inputs such as logos or colour, however, they can be 'more complex variations, such as aesthetics and form' (Jang et al., 2018; Tilburg et al., 2015; Vieira, 2013) (p. 4). According to Elder et al. (2009),

> when a product or ad is not presented in a visually vivid way, this impairs the fluency of consumption imagery, or the ease with which consumers can generate imagery of the consumption experience, leading to a negative effect of imagery appeals.

p. 1

Along with Elder et al.'s (2009) supposition, scholars have investigated different aspects of visual cues (e.g., colour, light, store design), and try to aid marketers by investigating in which conditions the certain aspects are preferred (e.g., dark colours vs light colours) and why. As one of the most influential aspects of visual cues in retail stores, colour has been investigated frequently by scholars (Babin et al., 2003; Osman et al., 2014): It has been found to influence consumers' mood, and therefore increase the money and time spent in the stores (Osman et al., 2014). Going further, Babin et al. (2003) investigated whether the use of cool and warm colours in fashion stores had different effects on consumers' emotional and behavioural responses. The striking conclusion was that store designs using cool colours influenced consumers' behavioural and emotional responses more than designs using warm colours.

Chebat and Morrin (2007) studied the influence of mall décor colour on consumer perceptions of the quality of the environment and products in two different groups: French-Canadians and Anglo-Canadians. The findings revealed that French-Canadian consumers perceived shopping mall environments and products to have a higher quality when the malls used warm colours in their design. However, for Anglo-Canadian consumers, the opposite was true: These consumers perceived shopping mall environments and products to be of a higher quality when cool colours were used in their design. Another study on store design, in Odeh and Abu-Rumman's (2014) study, store design is found to influence consumers' buying behaviour directly. Another study by Chen and Hsieh (2011) reveals that design factors integrated into retail stores influence consumers' cognitive evaluations such as service quality and product value, leading them to have a positive emotional state, and in turn, resulting in approach behaviour such as purchase intention.

Two other influential aspect of visual cues, layout and interior design, have often been noted as key factors in the *servicescape* used to attract consumers (Wakefield and Blodgett, 1996). They have been defined by Bitner (1992) as an approach for certain places to make them organised in terms of providing spatial coherence. According to Wakefield and Baker (1998), interior design and décor are significant aspects of visual cues and found to influence consumers' emotions and experience of 'pleasantness', which, in turn, lead consumers to have positive behavioural intentions (Holmqvist and Lunardo, 2015).

Another important aspect of visual cues, lighting, has been identified by Gifford (1988) as a tool to stimulate consumers' feelings during their shopping activities. The manipulation of lighting in retail stores has become one of the most intriguing topics for consumer stimulation leading to positive behavioural outcomes (Spence et al., 2014). To give empirical examples from the literature, Summers and Hebert (2001) revealed that lighting has a positive influence on consumers' willing to spend more time in a store. Areni and Kim (1994) examined the impact of lighting on consumers' patronage intentions, revealing that bright lighting increased the number of items examined by consumers in a wine store compared with soft lighting. Similarly, another study, conducted by Oberfeld et al. (2009), revealed that lighting manipulation in a winery positively influenced consumers' perceived value regarding wine they had been tasting positively: Consumers were willing to pay more money for wine tasted under blue and red lighting conditions than under green and white light.

Scrutiny of the literature reveals that research on different aspects of visual cues in the retail context has remained limited: Scholars have mainly investigated aspects such as colour (Babin et al., 2003; Chebat and Morrin, 2007), layout and design (Wakefield and Baker, 1998; Wakefield and Blodgett, 1996), and lighting (Spence et al., 2014). Based on the preceding discussion, it should be stressed that considering all aspects of visual cues is significant, since these cues may stimulate consumers and lead them to have better feelings, meaning they could experience a retail store in a more positive way.

Practical approach to visual cues

By being the dominant sense and the most dominantly used cue by brands to deliver their message, the concept of visual cues are evolving and changing, due to the attention spans of consumers (Marketingmag, 2020). With the blended technologies, to find out 'what is the most appealing' and 'why', marketers are widely using eclectic methods such as eye-tracking analysis. By using eye-tracking analysis researchers can gather aggregate data on how a shelf design, store layout, or retail setting influence consumer behaviour such as attention span, time spent, or willingness to stay (Huddleston et al., 2018), display elements (Behe et al., 2015), or in-store signage (Otterbring et al., 2014).

Another interesting method currently used by marketers is neuroimaging, to understand how the brain undertakes the sensory information and in turn, how that influences consumers perception towards a product, or service. Brands such as Frito-Lay and PepsiCo are frequently using neuroimaging to understand the products' and advertisements impact on consumer. According to Burkitt (2009):

> Executives at PepsiCo's Frito-Lay unit use neuromarketing to test commercials, products and packaging in the U.S. and overseas. They discovered that matte beige bags of potato chips picturing potatoes and other 'healthy' ingredients in the snack don't trigger activity in the anterior cingulate cortex--an area of the brain associated with feelings of guilt--as much as shiny bags with pictures of chips. Frito-Lay then switched out of shiny packaging in the U.S. at the end of February.

Audial cues: Background

Practical approach to audial cues

In terms of dealing with the audial cues, specialized advertising and design agencies on 'sound' such as *The Sound Agency*, *MetaDesign*, *A-Mnemonic*, and *Kalua* aims to deliver a sound-related identity to brands to enable more meaningful consumer/brand connections. According to *The Sound Agency*, 'A great audio brand has clear differentiation and direction, and these don't come about by accident' (The Sound Agency, 2020). According to the Claire Mitchell, the director of VaynerSmart- the digital agency that is a part of VaynerMedia, 'Sound design is the new packaging' (Marszalek, 2018).

When looking the practical approach to different facets of audial cues, *The Sound Agency* (2021) proposed eight key dimensions of audial cues which are: 1) brand voice; 2) brand music; 3) sonic logo; 4) soundscapes; 5) product sound; 6) advertising sound; 7) telephone sound; and 8) audio brand. Another approach from an agency, Boom (2007), conceptualises auditory cues as sound related touchpoint and later advocates that audial cues can be available in any context, 'from broadcast media to web-based communications, from the retail environment to custom cell phone rings'.

Considering its impact on attitude formation, emotion, and behaviour (Chang et al. 2011; Mattila and Wirtz, 2001; Yalch and Spangenberg, 1999), scholars and practitioners are in a consensus that music can be considered as one of the most important dimensions of auditory cues as it can be identified as 'brand signifier' (Balmer and Gray, 2003, p. 989). That is said, there are various evident examples from brands, where 'music' was utilized as a 'sonic logo' or namely 'brand signifier'. Intel® for example initiated their iconic sonic logo in 1994, or later called as Intel 'Bong' (Minsky and Fahey, 2014; Passman, 2016) and it has become one of the well-known identifiers used by a brand ever since. According to Passman (2016)'s articles in *Forbes*, Yogiraj Graham, Director of Production for Intel Global Production Labs stated that:

> The Intel bong is one of the most powerful assets we have. We're always looking for ways to showcase the amazing experiences that Intel enables, and the Intel bong sound helps keep our messaging consistent.

Other prominent examples of brands that are using their 'sonic logo' as their audial cues can be Siemens, Microsoft Windows, Apple, Allianz (Treasure, 2007), and McDonalds (Passman, 2016).

To understand 'audial cues' one should traced back to the definition of 'sound' which has defined as 'vibrations which travel through the air or another medium and can be heard when they reach a person's or animal's ear' and 'a thing that can be heard' (Oxford Dictionary, 2006, p. 1690). From this definition, the scholars in marketing had conceptualised 'audial' cues in various way. Jackson (2003), for instance, categorised voice, ambience, and music as sub-dimensions of audial cues. On the other hand, one of the early categorisations investigated by Treasure (2007), consider five different types of sound as audial cues, namely, (1) the sound of silence, (2) natural sounds, such as wind, water, (3) human voice, (4) music, and (5) noise. However, these early conceptualisations did not take into account sub-elements or various approaches such as volume or speed of music. Another conceptualisation highlighted by Fiore and Kelly (2007) through an empirical research investigating the applications of audial cues in online stores, revealed three sub-dimensions of audial cues, namely, (1) product sound, (2) noise in the atmosphere, and (3) conversation.

The scrutiny of literature reveals the fact that audial cues are found to influence on consumers' mood, evaluation, and behavioural, as well as emotional responses (Alpert et al., 2005; Bartholme and Melewar, 2016; Han and Ryu, 2009; Hulten, 2013; Kellaris and Kent, 2001). They have also been linked with other positive consumer-related variables, such as consumer loyalty (Walsh et al., 2011) and arousal of consumers' emotional states (El Sayed et al., 2004).

Looking into the 'audial' cues that each research has investigated, one can clearly see that there is no generalisability or a consensus on what 'audial' cues encapsulates. The reason can be the extended application and the variety in terms of its application practices. However, there one consensus contended that among other auditory related cues, music has been considered as one of the most widely used elements of audial cues, has an undeniable effect on consumers' satisfaction (Chang et al. 2011; Mattila and Wirtz, 2001). According to Krishna et al. (2016),

> Music in ads also has a referential meaning, which is context dependent and reflects a listener's personal associations. Most of the research on music also focuses on context, transportation, and familiarity.
>
> *p. 143*

Earlier to this approach, literature revealed prominent studies on the volume of music (Milliman, 1982; Smith and Curnow, 1966); the impact of familiar music (Yalch and Spangenberg, 2000), and the impact of background music (North and Hargreaves, 1999). To expand the knowledge here, according to Milliman (1982; 1986), the tempo of music has an impact on the sales volume in a supermarket and the length of stay in a restaurant. Grewal et al.'s (2003) empirical study investigating the relationship between classical music and customers' evaluations in a jewellery shop found that classical music had a significant influence on evaluation and led consumers to behavioural intention. Osman et al. (2014) concludes that music has a positive influence on customers' mood, leading to positive in-store behaviour, while El Sayed et al. (2004) also finds that music influences customers' emotions, leading to positive behavioural intention. North and Hargreaves (1999) revealed that the background music can decrease consumers' perception on time spent on waiting.

In that sense, Chang et al. (2011), highlighted that it should not be forgotten that managers need to understand the characteristics of the context and consumers as a starting point when integrating audial cues. Yalch and Spangenberg (1990) also emphasise that rather than utilising music appropriate to the target markets, manager and brands should investigate what consumers want and need before establishing the audial cues.

CASE STUDY – DIESEL: HOW TO ENGAGE CONSUMERS AT A DEEPER LEVEL THROUGH AUDITORY AND VISUAL CUES

Maria Palazzo, University of Salerno, Italy

Tugra Nazli Akarsu, University of Southampton, United Kingdom

Introduction

In 1978, with an intention of creating an innovative jean with its fabric and style that can reflect in every aspect of modern life, Renzo Rosso established 'Diesel' as a denim brand (Diesel, 2020). While Rosso was working on its brand's establishment, there was an ongoing oil crisis, where Diesel was considered as an alternative fuel, alternative energy and the idea of having his brand as an alternative jeans brand attracted Rosso (Sawai, 2016). By being an international term and easily pronounced, Rosso adopted name 'Diesel' to his brand.

Advertising campaign series that transformed Diesel

In 1990s, Diesel started to launch its 'Diesel for Successful Living' campaign, which lasted for a decade. During this advertising campaign series, Diesel took a provocative stance tackling themes on religion, politics, race, and sex by claiming the brand has its social conscious – on the contrary to the corporate heads. Within this series, unquestionably the most famous one is 'Kissing Sailors' where two male sailors are kissing while their shipmates are celebrating the end of World War II in the background. This campaign was actually tackling Clinton Administration's 'Don't ask, don't tell' policy, which was prohibiting military personnel to disclose their sexual orientation while they are working in the US army (US Congressional Research Service, 2013).

Starting from 1990 to 2001, Diesel has changed the game. Not only their campaign helped them to position the brand in the international market, the visual communication also inspired young generations to question the world they live in (Allwood, 2016). Aligned with this, Diesel has experienced extraordinary growth and has evolved from being a leading pioneer in denim into the world of premium casual wear, becoming a true alternative to the established luxury market. Diesel's philosophy has remained the same as the day of its creation: Renzo Rosso had envisaged a brand that would stand for passion, individuality, and self-expression. The Diesel manifesto reads:

> We decode the world around us, take it apart and unlock what we thought we knew. We see differently and unite with those who see it too. Draw your own path. March in the streets with us. Especially the ones our streets are on.
>
> *https://diesel.co.za/about*

The founder of the brand is Renzo Rosso, was born in Molvena in Italy and, here, he decided to create jeans which allowed him to show his personality in a very distinctive way. Diesel, in fact, not only sells jeans but it offers a lifestyle: Diesel promises to amuse and to offer the consumers original experiences, with jeans, fragrances, sunglasses, and bike helmets (Vianelli et al., 2016).

'Be stupid' campaign: How two senses are blended

In 2010, Diesel launched its provocative yet clever advertising campaign 'Be Stupid'. Aligned with its manifesto, the campaign was carrying a message to consumers that encourages them to take risks and move beyond smear and sensible with a slogan: 'Smart may have the brains, but stupid has the balls' (Campaign, 2010; Macleod, 2010)

With the phrase 'Be Stupid', fulcrum of the communication campaign of Diesel, the company refers to the fact that the brand is born thanks to Renzo Rosso, a man who decided to found an organisation as he was not able to find the kind of jeans he would like to wear. Renzo was so 'stupid' that he decided to create jeans, sells them in Italy, and also was even more stupid to reach the international market with his product. In addition to its edgy visual communication, Diesel launched 'Diesel U Music' in 2009 as the brand's internet radio station (Murray, 2009). The brand aimed to engage with its consumers in a deeper level, where the radio position itself as rich in content by allowing new groups, emerging artists, and indie bands to express themselves (Green, 2009). Diesel also extended the idea by organizing Diesel-U-Music Awards and Diesel-U: Music Tour, which gave alternative and local musicians to have live and recorded music opportunities under three music genres: urban/hip hop; electronic and rock/indie..

Looking to Diesel's effort in a way of implementing a two-way communication, Diesel aimed at connecting with its clients and their lifestyle. In reaching this goal, Diesel used music as an indissoluble part of its communication plans. Actually, music is able to express lifestyle and if it is linked with new music and new artists, it can offer something different to people allowing them to experiment unusual experiences. Leveraging on the link between the brand and acoustic/auditory cues, Diesel:U:Music was created by the company as an international music collaboration. Diesel:U:Music gives unsigned bands and artists a place where they can be noticed and a chance to have their musical ability acknowledged.

Today, the Diesel:U:Music is an online radio station and it carries on expressing how Diesel sustains unconventional lifestyles. The radio station, in fact, does not offer traditional playlists but it offers to customers the possibility to listen to music created by a resident DJ.

In conclusion, Diesel, leveraging on the original features of the product and mixing them with the right distribution channels and communication strategy, succeeded in attaining a clear position in the market (Barnum & Zajicek, 2008). This highlights that Diesel understands its customers and has created this differentiated product line to satisfy their needs expressing their unconventional lifestyles (Arning, 2009).

Case questions

1. After you have written down what corporate brand sensuality is, analyse the relationship between what this feature has to offer to brands and which company might be interested in it.
2. After you have written down what acoustic/auditory cues are, including all of their benefits, analyse the relationship between what they can offer to brands and which company might be interested in developing them.
3. List the reasons why Diesel uses acoustic/auditory cues to promote the products and brand.

References

Allwood, E. H. (2016). Finally, it all makes sense: Diesel adverts 1991–2001. *Dazed*. Available at: www.dazeddigital.com/fashion/article/33763/1/making-the-worlds-most-controversial-ad-campaigns-diesel-jocke-jonason

Arning, C. (2009). Kitsch, irony, and consumerism: A semiotic analysis of Diesel advertising 2000–2008. Semiotica, 2009(174), 21–48.

Barnum, A. J. and Zajicek, A. M. (2008). An intersectional analysis of visual media: A case of diesel advertisements. Social Thought & Research, 105–128.

Creed, W. D., Scully, M. A., and Austin, J. R. (2002). Clothes make the person? The tailoring of legitimating accounts and the social construction of identity. Organization Science, 13(5), 475–496.

Diesel. (2020). https://lu.diesel.com/en/diesel.html

Green, T. H. (2009). Diesel U Music: How to promote a funky brand through music, *The Telegraph*. Available at: www.telegraph.co.uk/culture/music/rockandpopfeatures/5497819/Diesel-U-Music-how-to-promote-a-funky-brand-through-music.html

Macleod, D. (2010). Diesel be stupid, *The Inspiration Room*. Available at: https://theinspirationroom.com/daily/2010/diesel-be-stupid/

Murray, R. (2009). Diesel U Music Radio launches, *Clash*. Available at: www.clashmusic.com/news/diesel-u-music-radio-launches

Sawai, A. (2016). Renzo Rosso reveals how the name 'Diesel' was chosen for his brand, *The Economic Times*. Available at: https://economictimes.indiatimes.com/magazines/panache/renzo-rosso-reveals-how-the-name-diesel-was-chosen-for-his-brand/articleshow/51680241.cms?from=mdr

The Campaign. (2010). Diesel 'be stupid' by Anomaly. Available at: www.campaignlive.co.uk/article/diesel-be-stupid-anomaly/977409

U.S. Congressional Research Service. (2013). 'Don't Ask, Don't Tell': A legal analysis (R40795; Aug. 6,2013), by Jody Feder.

Vianelli, D., Pegan, G., and Valta, M. (2016). Diesel: An unconventional, innovative, international-lifestyle, Italian company. In Fashion Brand Internationalization (pp. 65–88). New York: Palgrave Pivot.

Key terms and definitions

Audial cues are sound related cues that influence on consumers' mood, evaluation, and behavioural as well as emotional responses.

Visual cues are visual cues are the first sensorial cue noticeable by consumers and comprise the biggest part of branding strategies in environmental settings.

References

Alpert, M. I., Alpert, J. I., and Maltz, E. N. (2005). Purchase occasion influence on the role of music in advertising. Journal of Business Research, 58(3), 369–376.

Areni, C. S. and Kim, D. (1994). The influence of in-store lighting on consumers' examination of merchandise in a wine store. International Journal of Research in Marketing, 11(2), 117–125.

Babin, B. J., Hardesty, D., and Suter, T. (2003). Colour and shopping intentions: The intervening effect of price fairness and perceived affect. Journal of Business Research, 56(7), 541–552.

Balmer, J. M. T. and Gray, E. R. (2003). Corporate Brands – What are they? What of them? European Journal of Marketing, 37(7/8), pp. 972–997.

Bartholmé, R. H. and Melewar, T. C. (2016). The end of silence? Qualitative findings on corporate auditory identity from the UK. Journal of Marketing Communications, 22(4), 419–436.

Behe, B. K., Bae, M., Huddleston, P. T., and Sage, L. (2015). The effect of involvement on visual attention and product choice. Journal of Retailing and Consumer Services, 24, 10–21.

Biswas, D., Labrecque, L. I., Lehmann, D. R., and Markos, E. (2014). Making choices while smelling, tasting, and listening: The role of sensory (dis)similarity when dequentially sampling products. Journal of Marketing, 78(1), 112–126.

Boom (2007). Corporate Website. Available at: www.boomsonicbranding.com [Accessed 28 September 2017]

Burkitt, B. (2009). Neuromarketing: Companies Use Neuroscience for Consumer Insights. *Forbes*. Available at: www.forbes.com/forbes/2009/1116/marketing-hyundai-neurofocus-brain-waves-battle-for-the-brain.html?sh=4291382817bb [Accessed 27 September 2020]

Chang, H., Eckman, M., and Yan, R. (2011). Application of the stimulus–organism–response model to the retail environment: The role of hedonic motivation in impulse buying behaviour. The International Review of Retail, Distribution and Consumer Research, 21(3), 233–249.

Chebat, J. and Morrin, M. (2007). Colors and cultures: Exploring the effects of mall décor on consumer perceptions. Journal of Business Research, 60(3), 189–196.

Chen, H. S. and Hsieh, T. (2011). The effect of atmosphere on customer perceptions and customer behaviour responses in chain store supermarkets. African Journal of Business Management, 5(24), 10054–10066.

El Sayed, I. M., Farrag, D. A., and Belk, R. W. (2004). The effects of physical surroundings on Egyptian consumers' emotional states and buying intentions. Journal of International Consumer Marketing, 16(1), 5–27.

Fiore, S. G. and Kelly, S. (2007). Surveying the use of sound in online stores – practices, possibilities and pitfalls for user experience. International Journal of Retail and Distribution Management, 35 (7), pp. 600–611.

Gifford, R. (1988). Light, decor, arousal, comfort and communication. Journal of Environmental Psychology, 8(3), 177–189.

Han, H. and Ryu, K. (2009). The roles of the physical environment, price perception, and customer satisfaction in determining customer loyalty in the restaurant industry. Journal of Hospitality and Tourism Research, 33(4), 487–510.

Hargreaves, D. J. and North, A. C. (1999). The functions of music in everyday life: Redefining the social in music psychology. Psychology of Music, 27(1), 71–83.

Helmefalk, M. and Berndt, A. (2018). Shedding light on the use of single and multisensory cues and their effect on consumer behaviours. International Journal of Retail & Distribution Management, 46(11/12), 1077–1091.

Holmqvist, J. and Lunardo, R. (2015). The impact of an exciting store environment on consumer pleasure and shopping intentions. International Journal of Research in Marketing, 32(1), 117–119.

Huddleston, P. T., Behe, B. K., Driesener, C., and Minahan, S. (2018). Inside-outside: Using eye-tracking to investigate search-choice processes in the retail environment. Journal of Retailing and Consumer Services, 43, 85–93.

Hulten, B. (2013). Sensory cues as in-store innovations: Their impact on shopper approaches and touch behaviour. Journal of Innovation Management: The International Journal of Multidisciplinary Approaches to Innovation, 1(1), 17–37.

Jackson, D. M. (2003). Sonic Branding: An Introduction. New York: Palgrave Macmillan.

Jang, J. Y., Baek, E., and Choo, H. J. (2018). Managing the visual environment of a fashion store: Effects of visual complexity and order on sensation-seeking consumers. International Journal of Retail and Distribution Management, 46(2), 210–226.

Kahn, B. E. and Deng X. (2010). Effects on visual weight perceptions of product image locations on packaging. In Krishna, A. (Ed.), Sensory Marketing: Research on the Sensuality of Products. New York: Routledge.

Kellaris, J. J. and Kent, R. J. (2001). An exploratory investigation of responses elicited by music varying in tempo, tonality, and texture. Journal of Consumer Psychology, 2(4), 381–401.

Krishna, A. (2008). Spatial perception research: An integrative review of length, area, volume, and number perception. In Wedel, M. and Pieters, R. (Eds.), Visual Marketing: From Attention to Action (pp. 167–192). New York: Lawrence Erlbaum Associates.

Krishna, A., Cian, L., and Sokolova, T. (2016). The power of sensory marketing in advertising. Current Opinion in Psychology, 10, 142–147.

Grewal, D., Baker, J., Levy, M., and Voss, G. B. (2003). The effects of wait expectations and store atmosphere evaluations on patronage intentions in service-intensive retail stores. Journal of Retailing, 79(4), 259–268.

Marketingmag. (2020). How digital sensory marketing is key to appealing to today's consumer. Available at: www.marketingmag.com.au/hubs-c/how-digital-sensory-marketing-is-key-to-appealing-to-todays-consumer/

Marszalek, D. (2018). VoiceCon: 'Sound Design Is the New Packaging' Provoke Media. Available at: www.provokemedia.com/latest/article/voicecon-'sound-design-is-the-new-packaging [Accessed 27 September 2020]

Mattila, A. S. and Wirtz, J. (2001). Congruency of scent and music as a driver of in-store evaluations and behaviour. Journal of Retailing, 77(2), 273–289.

Milliman, R. E. (1982). Using background music to affect the behavior of supermarket shoppers. Journal of Marketing, 46(3), 86–91.

Milliman, R. E. (1986). The influence of background music on the behavior of restaurant patrons. Journal of Consumer Research, 13(2), 286–289.

Minsky, L. and Fahey, C. (2014). What does your brand sound like? HBR Blog Network. Harvard Business Review. Retrieved March, 13, 2014. Available at: https://hbr.org/2014/02/what-does-your-brand-sound-like

Oberfeld, D., Hecht, H., Allendorf, U., and Wickelmaier, F. (2009). Ambient lighting modifies the flavor of wine. Journal of Sensory Studies, 24(6), 797–832.

Odeh, M. R. and Abu-Rumman, H. A. (2014). The impact of Jordanian shopping malls' physical surrounding on consumer buying behavior: Field study. International Journal of Marketing Studies, 6(3), 135–141.

Osman, S., Sim Ong, F., Nor Othman, M., and Wei Khong, K. (2014). The mediating effect of mood on in-store behaviour among Muslim shoppers. Journal of Islamic Marketing, 5(2), 178–197.

Osman, S., Sim Ong, F., Nor Othman, M., and Wei Khong, K. (2014). The mediating effect of mood on in-store behaviour among Muslim shoppers. Journal of Islamic Marketing, 5(2), 178–197.

Otterbring, T., Wästlund, E., Gustafsson, A., and Shams, P. (2014). Vision (im) possible? The effects of in-store signage on customers' visual attention. Journal of Retailing and Consumer Services, 21(5), 676–684.

Oxford Dictionary of English (2006) 2nd ed., Oxford: Oxford University Press.

Passman, J. (2016). Intel, Netflix, Apple and the Power and Influence of Sonic Branding. *The Forbes*. Available at: www.forbes.com/sites/jordanpassman/2016/11/02/intel-netflix-apple-and-the-power-and-influence-of-sonic-branding/#5f1dab2f4836

Schiffman, H. R. (2001). Sensation and Perception: An Integrated Approach (5th ed.). New York: John Wiley & Sons (WIE).

Seock, Y.-K. and Lee, Y. E. (2013). Understanding the importance of visual merchandising on store image and shopper behaviours in home furnishings retail setting. European Journal of Business and Management, 5(4), 174–187.

Simpson, J. (2017). Finding brand success in the digital world. *Forbes*. Available at: www.forbes.com/sites/forbesagencycouncil/2017/08/25/finding-brand-success-in-the-digital-world/?sh=5c0ee72f626e [Accessed 27 September 2020]

Smith, P. C. and Curnow, R. (1966). 'Arousal hypothesis' and the effects of music on purchasing behavior. Journal of Applied Psychology, 50(3), 255–256.

Spence, C., Puccinelli, N. M., Grewal, D., and Roggeveen, A. L. (2014). Store atmospherics: A multisensory perspective. Psychology and Marketing, 31(7), 472–488.

Summers, T. A. and Hebert, P. R. (2001). Shedding some light on store atmospherics: Influence of illumination on consumer behavior. Journal of Business Research, 54(2), 145–150.

The Sound Agency (2020). Audio branding. Available at: www.thesoundagency.com/audio-branding/ [Accessed 27 September 2020]

The Sound Agency (n.d). Available at: www.thesoundagency.com/moodsonic// [Accessed 15 June 2021]

Tilburg, M., Lieven, T., Herrmann, A., and Townsend, C. (2015). Beyond 'Pink It and Shrink It' perceived product gender, aesthetics, and product evaluation. Psychology and Marketing, 32(4), 422–437.

Treasure, J. (2007). Sound Business. Kemble, Gloucestershire: Management Books 2000 Ltd.

Vieira, V. A. (2013). Stimuli–organism–response framework: A meta-analytic review in the store environment. Journal of Business Research, 66(9), 1420–1426.

Wakefield, K. L. and Baker, J. (1998). Excitement at the mall: Determinants and effects on shopping response. Journal of Retailing, 74(4), 515–539.

Wakefield, K. L. and Blodgett, J. G. (1996). The effect of the servicescape on customers' behavioural intentions in leisure service settings. Journal of Services Marketing, 10(6), 45–61.

Walsh, G., Shiu, E., Hassan, L. M., Michaelidou, N., and Beatty, S. E. (2011). Emotions, store-environmental cues, store-choice criteria, and marketing outcomes. Journal of Business Research, 64(7), 737–744.

Yalch, R. F. and Spangenberg, E. R. (1990). Effects of store music on shopping behaviour. Journal of Consumer Marketing, 7(2), 55–63.

Yalch, R. F. and Spangenberg, E. R. (2000). The effects of music in a retail setting on real and perceived shopping times. Journal of Business Research, 49(2), 139–147.

14

SENSORY MARKETING

Olfactory cues and haptic cues

Tugra Nazli Akarsu

Introduction

This chapter aims to present an overview to olfactory and haptic cues from sensory marketing literature, where the different elements of those cues and how those cues engage consumers and influence on consumers cognitive, affective attitudes, as well as judgements are also discussed via the chapter.

Olfactory cues: Background

Olfactory cues 'heighten awareness: [they alert] the organism to existence of agents in the air, to check their quality for guidance of behaviour on the basis of previous encounters, to avoid or approach certain substances' (Hvastja and Zanuttini, 1991, p. 883). Ambient scent is considered as one of the environmental characteristics in the marketing context that has a firm influence on consumers and refers to 'a scent that is not emanating from a particular object but is present in the environment' (Spangenberg et al., 1996, p. 67).

In the context of using sensorial cues to appeal to consumers, even though olfactory cues and their application to experiential marketing have attracted many industries, there has been little focus on them in the academic empirical research (Kivioja, 2017; Maille, 2001). Olfactory cues refer to the stimuli related to scent and freshness in the surrounding atmosphere (Areni and Kim, 1994). In the marketing domain, researchers first began to investigate the scent of specific products (Schneider, 1977; Schmitt and Schulz, 1995). However, this approach has evolved and shifted to the use of *ambient scent* to create a positive consumer experience in the store (Doucé and Janssens, 2013; Soars, 2009; Vinitzky and Mazursky, 2011).

Literature review

An examination of the relevant literature indicates that olfactory cues have been found to influence consumers' responses, such as influencing their revisit intentions (Spangenberg et al., 1996), leading them to have enhanced pleasure and, in turn, increasing their loyalty

(Walsh et al., 2011) and influencing their buying behaviour (Madzharov et al., 2015) as well as point of purchase (Kivioja, 2017). Spangenberg et al. (1996) found that pleasurable ambient scent could alter consumers' evaluations of their experience compared with a no-scent environment. Furthermore, Morrin and Ratneshwar's (2003) research concludes that a pleasant ambient scent alters consumers' recognition and recall towards the brand, and that pleasant scent increases the amount of time and money that consumers are willing to spend in the retail setting.

In another context, Walsh et al. (2011) found that aromas in coffee shops influenced consumer pleasure and satisfaction, which, in turn, enhanced customer loyalty. In another empirical study, Madzharov et al. (2015) concluded that ambient scent influenced consumers' preferences, which then led them to change their buying behaviour (e.g., money spent, number of items purchased).

Interestingly, when it comes to the resonation of memory, olfactory cues are found as an important denominator in terms of recall childhood memories (vividness, detail, and emotional intensity) compared to visual cues (images) (de Brujin and Bender, 2018)

Scrutiny of the literature indicates that ambient scent diffused into the retail context can influence consumer behaviour (Helmefalk and Berndt, 2018; Kivioja, 2017), specifically enhance the consumer experience, and the current literature supports this with findings that store scents are positively associated with positive consumer responses (Chebat and Michon, 2003; Michon et al., 2005; Michon et al., 2008; Spangenberg et al., 2005).

Haptic cues: Background

As the skin is the largest sensory organ and touch is the first human sense developed, the tactile sense or haptic cues are considered as a 'principal source of input to touch perceptual system' (Peck and Childers, 2003, p. 35). According to the existing body of knowledge (Klatzky and Lederman, 1992; McCabe and Nowlis, 2003), haptic cues are the least studied sensorial cues in the marketing discipline.

As highlighted by Littel and Orth (2013):

> A substantial amount of research has examined single-mode effects on brand evaluations. Research on visual cues has established effects for design elements including shapes (Folkes and Matta, 2004; Raghubir and Krishna, 1999; Wansink, 1996), colours (Garber et al., 2000), logos/typefaces (Henderson and Cote, 1998; Henderson et al., 2004), and pictures (Underwood and Klein, 2002). Subsequent research then established systematic relations between holistic types of visual design and consumer brand evaluations (Orth and Malkewitz, 2008). To a lesser extent research on haptic characteristics reported similar effects of touch (Grohmann et al., 2007; Peck and Childers, 2003.
>
> *p. 199*

Literature review

According to scholars (Hekkert, 2006; Lindstrom, 2005; Littel and Orth, 2013), even though haptic cues have had less attention than the other sensorial cues, practitioners and academics, rather than focusing on single sensorial cues to understand how consumers perceive brands or products, should lean on multiple senses to gain a better understanding. Peck and Childers

(2003) observe that in a retail setting, companies should utilise haptic cues to influence consumers in a positive manner by simply letting them touch the products. It has long been evident that haptic input provides consumers with substantial information that cannot be received simply by looking at products (Lindauer et al., 1986), where it has been emphasised that haptic cues has a vital standing for consumer emotion and behaviour (Streicher and Estes, 2016). As highlighted by Peck and Childers (2003), 'studying touch may lead to insights regarding brand judgements and choice preferences' (p. 430). McCabe and Nowlis (2003) also note that haptic cues are required by consumers to evaluate and explore information about products.

Even though haptic cues have been 'the most underappreciated sense in marketing' (Streicher, 2012; p. 920), previous studies have addressed crucial points such as touch being a necessity (Peck and Childers, 2003), and the influence of nondiagnostic haptic cues on the judgements of products (Krishna and Morrin, 2008). As discussed in Chapter II, the literature places haptic cues into two groups: diagnostic and nondiagnostic (Grohmann et al., 2007; Krishna and Morrin, 2008; Meyvis and Janiszewski, 2002). Diagnostic haptic cues are those involved when consumers specifically search for diagnostic information when evaluating a brand, product, or service (Meyvis and Janiszewski, 2002).

According to Krishna and Morrin (2008),

> haptic is diagnostic for the target task – that is, when it provides objective information relevant to product judgement, such as touching a sweater to assess its thickness or texture.
> *p. 807*

On the other hand, nondiagnostic haptic cues are those 'not objectively relevant to the judgement task' (ibid., p. 808). Furthermore, according to Krishna and Morrin (ibid.), nondiagnostic haptic cues are considered as a natural part of the consumption experience; their influence on consumer judgements has been long recognised by scholars (Broniarczyk and Gershoff, 1997; Meyvis and Janiszewski, 2002; Shiv et al., 2005; van Osselaer et al., 2004). For example, Grohmann et al. (2007) state that the sense of touch (or haptic cues) influences consumer response and perception of product quality. Another striking result from Hornik's (1992) study showed that consumers who had touched a product (while tasting a new snack being launched in a supermarket) tended to comply more than consumers who had not touched the product. Peck and Childers (2003) revealed the influence of individual-level differences in haptic orientation or preferences based on product-based haptic information.

As emphasised by Peck and Shu (2009), consumers feel more 'belongingness' towards products offered in touch situations than in no-touch situations. From the research discussed above, the results can be generalisable in terms of the idea that the use of haptic cues by consumers creates positive responses and in turn, affects behavioural responses such as increased rate of impulse purchases (Hulten, 2012; Peck and Childers, 2003).

Practical applications

Olfactory cues

When it comes to the olfactory and haptic cues in sensory marketing, there are still many different directions yet to be explored, and the reason can be supported with what Hone (2018) propagates as:

research shows that there's a 90–10 split between our subconscious and conscious minds – meaning that many of the decisions that we think are rational and analytical are, in fact, driven by something much more instinctive and emotional. The subconscious, anatomically known as the limbic system, is where we store our long-term memories, where we form our habits and patterns and where we get our intuition and creativity ... Sensory branding operates on the premise that if a brand stimulates multiple senses, we will experience the brand more profoundly, connecting on deeper emotional level.

p. 1

In the same vein, Elder et al. (2010) emphasised the importance of investigating individual differences in smell research as follows:

The study of individual differences should also constitute a further step in smell research. Anatomic and physiologic differences (gender, age, genetics) have been documented (Brand & Millot, 2001), and it is likely that other individual differences exist that affect scent perceptions. For example, do individuals differ in their need for smell (similar to the need for touch; Peck & Childers, 2003a), the centrality of smells in their lives, or in their emotional reaction to smells? Wrzesniewski, McCauley, and Rozin (1999) have developed a scale measuring individual differences in the affective impact of odors on places, objects, and persons, demonstrating that differences other than biologic one's influence scent perception. Among others, one promising direction for future research would be to develop a general scale measuring the susceptibility of an individual to using scent as an input for decisions and evaluations.

p. 9

In retail settings, brands may attempt different sensory strategies to gain a competitive advantage. Although visual and audial cues seem to be more important than the other sensorial cues, the findings provide evidence of increased attention to olfaction strategies. The reason has explained by Steven Semodd, co-president of Scent Marketing Institute as follows:

Because, when you think about it, in the world of product promotion, advertising and branding, everything is about sight and sound. Our senses are basically saturated. No one has really been tapping into smell, and the sense of smell is directly hardwired into your brain.

The Independent, 2011

With the increased attention to the olfaction strategies, brands have begun to formulate 'signature scents', where those scents are 'commercially viable' (White, 2011) within retail settings, and distributed through the ventilation systems. Although it seems quite new, companies formulated an already existed technology to distribute the scent; such as nebulisation technology to convert the fragranced oil into a vapour so that it can diffuse in the atmosphere (European Cleaning Journal (ECJ), 2019). According to European Cleaning Journal, 'the global air freshener market is set to increase from $10 billion (€9 billion) in 2016 to $12 billion dollars (€10.83 billion) by 2023' (2019).

Haptic cues

With the increasing online presence of retailers and the convenience of reaching the products through the e-commerce platforms such as Amazon, Alibaba, or Shopify, it can be assumed that the haptic cues can be compensated. As emphasised by Krishna and Morrin (2008), the influence of nondiagnostic haptic cues on consumer evaluation and judgement has long been recognised by the previous research (Broniarczyk and Gershoff 1997, Meyvis and Janiszewski 2002; Shiv et al., 2005; van Osselaer et al., 2004). In addition, Krishna and Morrin (2008) stress that nondiagnostic haptic cues are considered as a natural part of the consumption experience. According to Retail Dive's Consumer Survey, which has been conducted with 1,248 consumers on their brick-mortar and online shopping habits, despite the prevalence, ease of use and convenience, 56% of consumers stated 'need for touch' before buying the products online. Also, another important fact revealed by Peck and Shu (2009), is that haptic cues are more than an intuition or a need for evaluation, it also increases the perceived ownership of an object.

Considering these, the *need for touch* triggered the touch technologies, especially technologies enabling online retailers to replicate the 'retail experience' through emerging approaches to digital haptic experience. According to Wunderman Thompson's report on haptic ads (Laughlin, 2017), by no means haptic technology has 'invented', but renewed and altered through the needs of consumers in world of modern digital retailing, where the new technologies such as 'a programmable surface haptic technology that modulates electric fields to create textures on screens as users swipe their fingers' and 'screens that replicate textures using ultra-sonic vibrations' (Laughlin, 2017) has showcased at Consumer Electronic Show (CES) in 2017. In addition to these immersive techonolgies, Augmented reality (AR) and virtual reality (VR) begun to embed into digital retailing which allows brand to create a physical simulacrum (Magnarelli, 2018). Another interesting study conducted by IPG Media Lab confirms that adding the touch experience to the mobile advertisements increased the happiness and excitement level of consumers by 7% and 8% respectively, as well as increase the consumers' brand perception by 6% (IPG Lab, 2017).

CASE STUDY – NIVEA

Maria Palazzo, University of Salerno, Italy

Tugra Nazli Akarsu, University of Southampton, United Kingdom

Introduction

Having its name from a Latin adjective of 'snow white', and by inventing the modern skin care almost 100 years ago (Nivea, 2020), Nivea became a leading brand in beauty and cosmetic markets (Bilgram et al., 2011).

With its invention by chance in 1911, within just in three years, Nivea became available on every continent. In 1920s, with the increasing importance of the concept's 'youth' and 'holiday', Nivea redesigned its packaging and logo to the one we know today. To make itself accessible and distinguishable, they adopted today's simple yet distinctive blue tin and background with simple white Nivea letters.

Nivea experienced its groundbreaking expansion in the 1950s, where they launched their wide range sun cream products, which coincided with consumers increasing tendency to go on beach holidays and skiing holidays (Nivea, 2020). The availability and its expansion in products allowed them to be one of the most trustworthy brands in skincare. In 1990s, Nivea even expanded its products by having family products such as Nivea Visage, Nivea Bath Care, Nivea Q10, among many others.

The company describes itself as:

> As one of the leading companies in the field of skin care – with more than 130 years of experience – our products always cater for the needs of our consumers, who place a great deal of faith in us. (…) Reliability and quality – these are our most important values. Sustainability therefore plays an important role for NIVEA.
>
> *www.nivea.co.uk/about-us*

Nivea Visage Young

Nivea's aim is to create products that are able to answer to customers' needs. Thus, it launched Nivea Visage Young at the beginning of the 2000s trying to reach the new target of young women (aged 14–20).

Having found a gap in the skin care market, Nivea Visage Young was proposed as a new product with improved characteristics in terms of: Perfume, texture, formula, design, etc. (Alberti et al., 2019).

Nivea implemented different market research techniques to reach the selected market segments. Moreover, the new features of the Nivea Visage Young were created with the main scope of providing a benefit to the clients, instead of giving an answer to their skin problems. The company, in fact, enhanced the product using:

- A new formula (it removed alcohol and used sea salts and minerals).
- A new design with flowers.
- Soft colours.
- New perfumes to catch the attention of younger women.

In addition, the product was made available in retail outlets (i.e., supermarkets and street shops) and it was possible to buy it through direct mail and the internet.

Besides, the company used many communication channels to promote the product. The selected promotional activities were consumer-led, as Nivea decided to implement below-the-line tactics identifying new ways of appealing to young women and their mums.

These tactics allowed consumers to touch, feel, and smell the Nivea VISAGE Young. Among them, the company choose (Dessart & Pitardi, 2016):

- To distribute samples in stores in 'goody bags'.
- To take part in roadshows.
- To publish and interactive online magazine (titled FYI – Fun, Young & Independent).

- To promote during the Hit40UK chart show.
- To communicate using the TMF digital TV channel.
- To have its own pages on MySpace, Facebook, and Bebo.

In conclusion, Nivea Visage Young, leveraging on the original features of the product and mixing them with the right distribution channels and communication strategy, succeeded in attaining a clear position in the market. This highlights that Nivea understands its customers and has created this differentiated product line to satisfy their needs (Wulle, 2017).

Case questions

1. After you have written down what corporate brand sensuality is, analyse the relationship between what this feature has to offer to brands and which companies might be interested in it.
2. After you have written down what olfactory cues are, including all of their benefits, analyse the relationship between what they can offer to brands and which company might be interested in developing them.
3. List the reasons why Nivea does use olfactory cues to position its new product.

References

Alberti, B., Asgian, C., Caldwell, H., and DeFanti, M. (2019). A proposed brand portfolio strategy for Nivea to gain competitive advantage: A case study. Journal of Competitiveness Studies, 27(3/4), 190–199.

Bilgram, V., Bartl, M., and Biel, S. (2011). Getting closer to the consumer–how Nivea co-creates new products. Marketing Review St. Gallen, 28(1), 34–40.

Dessart, L., and Pitardi, V. (2016). How YouTube storytelling can win consumers' hearts: The case of Nivea. Advances in Consumer Research, 44, 728.

Nivea. (2020). www.nivea.co.uk/about-us/nivea-history

Wulle, M. (2017). Nivea and more: Digital value added instead of buzzword Bingo. NIM Marketing Intelligence Review, 9(1), 58.

Key terms and definitions

Haptic cues are the first human senses developed, the sense of touch. The tactile sense (or haptic cues) is considered as a primary source of input in our perceptual system.

Olfactory cues are the stimuli related to scent and freshness in the atmosphere.

References

Areni, C. S. and Kim, D. (1994). The influence of in-store lighting on consumers' examination of merchandise in a wine store. International Journal of Research in Marketing, 11(2), 117–125.

Broniarczyk, M. S. and Gershoff, A. D. (1997). "Meaningless Differentiation Revisited", in Brucks, M. and MacInnis, D. J. (Eds.), NA – Advances in Consumer Research Volume 24 (pp. 223–228). Provo, UT: Association for Consumer Research.

Chebat, J. and Michon, R. (2003). Impact of ambient odours on mall shoppers' emotions, cognition, and spending. Journal of Business Research, 56(7), 529–539.

de Bruijn, M. J. and Bender, M. (2018). Olfactory cues are more effective than visual cues in experimentally triggering autobiographical memories. Memory, 26(4), 547–558.

Doucé, L. and Janssens, W. (2013). The presence of a pleasant ambient scent in a fashion store: The moderating role of shopping motivation and affect intensity. Environment and Behavior, 45(2), 215–238.

Elder, R. S., Aydinoglu, N. Z., Barger, V., Caldara, C., Chin, H., Lee, C. J., and Mohr, G. S. (2010). "A Sense of Things to Come: Future Research Directions in Sensory Marketing", in Sensory Marketing: Research on the Sensuality of Products (pp. 361–376). New York: Taylor & Francis.

European Cleaning Journal (ECJ) (2019). The fragrance experience (September 18). Available at www.europeancleaningjournal.com/magazine/articles/product-features/the-fragrance-experience

Grohmann, B., Spangenberg, E. R., and Sprott, D. E. (2007). The influence of tactile input on the evaluation of retail product offerings. Journal of Retailing, 83(2), 237–245.

Helmefalk, M. and Berndt, A. (2018). Shedding light on the use of single and multisensory cues and their effect on consumer behaviours. International Journal of Retail and Distribution Management, 46, 1077–1091.

Hekkert, P. (2006). Design aesthetics: Principles of pleasure in design. Psychology Science, 48(2006), 157–172.

Hone, M. (2018). Using sensory branding will create more meaningful experiences for customers. The Drum. Available at: www.thedrum.com/opinion/2018/05/02/using-sensory-branding-will-create-more-meaningful-experiences-customers [Accessed 27 September 2020]

Hornik, J. (1992). Haptic stimulation and consumer response. Journal of Consumer Research, 19(3), 449–458.

Hulten, B. (2012). Sensory cues and shoppers' touching behaviour: The case of IKEA. International Journal of Retail and Distribution Management, 40(4), 273–289.

Hvastja, L. and Zanuttini, L. (1991). Recognition of nonexplicitly presented odors. Perceptual and Motor Skills, 72(3), 883–892.

IPG Lab (2017). Ads You Can Feel: Immersion, Magna, & IPG Media Lab Conduct In-Depth Analysis Of Haptic Tech In Video Ads, IPG Lab (August, 28). Available at: https://ipglab.com/2017/01/24/ads-you-can-feel-immersion-magna-ipg-media-lab-conduct-in-depth-analysis-of-haptic-tech-in-video-ads/

Kivioja, K. (2017). Impact of point-of-purchase olfactory cues on purchase behavior. Journal of Consumer Marketing, 34(2), 119–131.

Klatzky, R. L. and Lederman, S. J. (1992). Stages of manual exploration in haptic object identification. Perception and Psychophysics, 52(6), 661–670.

Krishna, A. and Morrin, M. (2008). Does touch affect taste? The perceptual transfer of product container haptic cues. Journal of Consumer Research, 34(6), 807–818.

Laughlin, S. (2017). Haptic ads. Wunderman Thompson (February 8). Available at: https://intelligence.wundermanthompson.com/2017/02/haptic-ads/

Lindauer, M. S., Stergiou, E. A., and Penn, D. L. (1986). Seeing and touching aesthetic objects: I. Judgments. Bulletin of the Psychonomic Society, 24(2), 121–124.

Lindstrom, M. (2005). Brand Sense: Build Powerful Brands through Touch, Taste, Smell, Sight and Sound. New York: Simon & Schuster Adult Publishing Group.

Littel, S. and Orth, U. R. (2013). Effects of package visuals and haptics on brand evaluations. European Journal of Marketing, 47(1/2), 198–217.

Madzharov, A. V., Block, L. G. and Morrin, M. (2015). The cool scent of power: Effects of ambient scent on consumer preferences and choice behaviours. Journal of Marketing, 79(1), 83–96.

Magnarelli, M. (2018). The next marketing skill you need to master: Touch, The Forbes. Available at: www.forbes.com/sites/margaretmagnarelli/2018/09/14/haptic-marketing/#4a5608987a3f

Maille, V. (2001). L'influence des stimuli olfactifs sur le comportement du consommateur: Un etat des recherches. Recherche et Applications en Marketing, 16(2), 51–75.

McCabe, D. B. and Nowlis, S. M. (2003). The effect of examining actual products or product descriptions on consumer preference. Journal of Consumer Psychology, 13(4), 431–439.

Meyvis, T. and Janiszewski, C. (2002). Consumers' beliefs about product benefits: The effect of obviously irrelevant product information. Journal of Consumer Research, 28(4), 618–635.

Michon, R., Chebat, J., and Turley, L. (2005). Mall atmospherics: The interaction effects of the mall environment on shopping behaviour. Journal of Business Research, 58(5), 576–583.

Michon, R., Yu, H., Smith, D., and Chebat, J. (2008). The influence of mall environment on female fashion shoppers' value and behaviour. Journal of Fashion Marketing and Management: An International Journal, 12(4), 456–468.

Morrin, M. and Ratneshwar, S. (2003). Does it make sense to use scents to enhance brand memory? Journal of Marketing Research, 40(1), 10–25.

Peck, J. and Childers, T. L. (2003). Individual differences in haptic information processing: The need for touch scale. Journal of Consumer Research, 30(3), 430–442.

Peck, J. and Shu, S. B. (2009). The effect of mere touch on perceived ownership. Journal of Consumer Research, 36(3), 434–447.

Schmitt, B. H. and Shultz, C. J. (1995). Situational effects on brand preferences for image products. Psychology and Marketing, 12(5), 433–446.

Schneider, K. C. (1977). Prevention of accidental poisoning through package and label design. Journal of Consumer Research, 4(2), 67–74.

Shiv, B., Carmon, Z., and Ariely, D. (2005). Placebo effects of marketing actions: Consumers may get what they pay for. Journal of Marketing Research, 9, 383–393.

Soars, B. (2009). Driving sales through shoppers' sense of sound, sight, smell and touch. International Journal of Retail and Distribution Management, 37(3), 286–298

Spangenberg, E. R., Crowley, A. E., and Henderson, P. W. (1996). Improving the store environment: Do olfactory cues affect evaluations and behaviors? Journal of Marketing, 60(2), 67–80.

Spangenberg, E. R., Grohmann, B., and Sprott, D. E. (2005). It's beginning to smell (and sound) a lot like Christmas: The interactive effects of ambient scent and music in a retail setting. Journal of Business Research, 58(11), 1583–1589.

Streicher, M. (2012). From the hands to the mind: Haptic brand signatures. In Zeynep Gürhan-Canli, Z., Otnes, C., and Zhu, R., Duluth, M. N. (Eds.), NA – Advances in Consumer Research, Volume 40. Association for Consumer Research, pp. 920–921.

Streicher, M. C. and Estes, Z. (2016). Multisensory interaction in product choice: Grasping a product affects choice of other seen products. Journal of Consumer Psychology, 26(4), 558–565.

Van Osselaer, S. M., Janiszewski, C., and Cunha, M. (2004). Stimulus generalization in two associative learning processes. Journal of Experimental Psychology: Learning, Memory, and Cognition, 30(3), 626–638.

Vinitzky, G. and Mazursky, D. (2011). The effects of cognitive thinking style and ambient scent on online consumer approach behaviour, experience approach behaviour, and search motivation. Psychology and Marketing, 28(5), 496–519.

Walsh, G., Shiu, E., Hassan, L. M., Michaelidou, N., and Beatty, S. E. (2011). Emotions, store-environmental cues, store-choice criteria, and marketing outcomes. Journal of Business Research, 64(7), 737–744.

White, C. (2011). The smell of commerce: How companies use scents to sell their products. *The Independent* (August 16). Available at: www.independent.co.uk/news/media/advertising/the-smell-of-commerce-how-companies-use-scents-to-sell-their-products-2338142.html

15
GUSTATIVE SIGNATURES AS CORPORATE BRAND IDENTIFIERS
Exploring the sensuality of taste as a marketing strategy

Dongmei Zha

Introduction

This chapter aim to introduce the concept of gustative signature as a corporate brand identifier enabling customers to recognise, identify, and recall a brand. By locating the gustative experience in the context of the mouth/brain relationship, the critical role of gustatory activities, and the creation of a customer-based brand identity is discussed.

Background

Brands have brand signatures, core and distinct aspects of a brand identity or brand personality that persist through different forms of communications, reflecting a *brand's image and reputation* (Foroudi, 2019). In the neuroscience literature, sensory signature is sensory/perceptual detailed with implicate memories (Fabiani and Wessels, 2000; Slotnick and Schacter, 2004). We assert that at the sensory level, brand signatures can also be experienced as sensory signatures via a set of sensory data (taste sensations, audio sensations, smell sensations, touch sensations) actualised and mined at the point of consumption, enabling the customer to recognise and identify the brand in his or her mind. Sensory signature is why you can you can tell right away whether its Taylor Swift or Beyonce singing on the radio just by the vocal timbre of their voice (e.g., clean or breathy sounds, vowel and diction, head voice or chesty voice, level of vibrato). Or why you can tell it's a Pepsi or Coke simply by mere savouring. Among the different catalogue of cues that represents a brand sensorially (e.g., audio signatures, visual signatures, olfactory signatures, haptic signatures) gustative signatures represent one of the most effective ways for a firm to build an enduring and sticky identity of the brand in the consumer's mind (Spence et al., 2014).

Gustative signatures

Gustative signatures are sets of sensory data (taste sensations, chemo-sensations, olfactory sensations, oral haptic sensations, sensorimotor sensations) actualised and mined at the point of consumption enabling the customer to recognise and identify the brand in his or her mind. In a nutshell, a gustative signature is the brand that pops up in your mind (e.g., brand name, recall of an experience with the brand), consistently and automatically, when you consume a product in your mouth. To understand gustative signatures, we have to first clarify two important relationships: i) the mouth and brain relationship; ii) the taste and flavour relationship.

The mouth/brain relationship

First, the relationship between the mouth and the brain. Taste is usually related with food-related products to explore how food product information affects sensory experience and well documented in sensory marketing and psychology literature. Tastes can be included five different types of elements that the sensory modality can evaluate are sweet, salty, bitter, sour and umami. Spence (2017) highlight the significance of this mouth/mind relationship by reminding us that *the pleasures of the table, it resides in the mind but not the mouth*. The taste sensation that we think we experience in our mouth is actually taking place in the brain. Information harvested by taste receptors imbedded in the tongue is immediately transmitted as neurophysiological data through multiple neural channels to the cortex region of the brain where the taste is coded and identified (Yamamoto, 1984). Think of the keyboard on your computer as the receptor and the hard disk in your computer as the brain. As Spence (2016) observed, most people think food contains flavour. Food only contain molecules that has the potential to trigger flavour. The flavour sensations are actually created in our brains. That said, while it is true flavour is only experienced in the brain, it is also worthwhile to note that everything taking place in the brain depends on what is going on in the mouth. To put it metaphorically, the mouth is the brain's taste laboratory, a *track and trace* centre, where information about the food we consume is harvested and sent to the brain.

Why does the brain require so much data about the food we eat? The answer is simple: This information is critical for our survival. Ingesting the right or wrong type of food can mean life or death. Without taste, we would not be able to assess the nutritional content of food to maintain a healthy diet (e.g., a sweet taste indicates energy-rich nutrients) or avoid ingesting substances that may be harmful to our bodies (e.g., a bitter taste is a signal that the content may be toxic) (Lindemann 2001). Besides determining whether the food we ingest is helpful or harmful, beneficial or detrimental, the receptors in the mouth also gather information about brands. The brain differentiates and compares sensations that comes from each different intake, determining whether we like and dislike, continue with the same brand, or discontinue and move on to another. A negative dining experience ingesting something harmful can trigger permanent avoidance of the restaurant (e.g., when you find you a cockroach in your bowl of noodles) while a positive experience can result in a craving for a repeat of such experiences.

The tools available in the cavity of the mouth for purposes of data gathering are multiple and highly sophisticated. They include *hardware* – intricate combination of bone and muscle structures, four types of teeth (incisors, canines, premolars and molars), the tongue, salivary gland, and *software* – a network of information-gathering receptors imbedded on the surface of the tongue, tissues lining the mouth, muscles, that function as a kind of receivers to monitor and capture data on behalf of the brain. From this perspective, mundane, day-to-day activities like eating, snacking, and drinking can be perceived as fact-finding activities. What are the types of information the brain harvest in your mouth?

Sensorimotor sensations

The sensorimotor activities, defined as sensations arising from bodily movements, used to move the food around in the mouth as people eat or drink is an essential part of gathering information about the food. Food is moved around the mouth to gather information about its size, texture, viscosity, granularity, and elasticity (Krishna and Elder, 2021). The delicate bone in your throat that anchors the tongue muscles allow movements of swelling and contraction to compress and churn the food in our mouth cavity ensuring that the multiple receptors have maximum exposure to the surface areas inside and outside the solids or volatiles we consume. What kind of food are we ingesting? Is it vegetable or meat, solid materials that require active chewing before swallowing. Is it water, liquid that can be swallowed or flavoured fluids like wine, coffee, and tea that requires additional olfactory functions. Although one of the most direct benefits of chewing is the breaking down of the substance to aid ingestion, the motor actions has the additional purpose of exposing the food to internal smell (Shepherd and Shepherd, 2011).

Olfactory sensations

Research has observed that as much as 75–95% of our tasting sensations are actually olfactory (Spence, 2015). There are two types of senses of smell at work: i) orthonasal smell – the smell when we inhale and whenever we swallow; and ii) retronasal smell – the little pulses of air that comes out of the back of the nostrils. That is where the flavour of food comes from. Orthonsal air comes exclusively from the environment and consists of the gases nitrogen, oxygen, and carbon dioxide, together with evaporated water varying with temperature and humidity. It includes various trace compounds, depending on the local environment and the levels of pollution, as well as particulate matter, such as smoke, pollen, dust, and lint. Depending on the levels of contamination, these external conditions do have an impact on flavour sensations, just as a smoking environment has an impact on the taste of food (Sanganahalli et al., 2020). In addition to nitrogen, oxygen, and carbon dioxide, it has high humidity due to moisturising by the airway mucus membranes and a warm temperature due to the body's temperature (Cavarretta et al., 2018).

Both senses of smell contribute to the gustative experience (Biswas et al., 2021). On most occasions, sniffing a coffee (orthonasal) and swallowing (retronasal), they are usually in alignment. But on some occasions, they are not. There are occasions when you experience of what smells like a great, freshly grounded coffee, great in the orthonasal sniff but on ingesting (retronasal), it's not quite the same, not quite as nice as the orthonasal smell has led you to believe. On the other hand, you may find the smell of an exotic brand of cheese a little repelling (orthonasal) but change your mind once you taste it in your mouth (retronasal).

Oral haptic sensations

In existing haptic studies (e.g., Peck and Childers, 2003) four haptic properties of objects has been identified (hardness, texture, temperature, and weight). These include haptic sensations relating to masticating actions to determine the quality of the food (Biswas et al., 2014). In gustative experience, thermo sensations play a very important role in determining the quality of the gustative experience (Zha et al., 2020; Zha et al., 2021). For example, you walk into a cafe, order a large flat-white. Even though the cafe got all the ingredients right. The temperature at which the product is made and delivered affects your judgement of the experience.

Chemo-sensations

Trigeminal receptors located in the tissues around the mouth collect chemo-sensation data for the brain in the process of biting and chewing. The spicy chemo-sensations fired up by a brand of Indian curry or the icy sensation of chewing a menthol sweet are typical sensations triggered by trigeminal receptors (Mukherjee et al. 2017).

The taste/flavour relationship

The complexities of the relationship between the brain and the mouth imply that many different processes are operative in an act of consumption. To understand the ontogenesis of a gustative signature simply examining the role of 'taste' is not sufficient. Taste is a member of a coalition of sensations that must be synchronised to elicit a representation of the brand in the consumer's mind. To evoke a gustative signature, taste needs to enlist the help of other sensory modalities such as oral haptic, olfactory, and sensorimotor. Strictly speaking, the taste sensation is the result of an impingement of external stimuli on the tongue resulting in one of five taste responses: salty, sweet, sour, bitter, and unami. Based on the definition, the brain would only gain very limited information about the food. A gustative signature on the other hand, requires the full complement of sensations defined within International Standards Organization lexicon as the equivalent of a flavour: A 'complex combination of the olfactory, gustatory and trigeminal sensations perceived during tasting. The flavour may be influenced by tactile, thermal, painful and/or kinaesthetic effects' (Spence, 2015, p. 4). Therefore, gustative signature should be understood with a consortium of sensations mobilised in an act of consumption where taste represents one component of the overall experience.

Discussion

Although all brands have sensory signatures, not all sensory signatures are created equal. It is obvious that some sensory signatures are more unique, more evocative, more effective at brand identification than others. Think of the audio mnemonic 'Ta-dum', the two 16th note timpani strikes on D2 and D3 that signals a night binge-watching with Netflix. Or the distinct oral haptic sensations evoked by a granular texture of a Ferrero Rocher chocolate ball strewn with roasted hazelnut pieces. Brand sensuality is the study of why some sensory signatures are more engaging, more arousing, and more memorable and why some are not. Therefore, we proposed a holistic approach to gustative signature (Figure 15.1).

Gustative sensuality and product consistency

To enhance gustative sensuality, a firm has to first identify its gustative signature. To be perceived as a gustative signature, the delivery of the gustative experience has to achieve a level of consistency and stability of response. It means the taste or experience of the product, whether it is a cup of coffee, a bowl of wanton noodles, a box of tikka curry, must be perceived by the customer as consistent and similar in experiential quality to the previous consumption of the

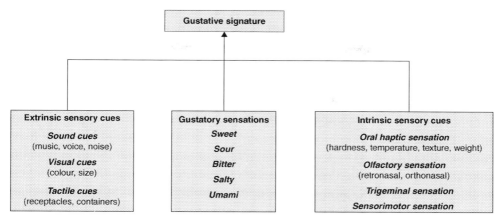

FIGURE 15.1 Gustative signature, gustatory sensations, extrinsic, and intrinsic sensory cues

same product. All of us have the same experience. We walk into a restaurant, have a wonderful gastronomic experience. The food was great. The taste was just right. A week, you go back to the same restaurant, this time the experience was a letdown. The food just didn't taste like before. What went wrong? Ensuring the consistent and stable preparation and delivery of a food experience is no easy task. Even a well-developed fast-food provider like McDonald's worldwide finds it a perennial challenge to ensure that the experience of consuming a double cheeseburger in Hawaii is consistent with the experience of consuming a double cheeseburger in Ho Chi Minh City in Vietnam.

Gustative sensuality and customer experience

Sensuality is enhanced when the gustative signature matches the needs, the wants, and the desires of the customer. Gustative signatures are co-created. It is at once a creation of the firm (what the firm intents it to be) and also a product of the subjectivities of the consumer (what the customer perceives it to be). A gustative offering can be the product of best intentions, best managerial efforts, best marketing strategies, but if it does not connect with the customer, it is still not a gustative signature. To enhance sensuality of gustative signatures, firms have to put their ears on the ground. Constantly be on the lookout for customer's responses, reactions, prevailing hearsay, media post, social media comments that infer to the evolving narrative of what the customer perceives as the signature of the brand. What aspects of the quality of the gustative experience that is most memorable? What unique features of the gustative experience brings them back as repeat customers?

Gustative sensuality and the consumption environment

External cues from the immediate brand setting also play a very important role in the enhancement of gustative signatures. Since food tasting usually takes place in a social setting our sensory experience is heavily dependent on what's taking place in the immediate external environment (see a summary in Table 15.1).

TABLE 15.1 Summary of Selected Business Studies Involving External Sensory Cues (2015–2020)

Author (s), year	Source	Methodology	Main construct	Theory	Sensory stimuli	Major implications
Knoeferle et al. 2015	*Psychology and Marketing*	Quantitative (3 online experiments)	– Music – Taste culture-specific	Mental imagery	Sound and taste (bitter, salty, sweet and sour) correspondence effect	– Understanding the cross-modal correspondences (taste and sound) – Providing more evidence between the auditory and gustatory modalities with shared underlying characteristics – Extending the knowledge about which cross-modal correspondences are 'strong' or 'weak'
Togawa et al. 2019	*Journal of Retailing*	Quantitative (4 experiments)	– Flavour heaviness – Location of food image – Purchase intention – Consumption quantity – subsequent – Food choice – Healthy eating decisions – Holistic	Embodied cognition	Visual-gustatory correspondence effect	– Examining the relationship between product image location (visual) and flavour heaviness (gustatory) correspondence – Adding to package design literature by identified cross-modal antecedent to flavour heaviness – First study to examined that the location of food image on the package façade
Biswas et al., 2019a	*Journal of Consumer Research*	Quantitative (6 experiments)	– Vestibular system – Posture – Food taste – Physical stress	Physiology	Vestibular system and food taste	– Adding physical stress-induced decreases in sensory sensitivity – Posture-related vestibular system – The important role of the nature of the stress and the pleasantness of the food and beverage consumption

Biswas et al., 2019b	*Journal of Marketing Research*	Quantitative (4 experiments)	– Ambient scent – Food purchases	Atmospherics	Smell and taste cross-modal sensory compensation effects	– Identifying a cue in olfaction modality could compensate (or satisfy) desires related to gustatory modality – First to investigate the impact of indulgent versus nonindulgent food-related ambient scents on preferences for healthy versus unhealthy food options
Pomirleanu et al. 2020	*Psychology and Marketing*	Quantitative (4 experiments)	– Temptation avoidance – Sour taste – Colour – Perceived muscle concentration	Embodied cognition	Sour and colour correspondence effect	– Identifying the body and the mind can influence temptation avoidance. – Exploring the relationship between embodied memories and subsequent reactions – Adding the role of a red-coloured background in the framework of embodied cognition

Auditory cues

Auditory cues related to the hearing and listening stimuli present in brand settings realised in the context of music, words or voices and ambient background sounds (noise, service or product sounds, noise levels by talking consumers or environmentally naturally occurring sounds), which are part of a brand's overall sensorial expression including jingles, voice and music atmosphere, attentiveness and thematic and signature sounds and sound brand. Numerous studies have already demonstrated the effect auditory cues derived from the consumption of dry food products (e.g., potato chips, biscuits, or pretzels) have on the perception of the product (Spence et al., 2011).

Researchers in Britain changed the music played in the wine section of the supermarket. When they played French music, the majority of shoppers bought French wine. Switch to German music and – you guessed it – we started filling our baskets with Riesling (North, 2012). In another test, researchers observe that when the background music is classical music, consumers spend more time in the store. In contrast, when the music is upbeat and rhythmic, consumers tend to be in a hurry and spend less time shopping or eating (Crisinel et al., 2012).

Visual cues

External marketing cues regarding taste, such as brand label (e.g., Bronnenberg et al., 2020), colour of juice, or price (e.g., Hogg and Alba, 2007), and even lighting (Biswas et al., 2014) also influence consumers' gustative experience. Studies have also shown that flavour is also affected by packaging design because visual cues do enhance or diminish our expectations and preference for the food we consume (Biswas et al., 2021; Krishna and Elder, 2021; Spence et al., 2019). Studies have shown conclusively that we have a tendency to pay more for food that are visually stimulating (Spence et al., 2019). In the same way, studies have shown that labels attached to food products predispose our food choices when we have dietary concerns (e.g., Piqueras-Fiszman and Spence, 2015).

Tactile cues

Studies have shown that the type of receptacles used for a drink influence our perception of the flavour of the substance we consume. The sense of touch (tactile sense) is the first of our human senses to develop and the largest sensory organ. Moreover, the tactile sense is regarded as one of our most intimate senses, involving physical contact with the skin, with the hands playing a major role as our 'principal source of input to the touch perceptual system' (Peck and Childers, 2003a, p. 35). Tactile sensations elicited from the feel of the glassware produce physico-chemical reactions which may be the result volatile aromatic molecules trapped in the surface of different types of glassware. The shape of the glassware can also influence the drinking experience by determining the pathway in which the liquid is physically ingested. Finally, some researchers have suggested that the shape of the glassware does evoke differing imaginings within the brain associated with the consumer's exposure to socio-cultural inferences. Based on the theory of cross-modal correspondence, the special tactile attributes do activate a variety of images to enhance a drinking experience (Spence et al., 2017).

Social cues

Social information, human perception of a product is often dependent on the social environment where the consumption is taking place. The social factor involves people, such as service personnel or other shoppers (Baker et al., 2002). The number of service personnel, their appearance, how affable they are, how helpful they are all can be relevant. Who are we sharing the gustative experience with? Who are the other customers in the store or restaurant? What do the other customers on the website comment about their experience?

Sensuality and place identity

Gustative sensuality is enhanced when the gustative signature is attached to a place or a physical location in the consumer's mind. Taste and place has always co-existed in human history. Gustative experiences grounded in a tangible, physical environment increase brand prominence and the ease of brand recall. Conversely, gustative signatures also adds value to the image and reputation of the place. Increasingly, practitioners in the hospitality industry such as hotels and shopping malls are recognising the contribution of gustative signature to destination branding and are looking for ways to integrate gustative signatures into their overall place branding strategies. For example, Kim et al. (2012) developed a scale to measure the motivation to consume local food to the tourist experience, and looking for ways to integrate gustative signatures into their overall place branding strategies. As the brick and mortar industry turn towards a more experience-centric model, mall operators worldwide are realising that integrating taste-related products, restaurants, bars, cafes, confectionary stores, increases visitor traffic. As a result, shopping mall mix and categories are changing as food and beverage category of shops are now featured more prominently at the entrance of the mall (Roggeveen et al. 2020).

Conclusion

As consumers' gastronomic interest and sophistication increase, gustative experiences assumes an increasingly important role to help firms connect with their customers. Therefore, investment of effort and resources to define a gustative signature will go a long way in ensuring the legacy and durability of a brand's identity remains vivid and prominent in both the consumer's mind and in the social consumption milieu.

CASE STUDY – COCA-COLA

Alfonso Siano, University of Salerno, Italy

Maria Palazzo, University of Salerno, Italy

Coca-Cola is one of the most well-known global brand and is considered the top producer and distributor of numerous beverages (Vrontis and Sharp, 2003; Dhar et al., 2005; Foster, 2014).

> On May 8, 1886, Dr. John Pemberton served the world's first Coca-Cola at Jacobs' Pharmacy in Atlanta, Ga. From that one iconic drink, we've evolved into a total beverage company.
>
> *www.coca-colacompany.com/company*

The market

The market of beverage has continually been affected by many issues raised by health conscious customers. In fact, flavourings, sugar, and additives affect the Cola products. Junk food and drink are considered as the main factor that can foster obesity and other food disorders (especially among young generations) and this creates negative publicity to all companies that are in this sector in recent years.

Coca-Cola Zero

Many producers face the issues by providing 'healthier' versions of their products such as a diet equivalent to the present brands: This strategy shows positive results among customers and the public opinion. In the UK, Diet Coke is, in fact, very appreciated. It must be said therefore that men do not want to buy it.

This pushed the company in 2005 to create Coke Zero: Coca Cola launched it in 2006 communicating the product and the brand as the most popular 'bloke coke'. Coke Zero's goal was to provide men (aged 18–34) a health beverage better than the original Coca-Cola.

However, many men (belonging to the selected target) highlighted that they do not like the taste of Diet Coke and that it was different from the original one, in addition, they carried on having mental associations of Diet Coke with female consumption. This was the Coke Zero main issue to take into account while it comes to create a successful communication plan (Brondoni, 2020; Harper et al., 2002).

Coke Zero was supported with a £10m advertising campaign and the organisation provided 5 million samples to prove consumers that the new coke tasted as good as the original.

On the other hand, Coke Zero has not always paid much attention to the taste of the drink. In this case, the taste was a key selling point and some researchers and practitioners highlight that not taking it into account has been the main Coca Cola Zero's downfall (Walsh and Dowding, 2012; Benjamin et al., 1991).

In these circumstances, actually, Coca-Cola had to face Pepsi Max. This product is synonymous with sugar-free coke and young males think that its tastes is great. Pepsi Max uses a simple message that this beverage has 'maximum taste with no sugar'. Besides, Pepsi has usually promoted concepts focusing on its male consumers with the tagline: 'live life to the max'.

During the launching phase of Coca-Cola Zero, the new product seems to be not as much appreciated than Pepsi Max. David Goudge (director of innovation and brand development) stated that creating a low sugar drink for the young target, who is loyal to Pepsi Max or easily decides to switching to other soft drinks, was the biggest mistake.

Older males should have been considered a more attractive segment in terms of life-style standards and potential revenues.

Despite struggling at the beginning to sell this new product, after two years of Coke Zero, AC Nielson data stated that 60 million litres have been sold in the UK. Moreover, Coke Zero now has more than 200,000 followers on Facebook and had the opportunity to partner Disney's Tron Legacy blockbuster.

After creating the Coke Zero, Coca-Cola has launched PowerAde Zero and many other Zero products (Fanta Zero, Sprite Zero, etc.). Nonetheless, does it show that we would be seeing more of Zero products in the market?

Case questions

1. Analyse the logo, design, typeface, and colour of Coke Zero.
2. Compare the logo, design, typeface, and colour of Coke Zero with that one of Coca-Cola.
3. Explain how Coca-Cola use the gustatory cues of Coke Zero in order to impact consumer evaluations, judgements, and purchase behaviour.

References

Benjamin Jr, L. T., Rogers, A. M., and Rosenbaum, A. (1991). Coca-Cola, caffeine, and mental deficiency: Harry Hollingworth and the Chattanooga trial of 1911. Journal of the History of the Behavioral Sciences, 27(1), 42–55.

Brondoni, S. M. (2020). Shareowners, stakeholders and the global oversize economy. The Coca-Cola Company case. Symphonya. Emerging Issues in Management, (1), 16–27.

Dhar, T., Chavas, J. P., Cotterill, R. W., and Gould, B. W. (2005). An econometric analysis of brand-level strategic pricing between Coca-Cola Company and PepsiCo. Journal of Economics & Management Strategy, 14(4), 905–931.

Foster, R. J. (2014). Corporations as partners: 'Connected capitalism' and the Coca-Cola Company. PoLAR: Political and Legal Anthropology Review, 37(2), 246–258.

Harper, L. A., Bettinger, J., Dismukes, R., and Kozarsky, P. E. (2002). Evaluation of the Coca-Cola company travel health kit. Journal of travel medicine, 9(5), 244–246.

Vrontis, D., and Sharp, I. (2003). The strategic positioning of Coca-Cola in their global marketing operation. The Marketing Review, 3(3), 289–309.

Walsh, H., and Dowding, T. J. (2012). Sustainability and the Coca-Cola Company: The global water crisis and Coca-Cola's Business case for water stewardship. International Journal of Business Insights & Transformation, 4.

Key terms and definitions

Brand signature is an original, distinctive design focused on the personality and identity of the brand that is expressed through all brand communications, it encompasses the critical connectivity, distinctiveness, and enduring characteristics of a brand that can represent the image and prestige of a brand globally (Foroudi et al., 2014; Foroudi, 2019; Melewar and Saunders, 1998).

Visual stimuli is the sense of vision, it includes functional and aesthetic elements, ambient elements, and social elements, have a predictive influence on how consumer evaluate a brand (Roggeveen et al., 2020; Krishna and Schwarz, 2014).

Tactile stimuli is the sense of touch which enables the perceptual differentiation of material, surface temperature, weight, and steadiness (Peck and Childers 2003).

Gustatory stimuli is taste attraction or taste aversion involving a multi-sensory inputs. A positive reaction to something eaten may recall a positive consumption experience, while a negative reaction may leads to long-term avoidance (Spence et al., 2014).

References

Baker, J., Parasuraman, A., Grewal, D., and Voss, G. B. (2002). The influence of multiple store environment cues on perceived merchandise value and patronage intentions. Journal of Marketing, 66(2), 120–141.

Biswas, D., Labrecque, L. I., and Lehmann, D. R. (2021). Effects of sequential sensory cues on food taste perception: Cross-modal interplay between visual and olfactory stimuli. Journal of Consumer Psychology. https://doi.org/10.1002/jcpy.123

Biswas, D., Lund, K., and Szocs, C. (2019a). Sounds like a healthy retail atmospheric strategy: Effects of ambient music and background noise on food sales. Journal of the Academy of Marketing Science, 47(1), 37–55.

Biswas, D., Szocs, C., and Abell, A. (2019b). Extending the boundaries of sensory marketing and examining the sixth sensory system: Effects of vestibular sensations for sitting versus standing postures on food taste perception. Journal of Consumer Research, 46(4), 708–724.

Biswas, D., Szocs, C., Krishna, A., and Lehmann, D. R. (2014). Something to chew on: The effects of oral haptics on mastication, orosensory perception, and calorie estimation. Journal of Consumer Research, 41(2), 261–273.

Bronnenberg, B. J., Dubé, J. P., and Sanders, R. E. (2020). Consumer misinformation and the brand premium: A private label blind taste test. Marketing Science, 39(2), 382–406.

Cavarretta, F., Burton, S. D., Igarashi, K. M., Shepherd, G. M., Hines, M. L., and Migliore, M. (2018). Parallel odor processing by mitral and middle tufted cells in the olfactory bulb. Scientific Reports, 8(1), 1–15.

Crisinel, A. S., Cosser, S., King, S., Jones, R., Petrie, J., and Spence, C. (2012). A bittersweet symphony: Systematically modulating the taste of food by changing the sonic properties of the soundtrack playing in the background. Food Quality and Preference, 24(1), 201–204.

Fabiani, M., Stadler, M. A., and Wessels, P. M. (2000). True but not false memories produce a sensory signature in human lateralized brain potentials. Journal of Cognitive Neuroscience, 12(6), 941–949.

Foroudi, P. (2019). Influence of brand signature, brand awareness, brand attitude, brand reputation on hotel industry's brand performance. International journal of hospitality management, 76, 271–285.

Foroudi, P., Melewar, T. C., and Gupta, S. (2014). Linking corporate logo, corporate image, and reputation: An examination of consumer perceptions in the financial setting. Journal of Business Research, 67(11), 2269–2281.

Hoegg, J. and Alba, J. W. (2007). Taste perception: More than meets the tongue. Journal of Consumer Research, 33(4), 490–498.

Kim, Y. G. and Eves, A. (2012). Construction and validation of a scale to measure tourist motivation to consume local food. Tourism management, 33(6), 1458–1467.

Krishna, A. and Elder, R. S. (2021). A review of the cognitive and sensory cues impacting taste perceptions and consumption. Consumer Psychology Review, 4(1), 121–134.

Krishna, A. and Schwarz, N. (2014). Sensory marketing, embodiment, and grounded cognition: A review and introduction. Journal of consumer psychology, 24(2), 159–168.

Lindemann, B. (2001). Receptors and transduction in taste. Nature, 413(6852), 219–225.

Mukherjee, S., Kramer, T., and Kulow, K. (2017). The effect of spicy gustatory sensations on variety-seeking. Psychology and Marketing, 34(8), 786–794.

North, A. C. (2012). The effect of background music on the taste of wine. British Journal of Psychology, 103(3), 293–301.

Peck, J. and Childers, T. L. (2003). Individual differences in haptic information processing: The 'need for touch' scale. Journal of Consumer Research, 30(3), 430–442.

Piqueras-Fiszman, B. and Spence, C. (2015). Sensory expectations based on product-extrinsic food cues: An interdisciplinary review of the empirical evidence and theoretical accounts. Food Quality and Preference, 40, 165–179.

Pomirleanu, N., Gustafson, B. M., and Bi, S. (2020). Ooh, that's sour: An investigation of the role of sour taste and color saturation in consumer temptation avoidance. Psychology and Marketing.

Roggeveen, A. L., Grewal, D., and Schweiger, E. B. (2020). The DAST framework for retail atmospherics: The impact of in-and out-of-store retail journey touchpoints on the customer experience. Journal of Retailing, 96(1), 128–137.

Sanganahalli, B. G., Baker, K. L., Thompson, G. J., Herman, P., Shepherd, G. M., Verhagen, J. V., and Hyder, F. (2020). Orthonasal versus retronasal glomerular activity in rat olfactory bulb by fMRI. NeuroImage, 212, 116664.

Shepherd, G. M. and Shepherd, G. (2012). Neurogastronomy. Columbia University Press.

Slotnick, S. D. and Schacter, D. L. (2004). A sensory signature that distinguishes true from false memories. Nature neuroscience, 7(6), 664–672.

Spence, C. (2013). Multisensory flavour perception. Current Biology, 23(9), 365–369.

Spence, C. (2015). Just how much of what we taste derives from the sense of smell?. Flavour, 4(1), 1–10.

Spence, C. (2016). "The neuroscience of flavour", in Multisensory Flavor Perception (pp. 235–248). Woodhead Publishing, Cambridge.

Spence, C. (2017). Gastrophysics: The new science of eating. Penguin, London.

Spence, C., Puccinelli, N. M., Grewal, D., and Roggeveen, A. L. (2014). Store atmospherics: A multisensory perspective. Psychology and Marketing, 31(7), 472–488.

Spence, C., Reinoso-Carvalho, F., Velasco, C., and Wang, Q. J. (2019). Extrinsic auditory contributions to food perception and consumer behaviour: An interdisciplinary review. Multisensory research, 32(4–5), 275–318.

Spence, C., Shankar, M. U., and Blumenthal, H. (2011). Sound bites': Auditory contributions to the perception and consumption of food and drink. Art and the Senses, 207–238.

Togawa, T., Park, J., Ishii, H., and Deng, X. (2019). A packaging visual-gustatory correspondence effect: Using visual packaging design to influence flavor perception and healthy eating decisions. Journal of Retailing, 95(4), 204–218.

Yamamoto, T. (1984). Taste responses of cortical neurons. Progress in Neurobiology, 23(4), 273–315.

Zha, D., Melewar, T. C., Foroudi, P., and Jin, Z. (2020). An assessment of brand experience knowledge literature: Using bibliometric data to identify future research direction. International Journal of Management Reviews, 22(3), 287–317.

Zha, D., Foroudi, P., Jin, Z., and Melewar, T. C. (2021). Making sense of sensory brand experience: Constructing an integrative framework for future research. International Journal of Management Reviews (forthcoming).

INDEX

Note: Entries in **bold** denote tables; entries in *italics* denote figures.

8 Cs 154

abbreviation names 55–6
ACID test 30
actual identity 30, 45
advertising: and corporate image 26, 70; rise of 204–5
advertising design 7–8
AEG (Allgemeine Elektrizitäts Gesellschaft) 9
aesthetic appeal 53, 81
aesthetic design 80–1, 83–4, 88, 105, 110
aesthetic objects, buildings as 101, 115
aesthetic value 29, 83, 102, 110
aesthetics 3, 100, 109–10; corporate 125; symbolic artifacts and 90, 95
algorithms, non-conscious 53
Alvarez, Domingo 83
AMA (American Marketing Association) 185
Amazon: company name of 117; discount codes on 159
ambient conditions 88, 92–3, 95, 116, 138; component of architecture 3, 79, 81, 116, 129, 135; impact on employees and consumers 130, 133–4; physiological reactions to 109; *see also* physical stimuli
approach behaviours 113, 223, 232
arbitrary names 56
architectural design 94, 101, 103; and control of space 105–6; influence on behaviour 113; meanings of 110–11
architectural perception 3, 100, 112, 116
architectural space 81–2, 108
architecture 93–4; and aesthetics 109–12; and ambient conditions/physical stimuli 92–3; and communication 114–15, 134–5; components of 81, 116; concept of 81–4, **85–90**, 95; decor and artifacts 84–91, 131; expressing underlying realities 104–6; and the human factor 100–2, 106–9, 113–14, 116; and identification 127; ideology of contemporary 102–3; perception and assessment 112–13; philosophy and mission 131–3; spatial layout and functionality 91–2; symbolism of 124; use of term 80, 138
Aristotle 155, 195, 204
artifacts 3, 79, 81, 84–90, 129; buildings as 101; idea-inspiring 79, 129; national 83; *see also* symbolic artifacts
artificial names 55
association/recognition 54
atmosphere: for consumption 205–6; decor and orientation in 116, 131; of an office 87, 103
atmospheric 205–7; use of term **208**, 214
atmospheric responsiveness 222
ATMs (Automated Teller Machines) 91, 134
attitudes 113–14, 189–90
attractiveness 175; and aesthetics 53, 112, 138; of organisational identity 126, 172; of physical environment 84, 95; of websites 146
attribution theory 16
audial cues 4, 233–5, 238; and gustative sensuality 258
audio brand 233
augmented reality (AR) 210–11, 246
authenticity, and reputation 66, 70
avoidance behaviours 113, 207, 222
Avon 195–7

Banana Republic 212
Bauhaus School 9
beauty, experience of 111
Behrens, Peter 8–9
belongingness 244
Berners-Lee, Tim 173
brand attachment 190, 197
brand attitude 190, 197
brand design 1, 71, 211
brand differentiation 26, 44, 137
brand experience 186, 192–3, 197–8; and brand attitude 190
brand extension 117
brand identification 27, 254
brand identity 251; Aaker's model of 27; corporate 30–1
brand image: and brand sensuality 196–7; corporate 2, 28, 66; of Dell 175; of Quiksilver 137; of Samsung 33–4; of Virgin 12
brand loyalty 158, 161, 169
brand mantra 27
brand personality 21, 251
brand recall 259
brand sensuality 2–3, 195–7, 254
brand signature 46, 49, 72, 251, 261–2; *see also* corporate brand signature
brand signifiers 234
brand touchpoint 193
brand value 12, 196
branded identity 19
branding: concept of 183–4; sensory 245; use of term 198
branding strategy 19, 136–7, 173, 231; multisensorial 194
brands: strong 28; as tactical tools 80
Branson, Richard 12
buildings: aesthetics of 81, 84, 101, 105–6, 110–11, 115; and architecture 79–80; and corporate identity 28; functionality of 102; landmark 86, 103; and space 81–3, 91, 105; symbolic meaning of 101; and visual identity 17–18, 20–1

Cadbury 57–8
Calvert, Gemma 210
chemo-sensations 254
client identification 85, 100–1, 127–8
coats of arms 52–3
Coca-Cola 259–61; trademark of 8; typeface of 49
cognitive strategies 101
cognitive structure 22, 191
coined names 56
colour: bright 131, 135; corporate brand 49–51; use of term 59; as visual cue 231–2; on websites 152
comfort: ambient conditions and 109, 116, 133; and architecture 80; of employees 91–2, 106, 130, 134; and natural light 93; and users' needs approach 114
commonalities 68, 132–3
communicated identity 30
communication: controlled and non-controlled 30; use of term 138
company name 17, 54–6, 117, 131
complaining behaviours 219, 227
conceived identity 31
consistency: in corporate brand signature 44, 49, 54; and corporate image 71; in integrated communications 20–1, 46; in marketing 24; and reputation 66, 70; website 149
constructive image 20, 169
consumer behaviour: and EPT 219–20; impact of information on 26; non-rational factors in 205–6
consumer experience 186, 218; and the senses 194
consumer loyalty 4, 169, 171–2, 234
consumer satisfaction 51, 92, 189, 193
consumer-brand relationship 204, 206
consumer-company identification 2–3, 81, 124, 171, 175
consumers, decision-making process of 16
consumption environment: creation of 206; and gustative sensuality 255
consumption experience 186, 231, 244, 246
consumption spaces, sensory marketing in 210–11
context effects 222
coping behaviour, emotion-focused 108
core values 17, 128, 138, 157
corporate architecture 103–4, 115, 124
corporate architecture design 2, 79, 112; and human factors 100
corporate architecture design management 3, 79–81
corporate associations 68–9, 129
corporate brand 1–2; and corporate identity 11, 16–17, 25, 27–8, 31; and corporate image 68; of Virgin 12; *see also* brand identity, corporate
corporate brand design 26; core disciplines in study of 15–19, 32; definition of 33; evaluation and audit 19; image and reputation 66–7, 70–1; internal interpretation of 29; levels of 19; major dimensions of 52–4; and marketing 25–8; origins of 7–9, *10*; use of term 74
corporate brand design management 2–3, 15, 31
corporate brand signature 3, 44–5, 56–7; concept of 46–8; elements of 48–56; impact of 45–6; main characteristics of 52; of Pampers 72–3
corporate brand signature management 2–3, 43–4
corporate brand website design 2, 4, 145–8; by Dell 175; favourability 148–52, 158, 160, 170, 172–3, 176; image, identification and loyalty 168–70

corporate branding, and identification 127
corporate branding design identity 2
corporate communications 9, 17–18, 20–1, 114–15
corporate culture: and corporate identity 17, 19; and corporate image 25; perceived 151, 157–8, 161; and physical environment 94
corporate giveaways 19
corporate identity 3–4; and architecture 79–80, 94, 100, 103–4, 112, 115–16, 124–6, 136; authenticity of 70; categories of 30–1; and communication 134–5; and corporate brand signature 46, 48; and culture 157; dimensions of 24–5, 46, 128–9; graphic design approach 16–19; and identification 126–7; and image 70–1, 170; integrated communication approach to 20–1; key elements of 1, 3, 124; marketing approach to 25–9; multi-disciplinary approach to 29–32; organisational and individual levels 44–5; organisational approach to 22–5; philosophy and mission 131–3; schools of thought on 17–18; use of term 11, 33, 67–9, 95, 138, 176; vision and values in 133; and visual identity 15–16; and website design 145–7, 169
corporate identity management 4; and architecture 128–9, 132; and corporate image 43–4, 70; dimensions of 24; and organisational behaviour 22; and website design 145, 158, 168
corporate identity mix 21, 29, 46
corporate image 3–4, 10; and architecture 79–80, 115–16; communicators of 20–1; concept of 67–9; and corporate brand design 15–16, 18, 28, 70–1; and corporate brand signature 45; and corporate identity 16, 24–6, 43, 48; and corporate name 55; and environmental elements 126; functionality of 132; organisational and individual levels 44–5; and performance outcomes 44; and reputation 66–7; use of term 11, 74, 176; and website design 146–7, 169–70
corporate image management process 21, 25
corporate logo see logo
corporate mind 30
corporate mission 25, 107, 125, 132–3, 158, 160–1
corporate name 19; and corporate brand signature 46, 48, 54–6; types of 55–6; use of term 59
corporate personality 3, 21
corporate reputation 4, 10; and conceived identity 31; concept of 69–70; and consumer-company identification 171; consumers' perception of 29; and corporate brand design 16, 29, 66–7; and corporate brand signature 46; and image 170–1; of Samsung 34; use of term 11, 67, 74, 176

corporate strategy: communicating 17; and corporate brand design 19
corporate values 25, 29, 114, 133–4, 158, 160–1
country of origin 33–4, 129, 158, 160–1, 191
covenanted identity see brand identity, corporate
COVID-19 211
CSR (corporate social responsibility), perceived 151, 156–7
cultural values 51, 89, 107
culture: and architecture 104, 107, 111; and website design 152
customer experience 186, 192; and gustative sensuality 255
customer loyalty: and architecture 80, 84, 92, 130; and corporate image 44; and olfactory cues 243; to Škoda 94; and websites 152, 154
customer perceptions: and architecture 128; of physical environment 92; and quality dimension 116
customer service 12, 151, 153–4, 156, 161, 174
CVI (corporate visual identity) 1, 15, 17–18, 32; and architecture 81, 130–1; colour in 50; and communications 21; and corporate brand signature 46–7; and corporate identity 129; and corporate name 54; and corporate reputation 70; forms of 19; and image 70–1; typeface in 49; use of term 138, 176; and websites 147, 168

da Vinci, Leonardo 53
Dapples, Louis 225
database processing 150
decor 95, 111; and architecture 3, 24, 79, 81, 84–90, 116, 129, 131, 134; and customer impressions 126, 133; interior 86, 104, 125, 207; of shopping malls 232; use of term 138; and visual identity 17
Dell 174–5
demographics 129, 222
descriptive names 55–6
design: and architecture 82, 100–1; and corporate values 114; and employees 106; use of term 59
design consultants 9, 45
design dimensions 48
design process 26, 88, 101, 129, 152
design technology 8
design-as-fashion 17–18
desired identity 31
destination branding 259
Deutscher Werkbund 9
Dewey, John 186
Diesel denim brand 235–7
distinctiveness 7, 9–11, 59, 66, 70
divine proportion 53

e-commerce 146, 148, 246; and discounting 159
Edwaybuy 159
e-loyalty 154

emotion, elements of 190
emotional intensity 187, 243
emotional reactions: to audial cues 234; and corporate brand design 28, 71; and corporate brand signature 44, 47; and physical environment 80; to sensory stimuli 93
emotional states 207; and audial cues 234; and design 232; in S-O-R model 219–20, 222
emotions, in retail environment 221
employees: identification with organisation 130; interactions with external audiences 20, 29; and organisational identity 17–18, 22–4, 27; and physical environment 79–81, 90–4, 103, 105–7, 109; social identities in the workplace 102; as stakeholders 21
endorsed identity 19
environment, social and cultural 103
environmental competence 114
environmental design 24, 89, 114, 131
environmental psychology 80; and architecture 100–1, 132, 134
environmental psychology theory (EPT) 4, 218–21, 226
environment-customer relationship 206
ergonomic design 80, 134
ethos 30, 132, 155
experience 18; and attitude 189–90; concept of 185–6, **187–9**; dimensions of 190, **191–3**; and emotion 190; in marketing 4, 185, 190–5, 206; and satisfaction 189; *see also* consumption experience; customer experience; shopping experience
eye-tracking 233

familiarity 17–18, 26, 46
first impressions 28, 44, 47, 132–3, 146
First World War, visual design in 9
flexibility, long-term 92
found names 55
founder of the company 133, 138, 157–8, 161, 236
Frito-Lay 233
functionalism 83
functionality 79, 81, 91–2, 96; and architecture 129–32; in service marketing 132, 134; and symbolism 102; use of term 138; *see also* physical structure

Galvanic Skin Response (GSR) 210
Gap, rebranding attempt 212–13
Gearbest 159
gender 126, 222, 224, 245
generic names 56
Gestalt approach 206–7
goal structure 220
Gothic architecture 82–4, 102–3
Goudge, David 260

Graham, Yogiraj 234
graphic communication 8
graphic design 3; and corporate brand design 15–19; and corporate brand signature 45, 47; and corporate image 68; and websites 147
graphic identity, modern 19
Gropius, Walter 9
group opinion 220
gustative experience 4, 251, 253–5, 258–9
gustative sensuality 254–9
gustative signatures 4, 251–2, 254, *255*, 259
gustatory stimuli 262

haptic cues 4, 248; background 243–4; and gustative sensuality 258; practical applications 246
haptic sensations, oral 253–4
hedonic features 146, 148–9
hedonic perception 220, 223
hedonism 146, 148–9, 205, 214, 220
Heinz, trademark of 8
Hendrich Gin 210
history, corporate 30, 158, 160–1
home page 150–1, 169
human interaction 94
human senses 2, 193–5, 211, 218, 243, 248, 258

IBAM (internet banking acceptance model) 148, 150
IBM 56, 174
icon, use of term 59
ideal identity 30–1
identification: and architecture 101; corporate 126–7; use of term 96, 138
identity design 8–10, 45
image, and reputation 3, 66–7, 69, 147, 169–70, 259
image formation, significance of personnel in 28
image positioning 32
imagery 9–11
IMC (integrated marketing communication) 20, 37, 147, 164
industrial design 8–9
Industrial Revolution 7–8, 103, 105, 184
information, on websites 150, 152–3, 161
information quality 150, 156
integrated communications 3, 15–16, 20–1, 25–6, 32; *see also* IMC
Intel 234
interdisciplinary approach 29, 31–2
interface 20–1
interior design 17, 105, 232
internal audiences 17, 20
internal spaces 82, 91, 102–3, 134
internet banking 147–50, 154, 156; *see also* IBAM

job satisfaction 80, 93, 106–7

Khan, Louis 105
Kodak, trademark of 8
Korea, and Samsung 33–4

language: colour as 50; corporate brand design as 7; and corporate names 55–6
Le Corbusier 83–4, 97, 110
lebensfuhl 83, 89
lighting 92–3; natural 91, 93, 131, 135; as visual cue 232
literacy 8
lithography 7–8
logo 3, 11; and coats of arms 52; colour appropriateness of 51; and corporate brand design 16–18, 28; and corporate brand signature 45–7; and CVI 70; of Gap 211–13; marketing studies approach to 25, 29; origins of 7–8; of Samsung 33; sonic 233–4; use of term 59; as visual cue 231; of Xiaomi Youpin 117
loyalty, use of term 176

macro-variables 207
management studies, corporate reputation and 69
managerial control 106, 128
managerial image 24
March, Lionel 83
marketing 3; consistency of messages 24; development of paradigms 203–4
marketing communication 135; colours in 50–1, 59; consistency in 20–1, 25; and corporate brand design 26
marketing studies: and architecture 115, 124–5; and corporate brand design 15–16, 25, 32; and corporate brand signature 44, 46–7; and corporate image 67–8
Marriott International 211
mass marketing 9
McConnell, David H. 195–6
McDonalds, visual identity of 18
meant-end actions 113
memorability 49
message sources 45
metaphoric names 55
micro-variables 207
mission, use of term 138
mission statement 25, 50, 132
Mitchell, Claire 233
moderating variables 222, 227
modernity 86, 108, 110
mouth/brain relationship 251–2, 254
multi-disciplinary approaches 3, 15–16, 29–32, 45
music: as auditory cue 234–5; and Diesel brand 236–7; and gustative sensuality 258

national identity 86, 103
natural architecture 101

natural sounds 234
navigation, contextual 151
Nescafé 225–6
neuroimaging 233
neuromarketing 210, 213
neuroscience 251
Nivea 246–8
noise 92–3, 106, 234
Nokia 72
no-nonsense era 4, 203–4

office chairs 111, 133
office decor 84, 90, 133
office design 79, 107–8
office layout 101, 104, 107–8, 131
office space 80; managerial enrichment of 106–7; psychosocial features of 92–3, 100, 109; redesigning 90–1, 129, 131
olfactory cues 4, 248; background 242–3; and gender 222; practical applications 244–5
olfactory sensations 253
online stores 159, 222, 234
open-plan offices 92; company preferences for 105–6; employee attitudes to 114; noise in 93
organisational attractiveness 172
organisational behaviour 17, 22
organisational change 102, 127–8
organisational communication 20–1, 134
organisational culture: communicating through facilities 94; and corporate identity 22; and employee behaviour 109; perceived 157; perceptions of 84–91; and symbolism 17; vision and values in 133
organisational efficiency 106, 108, 132
organisational identification 22, 24, 109, 126–8
organisational identity: and architecture 81, 116; creation of 17; of organisational members 22–4; use of term 11, 67
organisational image 23–4; and corporate image 69; use of term 11, 67
organisational nomenclature 17, 131
organisational studies approach 3; and corporate brand design 15–16, 21–3, 31–2; and corporate brand signature 43–4, 47–8; and corporate image 68
organisational values 133, 157
orthonasal smell 253

packaged goods 184
Pampers 72–3
paper-making machine 7
paradigm: shifts 103, 203–4; use of term 33
Peck, Art 213
PEOU (perceived ease of use) 148
PepsiCo 233, 260
perceived image 20, 71, 125
perception, use of term 214

perceptual curiosity 222
permanent media 20–1
Pernod Ricard UK 210
personal identification 128
philosophy: corporate 24–5, 30, 33, 132–4, 138, 158, 160–1; use of term 138
physical appearance 48, 50, 91, 96, 104, 112, 192
physical environment 79–81, 135; aesthetic element of 101–2, 111; in consumption settings 205–6; and customer behaviour 81; and employee productivity 106–8; factors of 3, 79; ideology of modern 104; management control over 135; and service failure 24; and situation 220; and social identity theory 112; and S-O-R theory 219
physical layout 89, 107–8, 113, 134, 138
physical setting 112; ambient conditions 92; artifacts in 84–90, 95; person as separate from 102, 104; privacy in 109
physical stimuli 90, 92–3, 95, 129–30, 134–5, 138
physical structure 3, 91–2, 96; and architecture 81–4, 129–31; communicating information 90; in service marketing 132, 134; and symbolism 102; use of term 138
pilotis 110
PIRQUAL (perceived internet retailing quality) 156
place: concept of 100–1; sense of 101, 112
place identification 123, 127–8
place identity, and gustative sensuality 259
pleasantness 232, 256
posters: scented 210; wood-type 7–8
principles, corporate 132, 158, 160–1
printing, revolution in 7–8
privacy 92–3, 105, 109, 150, 154
Procter & Gamble, boycott of 72
progression of economic value model 185, 198
promotional media 20–1
proportions: in architecture 82–3; divine 53
psychological situation 220–1
psychology, architectural 80
purchase intention: and corporate brand signature 47; and corporate image 44; in S-O-R model 219; and visual cues 232; and websites 152, 156
Pythagoras 53

Quiksilver 136–7

Rand, Paul 9
Rathenau, Walther 9
readability 49
rebranding 26
Redmi 117
repurchase intention 221
reputation: dimensions of 66, 70; *see also* corporate reputation
response time 150, 155
retail experience *see* shopping experience

retronasal smell 253
Rosso, Renzo 235–6
Rudofsky, Bernard 102

Samsung, corporate brand design 33–4
satisfaction 189; use of term 176, 198
scent 222; ambient 242–3, 257; signature 245; *see also* olfactory cues
self-esteem 127, 196
self-presentation 20, 134
Semodd, Steven 245
senses: definitions of **208**; evolution of 4, 203–4; *see also* human senses
sensorial stimuli *see* sensory cues
sensorimotor sensations 253–4
sensory cues: in advertising 204; brand signature as 47; business studies involving **256–7**; emotional reactions to 93; extrinsic and intrinsic *255*; in retail atmospheric 205, 210; in sensory marketing 195, 207, 218–19, 221
sensory marketing 4, 195, 218–19; future directions for 208–11, **209**; important terms in **208**; perception and sensation in 207; research directions in 221–2; rise of 204; use of term 214; visual and audial cues in 231
sensory signatures 251, 254
sensory strategies 206, 209–11, 245
service encounter: interactions during 132; physical setting of 24, 92, 130
service experience 156, 186–9, 192
service failure 24, 131
service industry, architecture in 81, 90–1, 94–6, 104, 129
service marketing 132
service organisations 28, 206
service quality, of websites 150–1
servicescape: consumer evaluation of 206–7; employee experience in 133; use of term 214; visual technologies in 208
shopping experience, replicating online 246
signalling theory 173
silence 234
Singer, trademark of 8
situation, and environment 220–1
Škoda 94–5
smell: senses of 245, 253, 263; *see also* olfactory cues
social cues, and gustative sensuality 259
social identification 23, 128
social identity 18; in organisational settings 22–4, 101
social identity theory 23, 43, 48; and architecture 101–2, 112–13; and corporate identity 126, 145; and corporate image 68; and place identification 127
social interaction: patterns of 89, 107, 134; and spatial layout 91, 130

social media interaction 174
social relations approach 105
sociotechnical approach 105
S-O-R (stimulus-organism-response) framework 4, 218–22, **223–4**, 227
soul 26–7, 30, 129
sound 234; *see also* audial cues
sound-related identity 233
space, managerial control of 105–6, 109, 124
spatial engagement, planned 92
spatial layout 79, 81, 91, 129; open-plan 105; in service marketing 132, 134; and symbolism 102; use of term 96, 138
spatial planning 82
stakeholders 1; favourable perceptions by 135; in integrated communication approach 21; and reputation 69–70; response to architecture 113, 116
Steadman, Philip 83
stimulant-free environments 210
stimulus cues 130
store environment 205
stress: and natural light 93; and office architecture 107–9
subculture 30, 158, 160–1
suggestive names 56
symbol, use of term 59
symbolic artifacts 84–90, 133–5; as component of architecture 3, 79, 81, 129; and office design 131; use of term 95, 138
symbolism: and architecture 101–2; corporate 17
system availability 155

tactile cues *see* haptic cues
tactile stimuli 262
TAM (technology acceptance model) 148, 150
taste sensations 251–3; *see also* gustatory signatures
taste/flavour relationship 254
technology, adoption of 150
temperature 92–3
territoriality 109, 131
tertiary communications 21, 30
touch: need for 246; *see also* haptic cues
TRA (theory of reasoned action) 148
trademarks 184; origins of 7–9; successful use of 16; use of term 59
transparency 66, 70
trigeminal sensations 254
trustworthiness 49, 94, 155, 161
typeface: and colour 50; corporate brand 48–9, 52; use of term 59
typography 7–8, 168

utilitarian features 146, 148

Valentine, Cathy 72
value 10–11
values, use of term 138
ventilation 130
Virgin, corporate image of 11–12
visibility: and corporate brand signature 45; and reputation 66, 70
vision, and mission 132–3
vision-driven approach 26
visual cues 4, 238; background 231–3; and gustative sensuality 258; practical approach to 233
visual design 9, 32, 152, 172, 243
visual identification 7, 9–11, 17, 25
visual identity 9; and colour 49; and corporate brand signature 43, 45; and corporate identity 24, 124–6, 129; employees grasping 27, 29; and identification 131; metaphors 32; objectives for 19; and websites 146, 152; *see also* CVI
visual identity paradigm 17, 131
visual impact 161
visual language 17, 26, 127
visual schools 18, 32, 45
visual stimuli 53, 211, 262
voice, human 234
VR (virtual reality) 208, 210–11, 246

Wallack, Pam 213
website development 173–4
website quality 149–50, 154, 156, 169
websites: availability of 155, 160; as buildings 147; characteristics of 146, 148–50; and communication 147–8; and corporate culture 157–8; credibility of 151, 155–6, 161; and customer service 156; customisation of 153–4, 161; information on 152–3; navigation of 151, 161; and perceived CSR 156–7; and reputation 170–1; security of 154, 161; significance of 169; usability of 153, 161; visual aspects of 151–2
Wolfe, H. D. 183
work environment 92, 106–7, 109
workplace: managerial control of 128; *see also* office space
workplace design 108–9, 129
workplace identity 90, 95, 102, 133, 138

Xiaomi 117

Printed in the United States
by Baker & Taylor Publisher Services